D1631254

THE WISDEN BOOK OF ONE-DAY INTERNATIONAL CRICKET 1971-1985

THE WISDEN BOOK OF ONE-DAY INTERNATIONAL CRICKET

1971-1985

Compiled by

Bill Frindall and Victor H. Isaacs

JOHN WISDEN · LONDON

First published in 1985 by John Wisden & Co Ltd
6 Warwick Court, London WC1R 5DJ

ISBN 0 947766 03 0

Computer typeset by SB Datagraphics, Colchester

Printed in Great Britain by Spottiswoode Ballantyne Printers Ltd

FOREWORD

The one-day international match is an integral part of the world cricketing scene and has been for some time. Argument and counter-argument rage backwards and forwards about the amount of international one-day cricket on offer in various parts of the world and whether the backbone of the game – the Test match – is in danger of being disjointed by its precocious and thrustful offspring.

While the member countries of the International Cricket Conference are almost to a man conscious of the need to safeguard the long-term future of the game by striking a reasonable balance between the two types of cricket, opinions do vary as to what is a suitable mixture. And of course conditions and appetites vary from one part of the world to another.

Be that as it may, there is no doubt that the income generated by these matches is of sufficient consequence to ensure that the one-day game at international level is here to stay. While there is no move within the International Cricket Conference to afford first-class status to these matches and thus to include relevant statistics in the first-class records, it has been felt, following promptings from Rob Vance of New Zealand, that records of matches, which are of considerable importance to both players and spectators alike, should be at least available here at Lord's. Thanks in no small measure to the compilers of this book this goal has been achieved.

I have no doubt that *The Wisden Book of One-Day International Cricket* will be welcomed as an indispensable record, for administrators, cricketers and the public alike. If the general interest engendered by these matches is any guide, it will be avidly received.

J.A. Bailey
Secretary MCC

CONTENTS

INTRODUCTION

The first one-day international was a hastily arranged affair, played on the final scheduled day of a rain-aborted Test match to appease the disappointed public. By coincidence, it not only took place on the very ground where Test cricket had begun 94 years earlier, but also resulted in an Australian victory against England. More significantly it attracted 46,000 spectators, produced receipts of $33,000, and began a revolution in international cricket.

When Australia toured England the following year, three limited-overs internationals replaced the extra (sixth) Test previously agreed by the respective Boards. In 1975 the same formula provided the basis for cricket's first world cup.

In Australia, the influence of television magnate Kerry Packer produced the dramatic advent of floodlit cricket, with such attendant innovations as white balls, black sightscreens, and coloured clothing. Skilful marketing of this instant formula produced a headlong proliferation of tournaments. The 1984-85 season saw the quite staggering total of 31 limited-overs internationals being staged in Australia during a period of just nine weeks.

Limited-overs cricket was conceived by an MCC committee established in 1956 to remedy the decline in attendances and the desperate financial positions of many of the first-class counties. Its proposal, that a one-day knock-out tournament be introduced, was implemented in 1963 when the Gillette Cup heralded a new era.

In 1981 the Limited-Overs Cricket Information Group published a list of matches it considered worthy of the status of one-day international. The ICC have yet to compile an official list of such matches and, like pre-1947 decisions concerning first-class status, the basic criteria for inclusion have been left to the chronicler. The 329 matches included in this volume are those played between full members of the ICC or involving associate members in Prudential World Cup tournaments. Five matches of dubious status have not been included: Gillette Cup Winners (New Zealand) v MCC at Melbourne 1974-75; Australia v New Zealand (Bushfire Appeal Challenge) at Sydney 1982-83; and three matches in India (v Pakistan at New Delhi 1983-84, and v Australia at Jamshedpur and v Pakistan at Rawalpindi 1984-85) which their Board of Control has declared unofficial.

An asterisk denotes the team's captain in the scores, and a not out innings or unbroken partnership in the records. A dagger signifies the appointed wicket-keeper. The matches are arranged chronologically by series, with each having a reference number to show its position in the general order and its place in the matches between these particular countries: e.g. 82/17 is the 82nd match listed and was the 17th match played between England and Australia.

We gratefully acknowledge the expertise of Graeme Wright (who commissioned this book) and Christine Forrest on behalf of the publishers, and the invaluable and enthusiastic assistance of Brenda and Richard Isaacs, Paula Dixon, Bapoo Mama, Simon Meadows, Francis Payne and Ken Piesse.

BILL FRINDALL and VICTOR ISAACS

June 1985

ONE-DAY INTERNATIONAL MATCHES 1970-71 to 1985

Match No. 1/1

AUSTRALIA v ENGLAND 1970-71 (Only Match)

At Melbourne Cricket Ground on 5 January 1971.
Toss: Australia. Result: AUSTRALIA won by 5 wickets.
40 eight-ball overs match. Award: J.H. Edrich.
Débuts: All.

See Introduction. Edrich, scorer of the first fifty in these matches, was adjudged the first international Man of the Match by C.S. Elliott, Derbyshire batsman and Test umpire, in Australia on a Churchill Fellowship.

ENGLAND		
G. Boycott	c Lawry b Thomson	8
J.H. Edrich	c Walters b Mallett	82
K.W.R. Fletcher	c G.S. Chappell b Mallett	24
B.L. D'Oliveira	run out	17
J.H. Hampshire	c McKenzie b Mallett	10
M.C. Cowdrey	c Marsh b Stackpole	1
R. Illingworth*	b Stackpole	1
A.P.E. Knott†	b McKenzie	24
J.A. Snow	b Stackpole	2
K. Shuttleworth	c Redpath b McKenzie	7
P. Lever	not out	4
Extras	(B 1, LB 9)	10
Total	(39.4 overs)	**190**

Fall of wickets: 1-21, 2-87, 3-124, 4-144, 5-148, 6-152, 7-156, 8-171, 9-183, 10-190.

AUSTRALIA	*O*	*M*	*R*	*W*
McKenzie	7.4	0	22	2
Thomson	8	2	22	1
Connolly	8	0	62	0
Mallett	8	1	34	3
Stackpole	8	0	40	3

AUSTRALIA		
W.M. Lawry*	c Knott b Illingworth	27
K.R. Stackpole	c and b Shuttleworth	13
I.M. Chappell	st Knott b Illingworth	60
K.D. Walters	c Knott b D'Oliveira	41
I.R. Redpath	b Illingworth	12
G.S. Chappell	not out	22
R.W. Marsh†	not out	10
A.A. Mallett		
G.D. McKenzie		
A.N. Connolly		
A.L. Thomson		
Extras	(LB 4, W 1, NB 1)	6
Total	(34.6 overs – 5 wickets)	**191**

Fall of wickets: 1-19, 2-51, 3-117, 4-158, 5-165.

ENGLAND	*O*	*M*	*R*	*W*
Snow	8	0	38	0
Shuttleworth	7	0	29	1
Lever	5.6	0	30	0
Illingworth	8	1	50	3
D'Oliveira	6	1	38	1

Umpires: T.F. Brooks and L.P. Rowan.

ENGLAND v AUSTRALIA 1972 (1st Match)
Prudential Trophy

At Old Trafford, Manchester on 24 August 1972.
Toss: Australia. Result: ENGLAND won by 6 wickets.
55 overs match. Award: D.L. Amiss.
Débuts: England – D.L. Amiss, G.G. Arnold, D.B. Close, A.W. Greig, R.A. Woolmer; Australia – R. Edwards, D.K. Lillee, R.A.L. Massie, A.P. Sheahan, G.D. Watson.

Amiss (134 balls, 161 minutes, 9 fours) completed the first century at this level off 130 balls in the 46th over. He shared the first hundred partnership with Fletcher, the pair adding 125 in 86 minutes (26.4 overs).

AUSTRALIA		
K.R. Stackpole	c D'Oliveira b Greig	37
G.D. Watson	b Arnold	0
I.M. Chappell*	b Woolmer	53
G.S. Chappell	b Woolmer	40
R. Edwards	run out	57
A.P. Sheahan	b Arnold	6
K.D. Walters	lbw b Woolmer	2
R.W. Marsh†	c Close b Snow	11
A.A. Mallett	not out	6
D.K. Lillee		
R.A.L. Massie		
Extras	(B 2, LB 3, NB 5)	10
Total	(55 overs – 8 wickets)	**222**

Fall of wickets: 1-4, 2-66, 3-125, 4-156, 5-167, 6-170, 7-205, 8-222.

ENGLAND	*O*	*M*	*R*	*W*
Snow	11	1	33	1
Arnold	11	0	38	2
Greig	11	0	50	1
Woolmer	10	1	33	3
D'Oliveira	9	1	37	0
Close	3	0	21	0

ENGLAND		
G. Boycott	c Marsh b Watson	25
D.L. Amiss	b Watson	103
K.W.R. Fletcher	b Massie	60
D.B. Close*	run out	1
J.H. Hampshire	not out	25
B.L. D'Oliveira	not out	5
A.W. Greig		
A.P.E. Knott†		
R.A. Woolmer		
J.A. Snow		
G.G. Arnold		
Extras	(B 1, LB 6)	7
Total	(49.1 overs – 4 wickets)	**226**

Fall of wickets: 1-48, 2-173, 3-174, 4-215.

AUSTRALIA	*O*	*M*	*R*	*W*
Lillee	11	2	49	0
Massie	11	1	49	1
Watson	8	1	28	2
Mallett	11	1	43	0
G.S. Chappell	3	0	20	0
Walters	3	1	16	0
Stackpole	2.1	0	14	0

Umpires: C.S. Elliott and A.E.G. Rhodes.

Match No. 3/3

ENGLAND v AUSTRALIA 1972 (2nd Match)

Prudential Trophy

At Lord's, London on 26 August 1972.
Toss: Australia. Result: AUSTRALIA won by 5 wickets.
55 overs match. Award: G.S. Chappell.
Débuts: Australia – D.J. Colley.

Australia's first hundred partnership in these matches took 78 minutes (21.2 overs).

ENGLAND		
G. Boycott	b Lillee	8
D.L. Amiss	b Mallett	25
D.B. Close*	run out	43
K.W.R. Fletcher	c Stackpole b G.S. Chappell	20
J.H. Hampshire	st Marsh b Mallett	13
B.L. D'Oliveira	c I.M. Chappell b Lillee	6
A.W. Greig	b Massie	31
A.P.E. Knott†	c Mallett b Massie	50
R.A. Woolmer	run out	9
J.A. Snow	not out	5
G.G. Arnold	not out	11
Extras	(B 1, LB 10, W 1, NB 3)	15
Total	(55 overs – 9 wickets)	**236**

Fall of wickets: 1-11, 2-65, 3-87, 4-114, 5-121, 6-121, 7-198, 8-217, 9-218.

AUSTRALIA	*O*	*M*	*R*	*W*
Lillee	11	0	56	2
Massie	11	1	35	2
Colley	11	1	72	0
Mallett	11	2	24	2
G.S. Chappell	11	0	34	1

AUSTRALIA		
K.R. Stackpole	lbw b D'Oliveira	52
R. Edwards	c Knott b Snow	6
I.M. Chappell*	c Knott b Woolmer	31
G.S. Chappell	lbw b Snow	48
A.P. Sheahan	c Knott b Snow	50
G.D. Watson	not out	11
R.W. Marsh†	not out	6
D.J. Colley		
A.A. Mallett		
D.K. Lillee		
R.A.L. Massie		
Extras	(B 6, LB 14, W 12, NB 4)	36
Total	(51.3 overs – 5 wickets)	**240**

Fall of wickets: 1-44, 2-112, 3-116, 4-219, 5-224.

ENGLAND	*O*	*M*	*R*	*W*
Snow	11	2	35	3
Arnold	11	0	47	0
D'Oliveira	11	0	46	1
Greig	9	1	29	0
Woolmer	9.3	1	47	1

Umpires: A.E. Fagg and T.W. Spencer.

ENGLAND v AUSTRALIA 1972 (3rd Match)

Prudential Trophy

At Edgbaston, Birmingham on 28 August 1972.
Toss: England. Result: ENGLAND won by 2 wickets.
55 overs match. Award: B. Wood.
Débuts: England – B. Wood; Australia – J.R. Hammond.

England became the first holders of a Prudential Trophy. They were to compete for a separate one against each visiting country until 1984, when Texaco took over the sponsorship – except in World Cup seasons.

AUSTRALIA		
K.R. Stackpole	b Woolmer	61
R. Edwards	b Arnold	6
I.M. Chappell*	run out	3
G.S. Chappell	c Wood b D'Oliveira	13
A.P. Sheahan	c Woolmer b Wood	19
K.D. Walters	b Wood	15
R.W. Marsh†	lbw b Arnold	0
A.A. Mallett	b Arnold	8
J.R. Hammond	not out	15
D.K. Lillee	c Wood b Arnold	13
R.A.L. Massie	not out	16
Extras	(LB 6, NB 4)	10
Total	(55 overs – 9 wickets)	**179**

Fall of wickets: 1-8, 2-15, 3-40, 4-87, 5-111, 6-112, 7-127, 8-136, 9-158.

ENGLAND	*O*	*M*	*R*	*W*
Snow	11	0	29	0
Arnold	11	3	27	4
Greig	10	3	24	0
D'Oliveira	6	1	19	1
Woolmer	11	1	50	1
Wood	6	0	20	2

ENGLAND		
G. Boycott	c Massie b Lillee	41
D.L. Amiss	c Marsh b G.S. Chappell	40
D.B. Close*	c Marsh b Lillee	5
K.W.R. Fletcher	c Marsh b Hammond	34
B.L. D'Oliveira	run out	2
B. Wood	lbw b Lillee	19
A.W. Greig	not out	24
A.P.E. Knott†	c Mallett b Walters	6
R.A. Woolmer	c Marsh b Walters	0
J.A. Snow	not out	0
G.G. Arnold		
Extras	(LB 5, W 4)	9
Total	(51.3 overs – 8 wickets)	**180**

Fall of wickets: 1-76, 2-89, 3-94, 4-104, 5-143, 6-154, 7-172, 8-172.

AUSTRALIA	*O*	*M*	*R*	*W*
Lillee	11	2	25	3
Massie	8.3	3	45	0
Mallett	4	0	16	0
Hammond	9	1	41	1
G.S. Chappell	11	3	20	1
Walters	8	1	24	2

Umpires: D.J. Constant and A.S.M. Oakman.

Match No. 5/1

NEW ZEALAND v PAKISTAN 1972-73 (Only Match)

At Lancaster Park, Christchurch on 11 February 1973.
Toss: Pakistan. Result: NEW ZEALAND won by 22 runs.
40 eight-ball overs match. Awards: batting – M.G. Burgess, Sadiq Mohammad; bowling – D.R. Hadlee, Sarfraz Nawaz; fielding – Asif Iqbal, G.M. Turner.
Débuts: All.

The first one-day international to be played on a Sunday began at noon and finished in dusk at 6.30 pm. Peter Coman, a 29-year-old right-handed batsman from Christchurch, was the first player to appear at this level who was destined not to play Test cricket.

NEW ZEALAND		
P.G. Coman	b Salim	24
G.M. Turner	c Majid b Sarfraz	10
B.E. Congdon*	c Wasim Bari b Sarfraz	3
B.F. Hastings	b Sarfraz	4
M.G. Burgess	c Asif Masood b Intikhab	47
G.E. Vivian	c Wasim Bari b Asif Iqbal	14
K.J. Wadsworth†	b Majid	30
D.R. Hadlee	run out	0
R.J. Hadlee	not out	21
H.J. Howarth	c Wasim Bari b Salim	1
R.O. Collinge	c Salim b Sarfraz	9
Extras	(B 5, LB 11, NB 8)	24
Total	(38.3 overs)	**187**

Fall of wickets: 1-35, 2-43, 3-45, 4-62, 5-98, 6-143, 7-152, 8-160, 9-176, 10-187.

PAKISTAN	*O*	*M*	*R*	*W*
Asif Masood	8	1	28	0
Salim Altaf	7	0	22	2
Sarfraz Nawaz	7.3	0	46	4
Asif Iqbal	5	0	32	1
Majid Khan	8	0	23	1
Intikhab Alam	3	1	12	1

PAKISTAN		
Intikhab Alam*	lbw b D.R. Hadlee	10
Sadiq Mohammad	lbw b Howarth	37
Majid Khan	lbw b D.R. Hadlee	8
Mushtaq Mohammad	b D.R. Hadlee	27
Asif Iqbal	c Coman b D.R. Hadlee	3
Wasim Raja	run out	4
Nasim-ul-Ghani	c and b Howarth	1
Wasim Bari†	b Congdon	21
Salim Altaf	c Hastings b Congdon	21
Sarfraz Nawaz	run out	17
Asif Masood	not out	4
Extras	(B 7, LB 1, NB 4)	12
Total	(33.3 overs)	**165**

Fall of wickets: 1-43, 2-52, 3-60, 4-71, 5-93, 6-99, 7-103, 8-136, 9-145, 10-165.

NEW ZEALAND	*O*	*M*	*R*	*W*
Collinge	8	1	35	0
R.J. Hadlee	5	0	37	0
D.R. Hadlee	8	0	34	4
Howarth	8	0	30	2
Congdon	4.3	1	17	2

Umpires: F.R. Goodall and E.G. Wainscott.

ENGLAND v NEW ZEALAND 1973 (1st Match)
Prudential Trophy

At St Helen's, Swansea on 18 July 1973.
Toss: New Zealand. Result: ENGLAND won by 7 wickets.
55 overs match. Award: D.L. Amiss.

Débuts: England – F.C. Hayes, G.R.J. Roope, D.L. Underwood; New Zealand – V. Pollard, R.E. Redmond, B.R. Taylor.

In the only Prudential Trophy match to be staged in Wales, Amiss continued his monopoly of centuries, reaching his second hundred off 116 balls in the 39th over.

NEW ZEALAND		
R.E. Redmond	lbw b Arnold	3
G.M. Turner	c and b Illingworth	26
B.E. Congdon*	c Knott b Snow	2
B.F. Hastings	c Roope b Snow	0
M.G. Burgess	c Knott b Arnold	1
V. Pollard	c Knott b Arnold	55
K.J. Wadsworth†	lbw b Underwood	3
B.R. Taylor	c Fletcher b Snow	22
R.J. Hadlee	c Snow b Greig	28
R.O. Collinge	c Knott b Snow	4
H.J. Howarth	not out	5
Extras	(LB 2, W 7)	9
Total	(52.5 overs)	**158**

Fall of wickets: 1-4, 2-9, 3-14, 4-15, 5-70, 6-81, 7-108, 8-133, 9-144, 10-158.

ENGLAND	*O*	*M*	*R*	*W*
Snow	10	0	32	4
Arnold	11	2	28	3
Greig	9.5	2	26	1
Underwood	11	3	29	1
Illingworth	11	1	34	1

ENGLAND		
G. Boycott	c Turner b Congdon	20
D.L. Amiss	c Pollard b Taylor	100
G.R.J. Roope	b Howarth	0
F.C. Hayes	not out	20
K.W.R. Fletcher	not out	16
A.W. Greig		
R. Illingworth*		
A.P.E. Knott†		
J.A. Snow		
G.G. Arnold		
D.L. Underwood		
Extras	(B 1, LB 1, W 1)	3
Total	(45.3 overs – 3 wickets)	**159**

Fall of wickets: 1-96, 2-97, 3-135.

NEW ZEALAND	*O*	*M*	*R*	*W*
Collinge	6	2	18	0
Hadlee	11	1	35	0
Taylor	8.3	1	37	1
Howarth	11	3	34	1
Congdon	9	2	32	1

Umpires: D.J. Constant and C.S. Elliott.

Match No. 7/2

ENGLAND v NEW ZEALAND 1973 (2nd Match)

Prudential Trophy

At Old Trafford, Manchester on 20 July 1973.

Toss: New Zealand. No result – rain.

55 overs match. No award.

No débuts.

Old Trafford, venue of the only two Test matches in England to be totally abandoned, staged the first aborted one-day international.

ENGLAND		
G. Boycott	lbw b Taylor	15
D.L. Amiss	c Wadsworth b Congdon	34
G.R.J. Roope	c Wadsworth b Hadlee	44
F.C. Hayes	b Congdon	9
K.W.R. Fletcher	c Hadlee b Taylor	25
A.W. Greig	c Taylor b Collinge	14
R. Illingworth*	c Turner b Hadlee	4
A.P.E. Knott†	c Wadsworth b Taylor	12
G.G. Arnold	not out	0
J.A. Snow		
P. Lever		
Extras	(LB 6, W 4)	10
Total	(48.3 overs – 8 wickets)	**167**

Fall of wickets: 1-23, 2-57, 3-75, 4-112, 5-150, 6-153, 7-160, 8-167.

NEW ZEALAND	*O*	*M*	*R*	*W*
Collinge	11	0	52	1
Taylor	10.3	3	25	3
Hadlee	8	1	23	2
Congdon	8	1	24	2
Howarth	11	1	33	0

NEW ZEALAND

G.M. Turner
R.E. Redmond
B.E. Congdon*
B.F. Hastings
M.G. Burgess
V. Pollard
K.J. Wadsworth†
B.R. Taylor
R.J. Hadlee
R.O. Collinge
H.J. Howarth

Umpires: H.D. Bird and A.E.G. Rhodes.

ENGLAND v WEST INDIES 1973 (1st Match)
Prudential Trophy

At Headingley, Leeds on 5 September 1973.
Toss: West Indies. Result: ENGLAND won by 1 wicket.
55 overs match. Award: M.H. Denness.

Débuts: England – M.H. Denness, M. Hendrick, C.M. Old, M.J. Smith, R.W. Taylor, R.G.D. Willis; West Indies – All.

On his début as England's captain, Denness made the highest contribution to the first of these contests to be decided by the final pair of batsmen. Sobers failed to score in his only one-day international.

WEST INDIES		
R.C. Fredericks	c Greig b Willis	4
M.L.C. Foster	c Greig b Old	25
R.B. Kanhai*	c Greig b Underwood	55
C.H. Lloyd	b Willis	31
A.I. Kallicharran	st Taylor b Underwood	26
G.St A. Sobers	c Taylor b Old	0
B.D. Julien	c Taylor b Old	0
K.D. Boyce	b Underwood	7
D.L. Murray†	run out	11
V.A. Holder	c Old b Hendrick	10
L.R. Gibbs	not out	0
Extras	(LB 12)	12
Total	(54 overs)	**181**

Fall of wickets: 1-4, 2-65, 3-115, 4-132, 5-133, 6-133, 7-158, 8-159, 9-181, 10-181.

ENGLAND	*O*	*M*	*R*	*W*
Willis	10	2	29	2
Hendrick	11	4	27	1
Old	11	1	43	3
Underwood	11	2	30	3
Greig	11	0	40	0

ENGLAND		
G. Boycott	c Kanhai b Holder	0
M.J. Smith	lbw b Julien	31
M.H. Denness*	b Gibbs	66
F.C. Hayes	c Murray b Julien	9
K.W.R. Fletcher	lbw b Holder	2
A.W. Greig	c Sobers b Boyce	48
C.M. Old	b Sobers	4
R.W. Taylor†	run out	8
M. Hendrick	b Boyce	1
R.G.D. Willis	not out	5
D.L. Underwood	not out	1
Extras	(B 1, LB 3, NB 3)	7
Total	(54.3 overs – 9 wickets)	**182**

Fall of wickets: 1-3, 2-74, 3-93, 4-95, 5-143, 6-157, 7-171, 8-176, 9-176.

WEST INDIES	*O*	*M*	*R*	*W*
Sobers	10.3	3	31	1
Holder	11	1	34	2
Boyce	11	1	40	2
Julien	11	1	40	2
Gibbs	11	0	30	1

Umpires: C.S. Elliott and A.E. Fagg.

Match No. 9/2

ENGLAND v WEST INDIES 1973 (2nd Match)

Prudential Trophy

At Kennington Oval, London on 7 September 1973.
Toss: England. Result: WEST INDIES won by 8 wickets.
55 overs match. Award: R.C. Fredericks.

Débuts: England – J.A. Jameson, D. Lloyd; West Indies – R.G.A. Headley, D.A. Murray.

West Indies won the Prudential Trophy on overall scoring rate. Fredericks reached his hundred off 113 balls in the 36th over to end the monopoly of D.L. Amiss.

ENGLAND		
M.J. Smith	b Lloyd	19
J.A. Jameson	c Holder b Gibbs	28
M.H. Denness*	lbw b Lloyd	0
D. Lloyd	run out	8
K.W.R. Fletcher	b Julien	63
A.W. Greig	c Lloyd b Foster	17
C.M. Old	c Murray b Holder	21
R.W. Taylor†	run out	3
G.G. Arnold	c Julien b Foster	17
R.G.D. Willis	not out	4
D.L. Underwood	not out	1
Extras	(B 2, LB 3, NB 3)	8
Total	(55 overs – 9 wickets)	**189**

Fall of wickets: 1-38, 2-39, 3-59, 4-59, 5-100, 6-135, 7-142, 8-177, 9-184.

WEST INDIES	*O*	*M*	*R*	*W*
Holder	11	0	40	1
Julien	11	2	35	1
Lloyd	11	2	25	2
Gibbs	11	4	12	1
Boyce	6	0	47	0
Foster	5	0	22	2

WEST INDIES		
R.C. Fredericks	b Arnold	105
R.G.A. Headley	c Taylor b Arnold	19
A.I. Kallicharran	not out	53
D.A. Murray†	not out	1
R.B. Kanhai*		
C.H. Lloyd		
M.L.C. Foster		
B.D. Julien		
K.D. Boyce		
V.A. Holder		
L.R. Gibbs		
Extras	(B 1, LB 6, NB 5)	12
Total	(42.2 overs – 2 wickets)	**190**

Fall of wickets: 1-43, 2-186.

ENGLAND	*O*	*M*	*R*	*W*
Willis	10.2	0	55	0
Arnold	9	1	24	2
Old	10	0	52	0
Underwood	7	0	26	0
Greig	6	2	21	0

Umpires: A.E.G. Rhodes and T.W. Spencer.

NEW ZEALAND v AUSTRALIA 1973-74 (1st Match)

At Carisbrook, Dunedin on 30 March 1974.
Toss: New Zealand. Result: AUSTRALIA won by 7 wickets.
35 eight-ball overs match. Awards: batting – I.M. Chappell, B.E. Congdon; bowling – G.J. Gilmour, D.R. O'Sullivan; fielding – K.J. Wadsworth, K.D. Walters.

Débuts: New Zealand – B.L. Cairns, D.R. O'Sullivan; Australia – R.J. Bright, I.C. Davis, G. Dymock, G.J. Gilmour, M.H.N. Walker.

NEW ZEALAND		
P.G. Coman	b Gilmour	0
G.M. Turner	c I.M. Chappell b Walker	5
B.E. Congdon*	c Marsh b G.S. Chappell	82
B.F. Hastings	b Walker	27
M.G. Burgess	c Dymock b G.S. Chappell	3
V. Pollard	c Walters b Gilmour	12
K.J. Wadsworth†	c Walters b Dymock	7
R.J. Hadlee	c Marsh b G.S. Chappell	3
D.R. Hadlee	c Walters b Dymock	8
B.L. Cairns	not out	30
D.R. O'Sullivan	not out	1
Extras	(LB 9, NB 7)	16
Total	(35 overs – 9 wickets)	**194**

Fall of wickets: 1-0, 2-12, 3-61, 4-94, 5-140, 6-145, 7-153, 8-153, 9-190.

AUSTRALIA	*O*	*M*	*R*	*W*
Walker	7	0	36	2
Gilmour	7	1	19	2
Dymock	7	0	28	2
Bright	7	0	44	0
G.S. Chappell	7	0	51	3

AUSTRALIA		
I.R. Redpath	run out	0
K.R. Stackpole	c Wadsworth b D.R. Hadlee	50
I.M. Chappell*	b O'Sullivan	83
G.S. Chappell	not out	42
I.C. Davis	not out	11
K.D. Walters		
R.W. Marsh†		
M.H.N. Walker		
G.J. Gilmour		
R.J. Bright		
G. Dymock		
Extras	(LB 3, NB 6)	9
Total	(24.3 overs – 3 wickets)	**195**

Fall of wickets: 1-0, 2-136, 3-160.

NEW ZEALAND	*O*	*M*	*R*	*W*
R.J. Hadlee	6	0	35	0
Cairns	4.3	0	38	0
Congdon	2	0	30	0
O'Sullivan	7	2	38	1
D.R. Hadlee	5	0	45	1

Umpires: E.W. Dempster and L.H.G. Harmer.

Match No. 11/2

NEW ZEALAND v AUSTRALIA 1973-74 (2nd Match)

At Lancaster Park, Christchurch on 31 March 1974.
Toss: Australia. Result: AUSTRALIA won by 31 runs.
35 eight-ball overs match. Awards: batting – K.J. Wadsworth, A.J. Woodcock; bowling – R.O. Collinge, A.A. Mallett; fielding – P.G. Coman, I.R. Redpath.
Débuts: New Zealand – J.M. Parker; Australia – A.J. Woodcock.

Wadsworth (92 minutes, 16 fours) recorded New Zealand's first century at this level and shared with Congdon his country's first hundred partnership.

AUSTRALIA		
A.J. Woodcock	b D.R. Hadlee	53
K.R. Stackpole	c Wadsworth b Collinge	11
I.M. Chappell*	c Wadsworth b Cairns	86
G.S. Chappell	not out	75
K.D. Walters	b Collinge	19
I.R. Redpath	c Coman b Congdon	8
R.W. Marsh†	not out	1
M.H.N. Walker		
G.J. Gilmour		
A.A. Mallett		
G. Dymock		
Extras	(B 2, LB 6, NB 4)	12
Total	(35 overs – 5 wickets)	**265**

Fall of wickets 1-39, 2-102, 3-176, 4-232, 5-261.

NEW ZEALAND	*O*	*M*	*R*	*W*
Collinge	7	1	38	2
Cairns	7	0	58	1
Congdon	7	0	77	1
O'Sullivan	7	0	43	0
Hadlee	7	1	37	1

NEW ZEALAND		
G.M. Turner	c I.M. Chappell b Gilmour	6
P.G. Coman	b Walker	38
J.M. Parker	c Gilmour b Mallett	14
B.F. Hastings	c G.S. Chappell b Mallett	7
M.G. Burgess	c Walters b Mallett	3
K.J. Wadsworth†	c I.M. Chappell b Walters	104
B.E. Congdon*	not out	49
D.R. Hadlee	not out	4
R.O. Collinge		
B.L. Cairns		
D.R. O'Sullivan		
Extras	(B 1, LB 1, NB 7)	9
Total	(35 overs – 6 wickets)	**234**

Fall of wickets 1-19, 2-58, 3-64, 4-70, 5-83, 6-213.

AUSTRALIA	*O*	*M*	*R*	*W*
Gilmour	7	0	36	1
Walker	7	1	35	1
Mallett	7	0	47	3
Dymock	7	1	49	0
Walters	7	0	58	1

Umpires: F.R. Goodall and E.G. Wainscott.

ENGLAND v INDIA 1974 (1st Match)

Prudential Trophy

At Headingley, Leeds on 13 July 1974.
Toss: England. Result: ENGLAND won by 4 wickets.
55 overs match. Award: J.H. Edrich.

Débuts: England – R.D. Jackman; India – All.

INDIA		
S.M. Gavaskar	b Arnold	28
S.S. Naik	lbw b Jackman	18
A.L. Wadekar*	b Jackman	67
G.R. Viswanath	b Woolmer	4
F.M. Engineer†	lbw b Old	32
B.P. Patel	c Fletcher b Greig	82
E.D. Solkar	lbw b Arnold	3
S. Abid Ali	c and b Woolmer	17
Madan Lal	b Old	2
S. Venkataraghavan	not out	1
B.S. Bedi	c Lloyd b Old	0
Extras	(B 8, NB 3)	11
Total	(53.5 overs)	**265**

Fall of wickets: 1-44, 2-50, 3-60, 4-130, 5-181, 6-194, 7-246, 8-264, 9-265, 10-265.

ENGLAND	*O*	*M*	*R*	*W*
Arnold	10	1	42	2
Old	10.5	0	43	3
Jackman	11	0	44	2
Woolmer	11	0	62	2
Greig	11	0	63	1

ENGLAND		
D.L. Amiss	lbw b Solkar	20
D. Lloyd	st Engineer b Solkar	34
J.H. Edrich	c Bedi b Venkataraghavan	90
M.H. Denness*	c Venkataraghavan b Madan Lal	8
K.W.R. Fletcher	c and b Bedi	39
A.W. Greig	c and b Bedi	40
A.P.E. Knott†	not out	15
C.M. Old	not out	5
R.A. Woolmer		
R.D. Jackman		
G.G. Arnold		
Extras	(LB 12, NB 3)	15
Total	(51.1 overs – 6 wickets)	**266**

Fall of wickets: 1-37, 2-84, 3-96, 4-179, 5-212, 6-254.

INDIA	*O*	*M*	*R*	*W*
Abid Ali	9	0	51	0
Solkar	11	1	31	2
Madan Lal	9.1	1	43	1
Venkataraghavan	11	0	58	1
Bedi	11	0	68	2

Umpires: W.E. Alley and H.D. Bird.

Match No. 13/2

ENGLAND v INDIA 1974 (2nd Match)

Prudential Trophy

At Kennington Oval, London on 15, 16 July 1974.
Toss: India. Result: ENGLAND won by 6 wickets.
55 overs match. Award: K.W.R. Fletcher.

Débuts: India – G. Bose, A.V. Mankad.

This was the first limited-overs international to involve play on a second day.

INDIA		
S.M. Gavaskar	c Arnold b Jackman	20
S.S. Naik	c Greig b Old	20
G. Bose	c Denness b Jackman	13
A.L. Wadekar*	c Lloyd b Underwood	6
G.R. Viswanath	c Knott b Old	32
F.M. Engineer†	lbw b Jackman	4
B.P. Patel	run out	12
A.V. Mankad	b Old	44
E.D. Solkar	c Knott b Greig	0
S. Abid Ali	c Smith b Greig	6
Madan Lal	not out	3
Extras	(LB 9, W 1, NB 1)	11
Total	(47.3 overs)	**171**

Fall of wickets 1-40, 2-48, 3-60, 4-64, 5-75, 6-94, 7-139, 8-142, 9-156, 10-171.

ENGLAND	*O*	*M*	*R*	*W*
Arnold	7	0	20	0
Old	9.3	0	36	3
Jackman	11	1	41	3
Underwood	11	0	36	1
Greig	9	0	27	2

ENGLAND		
M.J. Smith	c Engineer b Abid Ali	6
D. Lloyd	c sub (S.M.H. Kirmani) b Bose	39
J.H. Edrich	c Patel b Madan Lal	19
M.H. Denness*	c Wadekar b Mankad	24
K.W.R. Fletcher	not out	55
A.W. Greig	not out	24
A.P.E. Knott†		
C.M. Old		
R.D. Jackman		
G.G. Arnold		
D.L. Underwood		
Extras	(LB 4, W 1)	5
Total	(48.5 overs – 4 wickets)	**172**

Fall of wickets 1-19, 2-65, 3-71, 4-113.

INDIA	*O*	*M*	*R*	*W*
Abid Ali	11	3	21	1
Solkar	11	3	37	0
Madan Lal	10	0	23	1
Bose	11	2	39	1
Mankad	5.5	0	47	1

Umpires: C.S. Elliott and A. Jepson.

ENGLAND v PAKISTAN 1974 (1st Match)
Prudential Trophy

At Trent Bridge, Nottingham on 31 August 1974.
Toss: England. Result: PAKISTAN won by 7 wickets.
50 overs match. Award: Majid Khan.
Débuts: Pakistan – Imran Khan, Zaheer Abbas.

Lloyd became the first to bat throughout a one-day international innings. Two hundreds were scored in one of these matches for the first time, Majid reaching his century off only 88 balls.

ENGLAND		
D. Lloyd	not out	116
M.J. Smith	c Sadiq b Sarfraz	14
J.H. Edrich	c Wasim Bari b Asif Iqbal	18
M.H. Denness*	st Wasim Bari b Intikhab	32
C.M. Old	st Wasim Bari b Majid	39
A.W. Greig	not out	7
K.W.R. Fletcher		
A.P.E. Knott†		
P. Lever		
D.L. Underwood		
R.G.D. Willis		
Extras	(B 5, LB 11, NB 2)	18
Total	(50 overs – 4 wickets)	**244**

Fall of wickets 1-17, 2-59, 3-162, 4-226.

PAKISTAN	*O*	*M*	*R*	*W*
Asif Masood	10	2	31	0
Sarfraz Nawaz	10	0	46	1
Asif Iqbal	10	1	40	1
Imran Khan	10	0	36	0
Intikhab Alam	7	0	58	1
Majid Khan	3	0	15	1

PAKISTAN		
Sadiq Mohammad	b Lever	41
Majid Khan	c Old b Underwood	109
Zaheer Abbas	c and b Willis	31
Asif Iqbal	not out	24
Mushtaq Mohammad	not out	24
Wasim Raja		
Intikhab Alam*		
Imran Khan		
Sarfraz Nawaz		
Wasim Bari†		
Asif Masood		
Extras	(B 1, LB 11, NB 5)	17
Total	(42.5 overs – 3 wickets)	**246**

Fall of wickets 1-113, 2-187, 3-199.

ENGLAND	*O*	*M*	*R*	*W*
Willis	10	2	34	1
Lever	10	0	58	1
Old	10	0	65	0
Underwood	8	1	32	1
Greig	4.5	0	40	0

Umpires: W.L. Budd and D.J. Constant.

Match No. 15/2

ENGLAND v PAKISTAN 1974 (2nd Match)

Prudential Trophy

At Edgbaston, Birmingham on 3 September 1974.
Toss: Pakistan. Result: PAKISTAN won by 8 wickets.
35 overs match. Award: Asif Masood.
No débuts.

England recorded their lowest total in a one-day international, albeit in a match reduced to 35 overs each because of rain.

ENGLAND		
D. Lloyd	b Sarfraz	4
M.J. Smith	lbw b Asif Masood	0
J.H. Edrich	b Sarfraz	6
M.H. Denness*	b Imran	9
K.W.R. Fletcher	c Wasim Bari b Asif Masood	2
A.W. Greig	run out	1
C.M. Old	c Wasim Raja b Asif Iqbal	0
R.W. Taylor†	not out	26
G.G. Arnold	b Imran	2
D.L. Underwood	b Asif Iqbal	17
P. Lever	not out	8
Extras	(LB 6)	6
Total	(35 overs – 9 wickets)	**81**

Fall of wickets: 1-1, 2-12, 3-13, 4-20, 5-24, 6-25, 7-25, 8-28, 9-68.

PAKISTAN	*O*	*M*	*R*	*W*
Asif Masood	7	2	9	2
Sarfraz Nawaz	7	0	15	2
Imran Khan	7	2	16	2
Asif Iqbal	7	1	17	2
Intikhab Alam	6	1	12	0
Majid Khan	1	0	6	0

PAKISTAN		
Sadiq Mohammad	c Lloyd b Underwood	12
Majid Khan	lbw b Arnold	0
Zaheer Abbas	not out	57
Mushtaq Mohammad	not out	1
Asif Iqbal		
Wasim Raja		
Intikhab Alam*		
Sarfraz Nawaz		
Wasim Bari†		
Imran Khan		
Asif Masood		
Extras	(B 1, LB 7, NB 6)	14
Total	(18 overs – 2 wickets)	**84**

Fall of wickets: 1-1, 2-60.

ENGLAND	*O*	*M*	*R*	*W*
Arnold	6	3	7	1
Lever	4	0	22	0
Old	5	0	25	0
Underwood	3	0	16	1

Umpires: H.D. Bird and C.S. Elliott.

AUSTRALIA v ENGLAND 1974-75 (Only Match)

At Melbourne Cricket Ground on 1 January 1975.
Toss: England. Result: ENGLAND won by 3 wickets.
40 eight-ball overs match. Awards: D.L. Amiss and I.M. Chappell.

Débuts: Australia – W.J. Edwards, A.G. Hurst, T.J. Jenner, J.R. Thomson; England – B.W. Luckhurst.

AUSTRALIA		
I.R. Redpath	c Greig b Lever	2
W.J. Edwards	b Arnold	2
I.M. Chappell*	c Lever b Old	42
G.S. Chappell	b Old	44
R. Edwards	b Old	20
K.D. Walters	b Old	18
R.W. Marsh†	run out	14
T.J. Jenner	c Fletcher b Greig	12
M.H.N. Walker	b Greig	20
J.R. Thomson	b Arnold	4
A.G. Hurst	not out	1
Extras	(B 7, W 1, NB 3)	11
Total	(34.5 overs)	**190**

Fall of wickets 1-5, 2-11, 3-65, 4-105, 5-122, 6-139, 7-159, 8-173, 9-183, 10-190.

ENGLAND	*O*	*M*	*R*	*W*
Lever	5	0	24	1
Arnold	8	2	30	2
Greig	7.5	0	48	2
Old	8	0	57	4
Underwood	6	0	20	0

ENGLAND		
D.L. Amiss	b Walker	47
D. Lloyd	run out	49
B.W. Luckhurst	run out	14
K.W.R. Fletcher	c Redpath b Thomson	31
C.M. Old	b Hurst	12
A.W. Greig	run out	3
M.H. Denness*	c Walker b Hurst	12
A.P.E. Knott†	not out	2
D.L. Underwood	not out	1
G.G. Arnold		
P. Lever		
Extras	(B 5, LB 11, NB 4)	20
Total	(37.1 overs – 7 wickets)	**191**

Fall of wickets 1-70, 2-117, 3-124, 4-154, 5-157, 6-182, 7-182.

AUSTRALIA	*O*	*M*	*R*	*W*
Thomson	7	1	33	1
Hurst	8	0	27	2
Jenner	8	1	28	0
Walters	3	0	32	0
Walker	8	0	27	1
G.S. Chappell	3	0	24	0
W.J. Edwards	0.1	0	0	0

Umpires: R.C. Bailhache and T.F. Brooks.

Match No. 17/3

NEW ZEALAND v ENGLAND 1974-75 (1st Match)

At Carisbrook, Dunedin on 8 March 1975.
Toss: New Zealand. No result – rain.
35 eight-ball overs match. No award.
Débuts: New Zealand – G.P. Howarth, B.G. Hadlee; England – F.J. Titmus.

ENGLAND		
D.L. Amiss	c Wadsworth b R.J. Hadlee	3
B. Wood	b H.J. Howarth	33
B.W. Luckhurst	c G.P. Howarth b Collinge	0
K.W.R. Fletcher	c Turner b Congdon	11
J.H. Edrich*	c R.J. Hadlee b H.J. Howarth	8
C.M. Old	c Parker b H.J. Howarth	27
R.W. Taylor†	not out	23
F.J. Titmus	b D.R. Hadlee	11
G.G. Arnold	b D.R. Hadlee	0
D.L. Underwood	c Parker b R.J. Hadlee	2
M. Hendrick	b Collinge	1
Extras	(LB 12, NB 5)	17
Total	(34.1 overs)	**136**

Fall of wickets: 1-14, 2-17, 3-36, 4-51, 5-90, 6-90, 7-122, 8-122, 9-132, 10-136.

NEW ZEALAND	*O*	*M*	*R*	*W*
Collinge	6.1	0	17	2
R.J. Hadlee	7	0	21	2
H.J. Howarth	7	0	35	3
Congdon	7	0	25	1
D.R. Hadlee	7	1	21	2

NEW ZEALAND		
G.M. Turner	not out	8
B.G. Hadlee	not out	7
J.M. Parker		
G.P. Howarth		
B.E. Congdon*		
K.J. Wadsworth†		
B.F. Hastings		
R.J. Hadlee		
D.R. Hadlee		
R.O. Collinge		
H.J. Howarth		
Extras		0
Total	(4 overs – 0 wicket)	**15**

ENGLAND	*O*	*M*	*R*	*W*
Arnold	2	0	6	0
Hendrick	2	0	9	0

Umpires: E.W. Dempster and E.G. Wainscott.

NEW ZEALAND v ENGLAND 1974-75 (2nd Match)

At Basin Reserve, Wellington on 9 March 1975.
Toss: New Zealand. Result: No result – rain.
35 eight-ball overs match. No award.
Début: New Zealand – J.F.M. Morrison.

NEW ZEALAND		
G.M. Turner	b Hendrick	18
J.F.M. Morrison	c Taylor b Lever	5
B.E. Congdon*	lbw b Lever	101
B.F. Hastings	c Greig b Titmus	37
K.J. Wadsworth†	lbw b Titmus	0
J.M. Parker	c Wood b Titmus	25
G.P. Howarth	c sub (D.L. Amiss) b Old	13
R.J. Hadlee	not out	6
D.R. Hadlee	run out	0
R.O. Collinge	c Titmus b Lever	0
H.J. Howarth	b Lever	11
Extras	(B 6, LB 2, NB 3)	11
Total	(34.6 overs)	**227**

Fall of wickets 1-13, 2-46, 3-130, 4-130, 5-178, 6-206, 7-209, 8-209, 9-210, 10-227.

ENGLAND	*O*	*M*	*R*	*W*
Lever	6.6	0	35	4
Old	6	0	32	1
Hendrick	4	0	21	1
Greig	5	0	34	0
Titmus	7	0	53	3
Wood	6	0	41	0

ENGLAND		
B. Wood	not out	14
B.W. Luckhurst	c Wadsworth b Collinge	1
K.W.R. Fletcher	not out	18
J.H. Edrich		
M.H. Denness*		
A.W. Greig		
C.M. Old		
R.W. Taylor†		
F.J. Titmus		
P. Lever		
M. Hendrick		
Extras	(B 1, LB 1)	2
Total	(10 overs – 1 wicket)	**35**

Fall of wicket 1-3.

NEW ZEALAND	*O*	*M*	*R*	*W*
Collinge	4	1	9	1
D.R. Hadlee	3	0	6	0
Congdon	2	0	14	0
R.J. Hadlee	1	0	4	0

Umpires: J.B.R. Hastie and R.L. Monteith.

Match No. 19/3

ENGLAND v INDIA 1975

Prudential World Cup – 1st Match

At Lord's, London on 7 June 1975.
Toss: England. Result: ENGLAND won by 202 runs.
60 overs match. Award: D.L. Amiss.

Débuts: India – M. Amarnath, A.D. Gaekwad, K.D. Ghavri.

With Amiss contributing his third hundred, England achieved their highest total and became the first side to reach 300 in a one-day international. Their margin of victory, the second-largest at this level, owed much to an extraordinary display by Gavaskar, who batted throughout the innings as if hoping to gain a draw. Old reached his fifty off 30 balls.

ENGLAND		
J.A. Jameson	c Venkataraghavan b Amarnath	21
D.L. Amiss	b Madan Lal	137
K.W.R. Fletcher	b Abid Ali	68
A.W. Greig	lbw b Abid Ali	4
M.H. Denness*	not out	37
C.M. Old	not out	51
B. Wood		
A.P.E. Knott†		
J.A. Snow		
P. Lever		
G.G. Arnold		
Extras	(LB 12, W 2, NB 2)	16
Total	(60 overs – 4 wickets)	**334**

Fall of wickets 1-54, 2-230, 3-237, 4-245.

INDIA	*O*	*M*	*R*	*W*
Madan Lal	12	1	64	1
Amarnath	12	2	60	1
Abid Ali	12	0	58	2
Ghavri	11	1	83	0
Venkataraghavan	12	0	41	0
Solkar	1	0	12	0

INDIA		
S.M. Gavaskar	not out	36
E.D. Solkar	c Lever b Arnold	8
A.D. Gaekwad	c Knott b Lever	22
G.R. Viswanath	c Fletcher b Old	37
B.P. Patel	not out	16
M. Amarnath		
F.M. Engineer†		
S. Abid Ali		
Madan Lal		
S. Venkataraghavan*		
K.D. Ghavri		
Extras	(LB 3, W 1, NB 9)	13
Total	(60 overs – 3 wickets)	**132**

Fall of wickets 1-21, 2-50, 3-108.

ENGLAND	*O*	*M*	*R*	*W*
Snow	12	2	24	0
Arnold	10	2	20	1
Old	12	4	26	1
Greig	9	1	26	0
Wood	5	2	4	0
Lever	10	0	16	1
Jameson	2	1	3	0

Umpires: D.J. Constant and J.G. Langridge.

NEW ZEALAND v EAST AFRICA 1975
Prudential World Cup – 2nd Match

At Edgbaston, Birmingham on 7 June 1975.
Toss: New Zealand. Result: NEW ZEALAND won by 181 runs.
60 overs match. Award: G.M. Turner.
Débuts: New Zealand – B.J. McKechnie; East Africa – All.

Turner's innings, the first of 150 or more, was the highest in these matches until Kapil Dev scored 175* in 1983 (*Match No. 215*).

NEW ZEALAND		
G.M. Turner*	not out	171
J.F.M. Morrison	c and b Nana	14
G.P. Howarth	b Quaraishy	20
J.M. Parker	c Zulfiqar b Sethi	66
B.F. Hastings	c Sethi b Zulfiqar	8
K.J. Wadsworth†	b Nagenda	10
R.J. Hadlee	not out	6
B.J. McKechnie		
D.R. Hadlee		
H.J. Howarth		
R.O. Collinge		
Extras	(B 1, LB 8, W 5)	14
Total	(60 overs – 5 wickets)	**309**

Fall of wickets 1-51, 2-103, 3-252, 4-278, 5-292.

EAST AFRICA	*O*	*M*	*R*	*W*
Nagenda	9	1	50	1
Frasat	9	0	50	0
Nana	12	2	34	1
Sethi	10	1	51	1
Zulfiqar	12	0	71	1
Quaraishy	8	0	39	1

EAST AFRICA		
Frasat Ali	st Wadsworth b H.J. Howarth	45
S. Walusimba	b D.R. Hadlee	15
Ramesh Sethi	run out	1
Shiraz Sumar	b D.R. Hadlee	4
Jawahir Shah	c and b H.J. Howarth	5
Harilal R. Shah*	lbw b H.J. Howarth	0
Mehmood Quaraishy	not out	16
Zulfiqar Ali	b D.R. Hadlee	30
H. McLeod†	b Collinge	5
P.G. Nana	not out	1
J. Nagenda		
Extras	(LB 5, NB 1)	6
Total	(60 overs – 8 wickets)	**128**

Fall of wickets 1-30, 2-32, 3-36, 4-59, 5-59,
6-84, 7-121, 8-126.

NEW ZEALAND	*O*	*M*	*R*	*W*
Collinge	12	5	23	1
R.J. Hadlee	12	6	10	0
McKechnie	12	2	39	0
D.R. Hadlee	12	1	21	3
H.J. Howarth	12	3	29	3

Umpires: H.D. Bird and A.E. Fagg.

Match No. 21/1

AUSTRALIA v PAKISTAN 1975

Prudential World Cup – 3rd Match

At Headingley, Leeds on 7 June 1975.
Toss: Australia. Result: AUSTRALIA won by 73 runs.
60 overs match. Award: D.K. Lillee.
Débuts: Australia – R.B. McCosker, A. Turner; Pakistan – Naseer Malik.

Lillee became the first bowler to take five wickets in a one-day international.

AUSTRALIA		
A. Turner	c Mushtaq b Asif Iqbal	46
R.B. McCosker	c Wasim Bari b Naseer	25
I.M. Chappell*	c Wasim Raja b Sarfraz	28
G.S. Chappell	c Asif Iqbal b Imran	45
K.D. Walters	c Sarfraz b Naseer	2
R. Edwards	not out	80
R.W. Marsh†	c Wasim Bari b Imran	1
M.H.N. Walker	b Asif Masood	18
J.R. Thomson	not out	20
A.A. Mallett		
D.K. Lillee		
Extras	(LB 7, NB 6)	13
Total	(60 overs – 7 wickets)	**278**

Fall of wickets 1-63, 2-99, 3-110, 4-124, 5-184, 6-195, 7-243.

PAKISTAN	*O*	*M*	*R*	*W*
Naseer Malik	12	2	37	2
Asif Masood	12	0	50	1
Sarfraz Nawaz	12	0	63	1
Asif Iqbal	12	0	58	1
Imran Khan	10	0	44	2
Wasim Raja	2	0	13	0

PAKISTAN		
Sadiq Mohammad	b Lillee	4
Majid Khan	c Marsh b Mallett	65
Zaheer Abbas	c Turner b Thomson	8
Mushtaq Mohammad	c G.S. Chappell b Walters	8
Asif Iqbal*	b Lillee	53
Wasim Raja	c Thomson b Walker	31
Imran Khan	c Turner b Walker	9
Sarfraz Nawaz	c Marsh b Lillee	0
Wasim Bari†	c Marsh b Lillee	2
Asif Masood	c Walker b Lillee	6
Naseer Malik	not out	0
Extras	(LB 4, W 3, NB 12)	19
Total	(53 overs)	**205**

Fall of wickets 1-15, 2-27, 3-68, 4-104, 5-181, 6-189, 7-189, 8-195, 9-203, 10-205.

AUSTRALIA	*O*	*M*	*R*	*W*
Lillee	12	2	34	5
Thomson	8	2	25	1
Walker	12	3	32	2
Mallett	12	1	49	1
Walters	6	0	29	1
G.S. Chappell	3	0	17	0

Umpires: W.E. Alley and T.W. Spencer.

WEST INDIES v SRI LANKA 1975

Prudential World Cup – 4th Match

At Old Trafford, Manchester on 7 June 1975.
Toss: West Indies. Result: WEST INDIES won by 9 wickets.
60 overs match. Award: B.D. Julien.
Débuts: West Indies – I.V.A. Richards, A.M.E. Roberts; Sri Lanka – All.

Sri Lanka were dismissed for the first total of under 100 in one-day internationals, the match ending at 3.30 pm.

SRI LANKA		
E.R. Fernando†	c Murray b Julien	4
B. Warnapura	c Murray b Boyce	8
A.P.B. Tennekoon*	c Murray b Julien	0
P.D. Heyn	c Lloyd b Roberts	2
M.H. Tissera	c Kallicharran b Julien	14
L.R.D. Mendis	c Murray b Boyce	8
A.N. Ranasinghe	b Boyce	0
H.S.M. Pieris	c Lloyd b Julien	3
A.R.M. Opatha	b Roberts	11
D.S. De Silva	c Lloyd b Holder	21
L.W. Kaluperuma	not out	6
Extras	(B 3, LB 3, NB 3)	9
Total	(37.2 overs)	**86**

Fall of wickets: 1-5, 2-5, 3-16, 4-21, 5-41, 6-41, 7-42, 8-48, 9-58, 10-86.

WEST INDIES	*O*	*M*	*R*	*W*
Roberts	12	5	16	2
Boyce	8	1	22	3
Julien	12	3	20	4
Gibbs	4	0	17	0
Holder	1.2	0	2	1

WEST INDIES		
R.C. Fredericks	c Warnapura b De Silva	33
D.L. Murray†	not out	30
A.I. Kallicharran	not out	19
R.B. Kanhai		
C.H. Lloyd*		
I.V.A. Richards		
B.D. Julien		
K.D. Boyce		
V.A. Holder		
A.M.E. Roberts		
L.R. Gibbs		
Extras	(B 2, LB 1, W 1, NB 1)	5
Total	(20.4 overs – 1 wicket)	**87**

Fall of wicket: 1-52.

SRI LANKA	*O*	*M*	*R*	*W*
Opatha	4	0	19	0
De Silva	8	1	33	1
Pieris	2	0	13	0
Kaluperuma	6.4	1	17	0

Umpires: W.L. Budd and A. Jepson.

Match No. 23/5

ENGLAND v NEW ZEALAND 1975

Prudential World Cup – 5th Match

At Trent Bridge, Nottingham on 11 June 1975.
Toss: New Zealand. Result: ENGLAND won by 80 runs.
60 overs match. Award: K.W.R. Fletcher.
No débuts.

ENGLAND		
J.A. Jameson	c Wadsworth b Collinge	11
D.L. Amiss	b Collinge	16
K.W.R. Fletcher	run out	131
F.C. Hayes	lbw b R.J. Hadlee	34
M.H. Denness*	c Morrison b D.R. Hadlee	37
A.W. Greig	b D.R. Hadlee	9
C.M. Old	not out	20
A.P.E. Knott†		
D.L. Underwood		
G.G. Arnold		
P. Lever		
Extras	(LB 6, W 1, NB 1)	8
Total	(60 overs – 6 wickets)	**266**

Fall of wickets 1-27, 2-28, 3-111, 4-177, 5-200, 6-266.

NEW ZEALAND	*O*	*M*	*R*	*W*
Collinge	12	2	43	2
R.J. Hadlee	12	2	66	1
D.R. Hadlee	12	1	55	2
McKechnie	12	2	38	0
Howarth	12	2	56	0

NEW ZEALAND		
J.F.M. Morrison	c Old b Underwood	55
G.M. Turner*	b Lever	12
B.G. Hadlee	b Greig	19
J.M. Parker	b Greig	1
B.F. Hastings	c Underwood b Old	10
K.J. Wadsworth†	b Arnold	25
R.J. Hadlee	b Old	0
B.J. McKechnie	c Underwood b Greig	27
D.R. Hadlee	c Arnold b Greig	20
H.J. Howarth	not out	1
R.O. Collinge	b Underwood	6
Extras	(B 1, LB 4, W 1, NB 4)	10
Total	(60 overs)	**186**

Fall of wickets 1-30, 2-83, 3-91, 4-95, 5-129, 6-129, 7-129, 8-177, 9-180, 10-186.

ENGLAND	*O*	*M*	*R*	*W*
Arnold	12	3	35	1
Lever	12	0	37	1
Old	12	2	29	2
Greig	12	0	45	4
Underwood	12	2	30	2

Umpires: W.E. Alley and T.W. Spencer.

INDIA v EAST AFRICA 1975
Prudential World Cup – 6th Match

At Headingley, Leeds on 11 June 1975.
Toss: East Africa. Result: INDIA won by 10 wickets.
60 overs match. Award: F.M. Engineer.
Débuts: East Africa – Praful Mehta, D. Pringle, Yunus Badat.

Bedi's analysis remains the most economical at this level. India gained the first 10-wicket victory.

EAST AFRICA		
Frasat Ali	b Abid Ali	12
S. Walusimba	lbw b Abid Ali	16
Praful Mehta†	run out	12
Yunus Badat	b Bedi	1
Jawahir Shah	b Amarnath	37
Harilal R. Shah*	c Engineer b Amarnath	0
Ramesh Sethi	c Gaekwad b Madan Lal	23
Mehmood Quaraishy	run out	6
Zulfiqar Ali	not out	2
P.G. Nana	lbw b Madan Lal	0
D. Pringle	b Madan Lal	2
Extras	(LB 8, NB 1)	9
Total	(55.3 overs)	**120**

Fall of wickets: 1-26, 2-36, 3-37, 4-56, 5-56, 6-98, 7-116, 8-116, 9-116, 10-120.

INDIA	*O*	*M*	*R*	*W*
Abid Ali	12	5	22	2
Madan Lal	9.3	2	15	3
Bedi	12	8	6	1
Venkataraghavan	12	4	29	0
Amarnath	10	0	39	2

INDIA		
S.M. Gavaskar	not out	65
F.M. Engineer†	not out	54
A.D. Gaekwad		
G.R. Viswanath		
B.P. Patel		
E.D. Solkar		
S. Abid Ali		
Madan Lal		
M. Amarnath		
S. Venkataraghavan*		
B.S. Bedi		
Extras	(B 4)	4
Total	(29.5 overs – 0 wicket)	**123**

EAST AFRICA	*O*	*M*	*R*	*W*
Frasat	6	1	17	0
Pringle	3	0	14	0
Zulfiqar	11	3	32	0
Nana	4.5	0	36	0
Sethi	5	0	20	0

Umpires: H.D. Bird and A. Jepson.

Match No. 25/1

AUSTRALIA v SRI LANKA 1975

Prudential World Cup – 7th Match

At Kennington Oval, London on 11 June 1975.
Toss: Sri Lanka. Result: AUSTRALIA won by 52 runs.
60 overs match. Award: A. Turner.
Début: Sri Lanka – S.R. de S. Wettimuny.

Turner reached the only pre-lunch century in one-day internationals, out of 178, during the 34th over. Mendis and Wettimuny were injured by balls from Thomson and required treatment at St Thomas's Hospital.

AUSTRALIA		
R.B. McCosker	b De Silva	73
A. Turner	c Mendis b De Silva	101
I.M. Chappell*	b Kaluperuma	4
G.S. Chappell	c Opatha b Pieris	50
K.D. Walters	c Tennekoon b Pieris	59
J.R. Thomson	not out	9
R.W. Marsh†	not out	9
R. Edwards		
M.H.N. Walker		
D.K. Lillee		
A.A. Mallett		
Extras	(B 1, LB 20, W 1, NB 1)	23
Total	(60 overs – 5 wickets)	**328**

Fall of wickets 1-182, 2-187, 3-191, 4-308, 5-308.

SRI LANKA	*O*	*M*	*R*	*W*
Opatha	9	0	32	0
Pieris	11	0	68	2
Warnapura	9	0	40	0
Ranasinghe	7	0	55	0
De Silva	12	3	60	2
Kaluperuma	12	0	50	1

SRI LANKA		
S.R. de S. Wettimuny	retired hurt	53
E.R. Fernando†	b Thomson	22
B. Warnapura	st Marsh b Mallett	31
L.R.D. Mendis	retired hurt	32
A.P.B. Tennekoon*	b I.M. Chappell	48
M.H. Tissera	c Turner b I.M. Chappell	52
A.N. Ranasinghe	not out	14
H.S.M. Pieris	not out	0
A.R.M. Opatha		
D.S. De Silva		
L.W. Kaluperuma		
Extras	(B 6, LB 8, W 8, NB 2)	24
Total	(60 overs – 4 wickets)	**276**

Fall of wickets 1-30, 2-84, 3-246, 4-268.

AUSTRALIA	*O*	*M*	*R*	*W*
Lillee	10	0	42	0
Thomson	12	5	22	1
Mallett	12	0	72	1
Walters	6	1	33	0
Walker	12	1	44	0
G.S. Chappell	4	0	25	0
I.M. Chappell	4	0	14	2

Umpires: W.L. Budd and A.E. Fagg.

PAKISTAN v WEST INDIES 1975

Prudential World Cup – 8th Match

At Edgbaston, Birmingham on 11 June 1975.
Toss: Pakistan. Result: WEST INDIES won by 1 wicket.
60 overs match. Award: Sarfraz Nawaz.
Débuts: Pakistan – Javed Miandad, Parvez Mir; West Indies – C.G. Greenidge.

Joining forces at 203-9 in the 46th over, Murray and Roberts added 64 to clinch an astonishing victory with two balls to spare.

PAKISTAN		
Majid Khan*	c Murray b Lloyd	60
Sadiq Mohammad	c Kanhai b Julien	7
Zaheer Abbas	lbw b Richards	31
Mushtaq Mohammad	b Boyce	55
Wasim Raja	b Roberts	58
Javed Miandad	run out	24
Parvez Mir	run out	4
Wasim Bari†	not out	1
Sarfraz Nawaz	not out	0
Asif Masood		
Naseer Malik		
Extras	(B 1, LB 15, W 4, NB 6)	26
Total	(60 overs – 7 wickets)	**266**

Fall of wickets: 1-21, 2-83, 3-140, 4-202, 5-249, 6-263, 7-265.

WEST INDIES	*O*	*M*	*R*	*W*
Roberts	12	1	47	1
Boyce	12	2	44	1
Julien	12	1	41	1
Holder	12	3	56	0
Richards	4	0	21	1
Lloyd	8	1	31	1

WEST INDIES		
R.C. Fredericks	lbw b Sarfraz	12
C.G. Greenidge	c Wasim Bari b Sarfraz	4
A.I. Kallicharran	c Wasim Bari b Sarfraz	16
R.B. Kanhai	b Naseer	24
C.H. Lloyd*	c Wasim Bari b Miandad	53
I.V.A. Richards	c Zaheer b Parvez	13
B.D. Julien	c Miandad b Asif Masood	18
D.L. Murray†	not out	61
K.D. Boyce	b Naseer	7
V.A. Holder	c Parvez b Sarfraz	16
A.M.E. Roberts	not out	24
Extras	(LB 10, W 1, NB 8)	19
Total	(59.4 overs – 9 wickets)	**267**

Fall of wickets: 1-6, 2-31, 3-36, 4-84, 5-99, 6-145, 7-151, 8-166, 9-203.

PAKISTAN	*O*	*M*	*R*	*W*
Asif Masood	12	1	64	1
Sarfraz Nawaz	12	1	44	4
Naseer Malik	12	2	42	2
Parvez Mir	9	1	42	1
Javed Miandad	12	0	46	1
Mushtaq Mohammad	2	0	7	0
Wasim Raja	0.4	0	3	0

Umpires: D.J. Constant and J.G. Langridge.

Match No. 27/1

ENGLAND v EAST AFRICA 1975

Prudential World Cup – 9th Match

At Edgbaston, Birmingham on 14 June 1975.
Toss: East Africa. Result: ENGLAND won by 196 runs.
60 overs match. Award: J.A. Snow.
No débuts.

ENGLAND		
B. Wood	b Quaraishy	77
D.L. Amiss	c Nana b Zulfiqar	88
F.C. Hayes	b Zulfiqar	52
A.W. Greig	lbw b Zulfiqar	9
A.P.E. Knott†	not out	18
C.M. Old	b Quaraishy	18
M.H. Denness*	not out	12
K.W.R. Fletcher		
J.A. Snow		
P. Lever		
D.L. Underwood		
Extras	(B 7, LB 7, W 1, NB 1)	16
Total	(60 overs – 5 wickets)	**290**

Fall of wickets 1-158, 2-192, 3-234, 4-244, 5-277.

EAST AFRICA	*O*	*M*	*R*	*W*
Frasat	9	0	40	0
Pringle	12	0	41	0
Nana	12	2	46	0
Sethi	5	0	29	0
Zulfiqar	12	0	63	3
Quaraishy	10	0	55	2

EAST AFRICA		
Frasat Ali	b Snow	0
S. Walusimba	lbw b Snow	7
Yunus Badat	b Snow	0
Jawahir Shah	lbw b Snow	4
Ramesh Sethi	b Lever	30
Harilal R. Shah*	b Greig	6
Mehmood Quaraishy	c Amiss b Greig	19
Zulfiqar Ali	b Lever	7
H. McLeod†	b Lever	0
P.G. Nana	not out	8
D. Pringle	b Old	3
Extras	(LB 6, W 1, NB 3)	10
Total	(52.3 overs)	**94**

Fall of wickets 1-7, 2-7, 3-15, 4-21, 5-42,
6-72, 7-76, 8-79, 9-88, 10-94.

ENGLAND	*O*	*M*	*R*	*W*
Snow	12	6	11	4
Lever	12	3	32	3
Underwood	10	5	11	0
Wood	7	3	10	0
Greig	10	1	18	2
Old	1.3	0	2	1

Umpires: W.E. Alley and J.G. Langridge.

INDIA v NEW ZEALAND 1975
Prudential World Cup – 10th Match

At Old Trafford, Manchester on 14 June 1975.
Toss: India. Result: NEW ZEALAND won by 4 wickets.
60 overs match. Award: G.M. Turner.
No débuts.

INDIA		
S.M. Gavaskar	c R.J. Hadlee b D.R. Hadlee	12
F.M. Engineer†	lbw b R.J. Hadlee	24
A.D. Gaekwad	c Hastings b R.J. Hadlee	37
G.R. Viswanath	lbw b McKechnie	2
B.P. Patel	c Wadsworth b H.J. Howarth	9
E.D. Solkar	c Wadsworth b H.J. Howarth	13
S. Abid Ali	c H.J. Howarth b McKechnie	70
Madan Lal	c and b McKechnie	20
M. Amarnath	c Morrison b D.R. Hadlee	1
S. Venkataraghavan*	not out	26
B.S. Bedi	run out	6
Extras	(B 5, W 1, NB 4)	10
Total	(60 overs)	**230**

Fall of wickets: 1-17, 2-48, 3-59, 4-81, 5-94, 6-101, 7-156, 8-157, 9-217, 10-230.

NEW ZEALAND	*O*	*M*	*R*	*W*
Collinge	12	2	43	0
R.J. Hadlee	12	2	48	2
D.R. Hadlee	12	3	32	2
McKechnie	12	1	49	3
H.J. Howarth	12	0	48	2

NEW ZEALAND		
G.M. Turner*	not out	114
J.F.M. Morrison	c Engineer b Bedi	17
G.P. Howarth	run out	9
J.M. Parker	lbw b Abid Ali	1
B.F. Hastings	c Solkar b Amarnath	34
K.J. Wadsworth†	lbw b Madan Lal	22
R.J. Hadlee	b Abid Ali	15
D.R. Hadlee	not out	8
B.J. McKechnie		
H.J. Howarth		
R.O. Collinge		
Extras	(B 8, LB 5)	13
Total	(58.5 overs – 6 wickets)	**233**

Fall of wickets: 1-45, 2-62, 3-70, 4-135, 5-185, 6-224.

INDIA	*O*	*M*	*R*	*W*
Madan Lal	11.5	1	62	1
Amarnath	8	1	40	1
Bedi	12	6	28	1
Abid Ali	12	2	35	2
Venkataraghavan	12	0	39	0
Solkar	3	0	16	0

Umpires: W.L. Budd and A.E. Fagg.

Match No. 29/1

AUSTRALIA v WEST INDIES 1975
Prudential World Cup – 11th Match

At Kennington Oval, London on 14 June 1975.
Toss: West Indies. Result: WEST INDIES won by 7 wickets.
60 overs match. Award: A.I. Kallicharran.
No débuts.

AUSTRALIA		
R.B. McCosker	c Fredericks b Julien	0
A. Turner	lbw b Roberts	7
I.M. Chappell*	c Murray b Boyce	25
G.S. Chappell	c Murray b Boyce	15
K.D. Walters	run out	7
R. Edwards	b Richards	58
R.W. Marsh†	not out	52
M.H.N. Walker	lbw b Holder	8
J.R. Thomson	c Holder b Richards	1
D.K. Lillee	b Roberts	3
A.A. Mallett	c Murray b Roberts	0
Extras	(LB 9, W 1, NB 6)	16
Total	(53.4 overs)	**192**

Fall of wickets: 1-0, 2-21, 3-49, 4-56, 5-61, 6-160, 7-173, 8-174, 9-192, 10-192.

WEST INDIES	*O*	*M*	*R*	*W*
Julien	12	2	31	1
Roberts	10.4	1	39	3
Boyce	11	0	38	2
Holder	10	0	31	1
Lloyd	4	1	19	0
Richards	6	0	18	2

WEST INDIES		
R.C. Fredericks	c Marsh b Mallett	58
C.G. Greenidge	lbw b Walker	16
A.I. Kallicharran	c Mallett b Lillee	78
I.V.A. Richards	not out	15
R.B. Kanhai	not out	18
C.H. Lloyd*		
B.D. Julien		
D.L. Murray†		
K.D. Boyce		
V.A. Holder		
A.M.E. Roberts		
Extras	(B 4, LB 2, W 3, NB 1)	10
Total	(46 overs – 3 wickets)	**195**

Fall of wickets: 1-29, 2-153, 3-159.

AUSTRALIA	*O*	*M*	*R*	*W*
Lillee	10	0	66	1
Thomson	6	1	21	0
Walker	12	2	41	1
G.S. Chappell	4	0	13	0
Mallett	11	2	35	1
I.M. Chappell	3	1	9	0

Umpires: H.D. Bird and D.J. Constant.

PAKISTAN v SRI LANKA 1975

Prudential World Cup - 12th Match

At Trent Bridge, Nottingham on 14 June 1975.
Toss: Sri Lanka. Result: PAKISTAN won by 192 runs.
60 overs match. Award: Zaheer Abbas.
Début: Sri Lanka – G.R.A. De Silva.

PAKISTAN		
Sadiq Mohammad	c Opatha b Warnapura	74
Majid Khan*	c Tennekoon b D.S. De Silva	84
Zaheer Abbas	b Opatha	97
Mushtaq Mohammad	c Heyn b Warnapura	26
Wasim Raja	c Opatha b Warnapura	2
Javed Miandad	not out	28
Imran Khan	b Opatha	0
Parvez Mir	not out	4
Wasim Bari†		
Asif Masood		
Naseer Malik		
Extras	(B 4, LB 4, W 2, NB 5)	15
Total	(60 overs – 6 wickets)	**330**

Fall of wickets: 1-159, 2-168, 3-256, 4-268, 5-318, 6-318.

SRI LANKA	*O*	*M*	*R*	*W*
Opatha	12	0	67	2
Pieris	9	0	54	0
G.R.A. De Silva	7	1	46	0
D.S. De Silva	12	1	61	1
Kaluperuma	9	1	35	0
Warnapura	8	0	42	3
Ranasinghe	3	0	10	0

SRI LANKA		
E.R. Fernando†	c and b Miandad	21
B. Warnapura	b Imran	2
A.P.B. Tennekoon*	lbw b Naseer	30
M.H. Tissera	c Wasim Bari b Sadiq	12
P.D. Heyn	c Zaheer b Miandad	1
A.N. Ranasinghe	b Wasim Raja	9
H.S.M. Pieris	lbw b Parvez	16
A.R.M. Opatha	c Zaheer b Sadiq	0
D.S. De Silva	b Imran	26
L.W. Kaluperuma	not out	13
G.R.A. De Silva	c Wasim Raja b Imran	0
Extras	(LB 1, W 3, NB 4)	8
Total	(50.1 overs)	**138**

Fall of wickets: 1-5, 2-44, 3-60, 4-61, 5-75, 6-79, 7-90, 8-113, 9-135, 10-138.

PAKISTAN	*O*	*M*	*R*	*W*
Asif Masood	6	2	14	0
Imran Khan	7.1	3	15	3
Javed Miandad	7	2	22	2
Naseer Malik	6	1	19	1
Sadiq Mohammad	6	1	20	2
Wasim Raja	7	4	7	1
Mushtaq Mohammad	5	0	16	0
Parvez Mir	6	1	17	1

Umpires: A. Jepson and T.W. Spencer.

Match No. 31/6

ENGLAND v AUSTRALIA 1975

Prudential World Cup – Semi-Final

At Headingley, Leeds on 18 June 1975.
Toss: Australia. Result: AUSTRALIA won by 4 wickets.
60 overs match. Award: G.J. Gilmour.
No débuts.

Gilmour became the first bowler to take six wickets in a one-day international and held the record analysis until W.W. Davis took 7-51 in 1983 (*Match No. 202*).

ENGLAND		
D.L. Amiss	lbw b Gilmour	2
B. Wood	b Gilmour	6
K.W.R. Fletcher	lbw b Gilmour	8
A.W. Greig	c Marsh b Gilmour	7
F.C. Hayes	lbw b Gilmour	4
M.H. Denness*	b Walker	27
A.P.E. Knott†	lbw b Gilmour	0
C.M. Old	c G.S. Chappell b Walker	0
J.A. Snow	c Marsh b Lillee	2
G.G. Arnold	not out	18
P. Lever	lbw b Walker	5
Extras	(LB 5, W 7, NB 2)	14
Total	(36.2 overs)	**93**

Fall of wickets: 1-2, 2-11, 3-26, 4-33, 5-35, 6-36, 7-37, 8-52, 9-73, 10-93.

AUSTRALIA	*O*	*M*	*R*	*W*
Lillee	9	3	26	1
Gilmour	12	6	14	6
Walker	9.2	3	22	3
Thomson	6	0	17	0

AUSTRALIA		
A. Turner	lbw b Arnold	7
R.B. McCosker	b Old	15
I.M. Chappell*	lbw b Snow	2
G.S. Chappell	lbw b Snow	4
K.D. Walters	not out	20
R. Edwards	b Old	0
R.W. Marsh†	b Old	5
G.J. Gilmour	not out	28
M.H.N. Walker		
D.K. Lillee		
J.R. Thomson		
Extras	(B 1, LB 6, NB 6)	13
Total	(28.4 overs – 6 wickets)	**94**

Fall of wickets: 1-17, 2-24, 3-32, 4-32, 5-32, 6-39.

ENGLAND	*O*	*M*	*R*	*W*
Arnold	7.4	2	15	1
Snow	12	0	30	2
Old	7	2	29	3
Lever	2	0	7	0

Umpires: W.E. Alley and D.J. Constant.

NEW ZEALAND v WEST INDIES 1975

Prudential World Cup – Semi-Final

At Kennington Oval, London on 18 June 1975.
Toss: West Indies. Result: WEST INDIES won by 5 wickets.
60 overs match. Award: A.I. Kallicharran.
No débuts.

NEW ZEALAND		
G.M. Turner*	c Kanhai b Roberts	36
J.F.M. Morrison	lbw b Julien	5
G.P. Howarth	c Murray b Roberts	51
J.M. Parker	b Lloyd	3
B.F. Hastings	not out	24
K.J. Wadsworth†	c Lloyd b Julien	11
B.J. McKechnie	lbw b Julien	1
D.R. Hadlee	c Holder b Julien	0
B.L. Cairns	b Holder	10
H.J. Howarth	b Holder	0
R.O. Collinge	b Holder	2
Extras	(B 1, LB 5, W 2, NB 7)	15
Total	(52.2 overs)	**158**

Fall of wickets: 1-8, 2-98, 3-105, 4-106, 5-125, 6-133, 7-139, 8-155, 9-155, 10-158.

WEST INDIES	*O*	*M*	*R*	*W*
Julien	12	5	27	4
Roberts	11	3	18	2
Holder	8.2	0	30	3
Boyce	9	0	31	0
Lloyd	12	1	37	1

WEST INDIES		
R.C. Fredericks	c Hastings b Hadlee	6
C.G. Greenidge	lbw b Collinge	55
A.I. Kallicharran	c and b Collinge	72
I.V.A. Richards	lbw b Collinge	5
R.B. Kanhai	not out	12
C.H. Lloyd*	c Hastings b McKechnie	3
B.D. Julien	not out	4
D.L. Murray†		
K.D. Boyce		
V.A. Holder		
A.M.E. Roberts		
Extras	(LB 1, NB 1)	2
Total	(40.1 overs – 5 wickets)	**159**

Fall of wickets: 1-8, 2-133, 3-139, 4-142, 5-151.

NEW ZEALAND	*O*	*M*	*R*	*W*
Collinge	12	4	28	3
D.R. Hadlee	10	0	54	1
Cairns	6.1	2	23	0
McKechnie	8	0	37	1
H.J. Howarth	4	0	15	0

Umpires: W.L. Budd and A.E. Fagg.

Match No. 33/2

AUSTRALIA v WEST INDIES 1975

Prudential World Cup – Final

At Lord's, London on 21 June 1975.
Toss: Australia. Result: WEST INDIES won by 17 runs.
60 overs match. Award: C.H. Lloyd.
No débuts.

At 8.42 pm on the longest day of the year, West Indies became the first holders of the Prudential Cup. Lloyd reached his 100 off 82 balls.

WEST INDIES		
R.C. Fredericks	hit wicket b Lillee	7
C.G. Greenidge	c Marsh b Thomson	13
A.I. Kallicharran	c Marsh b Gilmour	12
R.B. Kanhai	b Gilmour	55
C.H. Lloyd*	c Marsh b Gilmour	102
I.V.A. Richards	b Gilmour	5
K.D. Boyce	c G.S. Chappell b Thomson	34
B.D. Julien	not out	26
D.L. Murray†	c and b Gilmour	14
V.A. Holder	not out	6
A.M.E. Roberts		
Extras	(LB 6, NB 11)	17
Total	(60 overs – 8 wickets)	**291**

Fall of wickets: 1-12, 2-27, 3-50, 4-199, 5-206, 6-209, 7-261, 8-285.

AUSTRALIA	*O*	*M*	*R*	*W*
Lillee	12	1	55	1
Gilmour	12	2	48	5
Thomson	12	1	44	2
Walker	12	1	71	0
G.S. Chappell	7	0	33	0
Walters	5	0	23	0

AUSTRALIA		
R.B. McCosker	c Kallicharran b Boyce	7
A. Turner	run out	40
I.M. Chappell*	run out	62
G.S. Chappell	run out	15
K.D. Walters	b Lloyd	35
R.W. Marsh†	b Boyce	11
R. Edwards	c Fredericks b Boyce	28
G.J. Gilmour	c Kanhai b Boyce	14
M.H.N. Walker	run out	7
J.R. Thomson	run out	21
D.K. Lillee	not out	16
Extras	(B 2, LB 9, NB 7)	18
Total	(58.4 overs)	**274**

Fall of wickets: 1-25, 2-81, 3-115, 4-162, 5-170, 6-195, 7-221, 8-231, 9-233, 10-274.

WEST INDIES	*O*	*M*	*R*	*W*
Julien	12	0	58	0
Roberts	11	1	45	0
Boyce	12	0	50	4
Holder	11.4	1	65	0
Lloyd	12	1	38	1

Umpires: H.D. Bird and T.W. Spencer.

AUSTRALIA v WEST INDIES 1975-76 (Only Match)

At Adelaide Oval on 20 December 1975.
Toss: Australia. Result: AUSTRALIA won by 5 wickets.
40 eight-ball overs match. Award: I.M. Chappell.
Débuts: Australia – G.J. Cosier; West Indies – L.G. Rowe.

WEST INDIES		
R.C. Fredericks	b Lillee	21
C.G. Greenidge	c and b Cosier	41
L.G. Rowe	c Marsh b Gilmour	5
I.V.A. Richards	c Cosier b Gilmour	74
C.H. Lloyd*	c Marsh b Walker	1
A.I. Kallicharran	c Mallett b G.S. Chappell	37
B.D. Julien	b G.S. Chappell	9
D.L. Murray†	b Walker	8
K.D. Boyce	c and b Walker	9
V.A. Holder	lbw b Walker	0
A.M.E. Roberts	not out	3
Extras	(B 1, LB 4, NB 11)	16
Total	(37.6 overs)	**224**

Fall of wickets: 1-39, 2-48, 3-86, 4-96, 5-188, 6-189, 7-201, 8-220, 9-220, 10-224.

AUSTRALIA	*O*	*M*	*R*	*W*
Lillee	8	1	44	1
Gilmour	8	0	48	2
Cosier	6	1	33	1
Walker	6.6	0	19	4
Mallett	2	0	21	0
G.S. Chappell	7	0	43	2

AUSTRALIA		
A. Turner	c Murray b Holder	46
R.B. McCosker	c Murray b Roberts	0
I.M. Chappell	c Greenidge b Boyce	63
G.S. Chappell*	c and b Holder	59
I.R. Redpath	run out	24
G.J. Cosier	not out	25
M.H.N. Walker	not out	3
R.W. Marsh†		
G.J. Gilmour		
D.K. Lillee		
A.A. Mallett		
Extras	(LB 3, NB 2)	5
Total	(31.5 overs – 5 wickets)	**225**

Fall of wickets: 1-1, 2-86, 3-119, 4-179, 5-214.

WEST INDIES	*O*	*M*	*R*	*W*
Roberts	4	0	22	1
Julien	8	0	66	0
Holder	7.5	1	53	2
Boyce	7	0	41	1
Lloyd	3	0	28	0
Richards	2	0	10	0

Umpires: R.C. Bailhache and M.G. O'Connell.

Match No. 35/2

NEW ZEALAND v INDIA 1975-76 (1st Match)

At Lancaster Park, Christchurch on 21 February 1976.
Toss: India. Result: NEW ZEALAND won by 9 wickets.
35 eight-ball overs match. Award: R.O. Collinge.
Débuts: New Zealand – G.N. Edwards; India – S.M.H. Kirmani, P. Sharma, D.B. Vengsarkar.

INDIA		
P. Sharma	b Collinge	6
D.B. Vengsarkar	run out	16
A.D. Gaekwad	c R.J. Hadlee b Cairns	3
G.R. Viswanath	c Turner b Cairns	56
B.P. Patel	c Wadsworth b D.R. Hadlee	17
M. Amarnath	b Collinge	26
E.D. Solkar	c Cairns b D.R. Hadlee	1
S.M.H. Kirmani†	c D.R. Hadlee b Collinge	8
Madan Lal	c Wadsworth b Collinge	8
S. Venkataraghavan	b Collinge	0
B.S. Bedi*	not out	4
Extras	(B 2, LB 6, NB 1)	9
Total	(35 overs)	**154**

Fall of wickets 1-7, 2-16, 3-30, 4-87, 5-113, 6-117, 7-138, 8-149, 9-149, 10-154.

NEW ZEALAND	*O*	*M*	*R*	*W*
Collinge	7	1	23	5
Cairns	7	1	20	2
R.J. Hadlee	6	0	28	0
McKechnie	5	0	16	0
D.R. Hadlee	7	0	41	2
Congdon	3	C	17	0

NEW ZEALAND		
G.M. Turner*	not out	63
G.N. Edwards	lbw b Bedi	41
B.E. Congdon	not out	45
J.M. Parker		
M.G. Burgess		
K.J. Wadsworth†		
B.L. Cairns		
R.J. Hadlee		
B.J. McKechnie		
R.O. Collinge		
D.R. Hadlee		
Extras	(LB 6)	6
Total	(30.3 overs – 1 wicket)	**155**

Fall of wicket 1-73.

INDIA	*O*	*M*	*R*	*W*
Madan Lal	4.3	1	22	0
Solkar	5	0	27	0
Bedi	7	0	24	1
Amarnath	7	0	37	0
Venkataraghavan	7	0	39	0

Umpires: E.W. Dempster and A.M. Rangi.

NEW ZEALAND v INDIA 1975-76 (2nd Match)

At Eden Park, Auckland on 22 February 1976.
Toss: New Zealand. Result: NEW ZEALAND won by 80 runs.
35 eight-ball overs match. Award: K.J. Wadsworth.
Débuts: India – B.S. Chandrasekhar, P. Krishnamurthy, Sudhakar Rao.

NEW ZEALAND		
G.M. Turner*	st Krishnamurthy b Venkataraghavan	52
G.N. Edwards	c Madan Lal b Chandrasekhar	32
B.L. Cairns	run out	31
B.E. Congdon	c and b Solkar	2
J.M. Parker	c Venkataraghavan b Solkar	14
M.G. Burgess	b Chandrasekhar	38
K.J. Wadsworth†	not out	46
R.J. Hadlee	c Krishnamurthy b Chandrasekhar	0
B.J. McKechnie	c Rao b Amarnath	8
R.O. Collinge	not out	0
D.R. Hadlee		
Extras	(B 2, LB 11)	13
Total	(35 overs – 8 wickets)	**236**

Fall of wickets: 1-71, 2-106, 3-109, 4-142, 5-142, 6-194, 7-194, 8-230.

INDIA	*O*	*M*	*R*	*W*
Madan Lal	7	0	37	0
Solkar	7	0	46	2
Amarnath	7	0	59	1
Chandrasekhar	7	0	36	3
Venkataraghavan	7	0	45	1

INDIA		
P. Sharma	b Cairns	14
D.B. Vengsarkar	c Turner b D.R. Hadlee	43
A.D. Gaekwad	st Wadsworth b McKechnie	13
B.P. Patel	c Turner b R.J. Hadlee	44
M. Amarnath	b D.R. Hadlee	3
E.D. Solkar	run out	2
Sudhakar Rao	run out	4
Madan Lal	c D.R. Hadlee b Parker	13
S. Venkataraghavan*	c Parker b Burgess	1
P. Krishnamurthy†	c and b Edwards	6
B.S. Chandrasekhar	not out	11
Extras	(LB 2)	2
Total	(31.6 overs)	**156**

Fall of wickets: 1-40, 2-66, 3-78, 4-97, 5-103, 6-120, 7-128, 8-139, 9-139, 10-156.

NEW ZEALAND	*O*	*M*	*R*	*W*
Collinge	3	0	19	0
R.J. Hadlee	7	0	35	1
Cairns	7	1	33	1
D.R. Hadlee	7	0	18	2
McKechnie	4	0	24	1
Parker	2	0	10	1
Burgess	1	0	10	1
Edwards	0.6	0	5	1

Umpires: W.R.C. Gardiner and J.B.R. Hastie.

Match No. 37/3

ENGLAND v WEST INDIES 1976 (1st Match)

Prudential Trophy

At Scarborough on 26 August 1976.
Toss: West Indies. Result: WEST INDIES won by 6 wickets.
55 overs match. Award: I.V.A. Richards.

Débuts: England – G.D. Barlow, I.T. Botham, G.A. Gooch, J.K. Lever, D.S. Steele; West Indies – M.A. Holding, C.L. King.

Knott made his only appearance as England's captain when Greig was unable to play because of a damaged finger.

ENGLAND		
B. Wood	b Roberts	0
D.L. Amiss	b Julien	34
D.S. Steele	c King b Roberts	8
R.A. Woolmer	c Murray b Holding	3
G.D. Barlow	not out	80
G.A. Gooch	c Holder b Roberts	32
I.T. Botham	c Fredericks b Holding	1
A.P.E. Knott*†	run out	16
D.L. Underwood	c Julien b Roberts	14
J.K. Lever		
M. Hendrick		
Extras	(LB 11, W 1, NB 2)	14
Total	(55 overs – 8 wickets)	**202**

Fall of wickets: 1-0, 2-18, 3-23, 4-72, 5-136, 6-145, 7-181, 8-202.

WEST INDIES	*O*	*M*	*R*	*W*
Roberts	11	0	32	4
Holding	11	1	38	2
Holder	11	3	30	0
Julien	11	2	37	1
King	6	0	25	0
Lloyd	5	1	26	0

WEST INDIES		
R.C. Fredericks	b Hendrick	1
C.G. Greenidge	b Wood	27
I.V.A. Richards	not out	119
C.H. Lloyd*	b Underwood	20
L.G. Rowe	c Hendrick b Botham	10
C.L. King	not out	14
D.L. Murray†		
B.D. Julien		
V.A. Holder		
M.A. Holding		
A.M.E. Roberts		
Extras	(B 8, LB 8)	16
Total	(41 overs – 4 wickets)	**207**

Fall of wickets: 1-3, 2-77, 3-116, 4-176.

ENGLAND	*O*	*M*	*R*	*W*
Lever	9	1	38	0
Hendrick	9	3	38	1
Wood	8	2	29	1
Underwood	9	1	35	1
Botham	3	0	26	1
Woolmer	2	0	16	0
Steele	1	0	9	0

Umpires: D.J. Constant and A. Jepson.

ENGLAND v WEST INDIES 1976 (2nd Match)
Prudential Trophy

At Lord's, London on 28, 29 August 1976.
Toss: England. Result: WEST INDIES won by 36 runs.
50 overs match. Award: I.V.A. Richards.
Début: England – D.W. Randall.

WEST INDIES		
R.C. Fredericks	c Randall b Hendrick	19
C.G. Greenidge	b Hendrick	29
I.V.A. Richards	c Woolmer b Greig	97
C.H. Lloyd*	c Barlow b Woolmer	27
C.L. King	c Wood b Woolmer	1
L.G. Rowe	b Underwood	4
D.L. Murray†	c and b Underwood	1
B.D. Julien	c Randall b Underwood	4
M.A. Holding	c Barlow b Wood	16
V.A. Holder	b Greig	2
A.M.E. Roberts	not out	7
Extras	(B 5, LB 5, W 1, NB 3)	14
Total	(47.5 overs)	**221**

Fall of wickets: 1-51, 2-53, 3-121, 4-124, 5-135, 6-143, 7-154, 8-193, 9-201, 10-221.

ENGLAND	*O*	*M*	*R*	*W*
Hendrick	9	2	34	2
Jackman	10	1	50	0
Woolmer	10	0	52	2
Underwood	10	0	27	3
Greig	5.5	0	31	2
Wood	3	0	13	1

ENGLAND		
B. Wood	c and b Roberts	4
D.L. Amiss	c Murray b Roberts	12
R.A. Woolmer	b Roberts	9
G.D. Barlow	c Holder b Roberts	0
G.A. Gooch	c Murray b Holder	5
D.W. Randall	c King b Lloyd	88
A.W. Greig*	c Richards b Julien	3
A.P.E. Knott†	run out	22
R.D. Jackman	b Holder	14
D.L. Underwood	c Greenidge b Lloyd	2
M. Hendrick	not out	0
Extras	(LB 14, W 4, NB 8)	26
Total	(45.3 overs)	**185**

Fall of wickets: 1-4, 2-25, 3-30, 4-31, 5-48, 6-62, 7-125, 8-180, 9-185, 10-185.

WEST INDIES	*O*	*M*	*R*	*W*
Roberts	8	1	27	4
Holding	8	0	26	0
Julien	10	4	22	1
Holder	10	0	35	2
King	8	0	45	0
Lloyd	1.3	0	4	2

Umpires: W.E. Alley and A.E. Fagg.

Match No. 39/5

ENGLAND v WEST INDIES 1976 (3rd Match)

Prudential Trophy

At Edgbaston, Birmingham on 30 (no play), 31 August 1976.

Toss: England.	Result: WEST INDIES won by 50 runs.
32 overs match.	Award: C.H. Lloyd.

No débuts.

WEST INDIES		
R.C. Fredericks	c Barlow b Lever	1
C.G. Greenidge	c Hendrick b Underwood	42
I.V.A. Richards	c Wood b Lever	0
C.H. Lloyd*	b Greig	79
L.G. Rowe	run out	45
C.L. King	lbw b Hendrick	7
B.D. Julien	b Hendrick	5
D.L. Murray†	run out	27
M.A. Holding	b Botham	3
A.M.E. Roberts	not out	0
V.A. Holder		
Extras	(LB 12, NB 2)	14
Total	(32 overs – 9 wickets)	**223**

Fall of wickets: 1-7, 2-7, 3-95, 4-145, 5-162, 6-174, 7-209, 8-223, 9-223.

ENGLAND	*O*	*M*	*R*	*W*
Hendrick	10	0	45	2
Lever	10	1	57	2
Botham	3	0	31	1
Underwood	3	0	28	1
Greig	6	0	48	1

ENGLAND		
B. Wood	b Julien	34
D.L. Amiss	b Julien	47
G.D. Barlow	lbw b Holder	0
G.A. Gooch	c Murray b Holder	3
D.W. Randall	c Murray b Holder	39
A.W. Greig*	b Holder	2
I.T. Botham	c Julien b Fredericks	20
A.P.E. Knott†	c Greenidge b Holder	10
D.L. Underwood	st Murray b Richards	6
J.K. Lever	b Fredericks	1
M. Hendrick	not out	1
Extras	(B 2, LB 6, NB 2)	10
Total	(31.4 overs)	**173**

Fall of wickets: 1-54, 2-59, 3-73, 4-89, 5-111, 6-138, 7-151, 8-171, 9-171, 10-173.

WEST INDIES	*O*	*M*	*R*	*W*
Roberts	5	1	9	0
Holding	7	1	34	0
Holder	10	0	50	5
Julien	7	0	56	2
Fredericks	1.4	0	10	2
Richards	1	0	4	1

Umpires: H.D. Bird and W.L. Budd.

PAKISTAN v NEW ZEALAND 1976-77 (Only Match)

At Jinnah Park, Sialkot on 16 October 1976.
Toss: New Zealand. Result: NEW ZEALAND won by 1 run.
35 eight-ball overs match. No award.

Débuts: New Zealand – R.W. Anderson, N.M. Parker, A.D.G. Roberts, G.B. Troup.

The first one-day international in Pakistan produced the first instance of a victory by only 1 run.

NEW ZEALAND		
J.F.M. Morrison	b Intikhab	15
G.M. Turner*	b Asif Masood	67
N.M. Parker	lbw b Intikhab	0
G.P. Howarth	b Miandad	43
A.D.G. Roberts	c Wasim Bari b Sarfraz	16
J.M. Parker†	c Mushtaq b Miandad	2
R.W. Anderson	not out	4
B.L. Cairns	c Zaheer b Imran	24
D.R. O'Sullivan	run out	1
R.O. Collinge	not out	5
G.B. Troup		
Extras	(B 3, LB 11, NB 7)	21
Total	(35 overs – 8 wickets)	**198**

Fall of wickets: 1-48, 2-48, 3-135, 4-143, 5-160, 6-161, 7-188, 8-189.

PAKISTAN	*O*	*M*	*R*	*W*
Sarfraz Nawaz	7	0	35	1
Imran Khan	7	0	36	1
Asif Masood	7	0	38	1
Intikhab Alam	7	0	36	2
Javed Miandad	6	0	31	2
Wasim Raja	1	0	1	0

PAKISTAN		
Majid Khan	b Roberts	20
Sadiq Mohammad	run out	17
Zaheer Abbas	st J.M. Parker b O'Sullivan	23
Mushtaq Mohammad*	c Roberts b Troup	46
Javed Miandad	b Cairns	47
Intikhab Alam	c N.M. Parker b Collinge	7
Wasim Raja	b Cairns	8
Imran Khan	not out	4
Sarfraz Nawaz	run out	0
Asif Masood	run out	0
Wasim Bari†	not out	2
Extras	(B 18, LB 5)	23
Total	(35 overs – 9 wickets)	**197**

Fall of wickets: 1-38, 2-43, 3-89, 4-139, 5-166, 6-188, 7-191, 8-192, 9-195.

NEW ZEALAND	*O*	*M*	*R*	*W*
Collinge	7	0	37	1
Cairns	7	0	36	2
Roberts	7	0	30	1
Troup	7	1	29	1
O'Sullivan	7	0	42	1

Umpires: Javed Akhtar and Mahboob Shah.

Match No. 41/2

WEST INDIES v PAKISTAN 1976-77 (Only Match)

Guinness Trophy

At Albion Sports Complex, Berbice, Guyana on 16 March 1977.
Toss: West Indies. Result: WEST INDIES won by 4 wickets.
45 overs match. Award: Asif Iqbal.

Débuts: West Indies – C.E.H. Croft, J. Garner; Pakistan – Mohsin Khan.

The first limited-overs international to be staged in the Caribbean.

PAKISTAN		
Majid Khan	c Lloyd b Garner	23
Sadiq Mohammad	c Murray b Croft	6
Zaheer Abbas	c Julien b Garner	10
Mohsin Khan	lbw b Julien	15
Wasim Raja	c Fredericks b Croft	0
Asif Iqbal*	not out	59
Javed Miandad	c Greenidge b Croft	15
Imran Khan	b Garner	39
Sarfraz Nawaz	not out	2
Wasim Bari†		
Salim Altaf		
Extras	(B 1, LB 4, W 1, NB 1)	7
Total	(45 overs – 7 wickets)	**176**

Fall of wickets: 1-32, 2-36, 3-46, 4-47, 5-67, 6-104, 7-171.

WEST INDIES	*O*	*M*	*R*	*W*
Roberts	9	3	27	0
Julien	9	1	30	1
Croft	9	2	50	3
Garner	9	3	27	3
King	9	0	35	0

WEST INDIES		
R.C. Fredericks	c Asif Iqbal b Majid	44
C.G. Greenidge	b Imran	8
I.V.A. Richards	c Mohsin b Sarfraz	20
A.I. Kallicharran	c Asif Iqbal b Sarfraz	24
C.H. Lloyd*	not out	45
C.L. King	c Wasim Bari b Asif Iqbal	0
B.D. Julien	c Wasim Bari b Sarfraz	20
D.L. Murray†	not out	11
J. Garner		
A.M.E. Roberts		
C.E.H. Croft		
Extras	(B 4, LB 4, W 1, NB 1)	10
Total	(43.2 overs – 6 wickets)	**182**

Fall of wickets: 1-27, 2-59, 3-96, 4-121, 5-122, 6-151.

PAKISTAN	*O*	*M*	*R*	*W*
Sarfraz Nawaz	9	1	42	3
Imran Khan	9	1	41	1
Salim Altaf	8	0	27	0
Asif Iqbal	8	0	30	1
Majid Khan	9	1	26	1
Sadiq Mohammad	0.2	0	6	0

Umpires: C. Paynter and C.F. Vyfhuis.

ENGLAND v AUSTRALIA 1977 (1st Match)
Prudential Trophy

At Old Trafford, Manchester on 2 June 1977.
Toss: Australia. Result: ENGLAND won by 2 wickets.
55 overs match. Award: R.W. Marsh.
Débuts: England – J.M. Brearley, P. Willey; Australia – D.W. Hookes, M.F. Malone, K.J. O'Keeffe, L.S. Pascoe, C.S. Serjeant.

AUSTRALIA		
R.B. McCosker	c Knott b Willis	1
I.C. Davis	c Greig b Lever	1
G.S. Chappell*	lbw b Underwood	30
C.S. Serjeant	c Randall b Greig	46
K.D. Walters	c Amiss b Old	0
D.W. Hookes	c Knott b Greig	11
R.W. Marsh†	b Lever	42
K.J. O'Keeffe	not out	16
M.H.N. Walker	c Barlow b Underwood	5
M.F. Malone	c Brearley b Underwood	4
L.S. Pascoe	not out	4
Extras	(B 4, LB 4, NB 1)	9
Total	(55 overs – 9 wickets)	**169**

Fall of wickets 1-2, 2-2, 3-55, 4-62, 5-93, 6-94, 7-145, 8-152, 9-156.

ENGLAND	*O*	*M*	*R*	*W*
Willis	8	2	16	1
Lever	10	1	45	2
Underwood	11	1	29	3
Old	11	3	30	1
Willey	11	1	29	0
Greig	4	0	11	2

ENGLAND		
D.L. Amiss	c Serjeant b Walker	8
J.M. Brearley*	lbw b Malone	29
D.W. Randall	c McCosker b Malone	19
G.D. Barlow	run out	42
P. Willey	c Walker b O'Keeffe	1
A.W. Greig	run out	22
A.P.E. Knott†	not out	21
C.M. Old	c Hookes b Walker	25
J.K. Lever	c Walters b Walker	1
D.L. Underwood	not out	0
R.G.D. Willis		
Extras	(B 1, LB 3, W 1)	5
Total	(45.2 overs – 8 wickets)	**173**

Fall of wickets 1-17, 2-51, 3-70, 4-71, 5-123, 6-125, 7-160, 8-168.

AUSTRALIA	*O*	*M*	*R*	*W*
Pascoe	10.2	1	44	0
Walker	7	3	20	3
Malone	11	1	37	2
O'Keeffe	11	3	36	1
Chappell	6	1	31	0

Umpires: D.J. Constant and B.J. Meyer.

Match No. 43/8

ENGLAND v AUSTRALIA 1977 (2nd Match)

Prudential Trophy

At Edgbaston, Birmingham on 4 June 1977.
Toss: Australia. Result: ENGLAND won by 101 runs.
55 overs match. Award: J.K. Lever.

Débuts: Australia – K.J. Hughes, R.D. Robinson.

Australia were dismissed for their lowest total in any one-day international after Chappell and Cosier had achieved the only instance of two bowlers taking five wickets in the same innings at this level.

ENGLAND		
D.L. Amiss	c Marsh b Chappell	35
J.M. Brearley*	lbw b Chappell	10
D.W. Randall	c Marsh b Chappell	0
G.D. Barlow	c Hughes b Chappell	25
P. Willey	c Marsh b Cosier	6
A.W. Greig	c Chappell b Cosier	0
A.P.E. Knott†	lbw b Cosier	0
C.M. Old	c Hughes b Chappell	35
J.K. Lever	not out	27
D.L. Underwood	b Cosier	0
R.G.D. Willis	c Marsh b Cosier	7
Extras	(LB 15, W 4, NB 7)	26
Total	(53.5 overs)	**171**

Fall of wickets: 1-19, 2-19, 3-67, 4-84, 5-84, 6-84, 7-90, 8-145, 9-160, 10-171.

AUSTRALIA	*O*	*M*	*R*	*W*
Thomson	9	0	46	0
Malone	11	2	27	0
Chappell	11	5	20	5
Walker	11	3	29	0
Cosier	8.5	3	18	5
Bright	3	0	5	0

AUSTRALIA		
I.C. Davis	c Old b Willis	0
C.S. Serjeant	b Willis	2
G.S. Chappell*	b Lever	19
G.J. Cosier	lbw b Lever	3
K.J. Hughes	c Knott b Lever	2
R.D. Robinson	b Old	12
R.W. Marsh†	c Old b Lever	1
R.J. Bright	not out	17
M.H.N. Walker	run out	0
M.F. Malone	run out	1
J.R. Thomson	b Greig	3
Extras	(B 4, LB 5, NB 1)	10
Total	(25.2 overs)	**70**

Fall of wickets: 1-0, 2-27, 3-31, 4-34, 5-35, 6-38, 7-58, 8-58, 9-60, 10-70.

ENGLAND	*O*	*M*	*R*	*W*
Willis	6	1	14	2
Lever	11	2	29	4
Old	7	2	15	1
Greig	1.2	0	2	1

Umpires: W.E. Alley and W.L. Budd.

ENGLAND v AUSTRALIA 1977 (3rd Match)
Prudential Trophy

At Kennington Oval, London on 6 June 1977.
Toss: Australia. Result: AUSTRALIA won by 2 wickets.
55 overs match. Award: G.S. Chappell.

Début: England – G. Miller.

Amiss became the first batsman to score four hundreds in these matches. Chappell's score remained the highest in Prudential Trophy matches. To avoid playing on Jubilee Day, the match was completed in torrential rain.

ENGLAND		
D.L. Amiss	b Pascoe	108
J.M. Brearley*	st Robinson b O'Keeffe	78
D.W. Randall	c and b Bright	6
G.D. Barlow	run out	2
A.W. Greig	c Robinson b Thomson	4
A.P.E. Knott†	c Robinson b Pascoe	4
G. Miller	c Robinson b Pascoe	4
C.M. Old	c Thomson b Chappell	20
J.K. Lever	b Thomson	2
D.L. Underwood	c Pascoe b Dymock	5
R.G.D. Willis	not out	0
Extras	(LB 1, W 2, NB 6)	9
Total	(54.2 overs)	**242**

Fall of wickets: 1-161, 2-168, 3-179, 4-196, 5-203, 6-207, 7-217, 8-227, 9-241, 10-242.

AUSTRALIA	*O*	*M*	*R*	*W*
Thomson	11	2	51	2
Dymock	10	0	39	1
Pascoe	11	0	44	3
O'Keeffe	11	0	43	1
Bright	11	1	56	1
Chappell	0.2	0	0	1

AUSTRALIA		
R.D. Robinson†	c Brearley b Willis	70
R.B. McCosker	lbw b Old	11
G.S. Chappell*	not out	125
K.J. Hughes	lbw b Willis	3
K.D. Walters	c Brearley b Underwood	12
D.W. Hookes	b Lever	3
R.J. Bright	c Randall b Old	0
K.J. O'Keeffe	run out	0
J.R. Thomson	run out	3
G. Dymock	not out	2
L.S. Pascoe		
Extras	(B 1, LB 14, W 1, NB 1)	17
Total	(53.2 overs – 8 wickets)	**246**

Fall of wickets: 1-33, 2-181, 3-186, 4-209, 5-225, 6-228, 7-228, 8-237.

ENGLAND	*O*	*M*	*R*	*W*
Willis	11	0	49	2
Lever	10	0	43	1
Old	10.2	0	56	2
Underwood	11	2	21	1
Miller	5	0	24	0
Greig	6	0	36	0

Umpires: H.D. Bird and K.E. Palmer.

Match No. 45/3

PAKISTAN v ENGLAND 1977-78 (1st Match)

At Sahiwal Stadium on 23 December 1977.
Toss: Pakistan. Result: ENGLAND won by 3 wickets.
35 eight-ball overs match. Awards: batting – Javed Miandad; bowling and fielding – I.T. Botham.

Débuts: Pakistan – Aamer Hameed, Hasan Jamil, Liaquat Ali, Mudassar Nazar, Shafiq Ahmed; England – P.R. Downton, P.H. Edmonds, M.W. Gatting, B.C. Rose.

PAKISTAN		
Mudassar Nazar	run out	20
Sadiq Mohammad	b Botham	2
Shafiq Ahmed	b Miller	29
Javed Miandad	not out	77
Wasim Raja	c Randall b Botham	36
Parvez Mir	lbw b Hendrick	18
Hasan Jamil	c Downton b Botham	20
Wasim Bari*†	not out	1
Salim Altaf		
Aamer Hameed		
Liaquat Ali		
Extras	(LB 3, NB 2)	5
Total	(35 overs – 6 wickets)	**208**

Fall of wickets: 1-4, 2-46, 3-63, 4-114, 5-167, 6-201.

ENGLAND	*O*	*M*	*R*	*W*
Hendrick	7	0	50	1
Botham	7	0	39	3
Old	7	0	49	0
Edmonds	7	0	19	0
Miller	7	0	46	1

ENGLAND		
J.M. Brearley*	c Parvez b Aamer	30
B.C. Rose	c and b Wasim Raja	54
M.W. Gatting	run out	17
D.W. Randall	c Wasim Bari b Salim	35
C.M. Old	lbw b Parvez	1
G.R.J. Roope	b Liaquat	29
I.T. Botham	not out	15
P.H. Edmonds	run out	5
G. Miller	not out	0
P.R. Downton†		
M. Hendrick		
Extras	(B 5, LB 14, NB 7)	26
Total	(35 overs – 7 wickets)	**212**

Fall of wickets: 1-66, 2-111, 3-127, 4-134, 5-181, 6-193, 7-205.

PAKISTAN	*O*	*M*	*R*	*W*
Salim Altaf	7	0	34	1
Liaquat Ali	7	0	50	1
Aamer Hameed	7	1	32	1
Parvez Mir	4	0	18	1
Javed Miandad	7	1	29	0
Wasim Raja	2	0	11	1
Mudassar Nazar	1	0	12	0

Umpires: Azhar Hussain and Shakoor Rana.

PAKISTAN v ENGLAND 1977-78 (2nd Match)

At Jinnah Park, Sialkot on 30 December 1977.
Toss: England. Result: ENGLAND won by 6 wickets.
35 eight-ball overs match. Awards: batting – Wasim Raja; bowling – J.K. Lever; fielding – D.W. Randall.

Débuts: Pakistan – Haroon Rashid, Iqbal Qasim, Sikander Bakht; England – G.A. Cope.

PAKISTAN		
Sadiq Mohammad	c Taylor b Lever	13
Mudassar Nazar	c Randall b Cope	33
Shafiq Ahmed	c and b Edmonds	9
Haroon Rashid	c Rose b Miller	5
Javed Miandad	run out	8
Wasim Raja	b Botham	43
Wasim Bari*†	b Edmonds	1
Hasan Jamil	c Taylor b Lever	28
Salim Altaf	not out	4
Iqbal Qasim	c and b Lever	0
Sikander Bakht	run out	0
Extras	(B 4, LB 2, NB 1)	7
Total	(33.7 overs)	**151**

Fall of wickets: 1-20, 2-55, 3-57, 4-65, 5-74, 6-76, 7-140, 8-150, 9-150, 10-151.

ENGLAND	*O*	*M*	*R*	*W*
Lever	6	1	18	3
Botham	6.7	0	21	1
Cope	7	0	19	1
Miller	6	1	43	1
Edmonds	7	0	28	2
Gatting	1	0	15	0

ENGLAND		
B.C. Rose	b Iqbal Qasim	45
G.R.J. Roope	c Haroon b Sikander	7
G. Miller	c Sikander b Iqbal Qasim	16
D.W. Randall	not out	51
M.W. Gatting	run out	5
I.T. Botham	not out	17
G. Boycott*		
R.W. Taylor†		
P.H. Edmonds		
J.K. Lever		
G.A. Cope		
Extras	(LB 4, W 1, NB 6)	11
Total	(32.7 overs – 4 wickets)	**152**

Fall of wickets: 1-17, 2-43, 3-104, 4-112.

PAKISTAN	*O*	*M*	*R*	*W*
Salim Altaf	5.7	0	20	0
Sikander Bakht	6	0	25	1
Javed Miandad	7	0	32	0
Iqbal Qasim	7	2	16	2
Hasan Jamil	6	0	39	0
Wasim Raja	1	0	9	0

Umpires: Javed Akhtar and Khalid Aziz.

Match No. 47/5

PAKISTAN v ENGLAND 1977-78 (3rd Match)

At Gaddafi Stadium, Lahore on 13 January 1978.
Toss: England. Result: PAKISTAN won by 36 runs.
35 eight-ball overs match. Award: Wasim Raja.
Début: Pakistan – Arshad Pervez.

PAKISTAN		
Mudassar Nazar	b Edmonds	30
Arshad Pervez	b Lever	8
Shafiq Ahmed	st Taylor b Edmonds	3
Javed Miandad	c Boycott b Lever	31
Wasim Raja	c Boycott b Cope	0
Mohsin Khan	not out	51
Hasan Jamil	c Boycott b Old	21
Sarfraz Nawaz	not out	1
Wasim Bari*†		
Aamer Hameed		
Iqbal Qasim		
Extras	(LB 11, NB 2)	13
Total	(35 overs – 6 wickets)	**158**

Fall of wickets: 1-22, 2-41, 3-52, 4-53, 5-112, 6-148.

ENGLAND	*O*	*M*	*R*	*W*
Old	7	0	35	1
Lever	7	1	25	2
Botham	7	0	41	0
Edmonds	7	1	28	2
Cope	7	0	16	1

ENGLAND		
G. Boycott	lbw b Sarfraz	6
J.M. Brearley*	c Shafiq b Sarfraz	1
D.W. Randall	c Mudassar b Wasim Raja	32
M.W. Gatting	c and b Jamil	3
I.T. Botham	c Wasim Bari b Iqbal Qasim	11
C.M. Old	c Wasim Raja b Jamil	4
G.R.J. Roope	run out	37
R.W. Taylor†	b Wasim Raja	12
P.H. Edmonds	run out	0
J.K. Lever	c Aamer b Wasim Raja	0
G.A. Cope	not out	1
Extras	(B 2, LB 6, W 1, NB 6)	15
Total	(31.6 overs)	**122**

Fall of wickets: 1-11, 2-15, 3-25, 4-42, 5-49, 6-97, 7-118, 8-119, 9-121, 10-122.

PAKISTAN	*O*	*M*	*R*	*W*
Sarfraz Nawaz	5	2	7	2
Aamer Hameed	4	1	6	0
Hasan Jamil	5	0	20	2
Iqbal Qasim	7	2	25	1
Javed Miandad	6	0	26	0
Wasim Raja	4.6	0	23	3

Umpires: Khalid Aziz and Shakoor Rana.

WEST INDIES v AUSTRALIA 1977-78 (1st Match)

Guinness Trophy

At Recreation Ground, St John's, Antigua on 22 February 1978.
Toss: Australia. Result: WEST INDIES won on scoring rate.
50 overs match. Award: D.L. Haynes.

Débuts: West Indies – R.A. Austin, S.F.A.F. Bacchus, W.W. Daniel, D.L. Haynes, I.T. Shillingford; Australia – I.W. Callen, W.M. Clark, W.M. Darling, T.J. Laughlin, S.J. Rixon, R.B. Simpson, P.M. Toohey, G.M. Wood, G.N. Yallop.

WEST INDIES		
R.A. Austin	c Simpson b Clark	8
D.L. Haynes	b Thomson	148
I.V.A. Richards	c sub (B. Yardley) b Callen	9
A.I. Kallicharran	c Rixon b Laughlin	7
S.F.A.F. Bacchus	hit wicket b Laughlin	0
I.T. Shillingford	b Thomson	24
D.L. Murray*†	c Simpson b Laughlin	51
J. Garner	c Rixon b Thomson	13
A.M.E. Roberts	c Callen b Thomson	3
W.W. Daniel	not out	14
C.E.H. Croft	not out	5
Extras	(B 3, LB 10, NB 18)	31
Total	(50 overs – 9 wickets)	**313**

Fall of wickets: 1-27, 2-56, 3-78, 4-78, 5-121, 6-247, 7-282, 8-288, 9-303.

AUSTRALIA	*O*	*M*	*R*	*W*
Thomson	10	0	67	4
Clark	10	3	22	1
Callen	7	1	42	1
Laughlin	9	2	54	3
Simpson	10	0	65	0
Cosier	4	0	32	0

AUSTRALIA		
G.M. Wood	c Shillingford b Croft	24
W.M. Darling	c Kallicharran b Croft	8
G.N. Yallop	c and b Garner	12
P.M. Toohey	lbw b Garner	5
G.J. Cosier	c Daniel b Croft	84
R.B. Simpson*	b Garner	13
T.J. Laughlin	c Richards b Daniel	2
S.J. Rixon†	not out	20
I.W. Callen	not out	3
J.R. Thomson		
W.M. Clark		
Extras	(NB 10)	10
Total	(36 overs – 7 wickets)	**181**

Fall of wickets: 1-20, 2-38, 3-48, 4-56, 5-94, 6-99, 7-172.

WEST INDIES	*O*	*M*	*R*	*W*
Roberts	7	0	38	0
Croft	10	1	44	3
Garner	8	0	29	3
Daniel	9	1	35	1
Austin	1	0	13	0
Richards	1	0	12	0

Umpires: R. Gosein and W. Malcolm.

Match No. 49/5

WEST INDIES v AUSTRALIA 1977-78 (2nd Match)

Guinness Trophy

At Mindoo Phillip Park, Castries, St Lucia on 12 April 1978.
Toss: West Indies. Result: AUSTRALIA won by 2 wickets.
35 overs match. Award: R.B. Simpson.

Débuts: West Indies – S.T. Clarke, H.A. Gomes, A.E. Greenidge, D.R. Parry, N. Phillip, S. Shivnarine; Australia – B. Yardley.

WEST INDIES		
A.E. Greenidge	run out	23
A.I. Kallicharran*	c Simpson b Yardley	34
H.A. Gomes	c Darling b Simpson	7
S.F.A.F. Bacchus	c and b Simpson	0
I.T. Shillingford	c Wood b Callen	6
D.A. Murray†	b Yardley	2
S. Shivnarine	not out	20
N. Phillip	c Rixon b Callen	0
D.R. Parry	c and b Callen	5
V.A. Holder	b Clark	30
S.T. Clarke	b Clark	0
Extras	(LB 4, NB 8)	12
Total	(34.4 overs)	**139**

Fall of wickets: 1-48, 2-69, 3-69, 4-69, 5-74, 6-80, 7-85, 8-92, 9-139, 10-139.

AUSTRALIA	*O*	*M*	*R*	*W*
Thomson	7	1	20	0
Callen	7	0	24	3
Clark	6.4	0	39	2
Simpson	7	0	30	2
Yardley	7	3	14	2

AUSTRALIA		
W.M. Darling	c Parry b Holder	21
G.M. Wood	c Murray b Clarke	9
P.M. Toohey	c Clarke b Parry	30
C.S. Serjeant	run out	25
G.N. Yallop	c Shillingford b Parry	7
R.B. Simpson*	c Parry b Phillip	23
S.J. Rixon†	c Murray b Holder	0
B. Yardley	run out	7
I.W. Callen	not out	3
J.R. Thomson	not out	1
W.M. Clark		
Extras	(B 5, LB 6, NB 3)	14
Total	(35 overs – 8 wickets)	**140**

Fall of wickets: 1-25, 2-61, 3-80, 4-95, 5-119, 6-120, 7-133, 8-138.

WEST INDIES	*O*	*M*	*R*	*W*
Clarke	7	1	15	1
Phillip	7	0	22	1
Gomes	4	0	18	0
Holder	7	0	28	2
Parry	7	1	27	2
Shivnarine	3	0	16	0

Umpires: P. Alleyne and R. Gosein.

ENGLAND v PAKISTAN 1978 (1st Match)

Prudential Trophy

At Old Trafford, Manchester on 24, 25 May 1978.
Toss: England. Result: ENGLAND won by 132 runs.
55 overs match. Award: R.G.D. Willis.

Débuts: England – D.I. Gower, C.T. Radley.

Pakistan's total remains their lowest in any one-day international.

ENGLAND		
B. Wood	c Miandad b Wasim Raja	26
G. Boycott*	c Wasim Bari b Sarfraz	3
C.T. Radley	c and b Mudassar	79
D.I. Gower	c Miandad b Mudassar	33
G.R.J. Roope	c Wasim Bari b Sikander	10
I.T. Botham	c Haroon b Sikander	31
G. Miller	b Sikander	0
C.M. Old	not out	6
P.H. Edmonds	not out	4
R.W. Taylor†		
R.G.D. Willis		
Extras	(B 2, LB 15, W 3, NB 5)	25
Total	(55 overs – 7 wickets)	**217**

Fall of wickets: 1-3, 2-86, 3-157, 4-158, 5-176, 6-185, 7-209.

PAKISTAN	*O*	*M*	*R*	*W*
Sarfraz Nawaz	11	6	13	1
Liaquat Ali	11	3	20	0
Sikander Bakht	11	0	56	3
Mudassar Nazar	11	1	52	2
Iqbal Qasim	4	1	24	0
Wasim Raja	7	1	27	1

PAKISTAN		
Mudassar Nazar	c Wood b Botham	8
Sadiq Mohammad	b Willis	3
Haroon Rashid	b Old	1
Javed Miandad	lbw b Willis	9
Mohsin Khan	c Roope b Willis	1
Wasim Raja	lbw b Willis	0
Sarfraz Nawaz	c Taylor b Botham	7
Wasim Bari*†	b Wood	19
Iqbal Qasim	b Wood	9
Sikander Bakht	not out	16
Liaquat Ali	b Old	7
Extras	(LB 3, W 1, NB 1)	5
Total	(47 overs)	**85**

Fall of wickets: 1-3, 2-7, 3-20, 4-21, 5-21, 6-31, 7-31, 8-60, 9-61, 10-85.

ENGLAND	*O*	*M*	*R*	*W*
Willis	11	5	15	4
Old	7	4	6	2
Botham	8	1	17	2
Wood	11	3	25	2
Edmonds	10	4	17	0

Umpires: D.J. Constant and K.E. Palmer.

Match No. 51/7

ENGLAND v PAKISTAN 1978 (2nd Match)

Prudential Trophy

At Kennington Oval, London on 26 May 1978.
Toss: Pakistan. Result: ENGLAND won by 94 runs.
55 overs match. Award: D.I. Gower.
Début: Pakistan – Naeem Ahmed.

On his second international appearance, Gower reached his first hundred for England off 116 balls.

ENGLAND		
D. Lloyd	b Wasim Raja	34
B. Wood	b Sarfraz	8
C.T. Radley	b Liaquat	13
D.I. Gower	not out	114
G.R.J. Roope	c Naeem b Mudassar	35
I.T. Botham	b Mudassar	1
G. Miller	lbw b Sikander	0
C.M. Old	not out	25
R.W. Taylor†		
J.K. Lever		
R.G.D. Willis*		
Extras	(B 5, LB 9, NB 4)	18
Total	(55 overs – 6 wickets)	**248**

Fall of wickets: 1-27, 2-60, 3-83, 4-188, 5-194, 6-195.

PAKISTAN	*O*	*M*	*R*	*W*
Sarfraz Nawaz	11	2	48	1
Liaquat Ali	11	1	41	1
Sikander Bakht	11	0	53	1
Wasim Raja	6	0	14	1
Naeem Ahmed	10	0	43	0
Mudassar Nazar	6	0	31	2

PAKISTAN		
Mudassar Nazar	c Willis b Botham	56
Sadiq Mohammad	c and b Old	9
Arshad Pervez	lbw b Miller	3
Javed Miandad	b Old	0
Haroon Rashid	st Taylor b Miller	20
Wasim Raja	c sub (P.H. Edmonds) b Lloyd	44
Wasim Bari*†	c Taylor b Wood	1
Sarfraz Nawaz	c Gower b Wood	12
Naeem Ahmed	not out	0
Sikander Bakht	not out	0
Liaquat Ali		
Extras	(B 1, LB 7, W 1)	9
Total	(55 overs – 8 wickets)	**154**

Fall of wickets: 1-27, 2-38, 3-39, 4-80, 5-117, 6-130, 7-154, 8-154.

ENGLAND	*O*	*M*	*R*	*W*
Willis	9	1	25	0
Old	11	1	26	2
Miller	11	3	24	2
Botham	11	2	36	1
Lever	7	1	17	0
Wood	4	0	14	2
Lloyd	2	1	3	1

Umpires: H.D. Bird and W.L. Budd.

ENGLAND v NEW ZEALAND 1978 (1st Match)

Prudential Trophy

At Scarborough on 15 July 1978.
Toss: New Zealand. Result: ENGLAND won by 19 runs.
55 overs match. Award: G.A. Gooch.
Débuts: New Zealand – S.L. Boock, J.G. Wright.

ENGLAND		
J.M. Brearley*	c Burgess b Boock	31
G.A. Gooch	c Parker b Cairns	94
C.T. Radley	c Parker b Cairns	41
D.I. Gower	c Burgess b Cairns	4
I.T. Botham	c Anderson b Cairns	3
G.R.J. Roope	b Cairns	11
G. Miller	c Edwards b Hadlee	2
R.W. Taylor†	lbw b Hadlee	0
J.K. Lever	not out	5
M. Hendrick	not out	2
R.G.D. Willis		
Extras	(B 2, LB 10, W 1)	13
Total	(55 overs – 8 wickets)	**206**

Fall of wickets: 1-67, 2-178, 3-181, 4-185, 5-185, 6-198, 7-198, 8-198.

NEW ZEALAND	*O*	*M*	*R*	*W*
Hadlee	11	3	22	2
Collinge	11	0	46	0
Cairns	11	3	28	5
Congdon	11	2	25	0
Boock	9	1	57	1
Howarth	2	0	15	0

NEW ZEALAND		
J.G. Wright	run out	18
R.W. Anderson	c Taylor b Hendrick	12
G.P. Howarth	c Taylor b Hendrick	42
M.G. Burgess*	b Botham	1
J.M. Parker	b Willis	7
G.N. Edwards†	c Gower b Gooch	12
R.J. Hadlee	st Taylor b Gooch	1
B.E. Congdon	not out	52
B.L. Cairns	run out	23
R.O. Collinge	not out	5
S.L. Boock		
Extras	(LB 13, W 1)	14
Total	(55 overs – 8 wickets)	**187**

Fall of wickets: 1-28, 2-43, 3-51, 4-62, 5-91, 6-97, 7-105, 8-173.

ENGLAND	*O*	*M*	*R*	*W*
Willis	11	1	35	1
Hendrick	11	1	35	2
Lever	11	2	25	0
Botham	11	1	43	1
Miller	1	0	6	0
Gooch	10	1	29	2

Umpires: D.J. Constant and J.G. Langridge.

Match No. 53/7

ENGLAND v NEW ZEALAND 1978 (2nd Match)

Prudential Trophy

At Old Trafford, Manchester on 17 July 1978.
Toss: England. Result: ENGLAND won by 126 runs.
55 overs match. Award: C.T. Radley.

Débuts: New Zealand – B.P. Bracewell, B.A. Edgar.

Cairns (43 balls, 47 minutes, 4 sixes and 4 fours) reached his fifty off 37 balls.

ENGLAND		
J.M. Brearley*	c Edwards b Bracewell	27
G.A. Gooch	run out	0
C.T. Radley	not out	117
D.I. Gower	run out	50
D.W. Randall	run out	41
I.T. Botham	c Edgar b Hadlee	34
G. Miller		
R.W. Taylor†		
J.K. Lever		
P.H. Edmonds		
R.G.D. Willis		
Extras	(LB 6, W 1, NB 2)	9
Total	(55 overs – 5 wickets)	**278**

Fall of wickets 1-0, 2-44, 3-149, 4-238, 5-278.

NEW ZEALAND	*O*	*M*	*R*	*W*
Hadlee	11	1	70	1
Collinge	11	0	48	0
Bracewell	11	0	41	1
Congdon	11	2	26	0
Cairns	11	0	84	0

NEW ZEALAND		
J.G. Wright	b Botham	30
B.A. Edgar	run out	31
G.P. Howarth	st Taylor b Edmonds	12
G.N. Edwards†	c Randall b Miller	0
M.G. Burgess*	c Taylor b Willis	0
B.E. Congdon	c Randall b Edmonds	2
R.J. Hadlee	c Gower b Miller	1
B.L. Cairns	c Botham b Edmonds	60
R.O. Collinge	c Gooch b Lever	3
B.P. Bracewell	not out	0
J.M. Parker	absent hurt	
Extras	(B 7, LB 6)	13
Total	(41.2 overs)	**152**

Fall of wickets 1-44, 2-80, 3-80, 4-84, 5-84,
6-85, 7-88, 8-133, 9-152.

ENGLAND	*O*	*M*	*R*	*W*
Willis	9	5	21	1
Lever	7	0	28	1
Miller	11	4	27	2
Botham	7	0	24	1
Edmonds	7.2	1	39	3

Umpires: H.D. Bird and B.J. Meyer.

PAKISTAN v INDIA 1978-79 (1st Match)

At Ayub Stadium, Quetta on 1 October 1978.
Toss: India. Result: INDIA won by 4 runs.
40 overs match. Award: M. Amarnath.
Débuts: India – S. Amarnath, C.P.S. Chauhan, Kapil Dev.

INDIA		
C.P.S. Chauhan	b Sarfraz	2
A.D. Gaekwad	c Imran b Jamil	16
S. Amarnath	c Zaheer b Jamil	37
G.R. Viswanath	run out	9
D.B. Vengsarkar	run out	34
M. Amarnath	c and b Sarfraz	51
Kapil Dev	not out	13
S.M.H. Kirmani†	b Sarfraz	0
K.D. Ghavri	not out	1
S. Venkataraghavan		
B.S. Bedi*		
Extras		7
Total	(40 overs – 7 wickets)	**170**

Fall of wickets 1-7, 2-60, 3-60, 4-72, 5-148, 6-163, 7-163.

PAKISTAN	*O*	*M*	*R*	*W*
Imran Khan	8	1	38	0
Sarfraz Nawaz	8	1	34	3
Hasan Jamil	8	1	29	2
Mudassar Nazar	8	0	32	0
Iqbal Qasim	8	1	30	0

PAKISTAN		
Majid Khan	b M. Amarnath	50
Mudassar Nazar	lbw b Ghavri	10
Zaheer Abbas	b M. Amarnath	26
Javed Miandad	lbw b Bedi	6
Mushtaq Mohammad*	run out	6
Hasan Jamil	c Gaekwad b Bedi	16
Mohsin Khan	run out	17
Imran Khan	b Kapil Dev	2
Wasim Bari†	not out	11
Sarfraz Nawaz	not out	14
Iqbal Qasim		
Extras		8
Total	(40 overs – 8 wickets)	**166**

Fall of wickets 1-22, 2-82, 3-89, 4-100, 5-100, 6-119, 7-134, 8-139.

INDIA	*O*	*M*	*R*	*W*
Kapil Dev	8	0	27	1
Ghavri	8	0	35	1
M. Amarnath	8	0	38	2
Bedi	8	0	44	2
Venkataraghavan	8	0	14	0

Umpires: Mahboob Shah and Shujauddin.

Match No. 55/2

PAKISTAN v INDIA 1978-79 (2nd Match)

At Jinnah Park, Sialkot on 13 October 1978.
Toss: Pakistan. Result: PAKISTAN won by 8 wickets.
40 overs match. Award: Hasan Jamil.
Débuts: Pakistan – Azmat Rana; India – Yashpal Sharma.

India's total remains the lowest in a limited-overs international in Pakistan.

INDIA		
S.M. Gavaskar	b Salim	4
D.B. Vengsarkar	c Wasim Raja b Sikander	3
S. Amarnath	run out	1
G.R. Viswanath	c Wasim Raja b Salim	0
M. Amarnath	not out	34
Yashpal Sharma	b Jamil	11
Kapil Dev	c Mushtaq b Jamil	5
S.M.H. Kirmani†	lbw b Jamil	5
K.D. Ghavri	run out	5
S. Venkataraghavan	b Sikander	0
B.S. Bedi*	c Miandad b Sarfraz	2
Extras		9
Total	(34.2 overs)	**79**

Fall of wickets: 1-7, 2-9, 3-11, 4-16, 5-36, 6-48, 7-60, 8-71, 9-71, 10-79.

PAKISTAN	*O*	*M*	*R*	*W*
Sarfraz Nawaz	5.2	2	6	1
Salim Altaf	5	2	7	2
Sikander Bakht	8	2	11	2
Hasan Jamil	8	2	18	3
Wasim Raja	8	0	28	0

PAKISTAN		
Sadiq Mohammad	c Yashpal b Kapil Dev	1
Azmat Rana	not out	22
Zaheer Abbas	c Kapil Dev b Gavaskar	48
Javed Miandad	not out	4
Wasim Raja		
Mushtaq Mohammad*		
Hasan Jamil		
Sarfraz Nawaz		
Wasim Bari†		
Salim Altaf		
Sikander Bakht		
Extras		8
Total	(16.5 overs – 2 wickets)	**83**

Fall of wickets: 1-2, 2-79.

INDIA	*O*	*M*	*R*	*W*
Kapil Dev	6	0	31	1
Ghavri	6	0	18	0
M. Amarnath	2	0	4	0
Bedi	2	0	12	0
Gavaskar	0.5	0	10	1

Umpires: Agha Saadat and Shakoor Rana.

PAKISTAN v INDIA 1978-79 (3rd Match)

At Sahiwal Stadium on 3 November 1978.
Toss: Pakistan. Result: PAKISTAN won (conceded by India).
40 overs match. Award: Asif Iqbal.
Début: India – B. Reddy.

Bedi called his batsmen from the field (when 23 runs were required from 20 balls) in protest against the bowling of Sarfraz, whose last four deliveries were bouncers.

PAKISTAN		
Majid Khan	b Venkataraghavan	37
Azmat Rana	b M. Amarnath	20
Zaheer Abbas	c Ghavri b Venkataraghavan	17
Asif Iqbal	c Bedi b Ghavri	62
Javed Miandad	lbw b M. Amarnath	7
Hasan Jamil	b Kapil Dev	26
Mushtaq Mohammad*	not out	16
Imran Khan	c S. Amarnath b Kapil Dev	10
Sarfraz Nawaz	not out	0
Wasim Bari†		
Salim Altaf		
Extras	(LB 7, NB 3)	10
Total	(40 overs – 7 wickets)	**205**

Fall of wickets: 1-38, 2-66, 3-93, 4-111, 5-167, 6-187, 7-201.

INDIA	*O*	*M*	*R*	*W*
Kapil Dev	8	0	49	2
Ghavri	8	0	33	1
Venkataraghavan	8	0	34	2
M. Amarnath	8	0	35	2
Bedi	8	0	44	0

INDIA		
C.P.S. Chauhan	c Wasim Bari b Jamil	23
A.D. Gaekwad	not out	78
S. Amarnath	c Imran b Asif Iqbal	62
G.R. Viswanath	not out	8
M. Amarnath		
Kapil Dev		
K.D. Ghavri		
B. Reddy†		
S. Venkataraghavan		
B.S. Bedi*		
Yashpal Sharma		
Extras	(B 2, LB 5, NB 5)	12
Total	(37.4 overs – 2 wickets)	**183**

Fall of wickets: 1-44, 2-163.

PAKISTAN	*O*	*M*	*R*	*W*
Imran Khan	7	0	22	0
Sarfraz Nawaz	6.4	0	16	0
Salim Altaf	8	0	41	0
Hasan Jamil	8	0	48	1
Asif Iqbal	8	0	44	1

Umpires: Javed Akhtar and Khizer Hayat.

Match No. 57/10

AUSTRALIA v ENGLAND 1978-79 (1st Match)

Benson and Hedges Cup

At Sydney Cricket Ground on 13 January 1979.
Toss: England. No result – rain.
40 eight-ball overs match. No award.

Débuts: Australia – A.R. Border, P.H. Carlson, J.A. Maclean; England – R.W. Tolchard.

This was the second one-day international of a scheduled three-match series, the first at Melbourne on 26 December 1978 having been abandoned without a ball bowled. When this match too was ended by rain, the tour itinerary was revised to incorporate two subsequent one-day internationals on 4 and 7 February in place of England's scheduled three-day fixture against Geelong and Districts XI.

AUSTRALIA		
G.M. Wood	c Tolchard b Old	6
W.M. Darling	not out	7
K.J. Hughes	not out	0
G.N. Yallop*		
G.J. Cosier		
P.M. Toohey		
A.R. Border		
P.H. Carlson		
J.A. Maclean†		
G. Dymock		
A.G. Hurst		
Extras	(LB 4)	4
Total	(7.2 overs – 1 wicket)	**17**

Fall of wicket 1-17.

ENGLAND	*O*	*M*	*R*	*W*
Lever	3	0	8	0
Old	3.2	1	5	1
Hendrick	1	1	0	0

ENGLAND
J.M. Brearley*
G. Boycott
D.W. Randall
D.I. Gower
G.A. Gooch
I.T. Botham
R.W. Tolchard†
P.H. Edmonds
C.M. Old
M. Hendrick
J.K. Lever

Umpires: A.R. Crafter and C.E. Harvey.

AUSTRALIA v ENGLAND 1978-79 (2nd Match)

Benson and Hedges Cup

At Melbourne Cricket Ground on 24 January 1979.
Toss: Australia. Result: ENGLAND won by 7 wickets.
40 eight-ball overs match. Award: M. Hendrick.
Débuts: Australia – A.M.J. Hilditch, R.M. Hogg; England – D.L. Bairstow.

AUSTRALIA		
G.M. Wood	c Gower b Edmonds	28
A.M.J. Hilditch	c Bairstow b Botham	10
A.R. Border	c Willis b Hendrick	11
G.N. Yallop*	run out	9
K.J. Hughes	lbw b Hendrick	0
P.H. Carlson	c Randall b Willis	11
T.J. Laughlin	c Willis b Hendrick	6
J.A. Maclean†	c Edmonds b Botham	11
R.M. Hogg	c Botham b Hendrick	4
G. Dymock	c and b Botham	1
A.G. Hurst	not out	0
Extras	(B 4, LB 2, NB 4)	10
Total	(33.5 overs)	**101**

Fall of wickets 1-27, 2-52, 3-54, 4-55, 5-76, 6-78, 7-94, 8-99, 9-101, 10-101.

ENGLAND	*O*	*M*	*R*	*W*
Willis	8	4	15	1
Lever	5	2	7	0
Hendrick	8	1	25	4
Botham	4.5	2	16	3
Edmonds	7	0	26	1
Gooch	1	0	2	0

ENGLAND		
G. Boycott	not out	39
J.M. Brearley*	b Hogg	0
D.W. Randall	c Yallop b Dymock	12
G.A. Gooch	b Carlson	23
D.I. Gower	not out	19
I.T. Botham		
P.H. Edmonds		
D.L. Bairstow†		
J.K. Lever		
R.G.D. Willis		
M. Hendrick		
Extras	(LB 5, NB 4)	9
Total	(28.2 overs – 3 wickets)	**102**

Fall of wickets 1-7, 2-29, 3-69.

AUSTRALIA	*O*	*M*	*R*	*W*
Hogg	6	1	20	1
Dymock	6	1	16	1
Laughlin	5	1	13	0
Carlson	5	0	21	1
Hurst	5.2	1	14	0
Border	1	0	9	0

Umpires: A.R. Crafter and C.E. Harvey.

Match No. 59/12

AUSTRALIA v ENGLAND 1978-79 (3rd Match)
Benson and Hedges Cup

At Melbourne Cricket Ground on 4 February 1979.
Toss: Australia. Result: AUSTRALIA won by 4 wickets.
40 eight-ball overs match. Award: D.I. Gower.
Début: Australia – K.J. Wright.

ENGLAND		
G. Boycott	lbw b Laughlin	33
J.M. Brearley*	c Wright b Dymock	0
D.W. Randall	lbw b Dymock	4
G.A. Gooch	c Hurst b Carlson	19
D.I. Gower	not out	101
I.T. Botham	c Wood b Hurst	31
D.L. Bairstow†	run out	1
C.M. Old	not out	16
R.G.D. Willis		
M. Hendrick		
J.K. Lever		
Extras	(B 3, LB 3, NB 1)	7
Total	(40 overs – 6 wickets)	**212**

Fall of wickets: 1-0, 2-7, 3-50, 4-89, 5-153, 6-158.

AUSTRALIA	*O*	*M*	*R*	*W*
Hurst	8	1	36	1
Dymock	8	1	31	2
Carlson	8	1	27	1
Cosier	8	0	48	0
Laughlin	8	0	63	1

AUSTRALIA		
G.M. Wood	b Old	23
W.M. Darling	c Old b Willis	7
K.J. Hughes	c Boycott b Lever	50
G.N. Yallop*	c Gower b Hendrick	31
P.M. Toohey	not out	54
G.J. Cosier	b Lever	28
P.H. Carlson	c Boycott b Lever	0
T.J. Laughlin	not out	15
K.J. Wright†		
G. Dymock		
A.G. Hurst		
Extras	(LB 6, NB 1)	7
Total	(38.6 overs – 6 wickets)	**215**

Fall of wickets: 1-7, 2-55, 3-90, 4-145, 5-185, 6-185.

ENGLAND	*O*	*M*	*R*	*W*
Willis	8	1	21	1
Lever	7	1	51	3
Hendrick	8	0	47	1
Old	8	1	31	1
Botham	7.6	0	58	0

Umpires: R.C. Bailhache and D.G. Weser.

AUSTRALIA v ENGLAND 1978-79 (4th Match)

Benson and Hedges Cup

At Melbourne Cricket Ground on 7 February 1979.
Toss: Australia. Result: AUSTRALIA won by 6 wickets.
40 eight-ball overs match. Award: G. Dymock.
No débuts.

Bairstow was run out while attempting a sixth run off an on-drive by Brearley.

ENGLAND		
G. Boycott	c Cosier b Dymock	2
J.M. Brearley*	c Wright b Cosier	46
D.W. Randall	c Hughes b Dymock	0
G.A. Gooch	c Hughes b Hurst	4
D.I. Gower	c Wood b Hurst	3
I.T. Botham	b Cosier	13
D.L. Bairstow†	run out	3
P.H. Edmonds	lbw b Laughlin	15
J.K. Lever	b Laughlin	1
R.G.D. Willis	c Wright b Cosier	2
M. Hendrick	not out	0
Extras	(LB 2, NB 3)	5
Total	(31.7 overs)	**94**

Fall of wickets: 1-10, 2-10, 3-17, 4-22, 5-42, 6-56, 7-91, 8-91, 9-94, 10-94.

AUSTRALIA	*O*	*M*	*R*	*W*
Hurst	5	3	7	2
Dymock	6	1	21	2
Carlson	8	2	22	0
Cosier	7	1	22	3
Laughlin	5.7	0	17	2

AUSTRALIA		
G.M. Wood	c Bairstow b Botham	30
W.M. Darling	c Brearley b Willis	14
K.J. Hughes	c Brearley b Willis	0
G.N. Yallop*	b Lever	25
P.M. Toohey	not out	16
G.J. Cosier	not out	8
P.H. Carlson		
T.J. Laughlin		
K.J. Wright†		
G. Dymock		
A.G. Hurst		
Extras	(NB 2)	2
Total	(21.5 overs – 4 wickets)	**95**

Fall of wickets: 1-29, 2-37, 3-54, 4-87.

ENGLAND	*O*	*M*	*R*	*W*
Willis	5	2	16	2
Hendrick	6	0	32	0
Botham	5.5	0	30	1
Lever	5	0	15	1

Umpires: R.C. Bailhache and D.G. Weser.

Match No. 61/1

INDIA v WEST INDIES 1979

Prudential World Cup – 1st Match

At Edgbaston, Birmingham on 9 June 1979.
Toss: West Indies. Result: WEST INDIES won by 9 wickets.
60 overs match. Award: C.G. Greenidge.
Début: India – S.C. Khanna.

INDIA		
S.M. Gavaskar	c Holding b Roberts	8
A.D. Gaekwad	c King b Holding	11
D.B. Vengsarkar	c Kallicharran b Holding	7
G.R. Viswanath	b Holding	75
B.P. Patel	run out	15
M. Amarnath	c Murray b Croft	8
Kapil Dev	b King	12
S.C. Khanna†	c Haynes b Holding	0
K.D. Ghavri	c Murray b Garner	12
S. Venkataraghavan*	not out	13
B.S. Bedi	c Lloyd b Roberts	13
Extras	(B 6, LB 3, W 3, NB 4)	16
Total	(53.1 overs)	**190**

Fall of wickets: 1-10, 2-24, 3-29, 4-56, 5-77, 6-112, 7-119, 8-155, 9-163, 10-190.

WEST INDIES	*O*	*M*	*R*	*W*
Roberts	9.1	0	32	2
Holding	12	2	33	4
Garner	12	1	42	1
Croft	10	1	31	1
King	10	1	36	1

WEST INDIES		
C.G. Greenidge	not out	106
D.L. Haynes	lbw b Kapil Dev	47
I.V.A. Richards	not out	28
A.I. Kallicharran		
C.H. Lloyd*		
C.L. King		
D.L. Murray†		
A.M.E. Roberts		
J. Garner		
M.A. Holding		
C.E.H. Croft		
Extras	(LB 6, NB 7)	13
Total	(51.3 overs – 1 wicket)	**194**

Fall of wicket: 1-138.

INDIA	*O*	*M*	*R*	*W*
Kapil Dev	10	1	46	1
Ghavri	10	2	25	0
Venkataraghavan	12	3	30	0
Bedi	12	0	45	0
Amarnath	7.3	0	35	0

Umpires: D.G.L. Evans and J.G. Langridge.

NEW ZEALAND v SRI LANKA 1979

Prudential World Cup – 2nd Match

At Trent Bridge, Nottingham on 9 June 1979.
Toss: New Zealand. Result: NEW ZEALAND won by 9 wickets.
60 overs match. Award: G.P. Howarth.

Débuts: New Zealand – J.V. Coney, W.K. Lees, L.W. Stott; Sri Lanka – D.L.S. De Silva, R.L. Dias, S.A. Jayasinghe, S.P. Pasqual.

SRI LANKA		
B. Warnapura	c and b McKechnie	20
S.R. de S. Wettimuny	b Cairns	16
A.P.B. Tennekoon*	b Stott	59
R.L. Dias	c and b Stott	25
L.R.D. Mendis	c Turner b Troup	14
D.S. De Silva	c Burgess b Stott	6
S.A. Jayasinghe†	run out	1
S.P. Pasqual	b Hadlee	1
A.R.M. Opatha	b McKechnie	18
D.L.S. De Silva	c Wright b McKechnie	10
G.R.A. De Silva	not out	2
Extras	(LB 13, W 2, NB 2)	17
Total	(56.5 overs)	**189**

Fall of wickets: 1-26, 2-57, 3-107, 4-137, 5-149, 6-150, 7-150, 8-154, 9-178, 10-189.

NEW ZEALAND	*O*	*M*	*R*	*W*
Hadlee	12	3	24	1
Troup	10	0	30	1
Cairns	12	1	45	1
McKechnie	10.5	2	25	3
Stott	12	1	48	3

NEW ZEALAND		
G.M. Turner	not out	83
J.G. Wright	c Tennekoon b G.R.A. De Silva	34
G.P. Howarth	not out	63
J.V. Coney		
M.G. Burgess*		
W.K. Lees†		
B.J. McKechnie		
B.L. Cairns		
R.J. Hadlee		
L.W. Stott		
G.B. Troup		
Extras	(LB 7, W 2, NB 1)	10
Total	(47.4 overs – 1 wicket)	**190**

Fall of wicket: 1-64.

SRI LANKA	*O*	*M*	*R*	*W*
Opatha	7	1	31	0
D.L.S. De Silva	8	2	18	0
Warnapura	7	0	30	0
D.S. De Silva	9	0	42	0
G.R.A. De Silva	12	1	39	1
Pasqual	4.4	0	20	0

Umpires: W.L. Budd and K.E. Palmer.

Match No. 63/14

ENGLAND v AUSTRALIA 1979

Prudential World Cup – 3rd Match

At Lord's, London on 9 June 1979.
Toss: England. Result: ENGLAND won by 6 wickets.
60 overs match. Award: G.A. Gooch.
No débuts.

AUSTRALIA		
A.M.J. Hilditch	b Boycott	47
W.M. Darling	lbw b Willis	25
A.R. Border	c Taylor b Edmonds	34
K.J. Hughes*	c Hendrick b Boycott	6
G.N. Yallop	run out	10
G.J. Cosier	run out	6
T.J. Laughlin	run out	8
K.J. Wright†	lbw b Old	6
R.M. Hogg	run out	0
A.G. Hurst	not out	3
G. Dymock	not out	4
Extras	(B 4, LB 5, W 1)	10
Total	(60 overs – 9 wickets)	**159**

Fall of wickets 1-56, 2-97, 3-111, 4-131, 5-132, 6-137, 7-150, 8-153, 9-153.

ENGLAND	*O*	*M*	*R*	*W*
Willis	11	2	20	1
Hendrick	12	2	24	0
Old	12	2	33	1
Botham	8	0	32	0
Edmonds	11	1	25	1
Boycott	6	0	15	2

ENGLAND		
J.M. Brearley*	c Wright b Laughlin	44
G. Boycott	lbw b Hogg	1
D.W. Randall	c Wright b Hurst	1
G.A. Gooch	lbw b Laughlin	53
D.I. Gower	not out	22
I.T. Botham	not out	18
P.H. Edmonds		
R.W. Taylor†		
C.M. Old		
M. Hendrick		
R.G.D. Willis		
Extras	(LB 10, NB 11)	21
Total	(47.1 overs – 4 wickets)	**160**

Fall of wickets 1-4, 2-5, 3-113, 4-124.

AUSTRALIA	*O*	*M*	*R*	*W*
Hogg	9	1	25	1
Hurst	10	3	33	1
Dymock	11	2	19	0
Cosier	8	1	24	0
Laughlin	9.1	0	38	2

Umpires: D.J. Constant and B.J. Meyer.

PAKISTAN v CANADA 1979

Prudential World Cup – 4th Match

At Headingley, Leeds on 9 June 1979.
Toss: Canada. Result: PAKISTAN won by 8 wickets.
60 overs match. Award: Sadiq Mohammad.
Débuts: Canada – All.

CANADA		
C.J.D. Chappell	c and b Sikander	14
G.R. Sealy	c and b Asif Iqbal	45
F.A. Dennis	c Wasim Bari b Sarfraz	25
M.P. Stead	c Zaheer b Asif Iqbal	10
C.A. Marshall	b Imran	8
J.C.B. Vaughan	c and b Asif Iqbal	0
B.M. Mauricette*†	c Zaheer b Sarfraz	15
Tariq Javed	st Wasim Bari b Majid	3
J.M. Patel	b Sarfraz	0
C.C. Henry	not out	1
J.N. Valentine		
Extras	(LB 10, W 5, NB 3)	18
Total	(60 overs – 9 wickets)	**139**

Fall of wickets: 1-54, 2-85, 3-103, 4-110, 5-110, 6-129, 7-134, 8-138, 9-139.

PAKISTAN	*O*	*M*	*R*	*W*
Imran Khan	11	1	27	1
Sarfraz Nawaz	10	1	26	3
Mudassar Nazar	4	1	11	0
Sikander Bakht	12	5	18	1
Majid Khan	11	4	11	1
Asif Iqbal	12	2	28	3

PAKISTAN		
Majid Khan	b Valentine	1
Sadiq Mohammad	not out	57
Zaheer Abbas	run out	36
Haroon Rashid	not out	37
Javed Miandad		
Asif Iqbal*		
Mudassar Nazar		
Imran Khan		
Sarfraz Nawaz		
Wasim Bari†		
Sikander Bakht		
Extras	(B 1, LB 3, W 1, NB 4)	9
Total	(40.1 overs – 2 wickets)	**140**

Fall of wickets: 1-4, 2-61.

CANADA	*O*	*M*	*R*	*W*
Valentine	9	3	18	1
Vaughan	5	1	21	0
Henry	5	0	26	0
Patel	11.1	0	27	0
Sealy	6	0	21	0
Stead	4	0	18	0

Umpires: H.D. Bird and A.G.T. Whitehead.

WEST INDIES v SRI LANKA (Prudential World Cup – 5th Match). At Kennington Oval on 13, 14, 15 June 1979. No result – abandoned without a ball bowled.

Match No. 65/4

INDIA v NEW ZEALAND 1979

Prudential World Cup – 6th Match

At Headingley, Leeds on 13 June 1979.
Toss: New Zealand. Result: NEW ZEALAND won by 8 wickets.
60 overs match. Award: B.A. Edgar.
No débuts.

INDIA

S.M. Gavaskar	c Lees b Hadlee	55
A.D. Gaekwad	b Hadlee	10
D.B. Vengsarkar	c Lees b McKechnie	1
G.R. Viswanath	c Turner b Cairns	9
B.P. Patel	b Troup	38
M. Amarnath	b Troup	1
Kapil Dev	c and b Cairns	25
K.D. Ghavri	c Coney b McKechnie	20
S.C. Khanna†	c Morrison b McKechnie	7
S. Venkataraghavan*	c Lees b Cairns	1
B.S. Bedi	not out	1
Extras	(LB 8, W 5, NB 1)	14
Total	(55.5 overs)	**182**

Fall of wickets 1-27, 2-38, 3-53, 4-104, 5-107, 6-147, 7-153, 8-180, 9-182, 10-182.

NEW ZEALAND	*O*	*M*	*R*	*W*
Hadlee	10	2	20	2
Troup	10	2	36	2
Cairns	11.5	0	36	3
McKechnie	12	1	24	3
Coney	7	0	33	0
Morrison	5	0	19	0

NEW ZEALAND

J.G. Wright	c and b Amarnath	48
B.A. Edgar	not out	84
B.L. Cairns	run out	2
G.M. Turner	not out	43
J.V. Coney		
M.G. Burgess*		
J.F.M. Morrison		
B.J. McKechnie		
W.K. Lees†		
R.J. Hadlee		
G.B. Troup		
Extras	(LB 3, NB 3)	6
Total	(57 overs – 2 wickets)	**183**

Fall of wickets 1-100, 2-103.

INDIA	*O*	*M*	*R*	*W*
Amarnath	12	1	39	1
Bedi	12	1	32	0
Venkataraghavan	12	0	34	0
Ghavri	10	1	34	0
Kapil Dev	11	3	38	0

Umpires: W.L. Budd and A.G.T. Whitehead.

AUSTRALIA v PAKISTAN 1979

Prudential World Cup – 7th Match

At Trent Bridge, Nottingham on 13, 14 June 1979.
Toss: Australia. Result: PAKISTAN won by 89 runs.
60 overs match. Award: Asif Iqbal.
Débuts: Australia – J.K. Moss, G.D. Porter.

PAKISTAN		
Sadiq Mohammad	c Moss b Porter	27
Majid Khan	b Dymock	61
Zaheer Abbas	c and b Cosier	16
Haroon Rashid	c Wright b Cosier	16
Javed Miandad	c Border b Cosier	46
Asif Iqbal*	c sub (D.F. Whatmore) b Hurst	61
Wasim Raja	c Moss b Border	18
Imran Khan	not out	15
Mudassar Nazar	not out	1
Wasim Bari†		
Sikander Bakht		
Extras	(B 6, LB 4, W 5, NB 10)	25
Total	(60 overs – 7 wickets)	**286**

Fall of wickets 1-99, 2-99, 3-133, 4-152, 5-239, 6-268, 7-274.

AUSTRALIA	*O*	*M*	*R*	*W*
Porter	12	3	20	1
Dymock	12	3	28	1
Cosier	12	1	54	3
Hurst	12	0	65	1
Yallop	8	0	56	0
Border	4	0	38	1

AUSTRALIA		
W.M. Darling	c Wasim Bari b Imran	13
A.M.J. Hilditch	c Sadiq b Mudassar	72
A.R. Border	b Sikander	0
K.J. Hughes*	lbw b Sikander	15
G.N. Yallop	b Majid	37
J.K. Moss	run out	7
G.J. Cosier	c and b Majid	0
K.J. Wright†	c Wasim Bari b Imran	23
G.D. Porter	c Sadiq b Majid	3
G. Dymock	lbw b Sikander	10
A.G. Hurst	not out	3
Extras	(B 1, LB 5, W 8)	14
Total	(57.1 overs)	**197**

Fall of wickets 1-22, 2-24, 3-46, 4-117, 5-136, 6-137, 7-172, 8-175, 9-193, 10-197.

PAKISTAN	*O*	*M*	*R*	*W*
Asif Iqbal	12	0	36	0
Majid Khan	12	0	53	3
Mudassar Nazar	12	0	31	1
Imran Khan	10.1	2	29	2
Sikander Bakht	11	1	34	3

Umpires: H.D. Bird and K.E. Palmer.

Match No. 67/1

ENGLAND v CANADA 1979

Prudential World Cup – 8th Match

At Old Trafford, Manchester on 13 (no play), 14 June 1979.
Toss: Canada. Result: ENGLAND won by 8 wickets.
60 overs match. Award: C.M. Old.
Début: Canada – R.G. Callender.

Electing to bat in reasonable conditions, Canada were dismissed in 157 minutes for the only total of less than 60 in a one-day international. The match aggregate of 91 runs remains the lowest at this level, while the actual playing time of 3 hours 35 minutes is easily the record for the shortest completed international match in England.

CANADA		
G.R. Sealy	c Botham b Hendrick	3
C.J.D. Chappell	lbw b Botham	5
F.A. Dennis	hit wicket b Willis	21
Tariq Javed	lbw b Old	4
J.C.B. Vaughan	b Old	1
C.A. Marshall	b Old	2
B.M. Mauricette*†	b Willis	0
M.P. Stead	b Old	0
J.M. Patel	b Willis	1
R.G. Callender	b Willis	0
J.N. Valentine	not out	3
Extras	(LB 4, NB 1)	5
Total	(40.3 overs)	**45**

Fall of wickets: 1-5, 2-13, 3-25, 4-29, 5-37, 6-38, 7-41, 8-41, 9-42, 10-45.

ENGLAND	*O*	*M*	*R*	*W*
Willis	10.3	3	11	4
Hendrick	8	4	5	1
Botham	9	5	12	1
Miller	2	1	1	0
Boycott	1	0	3	0
Old	10	5	8	4

ENGLAND		
J.M. Brearley*	lbw b Valentine	0
G. Boycott	not out	14
D.W. Randall	b Callender	5
G.A. Gooch	not out	21
D.I. Gower		
I.T. Botham		
G. Miller		
R.W. Taylor†		
C.M. Old		
R.G.D. Willis		
M. Hendrick		
Extras	(W 3, NB 3)	6
Total	(13.5 overs – 2 wickets)	**46**

Fall of wickets: 1-3, 2-11.

CANADA	*O*	*M*	*R*	*W*
Valentine	7	2	20	1
Callender	6	1	14	1
Stead	0.5	0	6	0

Umpires: J.G. Langridge and B.J. Meyer.

INDIA v SRI LANKA 1979
Prudential World Cup – 9th Match

At Old Trafford, Manchester on 16, 18 June 1979.
Toss: India. Result: SRI LANKA won by 47 runs.
60 overs match. Award: L.R.D. Mendis.
Débuts: Sri Lanka – F.R.M. Goonatillake, R.S. Madugalle.

SRI LANKA		
B. Warnapura*	c Gaekwad b Amarnath	18
S.R. de S. Wettimuny	c Vengsarkar b Kapil Dev	67
R.L. Dias	c and b Amarnath	50
L.R.D. Mendis	run out	64
R.S. Madugalle	c Khanna b Amarnath	4
S.P. Pasqual	not out	23
D.S. De Silva	not out	1
S.A. Jayasinghe†		
A.R.M. Opatha		
D.L.S. De Silva		
F.R.M. Goonatillake		
Extras	(LB 8, W 2, NB 1)	11
Total	(60 overs – 5 wickets)	**238**

Fall of wickets 1-31, 2-127, 3-147, 4-175, 5-227.

INDIA	*O*	*M*	*R*	*W*
Kapil Dev	12	2	53	1
Ghavri	12	0	53	0
Amarnath	12	3	40	3
Bedi	12	2	37	0
Venkataraghavan	12	0	44	0

INDIA		
S.M. Gavaskar	c Dias b Warnapura	26
A.D. Gaekwad	c sub (G.R.A. De Silva) b D.L.S. De Silva	33
D.B. Vengsarkar	c D.L.S. De Silva b D.S. De Silva	36
G.R. Viswanath	run out	22
B.P. Patel	b D.S. De Silva	10
Kapil Dev	c Warnapura b D.L.S. De Silva	16
M. Amarnath	b D.S. De Silva	7
K.D. Ghavri	c Warnapura b Opatha	3
S.C. Khanna†	c Dias b Opatha	10
S. Venkataraghavan*	not out	9
B.S. Bedi	c Jayasinghe b Opatha	5
Extras	(LB 10, W 3, NB 1)	14
Total	(54.1 overs)	**191**

Fall of wickets 1-60, 2-76, 3-119, 4-132, 5-147,
6-160, 7-162, 8-170, 9-185, 10-191.

SRI LANKA	*O*	*M*	*R*	*W*
Opatha	10.1	0	31	3
Goonatillake	9	1	34	0
Warnapura	12	0	47	1
D.L.S. De Silva	12	0	36	2
D.S. De Silva	11	1	29	3

Umpires: K.E. Palmer and A.G.T. Whitehead.

Match No. 69/2

NEW ZEALAND v WEST INDIES 1979

Prudential World Cup – 10th Match

At Trent Bridge, Nottingham on 16 June 1979.
Toss: New Zealand. Result: WEST INDIES won by 32 runs.
60 overs match. Award: C.H. Lloyd.
Début: New Zealand – E.J. Chatfield.

WEST INDIES		
C.G. Greenidge	c Edgar b Coney	65
D.L. Haynes	lbw b Hadlee	12
I.V.A. Richards	c Burgess b Coney	9
A.I. Kallicharran	b McKechnie	39
C.H. Lloyd*	not out	73
C.L. King	lbw b Cairns	12
D.L. Murray†	c Coney b Chatfield	12
A.M.E. Roberts	c Lees b Cairns	1
J. Garner	not out	9
M.A. Holding		
C.E.H. Croft		
Extras	(B 5, LB 7)	12
Total	(60 overs – 7 wickets)	**244**

Fall of wickets: 1-23, 2-61, 3-117, 4-152, 5-175, 6-202, 7-204.

NEW ZEALAND	*O*	*M*	*R*	*W*
Hadlee	11	2	41	1
Chatfield	11	0	45	1
Cairns	12	1	48	2
Coney	12	0	40	2
McKechnie	11	0	46	1
Morrison	3	0	12	0

NEW ZEALAND		
B.A. Edgar	run out	12
J.G. Wright	c Lloyd b Garner	15
J.V. Coney	c Garner b King	36
G.M. Turner	c Lloyd b Roberts	20
J.F.M. Morrison	c Murray b Garner	11
M.G. Burgess*	c Richards b Roberts	35
W.K. Lees†	b Croft	5
R.J. Hadlee	b Roberts	42
B.J. McKechnie	not out	13
B.L. Cairns	b Holding	1
E.J. Chatfield	not out	3
Extras	(LB 14, W 4, NB 1)	19
Total	(60 overs – 9 wickets)	**212**

Fall of wickets: 1-27, 2-38, 3-90, 4-91, 5-138, 6-143, 7-160, 8-199, 9-202.

WEST INDIES	*O*	*M*	*R*	*W*
Roberts	12	2	43	3
Holding	12	1	29	1
Croft	12	1	38	1
Garner	12	0	45	2
King	12	1	38	1

Umpires: H.D. Bird and B.J. Meyer.

AUSTRALIA v CANADA 1979

Prudential World Cup – 11th Match

At Edgbaston, Birmingham on 16 June 1979.
Toss: Australia. Result: AUSTRALIA won by 7 wickets.
60 overs match. Award: A.G. Hurst.
Début: Canada – S. Baksh.

CANADA		
G.R. Sealy	c Porter b Dymock	25
C.J.D. Chappell	lbw b Hurst	19
F.A. Dennis	lbw b Hurst	1
Tariq Javed	c Wright b Porter	8
S. Baksh	b Hurst	0
J.C.B. Vaughan	b Porter	29
B.M. Mauricette*†	c Hilditch b Cosier	5
J.M. Patel	b Cosier	2
R.G. Callender	c Wright b Hurst	0
C.C. Henry	c Hughes b Hurst	5
J.N. Valentine	not out	0
Extras	(B 4, LB 5, W 1, NB 1)	11
Total	(33.2 overs)	**105**

Fall of wickets: 1-44, 2-50, 3-51, 4-51, 5-78, 6-97, 7-97, 8-98, 9-104, 10-105.

AUSTRALIA	*O*	*M*	*R*	*W*
Hogg	2	0	26	0
Hurst	10	3	21	5
Dymock	8	2	17	1
Porter	6	2	13	2
Cosier	7.2	2	17	2

AUSTRALIA		
A.M.J. Hilditch	c Valentine b Henry	24
W.M. Darling	lbw b Valentine	13
A.R. Border	b Henry	25
K.J. Hughes*	not out	27
G.N. Yallop	not out	13
G.J. Cosier		
K.J. Wright†		
G.D. Porter		
R.M. Hogg		
G. Dymock		
A.G. Hurst		
Extras	(LB 1, NB 3)	4
Total	(26 overs – 3 wickets)	**106**

Fall of wickets: 1-23, 2-53, 3-72.

CANADA	*O*	*M*	*R*	*W*
Valentine	3	0	28	1
Callender	3	0	12	0
Henry	10	0	27	2
Vaughan	6	0	15	0
Patel	4	0	20	0

Umpires: D.J. Constant and J.G. Langridge.

Match No. 71/8

ENGLAND v PAKISTAN 1979

Prudential World Cup – 12th Match

At Headingley, Leeds on 16 June 1979.
Toss: Pakistan. Result: ENGLAND won by 14 runs.
60 overs match. Award: M. Hendrick.
No débuts.

ENGLAND		
J.M. Brearley*	c Wasim Bari b Imran	0
G. Boycott	lbw b Majid	18
D.W. Randall	c Wasim Bari b Sikander	1
G.A. Gooch	c Sadiq b Sikander	33
D.I. Gower	b Majid	27
I.T. Botham	b Majid	22
P.H. Edmonds	c Wasim Raja b Asif	2
R.W. Taylor†	not out	20
C.M. Old	c and b Asif	2
R.G.D. Willis	b Sikander	24
M. Hendrick	not out	1
Extras	(LB 3, W 7, NB 5)	15
Total	(60 overs – 9 wickets)	**165**

Fall of wickets: 1-0, 2-4, 3-51, 4-70, 5-99, 6-115, 7-115, 8-118, 9-161.

PAKISTAN	*O*	*M*	*R*	*W*
Imran Khan	12	3	34	1
Sikander Bakht	12	3	32	3
Mudassar Nazar	12	4	30	0
Asif Iqbal	12	3	37	2
Majid Khan	12	2	27	3

PAKISTAN		
Majid Khan	c Botham b Hendrick	7
Sadiq Mohammad	b Hendrick	18
Mudassar Nazar	lbw b Hendrick	0
Zaheer Abbas	c Taylor b Botham	3
Haroon Rashid	c Brearley b Hendrick	1
Javed Miandad	lbw b Botham	0
Asif Iqbal*	c Brearley b Willis	51
Wasim Raja	lbw b Old	21
Imran Khan	not out	21
Wasim Bari†	c Taylor b Boycott	17
Sikander Bakht	c Hendrick b Boycott	2
Extras	(LB 8, W 1, NB 1)	10
Total	(56 overs)	**151**

Fall of wickets: 1-27, 2-27, 3-28, 4-30, 5-31, 6-34, 7-86, 8-115, 9-145, 10-151.

ENGLAND	*O*	*M*	*R*	*W*
Willis	11	2	37	1
Hendrick	12	6	15	4
Botham	12	3	38	2
Old	12	2	28	1
Edmonds	3	0	8	0
Boycott	5	0	14	2
Gooch	1	0	1	0

Umpires: W.L. Budd and D.G.L. Evans.

ENGLAND v NEW ZEALAND 1979

Prudential World Cup - Semi-Final

At Old Trafford, Manchester on 20 June 1979.
Toss: New Zealand. Result: ENGLAND won by 9 runs.
60 overs match. Award: G.A. Gooch.
Début: England – W. Larkins.

ENGLAND		
J.M. Brearley*	c Lees b Coney	53
G. Boycott	c Howarth b Hadlee	2
W. Larkins	c Coney b McKechnie	7
G.A. Gooch	b McKechnie	71
D.I. Gower	run out	1
I.T. Botham	lbw b Cairns	21
D.W. Randall	not out	42
C.M. Old	c Lees b Troup	0
R.W. Taylor†	run out	12
R.G.D. Willis	not out	1
M. Hendrick		
Extras	(LB 8, W 3)	11
Total	(60 overs – 8 wickets)	**221**

Fall of wickets: 1-13, 2-38, 3-96, 4-98, 5-145, 6-177, 7-178, 8-219.

NEW ZEALAND	*O*	*M*	*R*	*W*
Hadlee	12	4	32	1
Troup	12	1	38	1
Cairns	12	2	47	1
Coney	12	0	47	1
McKechnie	12	1	46	2

NEW ZEALAND		
J.G. Wright	run out	69
B.A. Edgar	lbw b Old	17
G.P. Howarth	lbw b Boycott	7
J.V. Coney	lbw b Hendrick	11
G.M. Turner	lbw b Willis	30
M.G. Burgess*	run out	10
R.J. Hadlee	b Botham	15
W.K. Lees†	b Hendrick	23
B.L. Cairns	c Brearley b Hendrick	14
B.J. McKechnie	not out	4
G.B. Troup	not out	3
Extras	(B 5, W 4)	9
Total	(60 overs – 9 wickets)	**212**

Fall of wickets: 1-47, 2-58, 3-104, 4-112, 5-132, 6-162, 7-180, 8-195, 9-208.

ENGLAND	*O*	*M*	*R*	*W*
Botham	12	3	42	1
Hendrick	12	0	55	3
Old	12	1	33	1
Boycott	9	1	24	1
Gooch	3	1	8	0
Willis	12	1	41	1

Umpires: J.G. Langridge and K.E. Palmer.

Match No. 73/3

PAKISTAN v WEST INDIES 1979

Prudential World Cup – Semi-Final

At Kennington Oval, London on 20 June 1979.
Toss: Pakistan. Result: WEST INDIES won by 43 runs.
60 overs match. Award: C.G. Greenidge.
No débuts.

WEST INDIES		
C.G. Greenidge	c Wasim Bari b Asif	73
D.L. Haynes	c and b Asif	65
I.V.A. Richards	b Asif	42
C.H. Lloyd*	c Mudassar b Asif	37
C.L. King	c sub (Wasim Raja) b Sarfraz	34
A.I. Kallicharran	b Imran	11
A.M.E. Roberts	not out	7
J. Garner	not out	1
D.L. Murray†		
M.A. Holding		
C.E.H. Croft		
Extras	(B 1, LB 17, W 1, NB 4)	23
Total	(60 overs – 6 wickets)	**293**

Fall of wickets 1-132, 2-165, 3-233, 4-236, 5-285, 6-285.

PAKISTAN	*O*	*M*	*R*	*W*
Imran Khan	9	1	43	1
Sarfraz Nawaz	12	1	71	1
Sikander Bakht	6	1	24	0
Mudassar Nazar	10	0	50	0
Majid Khan	12	2	26	0
Asif Iqbal	11	0	56	4

PAKISTAN		
Majid Khan	c Kallicharran b Croft	81
Sadiq Mohammad	c Murray b Holding	2
Zaheer Abbas	c Murray b Croft	93
Haroon Rashid	run out	15
Javed Miandad	lbw b Croft	0
Asif Iqbal*	c Holding b Richards	17
Mudassar Nazar	c Kallicharran b Richards	2
Imran Khan	c and b Richards	6
Sarfraz Nawaz	c Haynes b Roberts	12
Wasim Bari†	c Murray b Roberts	9
Sikander Bakht	not out	1
Extras	(LB 9, W 2, NB 1)	12
Total	(56.2 overs)	**250**

Fall of wickets 1-10, 2-176, 3-187, 4-187, 5-208, 6-220, 7-221, 8-228, 9-246, 10-250.

WEST INDIES	*O*	*M*	*R*	*W*
Roberts	9.2	2	41	2
Holding	9	1	28	1
Croft	11	0	29	3
Garner	12	1	47	0
King	7	0	41	0
Richards	8	0	52	3

Umpires: W.L. Budd and D.J. Constant.

ENGLAND v WEST INDIES 1979

Prudential World Cup – Final

At Lord's, London on 23 June 1979.
Toss: England. Result: WEST INDIES won by 92 runs.
60 overs match. Award: I.V.A. Richards.

No débuts.

Richards (157 balls, 207 minutes, 3 sixes and 11 fours) recorded the highest score in a World Cup final, his partnership of 139 with King taking only 21 overs (77 minutes). Garner ended the match with a spell of five wickets for 4 runs in 11 balls.

WEST INDIES		
C.G. Greenidge	run out	9
D.L. Haynes	c Hendrick b Old	20
I.V.A. Richards	not out	138
A.I. Kallicharran	b Hendrick	4
C.H. Lloyd*	c and b Old	13
C.L. King	c Randall b Edmonds	86
D.L. Murray†	c Gower b Edmonds	5
A.M.E. Roberts	c Brearley b Hendrick	0
J. Garner	c Taylor b Botham	0
M.A. Holding	b Botham	0
C.E.H. Croft	not out	0
Extras	(B 1, LB 10)	11
Total	(60 overs – 9 wickets)	**286**

Fall of wickets: 1-22, 2-36, 3-55, 4-99, 5-238, 6-252, 7-258, 8-260, 9-272.

ENGLAND	*O*	*M*	*R*	*W*
Botham	12	2	44	2
Hendrick	12	2	50	2
Old	12	0	55	2
Boycott	6	0	38	0
Edmonds	12	2	40	2
Gooch	4	0	27	0
Larkins	2	0	21	0

ENGLAND		
J.M. Brearley*	c King b Holding	64
G. Boycott	c Kallicharran b Holding	57
D.W. Randall	b Croft	15
G.A. Gooch	b Garner	32
D.I. Gower	b Garner	0
I.T. Botham	c Richards b Croft	4
W. Larkins	b Garner	0
P.H. Edmonds	not out	5
C.M. Old	b Garner	0
R.W. Taylor†	c Murray b Garner	0
M. Hendrick	b Croft	0
Extras	(LB 12, W 2, NB 3)	17
Total	(51 overs)	**194**

Fall of wickets: 1-129, 2-135, 3-183, 4-183, 5-186, 6-186, 7-192, 8-192, 9-194, 10-194.

WEST INDIES	*O*	*M*	*R*	*W*
Roberts	9	2	33	0
Holding	8	1	16	2
Croft	10	1	42	3
Garner	11	0	38	5
Richards	10	0	35	0
King	3	0	13	0

Umpires: H.D. Bird and B.J. Meyer.

Match No. 75/6

AUSTRALIA v WEST INDIES 1979-80

Benson and Hedges World Series Cup – 1st Match

At Sydney Cricket Ground on 27 November 1979.

Toss: Australia.	Result: AUSTRALIA won by 5 wickets.
50 overs match (floodlit).	Award: G.S. Chappell.

Début: Australia – B.M. Laird.

The first official one-day international to be played under floodlights.

WEST INDIES		
C.G. Greenidge	b Lillee	5
D.L. Haynes	b Border	29
I.V.A. Richards	lbw b Lillee	9
A.I. Kallicharran	c and b Border	49
C.H. Lloyd*	c Marsh b Border	16
C.L. King	b Pascoe	29
D.L. Murray†	b Pascoe	27
A.M.E. Roberts	b Pascoe	16
J. Garner	run out	5
M.A. Holding	c McCosker b Pascoe	2
C.E.H. Croft	not out	0
Extras	(LB 3, NB 3)	6
Total	(49.3 overs)	**193**

Fall of wickets: 1-6, 2-18, 3-89, 4-112, 5-117, 6-164, 7-177, 8-187, 9-193, 10-193.

AUSTRALIA	*O*	*M*	*R*	*W*
Lillee	6	2	10	2
Pascoe	9.3	1	29	4
Bright	5	0	26	0
Hogg	10	0	49	0
Border	10	0	36	3
Chappell	9	0	37	0

AUSTRALIA		
B.M. Laird	b Croft	20
R.B. McCosker	lbw b Holding	1
A.R. Border	c Murray b Croft	17
G.S. Chappell*	not out	74
K.J. Hughes	b Richards	52
D.W. Hookes	b Richards	0
R.W. Marsh†	not out	18
R.J. Bright		
D.K. Lillee		
R.M. Hogg		
L.S. Pascoe		
Extras	(LB 14)	14
Total	(47.1 overs – 5 wickets)	**196**

Fall of wickets: 1-1, 2-37, 3-52, 4-144, 5-144.

WEST INDIES	*O*	*M*	*R*	*W*
Roberts	9	1	35	0
Holding	8.1	2	28	1
Croft	10	0	30	2
Garner	10	2	42	0
Richards	10	0	47	2

Umpires: R.G. Harris and C.E. Harvey.

ENGLAND v WEST INDIES 1979-80

Benson and Hedges World Series Cup – 2nd Match

At Sydney Cricket Ground on 28 November 1979.
Toss: West Indies. Result: ENGLAND won by 2 runs.
50 overs match (floodlit) – reduced to 47 overs. Award: P. Willey.
Début: England – G.R. Dilley.

Rain reduced West Indies' innings to 47 overs and their target to 199. With Croft needing 3 runs off Botham's final ball, Brearley positioned all his fielders, including Bairstow, on the boundary.

ENGLAND		
D.W. Randall	c Parry b Garner	49
J.M. Brearley*	c Greenidge b Parry	25
D.I. Gower	b Croft	44
G.A. Gooch	c and b Parry	2
P. Willey	not out	58
I.T. Botham	b Garner	11
D.L. Bairstow†	c Murray b Garner	0
G. Miller	b Roberts	4
G.R. Dilley	run out	1
D.L. Underwood		
R.G.D. Willis		
Extras	(B 4, LB 13)	17
Total	(50 overs – 8 wickets)	**211**

Fall of wickets: 1-79, 2-88, 3-91, 4-160, 5-195, 6-195, 7-210, 8-211.

WEST INDIES	*O*	*M*	*R*	*W*
Roberts	9	0	37	1
Holding	9	0	47	0
Croft	10	0	34	1
Garner	10	0	31	3
Parry	10	0	35	2
Kallicharran	2	0	10	0

WEST INDIES		
C.G. Greenidge	c Willis b Miller	42
D.L. Haynes	b Dilley	4
L.G. Rowe	lbw b Willis	60
A.I. Kallicharran	run out	44
C.H. Lloyd*	c Brearley b Willis	4
D.L. Murray†	c Gower b Underwood	3
D.R. Parry	b Underwood	4
A.M.E. Roberts	c Randall b Underwood	16
J. Garner	not out	8
M.A. Holding	c Gower b Underwood	0
C.E.H. Croft	b Botham	3
Extras	(B 1, LB 7)	8
Total	(47 overs)	**196**

Fall of wickets: 1-19, 2-68, 3-132, 4-143, 5-144, 6-155, 7-177, 8-185, 9-186, 10-196.

ENGLAND	*O*	*M*	*R*	*W*
Dilley	6	2	21	1
Botham	7	1	26	1
Underwood	10	0	44	4
Miller	10	0	33	1
Willey	8	0	29	0
Willis	6	0	35	2

Umpires: C.E. Harvey and A.G. Watson.

Match No. 77/15

AUSTRALIA v ENGLAND 1979-80

Benson and Hedges World Series Cup – 3rd Match

At Melbourne Cricket Ground on 8 December 1979.
Toss: England. Result: ENGLAND won by 3 wickets.
50 overs match. Award: G.S. Chappell.
Début: Australia – J.M. Wiener.

AUSTRALIA		
J.M. Wiener	b Botham	7
B.M. Laird	lbw b Dilley	7
A.R. Border	c Willey b Dilley	29
G.S. Chappell*	c Gooch b Willey	92
K.J. Hughes	st Bairstow b Gooch	23
K.D. Walters	c Randall b Gooch	12
R.W. Marsh†	c Bairstow b Willey	14
R.J. Bright	c Gooch b Willey	1
D.K. Lillee	not out	13
R.M. Hogg	c Brearley b Underwood	1
J.R. Thomson		
Extras	(B 1, LB 5, NB 2)	8
Total	(50 overs – 9 wickets)	**207**

Fall of wickets: 1-15, 2-15, 3-73, 4-114, 5-145, 6-184, 7-193, 8-193, 9-207.

ENGLAND	*O*	*M*	*R*	*W*
Dilley	10	1	30	2
Botham	9	2	27	1
Willis	7	0	28	0
Gooch	6	0	32	2
Underwood	10	0	49	1
Willey	8	0	33	3

ENGLAND		
D.W. Randall	lbw b Bright	28
G. Boycott	c Lillee b Hogg	68
P. Willey	c Marsh b Hogg	37
D.I. Gower	c Marsh b Lillee	17
G.A. Gooch	run out	1
I.T. Botham	c Walters b Hogg	10
J.M. Brearley*	c Marsh b Lillee	27
D.L. Bairstow†	not out	15
G.R. Dilley	not out	0
D.L. Underwood		
R.G.D. Willis		
Extras	(LB 3, NB 3)	6
Total	(49 overs – 7 wickets)	**209**

Fall of wickets: 1-71, 2-134, 3-137, 4-138, 5-148, 6-183, 7-205.

AUSTRALIA	*O*	*M*	*R*	*W*
Lillee	10	1	36	2
Hogg	10	2	26	3
Thomson	10	1	49	0
Chappell	8	0	40	0
Bright	9	1	40	1
Walters	2	0	12	0

Umpires: W.J. Copeland and R.A. French.

AUSTRALIA v WEST INDIES 1979-80

Benson and Hedges World Series Cup – 4th Match

At Melbourne Cricket Ground on 9 December 1979.
Toss: Australia. Result: WEST INDIES won by 80 runs.
48 overs match. Award: I.V.A. Richards.
No débuts.

Richards (131 balls, 1 six and 16 fours) became the first batsman to score 150 outside England in these matches. His partnership of 205 with Haynes was the first of 200 or more in one-day internationals and remained the record for any wicket until 1983-84 (*Match No. 228*).

WEST INDIES		
C.G. Greenidge	c Marsh b Lillee	11
D.L. Haynes	c Marsh b Thomson	80
I.V.A. Richards	not out	153
A.I. Kallicharran	not out	16
L.G. Rowe		
C.L. King		
D.L. Murray*†		
D.R. Parry		
A.M.E. Roberts		
J. Garner		
M.A. Holding		
Extras	(B 1, LB 10)	11
Total	(48 overs – 2 wickets)	**271**

Fall of wickets 1-28, 2-233.

AUSTRALIA	*O*	*M*	*R*	*W*
Lillee	10	1	48	1
Hogg	10	1	50	0
Chappell	4	0	24	0
Thomson	8	0	43	1
Bright	6	0	29	0
Hookes	1	0	10	0
Border	7	0	40	0
Wiener	2	0	16	0

AUSTRALIA		
B.M. Laird	b Holding	7
J.M. Wiener	c and b Parry	27
A.R. Border	run out	44
G.S. Chappell*	c Richards b King	31
K.J. Hughes	b Holding	12
D.W. Hookes	c Murray b Roberts	9
R.W. Marsh†	c Rowe b Roberts	13
R.J. Bright	not out	19
D.K. Lillee	b King	19
R.M. Hogg	not out	3
J.R. Thomson		
Extras	(B 1, LB 6)	7
Total	(48 overs – 8 wickets)	**191**

Fall of wickets 1-16, 2-54, 3-102, 4-119, 5-128, 6-147, 7-151, 8-185.

WEST INDIES	*O*	*M*	*R*	*W*
Roberts	8	1	33	2
Holding	10	2	29	2
Garner	10	1	26	0
King	10	0	40	2
Parry	10	0	56	1

Umpires: K. Carmody and R.V. Whitehead.

Match No. 79/16

AUSTRALIA v ENGLAND 1979-80

Benson and Hedges World Series Cup – 5th Match

At Sydney Cricket Ground on 11 December 1979.
Toss: England. Result: ENGLAND won by 72 runs.
49 overs match (floodlit). Award: G. Boycott.
No débuts.

ENGLAND		
D.W. Randall	run out	42
G. Boycott	b Lillee	105
P. Willey	c Walker b Chappell	64
D.I. Gower	c Wiener b Lillee	7
G.A. Gooch	b Thomson	11
I.T. Botham	c Walters b Lillee	5
D.L. Bairstow†	c sub (D.W. Hookes) b Lillee	18
J.M. Brearley*	not out	2
G.R. Dilley		
D.L. Underwood		
R.G.D. Willis		
Extras	(LB 6, W 1, NB 3)	10
Total	(49 overs – 7 wickets)	**264**

Fall of wickets: 1-78, 2-196, 3-220, 4-236, 5-242, 6-245, 7-264.

AUSTRALIA	*O*	*M*	*R*	*W*
Lillee	10	0	56	4
Thomson	9	0	53	1
Walker	10	1	30	0
Laughlin	8	0	39	0
Border	4	0	24	0
Chappell	5	0	28	1
Walters	3	0	24	0

AUSTRALIA		
J.M. Wiener	st Bairstow b Willey	14
W.M. Darling	c Randall b Willis	20
A.R. Border	b Willey	1
G.S. Chappell*	run out	0
K.J. Hughes	c Bairstow b Willis	1
K.D. Walters	c Bairstow b Botham	34
R.W. Marsh†	b Dilley	12
T.J. Laughlin	c Gooch b Randall	74
D.K. Lillee	b Botham	14
J.R. Thomson	run out	0
M.H.N. Walker	not out	9
Extras	(LB 10, W 2, NB 1)	13
Total	(47.2 overs)	**192**

Fall of wickets: 1-33, 2-36, 3-36, 4-38, 5-39, 6-63, 7-115, 8-146, 9-147, 10-192.

ENGLAND	*O*	*M*	*R*	*W*
Dilley	9	0	29	1
Botham	10	1	36	2
Willis	10	1	32	2
Willey	5	0	18	2
Underwood	6	1	29	0
Gooch	7	0	33	0
Randall	0.2	0	2	1

Umpires: J.R. Collins and L.J. Stevens.

AUSTRALIA v WEST INDIES 1979-80

Benson and Hedges World Series Cup – 6th Match

At Sydney Cricket Ground on 21 December 1979.
Toss: West Indies. Result: AUSTRALIA won by 7 runs.
50 overs match (floodlit). Award: I.M. Chappell.
No débuts.

AUSTRALIA		
J.M. Wiener	c Lloyd b Holding	7
B.M. Laird	c Rowe b Roberts	1
A.R. Border	c Murray b Garner	17
G.S. Chappell*	c Lloyd b Richards	24
K.J. Hughes	c Roberts b King	13
I.M. Chappell	not out	63
R.W. Marsh†	run out	33
D.K. Lillee	not out	12
L.S. Pascoe		
R.M. Hogg		
G. Dymock		
Extras	(LB 4, NB 2)	6
Total	(50 overs – 6 wickets)	**176**

Fall of wickets 1-1, 2-11, 3-28, 4-44, 5-94, 6-160.

WEST INDIES	*O*	*M*	*R*	*W*
Roberts	10	1	28	1
Holding	10	1	33	1
King	10	0	38	1
Garner	10	2	34	1
Richards	8	0	35	1
Lloyd	2	0	2	0

WEST INDIES		
C.G. Greenidge	c Marsh b Lillee	33
D.L. Haynes	c I.M. Chappell b Lillee	0
I.V.A. Richards	c Hogg b Dymock	62
A.I. Kallicharran	b Pascoe	19
L.G. Rowe	c Border b G.S. Chappell	5
C.H. Lloyd*	c Wiener b Dymock	0
C.L. King	c Marsh b G.S. Chappell	9
D.L. Murray†	not out	17
A.M.E. Roberts	lbw b Pascoe	8
J. Garner	c G.S. Chappell b Lillee	2
M.A. Holding	b Lillee	0
Extras	(LB 8, NB 6)	14
Total	(42.5 overs)	**169**

Fall of wickets 1-7, 2-74, 3-112, 4-124, 5-126, 6-139, 7-144, 8-158, 9-169, 10-169.

AUSTRALIA	*O*	*M*	*R*	*W*
Lillee	8.5	0	28	4
Pascoe	10	1	38	2
Hogg	10	3	47	0
Dymock	10	1	28	2
G.S. Chappell	4	0	14	2

Umpires: R.A. French and A.G. Watson.

Match No. 81/8

ENGLAND v WEST INDIES 1979-80

Benson and Hedges World Series Cup – 7th Match

At Woolloongabba, Brisbane on 23 December 1979.
Toss: West Indies. Result: WEST INDIES won by 9 wickets.
50 overs match. Award: C.G. Greenidge.
No débuts.

ENGLAND		
D.W. Randall	c Lloyd b Roberts	0
G. Boycott	c sub (M.D. Marshall) b Holding	68
P. Willey	run out	34
D.I. Gower	c Holding b Roberts	59
G.A. Gooch	b Garner	17
I.T. Botham	lbw b Holding	4
D.L. Bairstow†	c Lloyd b Roberts	12
J.M. Brearley*	not out	9
G.R. Dilley	b Garner	0
D.L. Underwood		
R.G.D. Willis		
Extras	(LB 8, W 5, NB 1)	14
Total	(50 overs – 8 wickets)	**217**

Fall of wickets: 1-0, 2-70, 3-167, 4-174, 5-191, 6-205, 7-209, 8-217.

WEST INDIES	*O*	*M*	*R*	*W*
Roberts	10	3	26	3
Holding	10	1	44	2
Garner	10	0	37	2
Richards	10	0	44	0
King	10	0	52	0

WEST INDIES		
C.G. Greenidge	not out	85
D.L. Haynes	c Underwood b Gooch	41
I.V.A. Richards	not out	85
A.I. Kallicharran		
L.G. Rowe		
C.H. Lloyd*		
C.L. King		
D.L. Murray†		
A.M.E. Roberts		
J. Garner		
M.A. Holding		
Extras	(LB 4, NB 3)	7
Total	(46.5 overs – 1 wicket)	**218**

Fall of wicket: 1-109.

ENGLAND	*O*	*M*	*R*	*W*
Botham	10	1	39	0
Dilley	8	1	25	0
Willis	10	2	27	0
Underwood	9	0	43	0
Willey	6	0	39	0
Gooch	3.5	0	38	1

Umpires: C.E. Harvey and M.W. Johnson.

AUSTRALIA v ENGLAND 1979-80

Benson and Hedges World Series Cup – 8th Match

At Sydney Cricket Ground on 26 December 1979.
Toss: Australia. Result: ENGLAND won by 4 wickets.
47 overs match (floodlit). Award: G. Boycott.
No débuts.

AUSTRALIA		
B.M. Laird	b Botham	6
J.M. Wiener	c Bairstow b Botham	2
A.R. Border	c Gower b Gooch	22
G.S. Chappell*	run out	52
K.J. Hughes	b Willis	23
I.M. Chappell	not out	60
R.W. Marsh†	c Bairstow b Dilley	10
D.K. Lillee	not out	2
R.M. Hogg		
G. Dymock		
L.S. Pascoe		
Extras	(B 3, LB 10, NB 4)	17
Total	(47 overs – 6 wickets)	**194**

Fall of wickets 1-5, 2-21, 3-50, 4-109, 5-135, 6-179.

ENGLAND	*O*	*M*	*R*	*W*
Dilley	10	1	32	1
Botham	9	1	33	2
Willis	10	1	38	1
Underwood	10	2	36	0
Gooch	8	0	38	1

ENGLAND		
G.A. Gooch	lbw b Hogg	29
G. Boycott	not out	86
P. Willey	b Pascoe	51
D.I. Gower	c Marsh b Hogg	2
D.W. Randall	c G.S. Chappell b Pascoe	1
I.T. Botham	lbw b Hogg	6
J.M. Brearley*	c Marsh b Hogg	0
D.L. Bairstow†	not out	7
G.R. Dilley		
D.L. Underwood		
R.G.D. Willis		
Extras	(LB 1, W 1, NB 11)	13
Total	(45.1 overs – 6 wickets)	**195**

Fall of wickets 1-41, 2-152, 3-157, 4-170, 5-179, 6-179.

AUSTRALIA	*O*	*M*	*R*	*W*
Lillee	10	0	47	0
Pascoe	10	2	28	2
Hogg	10	0	46	4
Dymock	10	1	38	0
G.S. Chappell	5.1	0	23	0

Umpires: P.M. Cronin and R.C. Isherwood.

ENGLAND v WEST INDIES (Benson and Hedges World Series Cup – 9th Match). At Melbourne Cricket Ground on 12 January 1980. No result - abandoned without a ball bowled.

Match No. 83/18

AUSTRALIA v ENGLAND 1979-80

Benson and Hedges World Series Cup – 10th Match

At Sydney Cricket Ground on 14 January 1980.
Toss: England. Result: ENGLAND won by 2 wickets.
50 overs match (floodlit). Award: D.K. Lillee.

Débuts: England – J.E. Emburey, G.B. Stevenson.

Stephenson celebrated his international début by taking 4-7 in 20 balls before leading England to a thrilling victory with seven balls to spare.

AUSTRALIA		
J.M. Wiener	st Bairstow b Emburey	33
R.B. McCosker	c Brearley b Willey	41
I.M. Chappell	c Randall b Emburey	8
G.S. Chappell*	c Randall b Stevenson	34
K.J. Hughes	c Larkins b Lever	34
A.R. Border	c Bairstow b Lever	0
R.W. Marsh†	c Bairstow b Stevenson	0
D.K. Lillee	lbw b Stevenson	0
G. Dymock	run out	0
J.R. Thomson	not out	3
L.S. Pascoe	b Stevenson	5
Extras	(LB 1, W 3, NB 1)	5
Total	(48.4 overs)	**163**

Fall of wickets 1-74, 2-82, 3-89, 4-148, 5-149, 6-150, 7-150, 8-152, 9-155, 10-163.

ENGLAND	*O*	*M*	*R*	*W*
Lever	9	1	11	2
Botham	7	0	33	0
Gooch	3	0	13	0
Stevenson	9.4	0	33	4
Emburey	10	1	33	2
Willey	10	0	35	1

ENGLAND		
G.A. Gooch	c McCosker b Pascoe	69
W. Larkins	c Thomson b Lillee	5
P. Willey	lbw b Lillee	0
D.I. Gower	c Marsh b Lillee	3
J.M. Brearley*	b G.S. Chappell	5
D.W. Randall	c Pascoe b G.S. Chappell	0
I.T. Botham	b Lillee	0
D.L. Bairstow†	not out	21
J.E. Emburey	c G.S. Chappell b Dymock	18
G.B. Stevenson	not out	28
J.K. Lever		
Extras	(LB 5, W 1, NB 9)	15
Total	(48.5 overs – 8 wickets)	**164**

Fall of wickets 1-31, 2-31, 3-40, 4-51, 5-56, 6-61, 7-105, 8-129.

AUSTRALIA	*O*	*M*	*R*	*W*
Thomson	9.5	0	46	0
Dymock	9	1	30	1
Lillee	10	6	12	4
Pascoe	10	0	38	1
G.S. Chappell	10	3	23	2

Umpires: R.C. Isherwood and R.V. Whitehead.

ENGLAND v WEST INDIES 1979-80

Benson and Hedges World Series Cup – 11th Match

At Adelaide Oval on 16 January 1980.
Toss: England. Result: WEST INDIES won by 107 runs.
50 overs match. Award: A.M.E. Roberts.
No débuts.

WEST INDIES		
C.G. Greenidge	c Emburey b Willey	50
D.L. Haynes	c Gooch b Stevenson	26
I.V.A. Richards	b Botham	88
A.I. Kallicharran	c and b Botham	57
C.L. King	run out	12
J. Garner	not out	7
A.M.E. Roberts	not out	0
C.H. Lloyd*		
L.G. Rowe		
D.L. Murray†		
M.A. Holding		
Extras	(B 1, LB 4, NB 1)	6
Total	(50 overs – 5 wickets)	**246**

Fall of wickets 1-58, 2-115, 3-224, 4-227, 5-245.

ENGLAND	*O*	*M*	*R*	*W*
Lever	10	1	54	0
Botham	10	0	35	2
Gooch	2	0	22	0
Stevenson	8	1	53	1
Emburey	10	0	39	0
Willey	10	1	37	1

ENGLAND		
G.A. Gooch	b King	20
J.M. Brearley*	c Murray b Roberts	0
P. Willey	c Lloyd b King	5
W. Larkins	c Lloyd b King	24
D.I. Gower	c sub (D.R. Parry) b King	12
D.W. Randall	b Roberts	16
I.T. Botham	c Haynes b Roberts	22
D.L. Bairstow†	not out	23
G.B. Stevenson	b Roberts	1
J.E. Emburey	c Murray b Roberts	1
J.K. Lever	b Garner	11
Extras	(LB 2, W 1, NB 1)	4
Total	(42.5 overs)	**139**

Fall of wickets 1-5, 2-24, 3-31, 4-52, 5-68,
6-98, 7-100, 8-105, 9-109, 10-139.

WEST INDIES	*O*	*M*	*R*	*W*
Roberts	10	5	22	5
Holding	7	0	16	0
King	9	3	23	4
Garner	7.5	3	9	1
Richards	7	0	46	0
Kallicharran	2	0	19	0

Umpires: P.M. Cronin and G. Duperouzel.

Match No. 85/9

AUSTRALIA v WEST INDIES 1979-80

Benson and Hedges World Series Cup – 12th Match

At Sydney Cricket Ground on 18 January 1980.
Toss: Australia. Result: AUSTRALIA won by 9 runs.
50 overs match (floodlit). Award: R.B. McCosker.
Début: Australia – D.F. Whatmore.

AUSTRALIA		
J.M. Wiener	c Gomes b Parry	50
R.B. McCosker	c Lloyd b Holding	95
K.J. Hughes	b Parry	4
G.S. Chappell*	c and b Parry	2
G.N. Yallop	b Roberts	11
D.F. Whatmore	c Murray b Holding	2
R.W. Marsh†	c Lloyd b Roberts	5
D.K. Lillee	c Murray b Holding	0
G. Dymock	not out	4
M.H.N. Walker	run out	5
L.S. Pascoe	b Holding	0
Extras	(B 1, LB 10, W 1)	12
Total	(48.3 overs)	**190**

Fall of wickets: 1-103, 2-124, 3-134, 4-161, 5-166, 6-177, 7-177, 8-177, 9-190, 10-190.

WEST INDIES	*O*	*M*	*R*	*W*
Holding	9.3	2	17	4
Croft	10	0	22	0
King	9	0	40	0
Roberts	10	0	38	2
Parry	10	0	61	3

WEST INDIES		
L.G. Rowe	lbw b Dymock	3
D.L. Haynes	c Marsh b Lillee	1
A.I. Kallicharran	lbw b Chappell	66
D.A. Murray†	c Chappell b Pascoe	35
C.H. Lloyd*	not out	34
C.L. King	lbw b Walker	0
H.A. Gomes	lbw b Lillee	4
D.R. Parry	b Pascoe	9
A.M.E. Roberts	c Marsh b Lillee	2
M.A. Holding	c and b Pascoe	8
C.E.H. Croft	c Lillee b Chappell	8
Extras	(B 3, NB 8)	11
Total	(49.1 overs)	**181**

Fall of wickets: 1-4, 2-8, 3-91, 4-134, 5-135, 6-140, 7-152, 8-157, 9-166, 10-181.

AUSTRALIA	*O*	*M*	*R*	*W*
Lillee	10	3	17	3
Dymock	10	2	18	1
Walker	10	2	46	1
Pascoe	10	0	34	3
Chappell	7.1	0	37	2
Wiener	2	0	18	0

Umpires: K. Carmody and A.G. Watson.

ENGLAND v WEST INDIES 1979-80

Benson and Hedges World Series Cup – 1st Final

At Melbourne Cricket Ground on 20 January 1980.
Toss: England. Result: WEST INDIES won by 2 runs.
50 overs match. No award.
No débuts.

WEST INDIES		
C.G. Greenidge	c Larkins b Botham	80
D.L. Haynes	c Bairstow b Willis	9
I.V.A. Richards	c Bairstow b Dilley	23
A.I. Kallicharran	b Botham	42
C.H. Lloyd*	b Botham	4
C.L. King	not out	31
D.L. Murray†	c Bairstow b Dilley	4
A.M.E. Roberts	run out	1
J. Garner	run out	3
M.A. Holding	not out	5
C.E.H. Croft		
Extras	(LB 11, W 1, NB 1)	13
Total	(50 overs – 8 wickets)	**215**

Fall of wickets: 1-17, 2-66, 3-161, 4-168, 5-168, 6-181, 7-183, 8-197.

ENGLAND	*O*	*M*	*R*	*W*
Willis	10	1	51	1
Botham	10	2	33	3
Emburey	10	0	31	0
Dilley	10	0	39	2
Willey	10	0	48	0

ENGLAND		
G.A. Gooch	c King b Holding	9
G. Boycott	c Greenidge b Roberts	35
P. Willey	run out	51
D.I. Gower	c Holding b Roberts	10
W. Larkins	run out	34
I.T. Botham	c Lloyd b Roberts	19
J.M. Brearley*	not out	25
D.L. Bairstow†	run out	4
J.E. Emburey		
G.R. Dilley		
R.G.D. Willis		
Extras	(B 12, LB 12, W 1, NB 1)	26
Total	(50 overs – 7 wickets)	**213**

Fall of wickets: 1-13, 2-74, 3-96, 4-152, 5-164, 6-190, 7-213.

WEST INDIES	*O*	*M*	*R*	*W*
Roberts	10	1	30	3
Holding	10	1	43	1
Garner	10	1	27	0
Croft	10	1	23	0
King	4	0	30	0
Richards	6	1	34	0

Umpires: R.C. Bailhache and C.E. Harvey.

Match No. 87/11

ENGLAND v WEST INDIES 1979-80

Benson and Hedges World Series Cup – 2nd Final

At Sydney Cricket Ground on 22 January 1980.

Toss: England. Result: WEST INDIES won by 8 wickets.

50 overs match. Finals award: C.G. Greenidge.

No débuts.

ENGLAND		
G.A. Gooch	lbw b Garner	23
G. Boycott	c Greenidge b Roberts	63
P. Willey	b Garner	3
D.I. Gower	c Murray b Holding	27
W. Larkins	b Croft	14
I.T. Botham	c King b Roberts	37
D.L. Bairstow†	not out	18
J.M. Brearley*	run out	4
J.E. Emburey	run out	6
G.R. Dilley		
R.G.D. Willis		
Extras	(B 1, LB 11, NB 1)	13
Total	(50 overs – 8 wickets)	**208**

Fall of wickets 1-40, 2-54, 3-118, 4-126, 5-155, 6-188, 7-194, 8-208.

WEST INDIES	*O*	*M*	*R*	*W*
Roberts	10	3	31	2
Holding	10	1	34	1
Croft	10	3	29	1
Garner	10	0	44	2
Richards	3	0	19	0
King	7	1	38	0

WEST INDIES		
C.G. Greenidge	not out	98
D.L. Haynes	lbw b Botham	17
I.V.A. Richards	c Botham b Willey	65
A.I. Kallicharran	not out	8
C.H. Lloyd*		
C.L. King		
D.L. Murray†		
A.M.E. Roberts		
J. Garner		
M.A. Holding		
C.E.H. Croft		
Extras	(B 5, LB 10, W 5, NB 1)	21
Total	(47.3 overs – 2 wickets)	**209**

Fall of wickets 1-61, 2-180.

ENGLAND	*O*	*M*	*R*	*W*
Willis	10	0	35	0
Dilley	7	0	37	0
Botham	10	1	28	1
Emburey	9.3	0	48	0
Willey	10	2	35	1
Gooch	1	0	5	0

Umpires: A.R. Crafter and M.G. O'Connell.

NEW ZEALAND v WEST INDIES 1979-80 (Only Match)

At Lancaster Park, Christchurch on 6 February 1980.
Toss: New Zealand. Result: NEW ZEALAND won by 1 wicket.
50 overs match. Award: R.J. Hadlee.
Débuts: New Zealand – P.E. McEwan, J.F. Reid.

WEST INDIES		
D.L. Haynes	lbw b Coney	27
C.G. Greenidge	b Cairns	103
L.G. Rowe	run out	4
A.I. Kallicharran	run out	6
C.H. Lloyd*	b Hadlee	14
C.L. King	c Lees b Cairns	12
D.R. Parry	not out	11
J. Garner	c Coney b Hadlee	5
D.L. Murray†	not out	3
M.A. Holding		
C.E.H. Croft		
Extras	(B 4, LB 10, NB 4)	18
Total	(50 overs – 7 wickets)	**203**

Fall of wickets: 1-81, 2-94, 3-126, 4-165, 5-175, 6-185, 7-196.

NEW ZEALAND	*O*	*M*	*R*	*W*
Hadlee	10	3	28	2
Troup	10	0	30	0
Cairns	10	1	37	2
McEwan	10	0	40	0
Coney	8	0	41	1
Howarth	2	0	9	0

NEW ZEALAND		
J.G. Wright	c Lloyd b King	20
B.A. Edgar	c Murray b Garner	18
J.F. Reid	c Murray b Parry	5
J.M. Parker	c Lloyd b Garner	0
G.P. Howarth*	c Parry b King	18
P.E. McEwan	c and b Parry	12
J.V. Coney	not out	53
W.K. Lees†	b Parry	25
R.J. Hadlee	c Garner b Holding	41
B.L. Cairns	run out	1
G.B. Troup	not out	0
Extras	(B 1, LB 10, W 1, NB 2)	14
Total	(49.4 overs – 9 wickets)	**207**

Fall of wickets: 1-28, 2-40, 3-41, 4-56, 5-78, 6-80, 7-134, 8-194, 9-203.

WEST INDIES	*O*	*M*	*R*	*W*
Holding	9.4	1	23	1
Croft	10	2	46	0
Garner	10	2	42	2
King	10	1	35	2
Parry	10	0	47	3

Umpires: F.R. Goodall and R.L. Monteith.

Match No. 89/12

ENGLAND v WEST INDIES 1980 (1st Match)

Prudential Trophy

At Headingley, Leeds on 28, 29 May 1980.
Toss: England. Result: WEST INDIES won by 24 runs.
55 overs match. Award: C.J. Tavaré.
Débuts: England – C.J. Tavaré; West Indies – M.D. Marshall.

WEST INDIES		
C.G. Greenidge	b Botham	78
D.L. Haynes	c Tavaré b Old	19
I.V.A. Richards	c Gower b Gooch	7
S.F.A.F. Bacchus	c Lever b Gooch	2
A.I. Kallicharran	c Botham b Old	10
C.H. Lloyd*	c and b Lever	21
M.D. Marshall	b Botham	6
D.L. Murray†	run out	9
A.M.E. Roberts	c Botham b Dilley	10
J. Garner	run out	14
M.A. Holding	not out	0
Extras	(B 5, LB 15, W 2)	22
Total	(55 overs)	**198**

Fall of wickets 1-36, 2-49, 3-51, 4-110, 5-151, 6-161, 7-163, 8-178, 9-197, 10-198.

ENGLAND	*O*	*M*	*R*	*W*
Dilley	11	3	41	1
Lever	11	3	36	1
Botham	11	1	45	2
Old	11	4	12	2
Gooch	7	2	30	2
Willey	4	0	12	0

ENGLAND		
P. Willey	c Richards b Marshall	7
G. Boycott	c Kallicharran b Garner	5
C.J. Tavaré	not out	82
G.A. Gooch	c Murray b Richards	2
D.I. Gower	c Murray b Holding	12
I.T. Botham*	c Murray b Marshall	30
D. Lloyd	b Greenidge	1
D.L. Bairstow†	c Garner b Holding	16
C.M. Old	b Marshall	4
G.R. Dilley	c Haynes b Roberts	0
J.K. Lever	run out	6
Extras	(B 3, LB 4, W 2)	9
Total	(51.2 overs)	**174**

Fall of wickets 1-11, 2-15, 3-23, 4-38, 5-81, 6-86, 7-130, 8-149, 9-150, 10-174.

WEST INDIES	*O*	*M*	*R*	*W*
Holding	9	3	16	2
Roberts	11	4	30	1
Garner	9.2	0	20	1
Marshall	11	2	28	3
Richards	7	0	50	1
Greenidge	4	0	21	1

Umpires: B.J. Meyer and K.E. Palmer.

ENGLAND v WEST INDIES 1980 (2nd Match)
Prudential Trophy

At Lord's, London on 30 May 1980.
Toss: England. Result: ENGLAND won by 3 wickets.
55 overs match. Award: G. Boycott.
Début: England – V.J. Marks.

WEST INDIES		
C.G. Greenidge	c Lever b Marks	39
D.L. Haynes	c Willis b Marks	50
S.F.A.F. Bacchus	run out	40
I.V.A. Richards*	c Lever b Botham	26
A.I. Kallicharran	c Willis b Old	11
C.L. King	run out	33
A.M.E. Roberts	not out	25
J. Garner	run out	0
M.D. Marshall	b Willis	0
M.A. Holding	b Willis	0
D.A. Murray†		
Extras	(LB 9, NB 2)	11
Total	(55 overs – 9 wickets)	**235**

Fall of wickets: 1-86, 2-113, 3-147, 4-169, 5-186, 6-231, 7-233, 8-233, 9-235.

ENGLAND	*O*	*M*	*R*	*W*
Willis	10	1	25	2
Lever	7	1	23	0
Botham	11	2	71	1
Old	11	1	43	1
Marks	11	1	44	2
Willey	5	0	18	0

ENGLAND		
P. Willey	c and b Holding	56
G. Boycott	run out	70
C.J. Tavaré	c Murray b Holding	5
G.A. Gooch	c Bacchus b Marshall	12
D.I. Gower	c Bacchus b Roberts	12
I.T. Botham*	not out	42
V.J. Marks	b Holding	9
D.L. Bairstow†	run out	2
J.K. Lever	not out	0
C.M. Old		
R.G.D. Willis		
Extras	(LB 22, W 4, NB 2)	28
Total	(54.3 overs – 7 wickets)	**236**

Fall of wickets: 1-135, 2-143, 3-156, 4-160, 5-176, 6-212, 7-231.

WEST INDIES	*O*	*M*	*R*	*W*
Roberts	11	3	42	1
Holding	11	0	28	3
Garner	10.3	0	41	0
Marshall	11	1	45	1
Richards	5	0	28	0
Greenidge	6	0	24	0

Umpires: D.J. Constant and D.G.L. Evans.

Match No. 91/19

ENGLAND v AUSTRALIA 1980 (1st Match)

Prudential Trophy

At Kennington Oval, London on 20 August 1980.
Toss: Australia. Result: ENGLAND won by 23 runs.
55 overs match. Award: M. Hendrick.

Débuts: England – C.W.J. Athey, A.R. Butcher.

Hendrick became the first bowler to take five wickets for England in a limited-overs international. Surprisingly this feat eluded him during his 30-match Test career.

ENGLAND		
G.A. Gooch	b Border	54
G. Boycott	c Hughes b Lillee	99
A.R. Butcher	lbw b Dymock	14
C.W.J. Athey	c Chappell b Lillee	32
M.W. Gatting	not out	17
I.T. Botham*	c Yallop b Lillee	4
P. Willey	c Yallop b Lillee	2
D.L. Bairstow†	not out	9
R.D. Jackman		
C.M. Old		
M. Hendrick		
Extras	(B 2, LB 8, W 3, NB 4)	17
Total	(55 overs – 6 wickets)	**248**

Fall of wickets: 1-108, 2-140, 3-212, 4-221, 5-225, 6-232.

AUSTRALIA	*O*	*M*	*R*	*W*
Lillee	11	1	35	4
Thomson	11	3	25	0
Dymock	9	0	50	1
Pascoe	11	1	50	0
Border	11	2	61	1
Chappell	2	0	10	0

AUSTRALIA		
B.M. Laird	lbw b Gooch	15
G.M. Wood	c Athey b Jackman	4
G.S. Chappell*	c Bairstow b Hendrick	36
A.R. Border	b Hendrick	13
K.J. Hughes	not out	73
G.N. Yallop	b Hendrick	0
R.W. Marsh†	c Bairstow b Hendrick	41
D.K. Lillee	c Willey b Hendrick	0
J.R. Thomson	run out	15
G. Dymock	not out	14
L.S. Pascoe		
Extras	(B 3, LB 10, W 1)	14
Total	(55 overs – 8 wickets)	**225**

Fall of wickets: 1-11, 2-36, 3-68, 4-71, 5-75, 6-161, 7-161, 8-192.

ENGLAND	*O*	*M*	*R*	*W*
Old	9	0	43	0
Jackman	11	0	46	1
Botham	9	1	28	0
Gooch	7	0	29	1
Hendrick	11	3	31	5
Willey	8	0	34	0

Umpires: W.E. Alley and D.G.L. Evans.

ENGLAND v AUSTRALIA 1980 (2nd Match)
Prudential Trophy

At Edgbaston, Birmingham on 22 August 1980.
Toss: Australia. Result: ENGLAND won by 47 runs.
55 overs match. Award: G.A. Gooch.

Débuts: England – R.O. Butcher; Australia – J. Dyson.

Butcher reached his fifty off 35 balls – the fastest in Prudential Trophy matches.

ENGLAND		
G.A. Gooch	b Thomson	108
G. Boycott	c Marsh b Border	78
C.W.J. Athey	b Pascoe	51
R.O. Butcher	c Dyson b Pascoe	52
M.W. Gatting	run out	2
I.T. Botham*	b Pascoe	2
D.L. Bairstow†	b Lillee	6
R.D. Jackman	c Marsh b Pascoe	6
J.E. Emburey	not out	1
C.M. Old	not out	2
M. Hendrick		
Extras	(B 4, LB 3, W 1, NB 4)	12
Total	(55 overs – 8 wickets)	**320**

Fall of wickets: 1-154, 2-215, 3-292, 4-298, 5-302, 6-311, 7-313, 8-318.

AUSTRALIA	*O*	*M*	*R*	*W*
Thomson	11	1	69	1
Lillee	11	0	43	1
Pascoe	11	0	69	4
Bright	8	0	48	0
Chappell	11	0	65	0
Border	3	0	14	1

AUSTRALIA		
B.M. Laird	c Emburey b Hendrick	36
J. Dyson	b Hendrick	24
K.J. Hughes	c and b Gooch	98
A.R. Border	run out	26
G.N. Yallop	not out	52
D.K. Lillee	b Hendrick	21
R.J. Bright	not out	5
G.S. Chappell*		
R.W. Marsh†		
J.R. Thomson		
L.S. Pascoe		
Extras	(B 1, LB 9, W 1)	11
Total	(55 overs – 5 wickets)	**273**

Fall of wickets: 1-53, 2-80, 3-119, 4-222, 5-229.

ENGLAND	*O*	*M*	*R*	*W*
Old	11	2	44	0
Jackman	11	1	45	0
Botham	11	1	41	0
Hendrick	10	0	54	3
Emburey	8	0	51	0
Gooch	3	0	16	1
Boycott	1	0	11	0

Umpires: H.D. Bird and D.O. Oslear.

Match No. 93/4

PAKISTAN v WEST INDIES 1980-81 (1st Match)

At National Stadium, Karachi on 21 November 1980.
Toss: West Indies. Result: WEST INDIES won by 4 wickets.
40 overs match. Award: I.V.A. Richards.

Débuts: Pakistan – Mansoor Akhtar, Mohammad Nazir, Taslim Arif; West Indies – M.R. Pydanna.

PAKISTAN		
Taslim Arif†	c Marshall b Croft	4
Sadiq Mohammad	c Holding b Richards	40
Mansoor Akhtar	b Garner	24
Javed Miandad*	c Pydanna b Croft	8
Wasim Raja	c Holding b Richards	2
Majid Khan	c Lloyd b Kallicharran	16
Mudassar Nazar	c and b Holding	4
Imran Khan	c Bacchus b Kallicharran	2
Sarfraz Nawaz	run out	8
Iqbal Qasim	not out	6
Mohammad Nazir	not out	2
Extras	(B 1, LB 5, W 4, NB 1)	11
Total	(40 overs – 9 wickets)	**127**

Fall of wickets: 1-5, 2-59, 3-74, 4-81, 5-83, 6-97, 7-102, 8-114, 9-119.

WEST INDIES	*O*	*M*	*R*	*W*
Holding	5.3	3	5	1
Croft	7	1	17	2
Marshall	8	0	34	0
Garner	8	0	26	1
Richards	8	0	24	2
Kallicharran	3.3	0	10	2

WEST INDIES		
D.L. Haynes	b Iqbal Qasim	4
S.F.A.F. Bacchus	hit wicket b Mudassar	36
I.V.A. Richards	st Taslim b Majid	36
C.H. Lloyd*	c Sadiq b Mudassar	9
A.I. Kallicharran	lbw b Imran	14
C.G. Greenidge	not out	21
M.D. Marshall	run out	0
J. Garner	not out	0
M.R. Pydanna†		
M.A. Holding		
C.E.H. Croft		
Extras	(B 2, LB 4, W 1, NB 1)	8
Total	(40 overs – 6 wickets)	**128**

Fall of wickets: 1-18, 2-69, 3-85, 4-93, 5-124, 6-124.

PAKISTAN	*O*	*M*	*R*	*W*
Imran Khan	7	3	14	1
Sarfraz Nawaz	6	0	25	0
Iqbal Qasim	8	2	21	1
Mohammad Nazir	8	1	25	0
Mudassar Nazar	4	0	13	2
Majid Khan	7	1	22	1

Umpires: Javed Akhtar and Khalid Aziz.

PAKISTAN v WEST INDIES 1980-81 (2nd Match)

At Jinnah Park, Sialkot on 5 December 1980.
Toss: West Indies. Result: WEST INDIES won by 7 wickets.
40 overs match. Award: I.V.A. Richards.
Début: Pakistan – Ashraf Ali.

PAKISTAN		
Mudassar Nazar	c Marshall b Croft	3
Sadiq Mohammad	c Lloyd b Garner	13
Zaheer Abbas	not out	95
Javed Miandad*	st Pydanna b Richards	16
Majid Khan	c Clarke b Richards	34
Wasim Raja	not out	22
Imran Khan		
Ashraf Ali†		
Sarfraz Nawaz		
Iqbal Qasim		
Sikander Bakht		
Extras		17
Total	(40 overs – 4 wickets)	**200**

Fall of wickets 1-5, 2-35, 3-80, 4-138.

WEST INDIES	*O*	*M*	*R*	*W*
Clarke	8	1	28	0
Croft	8	2	28	1
Garner	8	2	36	1
Marshall	8	1	38	0
Richards	8	0	53	2

WEST INDIES		
D.L. Haynes	c Iqbal Qasim b Imran	16
S.F.A.F. Bacchus	lbw b Sarfraz	79
I.V.A. Richards	lbw b Sikander	83
M.R. Pydanna†	not out	2
C.H. Lloyd*	not out	1
A.I. Kallicharran		
H.A. Gomes		
S.T. Clarke		
M.D. Marshall		
J. Garner		
C.E.H. Croft		
Extras		20
Total	(35.3 overs – 3 wickets)	**201**

Fall of wickets 1-22, 2-198, 3-198.

PAKISTAN	*O*	*M*	*R*	*W*
Imran Khan	8	1	30	1
Sarfraz Nawaz	7.3	0	29	1
Sikander Bakht	4	0	22	1
Iqbal Qasim	8	0	37	0
Majid Khan	2	0	20	0
Wasim Raja	4	0	27	0
Mudassar Nazar	2	0	16	0

Umpires: Amanullah Khan and Shakoor Rana.

Match No. 95/6

PAKISTAN v WEST INDIES 1980-81 (3rd Match)

At Gaddafi Stadium, Lahore on 19 December 1980.
Toss: Pakistan. Result: WEST INDIES won by 7 runs.
40 overs match. Award: S.T. Clarke.
Débuts: Pakistan – Ijaz Faqih, Rashid Khan, Salim Pervez, Tahir Naqqash.

WEST INDIES		
A.I. Kallicharran	lbw b Wasim Raja	50
D.L. Haynes	b Rashid	2
I.V.A. Richards	c Taslim b Rashid	0
C.H. Lloyd*	c Wasim Bari b Wasim Raja	13
H.A. Gomes	c and b Majid	32
D.R. Parry	run out	32
S.T. Clarke	b Majid	20
M.D. Marshall	run out	12
J. Garner	not out	3
D.A. Murray†		
C.E.H. Croft		
Extras	(LB 3, W 3)	6
Total	(40 overs – 8 wickets)	**170**

Fall of wickets: 1-10, 2-10, 3-36, 4-92, 5-110, 6-134, 7-164, 8-170.

PAKISTAN	*O*	*M*	*R*	*W*
Sikander Bakht	1	0	3	0
Rashid Khan	8	2	31	2
Tahir Naqqash	8	1	37	0
Ijaz Faqih	8	1	30	0
Wasim Raja	8	0	28	2
Majid Khan	7	0	35	2

PAKISTAN		
Salim Pervez	c Murray b Garner	18
Taslim Arif	run out	24
Zaheer Abbas	b Clarke	42
Javed Miandad*	b Clarke	23
Wasim Raja	not out	22
Majid Khan	run out	16
Ijaz Faqih	run out	0
Rashid Khan	not out	4
Wasim Bari†		
Tahir Naqqash		
Sikander Bakht		
Extras	(B 1, LB 8, NB 5)	14
Total	(40 overs – 6 wickets)	**163**

Fall of wickets: 1-44, 2-63, 3-116, 4-123, 5-155, 6-157.

WEST INDIES	*O*	*M*	*R*	*W*
Clarke	8	0	25	2
Croft	7	0	28	0
Garner	8	2	18	1
Marshall	6	0	27	0
Parry	8	1	33	0
Richards	3	0	18	0

Umpires: Khizer Hayat and Mahboob Shah.

AUSTRALIA v NEW ZEALAND 1980-81

Benson and Hedges World Series Cup – 1st Match

At Adelaide Oval on 23 November 1980.
Toss: New Zealand. Result: NEW ZEALAND won by 3 wickets.
50 overs match. Award: E.J. Chatfield.

Débuts: Australia – T.M. Chappell, S.F. Graf, G.F. Lawson; New Zealand – M.C. Snedden.

Substitute John Bracewell became the first non-wicket-keeper to hold four catches in a one-day international.

AUSTRALIA		
J. Dyson	c sub (J.G. Bracewell) b Chatfield	69
G.M. Wood	c sub (J.G. Bracewell) b Chatfield	19
G.S. Chappell*	c Lees b Chatfield	25
K.J. Hughes	c Wright b McEwan	20
A.R. Border	c Lees b Chatfield	5
R.W. Marsh†	c sub (J.G. Bracewell) b Cairns	44
S.F. Graf	c sub (J.G. Bracewell) b Chatfield	0
T.M. Chappell	c Hadlee b Cairns	12
D.K. Lillee	c Wright b Cairns	3
G.F. Lawson	not out	4
L.S. Pascoe		
Extras	(LB 1, NB 15)	16
Total	(50 overs – 9 wickets)	**217**

Fall of wickets: 1-37, 2-92, 3-142, 4-147, 5-150, 6-150, 7-167, 8-171, 9-217.

NEW ZEALAND	*O*	*M*	*R*	*W*
Hadlee	10	1	25	0
Snedden	10	1	34	0
Coney	4	0	14	0
Cairns	10	0	58	3
Chatfield	10	1	34	5
McEwan	6	0	36	1

NEW ZEALAND		
J.G. Wright	c Dyson b G.S. Chappell	60
B.A. Edgar	c T.M. Chappell b Graf	25
P.E. McEwan	run out	3
G.P. Howarth*	run out	37
R.J. Hadlee	lbw b Lillee	39
J.M. Parker	c and b Lillee	16
J.V. Coney	not out	10
W.K. Lees†	c Lawson b Lillee	2
B.L. Cairns	not out	4
E.J. Chatfield		
M.C. Snedden		
Extras	(LB 15, NB 8)	23
Total	(49.1 overs – 7 wickets)	**219**

Fall of wickets: 1-61, 2-67, 3-140, 4-151, 5-198, 6-203, 7-211.

AUSTRALIA	*O*	*M*	*R*	*W*
Lillee	10	2	40	3
Pascoe	10	3	30	0
Lawson	9.1	1	42	0
T.M. Chappell	5	0	21	0
Graf	10	1	40	1
G.S. Chappell	5	0	23	1

Umpires: A.R. Crafter and P.M. Cronin.

Match No. 97/4

AUSTRALIA v NEW ZEALAND 1980-81

Benson and Hedges World Series Cup – 2nd Match

At Sydney Cricket Ground on 25 November 1980.
Toss: Australia. Result: AUSTRALIA won by 94 runs.
50 overs match (floodlit). Award: G.S. Chappell.
Début: New Zealand – I.D.S. Smith.

AUSTRALIA		
K.J. Hughes	c Smith b McEwan	19
J. Dyson	b Hadlee	79
G.S. Chappell*	not out	138
A.R. Border	c Snedden b Chatfield	9
K.D. Walters	not out	26
T.M. Chappell		
R.W. Marsh†		
D.K. Lillee		
L.S. Pascoe		
G.F. Lawson		
S.F. Graf		
Extras	(B 6, LB 12)	18
Total	(50 overs – 3 wickets)	**289**

Fall of wickets 1-29, 2-180, 3-207.

NEW ZEALAND	*O*	*M*	*R*	*W*
Hadlee	10	1	66	1
Snedden	10	1	58	0
Cairns	10	0	41	0
Chatfield	10	0	55	1
McEwan	10	0	51	1

NEW ZEALAND		
B.A. Edgar	lbw b G.S. Chappell	34
J.M. Parker	c Dyson b Pascoe	6
P.E. McEwan	c G.S. Chappell b Lawson	23
G.P. Howarth*	c Marsh b Pascoe	46
M.G. Burgess	b Lillee	29
R.J. Hadlee	c Dyson b Graf	10
B.L. Cairns	c Border b Pascoe	16
I.D.S. Smith	c Marsh b Graf	1
W.K. Lees†	c Dyson b Pascoe	8
M.C. Snedden	b Pascoe	3
E.J. Chatfield	not out	4
Extras	(LB 11, W 1, NB 3)	15
Total	(42.5 overs)	**195**

Fall of wickets 1-14, 2-63, 3-73, 4-138, 5-155,
6-173, 7-176, 8-181, 9-190, 10-195.

AUSTRALIA	*O*	*M*	*R*	*W*
Lillee	7	0	26	1
Pascoe	7.5	1	30	5
Lawson	10	0	43	1
G.S. Chappell	10	1	41	1
Graf	8	0	40	2

Umpires: R.C. Bailhache and M.W. Johnson.

AUSTRALIA v INDIA 1980-81

Benson and Hedges World Series Cup – 3rd Match

At Melbourne Cricket Ground on 6 December 1980.
Toss: Australia. Result: INDIA won by 66 runs.
49 overs match. Award: S.M. Patil.
Débuts: India – K. Azad, R.M.H. Binny, D.R. Doshi, S.M. Patil, T.E. Srinivasan.

INDIA		
S.M. Gavaskar*	c Lawson b Lillee	4
D.B. Vengsarkar	b G.S. Chappell	22
T.E. Srinivasan	c G.S. Chappell b Lillee	6
G.R. Viswanath	b T.M. Chappell	22
K. Azad	c Lawson b Pascoe	4
S.M. Patil	b G.S. Chappell	64
Kapil Dev	b Lawson	6
S.M.H. Kirmani†	not out	48
R.M.H. Binny	run out	0
K.D. Ghavri	run out	0
D.R. Doshi		
Extras	(B 11, LB 15, NB 6)	32
Total	(49 overs – 9 wickets)	**208**

Fall of wickets: 1-12, 2-22, 3-58, 4-65, 5-73, 6-111, 7-203, 8-208, 9-208.

AUSTRALIA	*O*	*M*	*R*	*W*
Lillee	7	1	22	2
Pascoe	10	0	32	1
Graf	10	0	30	0
Lawson	9	0	46	1
T.M. Chappell	5	0	14	1
G.S. Chappell	8	1	32	2

AUSTRALIA		
K.J. Hughes	b Patil	35
J. Dyson	run out	23
G.S. Chappell*	c Gavaskar b Doshi	11
A.R. Border	c Azad b Doshi	6
K.D. Walters	st Kirmani b Doshi	27
T.M. Chappell	run out	14
R.W. Marsh†	b Ghavri	7
S.F. Graf	b Binny	5
D.K. Lillee	run out	5
G.F. Lawson	c Doshi b Binny	0
L.S. Pascoe	not out	0
Extras	(LB 2, NB 7)	9
Total	(42.1 overs)	**142**

Fall of wickets: 1-60, 2-62, 3-73, 4-80, 5-118, 6-129, 7-137, 8-139, 9-139, 10-142.

INDIA	*O*	*M*	*R*	*W*
Ghavri	9.1	1	32	1
Binny	6	0	23	2
Kapil Dev	7	2	15	0
Doshi	10	1	32	3
Patil	10	1	31	1

Umpires: M.G. O'Connell and R.V. Whitehead.

Match No. 99/5

AUSTRALIA v NEW ZEALAND 1980-81

Benson and Hedges World Series Cup – 4th Match

At Melbourne Cricket Ground on 7 December 1980.
Toss: New Zealand. Result: AUSTRALIA won by 4 wickets.
50 overs match. Award: A.R. Border.
No débuts.

NEW ZEALAND		
B.A. Edgar	run out	33
J.G. Wright	b Pascoe	57
J.V. Coney	run out	9
P.E. McEwan	b Lillee	17
R.J. Hadlee	c T.M. Chappell b Pascoe	1
M.G. Burgess*	c Border b Pascoe	14
J.M. Parker	lbw b G.S. Chappell	3
W.K. Lees†	c G.S. Chappell b Lillee	0
G.B. Troup	not out	7
S.L. Boock	lbw b Lillee	2
E.J. Chatfield	lbw b Pascoe	0
Extras	(B 2, LB 10, W 1)	13
Total	(49.5 overs)	**156**

Fall of wickets: 1-74, 2-95, 3-112, 4-116, 5-138, 6-141, 7-142, 8-147, 9-153, 10-156.

AUSTRALIA	*O*	*M*	*R*	*W*
Lillee	10	3	19	3
Pascoe	9.5	3	37	4
Graf	4	0	15	0
G.S. Chappell	10	1	23	1
T.M. Chappell	10	2	27	0
Walters	6	0	22	0

AUSTRALIA		
J. Dyson	lbw b Hadlee	3
A.R. Border	c Edgar b Chatfield	55
G.S. Chappell*	st Lees b Boock	48
K.J. Hughes	run out	19
K.D. Walters	lbw b Boock	7
T.M. Chappell	b Hadlee	6
G.M. Wood	not out	1
R.W. Marsh†	not out	10
D.K. Lillee		
S.F. Graf		
L.S. Pascoe		
Extras	(B 2, LB 8)	10
Total	(47.2 overs – 6 wickets)	**159**

Fall of wickets: 1-15, 2-107, 3-116, 4-124, 5-143, 6-145.

NEW ZEALAND	*O*	*M*	*R*	*W*
Troup	9	3	15	0
Hadlee	10	0	34	2
Chatfield	9.2	1	34	1
McEwan	5	0	18	0
Boock	10	1	30	2
Coney	4	0	18	0

Umpires: R.C. Bailhache and R.A. French.

INDIA v NEW ZEALAND 1980-81

Benson and Hedges World Series Cup – 5th Match

At WACA Ground, Perth on 9 December 1980.

Toss: India.	Result: INDIA won by 5 runs.
50 overs match.	Award: R.J. Hadlee.

No débuts.

INDIA

S.M. Gavaskar*	c Lees b Hadlee	0
R.M.H. Binny	c Parker b Chatfield	14
D.B. Vengsarkar	c Coney b Troup	12
G.R. Viswanath	c Coney b Hadlee	10
Yashpal Sharma	b Cairns	23
S.M. Patil	c Parker b Hadlee	39
Kapil Dev	c Lees b Hadlee	0
S.M.H. Kirmani†	c Parker b Cairns	1
K. Azad	c and b Chatfield	29
K.D. Ghavri	b Hadlee	14
D.R. Doshi	not out	2
Extras	(B 9, LB 6, W 2, NB 1)	18
Total	(47.4 overs)	**162**

Fall of wickets: 1-0, 2-27, 3-35, 4-46, 5-116, 6-116, 7-116, 8-119, 9-157, 10-162.

NEW ZEALAND	*O*	*M*	*R*	*W*
Hadlee	9	1	32	5
Chatfield	8.4	0	33	2
Troup	10	2	36	1
Coney	10	1	25	0
Cairns	10	2	18	2

NEW ZEALAND

J.G. Wright	c Vengsarkar b Kapil Dev	4
B.A. Edgar	b Binny	16
P.E. McEwan	c Yashpal b Doshi	41
J.M. Parker	c Kapil Dev b Binny	1
J.V. Coney	c Kirmani b Patil	5
M.G. Burgess*	c sub (N.S. Yadav) b Doshi	10
R.J. Hadlee	c Kirmani b Binny	20
B.L. Cairns	c Vengsarkar b Ghavri	26
W.K. Lees†	c Vengsarkar b Binny	16
G.B. Troup	run out	5
E.J. Chatfield	not out	6
Extras	(LB 4, W 1, NB 2)	7
Total	(49.5 overs)	**157**

Fall of wickets: 1-13, 2-22, 3-38, 4-50, 5-80, 6-80, 7-130, 8-136, 9-157, 10-157.

INDIA	*O*	*M*	*R*	*W*
Kapil Dev	10	2	33	1
Ghavri	10	0	30	1
Binny	9.5	1	41	4
Patil	10	3	24	1
Doshi	10	4	22	2

Umpires: A.R. Crafter and D.G. Weser.

Match No. 101/2

AUSTRALIA v INDIA 1980-81

Benson and Hedges World Series Cup – 6th Match

At Sydney Cricket Ground on 18 December 1980.
Toss: Australia. Result: AUSTRALIA won by 9 wickets.
49 overs match (floodlit). Award: A.R. Border.
No débuts.

INDIA		
S.M. Gavaskar*	b Pascoe	22
R.M.H. Binny	c Marsh b Graf	31
D.B. Vengsarkar	c Marsh b Pascoe	4
G.R. Viswanath	b Graf	43
Yashpal Sharma	b Lillee	34
S.M. Patil	b T.M. Chappell	0
K. Azad	lbw b Lillee	1
Kapil Dev	c Dyson b Hogg	4
S.M.H. Kirmani†	run out	24
K.D. Ghavri	not out	11
D.R. Doshi		
Extras	(B 1, LB 3, NB 2)	6
Total	(49 overs – 9 wickets)	**180**

Fall of wickets: 1-31, 2-42, 3-64, 4-129, 5-130, 6-133, 7-139, 8-151, 9-180.

AUSTRALIA	*O*	*M*	*R*	*W*
Lillee	10	1	29	2
Hogg	10	1	48	1
Pascoe	9	2	34	2
Graf	10	1	23	2
T.M. Chappell	10	0	40	1

AUSTRALIA		
J. Dyson	c Kirmani b Kapil Dev	20
A.R. Border	not out	105
G.S. Chappell*	not out	52
K.J. Hughes		
T.M. Chappell		
K.D. Walters		
R.W. Marsh†		
S.F. Graf		
D.K. Lillee		
L.S. Pascoe		
R.M. Hogg		
Extras	(LB 4, NB 2)	6
Total	(42.2 overs – 1 wicket)	**183**

Fall of wicket: 1-56.

INDIA	*O*	*M*	*R*	*W*
Ghavri	8	0	25	0
Binny	7	0	29	0
Kapil Dev	8	1	27	1
Patil	8	0	49	0
Doshi	10	0	40	0
Gavaskar	1.2	0	7	0

Umpires: R.A. French and R.V. Whitehead.

INDIA v NEW ZEALAND 1980-81

Benson and Hedges World Series Cup – 7th Match

At Woolloongabba, Brisbane on 21 December 1980.
Toss: India. Result: NEW ZEALAND won by 3 wickets.
50 overs match. Award: Kapil Dev.
Début: India – Yograj Singh.

INDIA		
S.M. Gavaskar*	c Coney b Troup	1
C.P.S. Chauhan	c Hadlee b Snedden	46
D.B. Vengsarkar	c Lees b Cairns	13
G.R. Viswanath	b Snedden	2
Yashpal Sharma	c Wright b Snedden	16
S.M. Patil	c Wright b Cairns	16
Kapil Dev	c Cairns b Troup	75
S.M.H. Kirmani†	c Edgar b Troup	18
K.D. Ghavri	not out	9
Yograj Singh	c Burgess b Troup	0
D.R. Doshi	run out	0
Extras	(B 2, LB 6)	8
Total	(48.5 overs)	**204**

Fall of wickets: 1-3, 2-45, 3-52, 4-79, 5-84, 6-136, 7-190, 8-203, 9-204, 10-204.

NEW ZEALAND	*O*	*M*	*R*	*W*
Hadlee	9.5	1	21	0
Troup	9	2	19	4
Snedden	10	0	33	3
Cairns	10	1	53	2
Coney	10	0	70	0

NEW ZEALAND		
J.G. Wright	c sub (K. Azad) b Kapil Dev	42
B.A. Edgar	b Doshi	28
W.K. Lees†	c Yograj b Doshi	20
G.P. Howarth*	c Kapil Dev b Doshi	0
J.M. Parker	c Kirmani b Doshi	11
J.V. Coney	not out	47
M.G. Burgess	b Yograj	13
R.J. Hadlee	c Vengsarkar b Yograj	0
B.L. Cairns	not out	27
M.C. Snedden		
G.B. Troup		
Extras	(B 6, LB 9, W 1, NB 1)	17
Total	(48.4 overs – 7 wickets)	**205**

Fall of wickets: 1-67, 2-93, 3-97, 4-103, 5-130, 6-158, 7-166.

INDIA	*O*	*M*	*R*	*W*
Yograj Singh	8.4	0	44	2
Ghavri	10	1	38	0
Kapil Dev	10	0	37	1
Patil	10	1	39	0
Doshi	10	0	30	4

Umpires: R.A. French and M.W. Johnson.

Match No. 103/7

INDIA v NEW ZEALAND 1980-81

Benson and Hedges World Series Cup – 8th Match

At Adelaide Oval on 23 December 1980.
Toss: India. Result: INDIA won by 6 runs.
50 overs match. Award: Yashpal Sharma.
No débuts.

INDIA		
S.M. Gavaskar*	c Lees b Troup	17
C.P.S. Chauhan	c Coney b Snedden	43
D.B. Vengsarkar	b Snedden	3
Yashpal Sharma	c Cairns b Troup	72
S.M. Patil	c Coney b Chatfield	6
Kapil Dev	c Lees b Snedden	27
S.M.H. Kirmani†	not out	39
R.M.H. Binny	c Wright b Troup	4
K.D. Ghavri	not out	10
Yograj Singh		
D.R. Doshi		
Extras	(LB 8, NB 1)	9
Total	(50 overs – 7 wickets)	**230**

Fall of wickets: 1-23, 2-30, 3-95, 4-102, 5-153, 6-192, 7-209.

NEW ZEALAND	*O*	*M*	*R*	*W*
Hadlee	10	2	42	0
Troup	10	0	65	3
Snedden	10	2	30	3
Cairns	10	3	30	0
Chatfield	10	0	54	1

NEW ZEALAND		
J.G. Wright	b Patil	18
J.M. Parker	c Chauhan b Yograj	13
G.P. Howarth*	st Kirmani b Doshi	26
J.V. Coney	run out	49
W.K. Lees†	lbw b Ghavri	6
M.G. Burgess	run out	42
R.J. Hadlee	c Gavaskar b Doshi	4
B.L. Cairns	b Ghavri	39
M.C. Snedden	c Ghavri b Kapil Dev	4
G.B. Troup	b Kapil Dev	5
E.J. Chatfield	not out	0
Extras	(B 2, LB 12, NB 4)	18
Total	(49.3 overs)	**224**

Fall of wickets: 1-36, 2-36, 3-105, 4-123, 5-125, 6-134, 7-213, 8-213, 9-224, 10-224.

INDIA	*O*	*M*	*R*	*W*
Yograj Singh	9	1	39	1
Binny	10	0	47	0
Ghavri	10	1	49	2
Kapil Dev	9.3	1	34	2
Patil	1	0	3	1
Doshi	10	1	34	2

Umpires: A.R. Crafter and M.G. O'Connell.

AUSTRALIA v INDIA 1980-81

Benson and Hedges World Series Cup – 9th Match

At Sydney Cricket Ground on 8 January 1981.
Toss: Australia. Result: AUSTRALIA won by 9 wickets.
50 overs match. Award: G.S. Chappell.
No débuts.

India were dismissed on a rain-affected pitch in 113 minutes for their lowest total in these matches. This remains the shortest completed one-day international, actual playing time totalling 3 hours 26 minutes.

INDIA		
C.P.S. Chauhan	b Lillee	2
R.M.H. Binny	c Marsh b G.S. Chappell	16
D.B. Vengsarkar	c Marsh b Pascoe	3
G.R. Viswanath	c Marsh b Hogg	23
S.M. Gavaskar*	b G.S. Chappell	1
Yashpal Sharma	lbw b G.S. Chappell	6
Kapil Dev	lbw b Hogg	0
S.M.H. Kirmani†	run out	4
K.D. Ghavri	c Marsh b G.S. Chappell	1
Yograj Singh	not out	0
D.R. Doshi	b G.S. Chappell	2
Extras	(LB 3, W 1, NB 1)	5
Total	(25.5 overs)	**63**

Fall of wickets 1-2, 2-24, 3-26, 4-32, 5-50, 6-54, 7-55, 8-60, 9-61, 10-63.

AUSTRALIA	*O*	*M*	*R*	*W*
Lillee	5	2	3	1
Hogg	7	2	14	2
G.S. Chappell	9.5	5	15	5
Pascoe	4	0	26	1

AUSTRALIA		
J. Dyson	not out	13
G.M. Wood	c Binny b Kapil Dev	11
G.S. Chappell*	not out	33
K.J. Hughes		
A.R. Border		
K.D. Walters		
T.M. Chappell		
R.W. Marsh†		
D.K. Lillee		
L.S. Pascoe		
R.M. Hogg		
Extras	(LB 3, W 1, NB 3)	7
Total	(21 overs – 1 wicket)	**64**

Fall of wicket 1-18.

INDIA	*O*	*M*	*R*	*W*
Kapil Dev	9	5	15	1
Ghavri	4	0	14	0
Yograj Singh	4	1	9	0
Doshi	1	0	6	0
Binny	3	1	13	0

Umpires: M.G. O'Connell and D.G. Weser.

Match No. 105/8

INDIA v NEW ZEALAND 1980-81

Benson and Hedges World Series Cup – 10th Match

At Melbourne Cricket Ground on 10 January 1981.
Toss: New Zealand. Result: NEW ZEALAND won by 10 wickets.
34 overs match. Award: B.A. Edgar.
No débuts.

INDIA		
S.M. Gavaskar*	lbw b Chatfield	8
T.E. Srinivasan	b Coney	4
D.B. Vengsarkar	c Parker b Coney	0
G.R. Viswanath	run out	33
S.M. Patil	c Coney b Snedden	8
Yashpal Sharma	c Coney b Cairns	5
Kapil Dev	run out	21
S.M.H. Kirmani†	run out	7
K.D. Ghavri	c Howarth b Snedden	6
R.M.H. Binny	not out	5
D.R. Doshi	not out	5
Extras	(LB 10)	10
Total	(34 overs – 9 wickets)	**112**

Fall of wickets: 1-13, 2-13, 3-13, 4-46, 5-60, 6-66, 7-82, 8-98, 9-100.

NEW ZEALAND	*O*	*M*	*R*	*W*
Hadlee	8	3	15	0
Chatfield	8	2	14	1
Coney	6	3	18	2
Cairns	7	0	39	1
Snedden	5	0	16	2

NEW ZEALAND		
J.G. Wright	not out	39
B.A. Edgar	not out	65
J.M. Parker		
G.P. Howarth*		
J.V. Coney		
W.K. Lees†		
M.G. Burgess		
R.J. Hadlee		
B.L. Cairns		
E.J. Chatfield		
M.C. Snedden		
Extras	(LB 8, NB 1)	9
Total	(29 overs – 0 wicket)	**113**

INDIA	*O*	*M*	*R*	*W*
Kapil Dev	8	0	29	0
Ghavri	7	2	15	0
Binny	4	0	23	0
Patil	2	0	10	0
Doshi	8	0	27	0

Umpires: R.C. Bailhache and R.V. Whitehead.

AUSTRALIA v INDIA 1980-81

Benson and Hedges World Series Cup – 11th Match

At Melbourne Cricket Ground on 11 January 1981.

Toss: Australia.	Result: AUSTRALIA won by 7 wickets.
50 overs match.	Award: G.M. Wood.

No débuts.

INDIA

S.M. Gavaskar*	b T.M. Chappell	80
R.M.H. Binny	c G.S. Chappell b T.M. Chappell	21
D.B. Vengsarkar	c Hughes b Lillee	46
Kapil Dev	c T.M. Chappell b G.S. Chappell	4
S.M. Patil	b G.S. Chappell	3
Yashpal Sharma	not out	21
S.M.H. Kirmani†	not out	3
G.R. Viswanath		
K.D. Ghavri		
Yograj Singh		
D.R. Doshi		
Extras	(B 2, LB 11, NB 1)	14
Total	(50 overs – 5 wickets)	**192**

Fall of wickets 1-57, 2-158, 3-165, 4-165, 5-169.

AUSTRALIA	*O*	*M*	*R*	*W*
Lillee	10	1	29	1
Pascoe	9	1	33	0
Graf	6	0	31	0
G.S. Chappell	10	4	23	2
T.M. Chappell	9	0	41	2
Border	6	0	21	0

AUSTRALIA

A.R. Border	b Patil	39
G.M. Wood	not out	98
G.S. Chappell*	c Viswanath b Doshi	7
K.J. Hughes	run out	0
K.D. Walters	not out	43
J. Dyson		
T.M. Chappell		
R.W. Marsh†		
D.K. Lillee		
S.F. Graf		
L.S. Pascoe		
Extras	(B 1, LB 5)	6
Total	(47.2 overs – 3 wickets)	**193**

Fall of wickets 1-69, 2-96, 3-97.

INDIA	*O*	*M*	*R*	*W*
Binny	9.2	1	42	0
Ghavri	9	1	37	0
Kapil Dev	9	1	27	0
Patil	10	0	43	1
Doshi	10	0	38	1

Umpires: P.M. Cronin and R.A. French.

Match No. 107/6

AUSTRALIA v NEW ZEALAND 1980-81

Benson and Hedges World Series Cup – 12th Match

At Sydney Cricket Ground on 13 January 1981.
Toss: New Zealand. Result: NEW ZEALAND won by 1 run.
50 overs match (floodlit). Award: J.G. Wright.
No débuts.

NEW ZEALAND		
J.G. Wright	c T.M. Chappell b G.S. Chappell	78
B.A. Edgar	b Hogg	0
G.P. Howarth*	lbw b Pascoe	20
J.M. Parker	c Pascoe b T.M. Chappell	23
M.G. Burgess	c Walters b Graf	14
J.V. Coney	c Marsh b Pascoe	18
R.J. Hadlee	c Hogg b Graf	9
B.L. Cairns	b Pascoe	7
I.D.S. Smith†	not out	23
M.C. Snedden	not out	8
E.J. Chatfield		
Extras	(LB 16, W 1, NB 3)	20
Total	(50 overs – 8 wickets)	**220**

Fall of wickets: 1-2, 2-30, 3-75, 4-105, 5-134, 6-176, 7-181, 8-191.

AUSTRALIA	*O*	*M*	*R*	*W*
Lillee	10	2	27	0
Hogg	8	0	40	1
Pascoe	10	0	37	3
G.S. Chappell	9	2	35	1
Graf	10	0	40	2
T.M. Chappell	3	0	21	1

AUSTRALIA		
A.R. Border	b Chatfield	8
G.M. Wood	c Smith b Coney	37
G.S. Chappell*	c Coney b Cairns	30
K.J. Hughes	c Smith b Snedden	21
K.D. Walters	not out	50
T.M. Chappell	run out	0
R.W. Marsh†	c Smith b Hadlee	49
S.F. Graf	run out	7
D.K. Lillee		
R.M. Hogg		
L.S. Pascoe		
Extras	(B 3, LB 12, W 1, NB 1)	17
Total	(50 overs – 7 wickets)	**219**

Fall of wickets: 1-18, 2-74, 3-90, 4-122, 5-123, 6-201, 7-219.

NEW ZEALAND	*O*	*M*	*R*	*W*
Hadlee	10	1	46	1
Chatfield	10	2	26	1
Coney	10	0	41	1
Cairns	10	1	48	1
Snedden	10	0	41	1

Umpires: M.W. Johnson and D.G. Weser.

AUSTRALIA v INDIA 1980-81

Benson and Hedges World Series Cup – 13th Match

At Sydney Cricket Ground on 15 January 1981.
Toss: India. Result: AUSTRALIA won by 27 runs.
50 overs match. Award: A.R. Border.
No débuts.

AUSTRALIA		
G.M. Wood	c Binny b Patil	26
A.R. Border	c Azad b Doshi	85
G.S. Chappell*	c Sharma b Patil	2
K.J. Hughes	c Kapil Dev b Binny	39
K.D. Walters	b Ghavri	38
T.M. Chappell	c Vengsarkar b Kapil Dev	14
R.W. Marsh†	c Reddy b Ghavri	12
S.F. Graf	c Azad b Kapil Dev	2
D.K. Lillee	not out	4
R.M. Hogg	not out	1
L.S. Pascoe		
Extras	(B 1, LB 16, NB 2)	19
Total	(50 overs – 8 wickets)	**242**

Fall of wickets: 1-48, 2-55, 3-155, 4-181, 5-216, 6-230, 7-233, 8-240.

INDIA	*O*	*M*	*R*	*W*
Kapil Dev	10	1	46	2
Ghavri	10	0	39	2
Binny	10	0	45	1
Patil	10	2	34	2
Doshi	10	0	59	1

INDIA		
S.M. Gavaskar*	lbw b Lillee	1
R.M.H. Binny	lbw b Graf	34
D.B. Vengsarkar	c Marsh b Hogg	52
G.R. Viswanath	c and b G.S. Chappell	7
Yashpal Sharma	c and b G.S. Chappell	25
S.M. Patil	b Lillee	27
Kapil Dev	c Marsh b Lillee	20
K. Azad	b Lillee	19
K.D. Ghavri	not out	11
B. Reddy†	not out	8
D.R. Doshi		
Extras	(LB 10, NB 1)	11
Total	(50 overs – 8 wickets)	**215**

Fall of wickets: 1-2, 2-59, 3-78, 4-112, 5-135, 6-161, 7-196, 8-197.

AUSTRALIA	*O*	*M*	*R*	*W*
Lillee	10	1	32	4
Hogg	10	1	34	1
Pascoe	10	0	64	0
Graf	10	2	36	1
G.S. Chappell	10	0	38	2

Umpires: D.G. Weser and R.V. Whitehead.

Match No. 109/9

INDIA v NEW ZEALAND 1980-81

Benson and Hedges World Series Cup – 14th Match

At Woolloongabba, Brisbane on 18 January 1981.
Toss: India. Result: NEW ZEALAND won by 22 runs.
50 overs match. Award: J.V. Coney.
No débuts.

NEW ZEALAND		
J.G. Wright	b Ghavri	14
B.A. Edgar	b Doshi	34
G.P. Howarth*	c Patil b Doshi	45
J.M. Parker	c Reddy b Kapil Dev	6
M.G. Burgess	c Viswanath b Azad	26
J.V. Coney	run out	49
I.D.S. Smith†	c sub (N.S. Yadav) b Kapil Dev	12
R.J. Hadlee	b Ghavri	32
B.L. Cairns	b Kapil Dev	0
M.C. Snedden	not out	6
E.J. Chatfield	not out	0
Extras	(B 1, LB 13, W 1, NB 3)	18
Total	(50 overs – 9 wickets)	**242**

Fall of wickets: 1-28, 2-95, 3-108, 4-108, 5-166, 6-199, 7-207, 8-207, 9-241.

INDIA	*O*	*M*	*R*	*W*
Kapil Dev	10	3	37	3
Ghavri	10	0	61	2
Binny	4	0	25	0
Patil	10	0	38	0
Doshi	10	0	25	2
Azad	3	1	26	1
Yashpal Sharma	3	0	12	0

INDIA		
R.M.H. Binny	c Cairns b Coney	35
S.M. Gavaskar*	run out	9
D.B. Vengsarkar	run out	66
G.R. Viswanath	b Coney	9
Kapil Dev	b Coney	0
S.M. Patil	run out	48
Yashpal Sharma	c Smith b Snedden	13
K. Azad	c Parker b Snedden	19
K.D. Ghavri	b Snedden	2
B. Reddy†	not out	3
D.R. Doshi	lbw b Hadlee	0
Extras	(B 4, LB 11, NB 1)	16
Total	(48.1 overs)	**220**

Fall of wickets: 1-32, 2-73, 3-86, 4-86, 5-178, 6-179, 7-197, 8-213, 9-220, 10-220.

NEW ZEALAND	*O*	*M*	*R*	*W*
Hadlee	9.1	2	15	1
Chatfield	10	1	42	0
Coney	10	1	28	3
Cairns	10	0	54	0
Snedden	8	0	57	3
Burgess	1	0	8	0

Umpires: P.M. Cronin and M.W. Johnson.

AUSTRALIA v NEW ZEALAND 1980-81

Benson and Hedges World Series Cup – 15th Match

At Sydney Cricket Ground on 21 January 1981.
Toss: Australia. No result – rain.
50 overs match (floodlit). No award.
No débuts.

AUSTRALIA		
A.R. Border	c Hadlee b McKechnie	40
G.M. Wood	c Smith b Chatfield	5
G.S. Chappell*	c Burgess b McEwan	74
K.J. Hughes	c Coney b McEwan	14
K.D. Walters	run out	16
T.M. Chappell	lbw b Cairns	14
R.W. Marsh†	c Hadlee b McKechnie	0
S.F. Graf	lbw b Hadlee	2
D.K. Lillee	c Coney b Cairns	0
R.M. Hogg	run out	1
M.H.N. Walker	not out	0
Extras	(LB 12, W 2)	14
Total	(43.1 overs)	**180**

Fall of wickets: 1-10, 2-98, 3-125, 4-149, 5-173, 6-175, 7-179, 8-179, 9-179, 10-180.

NEW ZEALAND	*O*	*M*	*R*	*W*
Hadlee	8	4	13	1
Chatfield	8.1	2	15	1
Coney	4	0	19	0
Cairns	8	2	37	2
McKechnie	10	0	53	2
McEwan	5	0	29	2

NEW ZEALAND		
B.A. Edgar	not out	2
J.G. Wright	c Marsh b G.S. Chappell	8
G.P. Howarth*	not out	0
M.G. Burgess		
P.E. McEwan		
J.V. Coney		
I.D.S. Smith†		
B.J. McKechnie		
R.J. Hadlee		
B.L. Cairns		
E.J. Chatfield		
Extras	(B 8, LB 4, NB 1)	13
Total	(8 overs – 1 wicket)	**23**

Fall of wicket: 1-22.

AUSTRALIA	*O*	*M*	*R*	*W*
Lillee	3	1	6	0
Walker	4	3	3	0
G.S. Chappell	1	0	1	1

Umpires: R.A. French and M.G. O'Connell.

Match No. 111/8

AUSTRALIA v NEW ZEALAND 1980-81

Benson and Hedges World Series Cup – 1st Final

At Sydney Cricket Ground on 29 January 1981.
Toss: Australia. Result: NEW ZEALAND won by 78 runs.
50 overs match (floodlit). No award.
Début: Australia – M.F. Kent.

NEW ZEALAND		
J.G. Wright	b G.S. Chappell	81
B.A. Edgar	c Walters b Lillee	21
G.P. Howarth*	c Border b Walker	47
J.V. Coney	c and b Pascoe	0
M.G. Burgess	lbw b Lillee	15
R.J. Hadlee	not out	23
B.L. Cairns	c Walker b Pascoe	18
B.J. McKechnie	not out	1
I.D.S. Smith†		
M.C. Snedden		
E.J. Chatfield		
Extras	(B 18, W 7, NB 2)	27
Total	(50 overs – 6 wickets)	**233**

Fall of wickets 1-45, 2-148, 3-152, 4-172, 5-198, 6-231.

AUSTRALIA	*O*	*M*	*R*	*W*
Hogg	10	1	37	0
Walker	10	1	31	1
Lillee	10	0	47	2
Pascoe	10	0	48	2
G.S. Chappell	10	0	43	1

AUSTRALIA		
G.M. Wood	c Burgess b Hadlee	13
M.F. Kent	c Howarth b Hadlee	12
R.W. Marsh†	c Coney b Chatfield	0
G.S. Chappell*	c Wright b Chatfield	31
K.J. Hughes	lbw b Hadlee	0
A.R. Border	c Coney b McKechnie	55
K.D. Walters	b McKechnie	20
D.K. Lillee	c Cairns b McKechnie	7
M.H.N. Walker	c Smith b Hadlee	4
R.M. Hogg	c Smith b Hadlee	1
L.S. Pascoe	not out	3
Extras	(B 2, LB 6, W 1)	9
Total	(39.3 overs)	**155**

Fall of wickets 1-28, 2-28, 3-28, 4-28, 5-93, 6-135, 7-145, 8-147, 9-148, 10-155.

NEW ZEALAND	*O*	*M*	*R*	*W*
Chatfield	10	3	38	2
Hadlee	8.3	4	26	5
McKechnie	9	1	23	3
Snedden	6	1	25	0
Cairns	6	0	34	0

Umpires: R.C. Bailhache and M.W. Johnson.

AUSTRALIA v NEW ZEALAND 1980-81
Benson and Hedges World Series Cup – 2nd Final

At Melbourne Cricket Ground on 31 January 1981.
Toss: Australia. Result: AUSTRALIA won by 7 wickets.
50 overs match. No award.
Début: Australia – G.R. Beard.

NEW ZEALAND		
J.G. Wright	c Marsh b Lillee	11
B.A. Edgar	c Border b T.M. Chappell	28
G.P. Howarth*	b Walker	7
J.V. Coney	lbw b Lillee	4
M.G. Burgess	run out	13
P.E. McEwan	run out	12
B.J. McKechnie	lbw b T.M. Chappell	0
I.D.S. Smith†	b G.S. Chappell	13
R.J. Hadlee	c G.S. Chappell b Beard	16
B.L. Cairns	c T.M. Chappell b Beard	14
E.J. Chatfield	not out	2
Extras	(LB 4, W 1, NB 1)	6
Total	(46.4 overs)	**126**

Fall of wickets 1-14, 2-21, 3-30, 4-62, 5-70, 6-71, 7-92, 8-95, 9-113, 10-126.

AUSTRALIA	*O*	*M*	*R*	*W*
Lillee	8	0	25	2
Walker	10	0	25	1
Beard	8.4	3	20	2
G.S. Chappell	10	2	22	1
T.M. Chappell	10	1	28	2

AUSTRALIA		
G.M. Wood	c Smith b Chatfield	32
A.R. Border	c Burgess b Howarth	19
G.S. Chappell*	not out	58
K.J. Hughes	st Smith b Cairns	12
K.D. Walters	not out	4
G.R. Beard		
T.M. Chappell		
R.W. Marsh†		
D.K. Lillee		
M.H.N. Walker		
L.S. Pascoe		
Extras	(B 2, LB 2, W 1)	5
Total	(39.3 overs – 3 wickets)	**130**

Fall of wickets 1-30, 2-85, 3-118.

NEW ZEALAND	*O*	*M*	*R*	*W*
Hadlee	10	2	29	0
Chatfield	6	1	21	1
McEwan	4	0	18	0
Howarth	4	0	13	1
Cairns	10	1	23	1
McKechnie	5.3	1	21	0

Umpires: R.A. French and D.G. Weser.

Match No. 113/10

AUSTRALIA v NEW ZEALAND 1980-81

Benson and Hedges World Series Cup – 3rd Final

At Melbourne Cricket Ground on 1 February 1981.
Toss: Australia. Result: AUSTRALIA won by 6 runs.
50 overs match. No award.
No débuts.

With his score 58, Chappell was spectacularly caught by Snedden on the mid-wicket boundary but stood his ground even after the fielder had signalled that he had completed the catch. The umpires gave the batsman not out because they had been watching for short runs and not seen the catch. With New Zealand needing 6 runs off the final ball to tie the match, Greg Chappell ordered his younger brother, Trevor, to bowl it underarm along the ground. Such tactics, condemned by New Zealand's Prime Minister, were subsequently banned.

AUSTRALIA		
A.R. Border	c Parker b Hadlee	5
G.M. Wood	b McEwan	72
G.S. Chappell*	c Edgar b Snedden	90
M.F. Kent	c Edgar b Snedden	33
R.W. Marsh†	not out	18
K.D. Walters	not out	6
K.J. Hughes		
G.R. Beard		
T.M. Chappell		
D.K. Lillee		
M.H.N. Walker		
Extras	(B 8, LB 3)	11
Total	(50 overs – 4 wickets)	**235**
Fall of wickets	1-8, 2-153, 3-199, 4-215.	

NEW ZEALAND	*O*	*M*	*R*	*W*
Hadlee	10	0	41	1
Snedden	10	0	52	2
Cairns	10	0	34	0
McKechnie	10	0	54	0
McEwan	7	1	31	1
Howarth	3	0	12	0

NEW ZEALAND		
J.G. Wright	c Kent b G.S. Chappell	42
B.A. Edgar	not out	102
G.P. Howarth*	c Marsh b G.S. Chappell	18
B.L. Cairns	b Beard	12
M.G. Burgess	c T.M. Chappell b G.S. Chappell	2
P.E. McEwan	c Wood b Beard	11
J.M. Parker	c T.M. Chappell b Lillee	24
R.J. Hadlee	lbw b T.M. Chappell	4
I.D.S. Smith†	b T.M. Chappell	4
B.J. McKechnie	not out	0
M.C. Snedden		
Extras	(LB 10)	10
Total	(50 overs – 8 wickets)	**229**
Fall of wickets	1-85, 2-117, 3-136, 4-139, 5-172, 6-221, 7-225, 8-229.	

AUSTRALIA	*O*	*M*	*R*	*W*
Lillee	10	1	34	1
Walker	10	0	35	0
Beard	10	0	50	2
G.S. Chappell	10	0	43	3
T.M. Chappell	10	0	57	2

Umpires: P.M. Cronin and D.G. Weser.

AUSTRALIA v NEW ZEALAND 1980-81

Benson and Hedges World Series Cup – 4th Final

At Sydney Cricket Ground on 3 February 1981.
Toss: New Zealand. Result: AUSTRALIA won by 6 wickets.
50 overs match (floodlit). Finals award: G.S. Chappell.
No débuts.

NEW ZEALAND		
J.G. Wright	c Border b T.M. Chappell	57
B.A. Edgar	run out	38
G.P. Howarth*	c Kent b Hogg	46
M.G. Burgess	b G.S. Chappell	20
R.J. Hadlee	c Border b Lillee	15
J.M. Parker	c Marsh b Lillee	12
P.E. McEwan	c Hogg b Lillee	4
B.L. Cairns	b Pascoe	7
I.D.S. Smith†	not out	2
M.C. Snedden		
E.J. Chatfield		
Extras	(LB 9, NB 5)	14
Total	(50 overs – 8 wickets)	**215**

Fall of wickets: 1-90, 2-119, 3-171, 4-177, 5-200, 6-201, 7-210, 8-215.

AUSTRALIA	*O*	*M*	*R*	*W*
Lillee	10	2	27	3
Hogg	10	0	46	1
Pascoe	10	0	51	1
G.S. Chappell	10	1	36	1
T.M. Chappell	10	0	41	1

AUSTRALIA		
G.M. Wood	run out	34
A.R. Border	b Snedden	19
G.S. Chappell*	b Snedden	87
K.J. Hughes	b Snedden	47
R.W. Marsh†	not out	18
M.F. Kent	not out	4
K.D. Walters		
T.M. Chappell		
D.K. Lillee		
R.M. Hogg		
L.S. Pascoe		
Extras	(LB 8, W 1)	9
Total	(47.4 overs – 4 wickets)	**218**

Fall of wickets: 1-37, 2-89, 3-188, 4-209.

NEW ZEALAND	*O*	*M*	*R*	*W*
Chatfield	10	1	30	0
Hadlee	8.4	1	43	0
Snedden	9	0	27	3
McEwan	10	1	58	0
Burgess	10	0	51	0

Umpires: R.C. Bailhache and A.R. Crafter.

Match No. 115/14

WEST INDIES v ENGLAND 1980-81 (1st Match)

At Arnos Vale, St Vincent on 4 February 1981.
Toss: England. Result: WEST INDIES won by 2 runs.
50 overs match. Award: C.E.H. Croft.

Début: West Indies – E.H. Mattis.

Croft became the second bowler after G.J. Gilmour (*Match No. 31*) to take six wickets in a one-day international.

WEST INDIES		
D.L. Haynes	c Emburey b Stevenson	34
S.F.A.F. Bacchus	c Stevenson b Old	1
E.H. Mattis	run out	62
A.I. Kallicharran	b Emburey	2
C.H. Lloyd*	c Willey b Stevenson	2
H.A. Gomes	b Willey	8
D.A. Murray†	b Gooch	1
A.M.E. Roberts	st Bairstow b Gooch	2
J. Garner	run out	4
M.A. Holding	b Botham	1
C.E.H. Croft	not out	2
Extras	(LB 4, W 1, NB 3)	8
Total	(47.2 overs)	**127**

Fall of wickets: 1-5, 2-48, 3-51, 4-58, 5-89, 6-90, 7-102, 8-110, 9-120, 10-127.

ENGLAND	*O*	*M*	*R*	*W*
Old	5	4	8	1
Botham	8	1	32	1
Stevenson	8.2	2	18	2
Emburey	10	4	20	1
Willey	10	1	29	1
Gooch	6	1	12	2

ENGLAND		
G. Boycott	c Mattis b Croft	2
G.A. Gooch	c Lloyd b Roberts	11
P. Willey	c Murray b Croft	0
D.I. Gower	c Haynes b Kallicharran	23
R.O. Butcher	c Murray b Croft	1
I.T. Botham*	c Murray b Croft	60
M.W. Gatting	b Croft	3
D.L. Bairstow†	b Croft	5
J.E. Emburey	b Holding	5
G.B. Stevenson	not out	6
C.M. Old	b Holding	1
Extras	(LB 8)	8
Total	(48.2 overs)	**125**

Fall of wickets: 1-14, 2-14, 3-14, 4-15, 5-80, 6-88, 7-111, 8-114, 9-123, 10-125.

WEST INDIES	*O*	*M*	*R*	*W*
Roberts	10	1	30	1
Holding	9.2	2	30	2
Croft	9	4	15	6
Garner	10	2	17	0
Kallicharran	10	3	25	1

Umpires: D.M. Archer and S. Mohammed.

WEST INDIES v ENGLAND 1980-81 (2nd Match)

At Albion Sports Complex, Berbice, Guyana on 26 February 1981.
Toss: West Indies. Result: WEST INDIES won by 6 wickets.
50 overs match. Award: H.A. Gomes.
No débuts.

ENGLAND		
G. Boycott	b Richards	7
G.A. Gooch	c Murray b Roberts	11
M.W. Gatting	c Mattis b Gomes	29
D.I. Gower	b Gomes	3
R.O. Butcher	c Haynes b Gomes	5
I.T. Botham*	b Roberts	27
P. Willey	b Croft	21
D.L. Bairstow†	b Croft	16
J.E. Emburey	c Croft b Holding	0
G.B. Stevenson	not out	8
G.R. Dilley	b Croft	3
Extras	(B 4, LB 2, NB 1)	7
Total	(47.2 overs)	**137**

Fall of wickets: 1-16, 2-27, 3-34, 4-59, 5-62, 6-108, 7-112, 8-119, 9-132, 10-137.

WEST INDIES	*O*	*M*	*R*	*W*
Roberts	7	0	17	2
Holding	7	1	13	1
Richards	10	0	26	1
Croft	6.2	1	9	3
Gomes	10	2	30	3
Garner	7	2	35	0

WEST INDIES		
C.G. Greenidge	run out	2
D.L. Haynes	c Gooch b Emburey	48
I.V.A. Richards	c Stevenson b Dilley	3
E.H. Mattis	b Emburey	24
H.A. Gomes	not out	22
C.H. Lloyd*	not out	25
D.A. Murray†		
A.M.E. Roberts		
M.A. Holding		
J. Garner		
C.E.H. Croft		
Extras	(B 4, LB 8, NB 2)	14
Total	(39.3 overs – 4 wickets)	**138**

Fall of wickets: 1-6, 2-11, 3-85, 4-90.

ENGLAND	*O*	*M*	*R*	*W*
Dilley	5	0	21	1
Botham	7	1	24	0
Stevenson	6	0	21	0
Emburey	10	4	22	2
Gooch	2	0	8	0
Willey	9	0	23	0
Gower	0.3	0	5	0

Umpires: D.J. Narine and P.J. McConnell.

Match No. 117/10

NEW ZEALAND v INDIA 1980-81 (1st Match)

At Eden Park, Auckland on 14 February 1981.
Toss: India. Result: NEW ZEALAND won by 78 runs.
45 overs match. Award: B.A. Edgar.
No débuts.

NEW ZEALAND		
J.G. Wright	c Binny b Ghavri	10
B.A. Edgar	not out	99
G.N. Edwards	c Chauhan b Ghavri	36
G.P. Howarth*	c Yograj b Patil	11
J.V. Coney	c and b Kapil Dev	2
I.D.S. Smith†	lbw b Patil	10
R.J. Hadlee	c Vengsarkar b Ghavri	22
B.L. Cairns	not out	12
M.C. Snedden		
G.B. Troup		
E.J. Chatfield		
Extras	(LB 11, W 1, NB 4)	16
Total	(45 overs – 6 wickets)	**218**

Fall of wickets: 1-24, 2-112, 3-127, 4-132, 5-156, 6-196.

INDIA	*O*	*M*	*R*	*W*
Kapil Dev	10	1	40	1
Ghavri	10	1	40	3
Binny	6	2	26	0
Yograj Singh	9	0	57	0
Patil	10	1	39	2

INDIA		
C.P.S. Chauhan	b Hadlee	6
S.M. Gavaskar*	c Smith b Snedden	14
D.B. Vengsarkar	run out	0
G.R. Viswanath	b Chatfield	14
S.M. Patil	b Chatfield	4
Yashpal Sharma	c Edwards b Cairns	17
Kapil Dev	run out	50
R.M.H. Binny	c Edwards b Cairns	12
K.D. Ghavri	not out	6
Yograj Singh	c Hadlee b Troup	1
S.M.H. Kirmani†	not out	10
Extras	(LB 5, NB 1)	6
Total	(45 overs – 9 wickets)	**140**

Fall of wickets: 1-9, 2-10, 3-31, 4-40, 5-41, 6-86, 7-122, 8-122, 9-124.

NEW ZEALAND	*O*	*M*	*R*	*W*
Hadlee	6	3	6	1
Troup	10	3	21	1
Chatfield	10	2	36	2
Snedden	8	2	26	1
Coney	3	0	7	0
Cairns	7	2	33	2
Howarth	1	0	5	0

Umpires: B.A. Bricknell and F.R. Goodall.

NEW ZEALAND v INDIA 1980-81 (2nd Match)

At Seddon Park, Hamilton on 15 February 1981.
Toss: India. Result: NEW ZEALAND won by 57 runs.
50 overs match. Award: J.V. Coney.
Début: New Zealand – G.K. Robertson.

NEW ZEALAND		
J.G. Wright	c Kirmani b Binny	38
B.A. Edgar	b Kapil Dev	1
G.N. Edwards	c Vengsarkar b Yograj	17
G.P. Howarth*	c Chauhan b Patil	17
J.V. Coney	c Vengsarkar b Ghavri	46
I.D.S. Smith†	c Vengsarkar b Patil	0
R.J. Hadlee	c Azad b Ghavri	23
G.K. Robertson	c Patil b Kapil Dev	17
M.C. Snedden	not out	11
G.B. Troup	not out	14
E.J. Chatfield		
Extras	(B 1, LB 10, W 10, NB 5)	26
Total	(50 overs – 8 wickets)	**210**

Fall of wickets: 1-13, 2-43, 3-89, 4-91, 5-92, 6-165, 7-166, 8-185.

INDIA	*O*	*M*	*R*	*W*
Kapil Dev	10	1	34	2
Yograj Singh	10	2	37	1
Ghavri	10	1	47	2
Binny	10	2	38	1
Patil	10	1	28	2

INDIA		
C.P.S. Chauhan	b Snedden	31
R.M.H. Binny	c Howarth b Chatfield	18
D.B. Vengsarkar	b Hadlee	41
K. Azad	b Robertson	10
G.R. Viswanath*	b Snedden	5
S.M. Patil	b Robertson	20
Yashpal Sharma	b Hadlee	9
Kapil Dev	lbw b Troup	1
S.M.H. Kirmani†	c Smith b Troup	2
K.D. Ghavri	c Wright b Troup	3
Yograj Singh	not out	0
Extras	(B 6, LB 4, W 2, NB 1)	13
Total	(45.2 overs)	**153**

Fall of wickets: 1-34, 2-82, 3-104, 4-111, 5-127, 6-140, 7-141, 8-149, 9-153, 10-153.

NEW ZEALAND	*O*	*M*	*R*	*W*
Hadlee	8	1	27	2
Troup	9.2	2	18	3
Chatfield	10	1	31	1
Robertson	10	1	29	2
Snedden	8	1	35	2

Umpires: J.B.R. Hastie and R.L. Monteith.

Match No. 119/21

ENGLAND v AUSTRALIA 1981 (1st Match)

Prudential Trophy

At Lord's, London on 4 June 1981.
Toss: England. Result: ENGLAND won by 6 wickets.
55 overs match. Award: G. Boycott.
Débuts: England – G.W. Humpage, J.D. Love.

AUSTRALIA		
J. Dyson	lbw b Willis	2
G.M. Wood	run out	22
T.M. Chappell	run out	16
K.J. Hughes*	lbw b Jackman	12
A.R. Border	not out	73
M.F. Kent	c Gooch b Botham	28
R.W. Marsh†	b Botham	18
R.J. Bright	b Willis	18
G.F. Lawson	not out	12
D.K. Lillee		
R.M. Hogg		
Extras	(B 1, LB 8)	9
Total	(55 overs – 7 wickets)	**210**

Fall of wickets: 1-2, 2-36, 3-48, 4-60, 5-134, 6-162, 7-189.

ENGLAND	*O*	*M*	*R*	*W*
Willis	11	0	56	2
Botham	11	1	39	2
Hendrick	11	2	32	0
Jackman	11	1	27	1
Willey	6	1	26	0
Gooch	5	1	21	0

ENGLAND		
G.A. Gooch	c Kent b Lillee	53
G. Boycott	not out	75
M.W. Gatting	lbw b Lillee	0
D.I. Gower	c Kent b Chappell	47
J.D. Love	c Bright b Lawson	15
I.T. Botham*	not out	13
P. Willey		
G.W. Humpage†		
R.D. Jackman		
R.G.D. Willis		
M. Hendrick		
Extras	(B 5, LB 4)	9
Total	(51.4 overs – 4 wickets)	**212**

Fall of wickets: 1-86, 2-86, 3-172, 4-199.

AUSTRALIA	*O*	*M*	*R*	*W*
Hogg	11	1	36	0
Lillee	11	3	23	2
Lawson	9	0	51	1
Chappell	11	1	50	1
Bright	9.4	0	43	0

Umpires: W.E. Alley and H.D. Bird.

ENGLAND v AUSTRALIA 1981 (2nd Match)

Prudential Trophy

At Edgbaston, Birmingham on 6 June 1981.
Toss: England. Result: AUSTRALIA won by 2 runs.
55 overs match. Award: M.W. Gatting.
Début: Australia – T.M. Alderman.

AUSTRALIA		
G.M. Wood	c Willis b Jackman	55
T.M. Chappell	c Humpage b Botham	0
G.N. Yallop	b Hendrick	63
K.J. Hughes*	run out	34
A.R. Border	run out	17
R.W. Marsh†	c Love b Botham	20
M.F. Kent	lbw b Willis	1
G.F. Lawson	not out	29
D.K. Lillee	run out	8
R.M. Hogg	not out	0
T.M. Alderman		
Extras	(B 1, LB 18, W 1, NB 2)	22
Total	(55 overs – 8 wickets)	**249**

Fall of wickets: 1-10, 2-96, 3-160, 4-171, 5-183, 6-193, 7-213, 8-248.

ENGLAND	*O*	*M*	*R*	*W*
Willis	11	3	41	1
Botham	11	1	44	2
Hendrick	11	2	21	1
Jackman	11	0	47	1
Willey	6	0	36	0
Gooch	5	0	38	0

ENGLAND		
G.A. Gooch	b Hogg	11
G. Boycott	b Lawson	14
M.W. Gatting	c Lawson b Lillee	96
D.I. Gower	b Alderman	2
J.D. Love	b Lawson	43
P. Willey	c Wood b Chappell	37
I.T. Botham*	c Hughes b Lawson	24
G.W. Humpage†	b Lillee	5
R.D. Jackman	run out	2
R.G.D. Willis	not out	1
M. Hendrick	c Marsh b Lillee	0
Extras	(LB 12)	12
Total	(54.5 overs)	**247**

Fall of wickets: 1-20, 2-27, 3-36, 4-111, 5-177, 6-224, 7-232, 8-244, 9-244, 10-247.

AUSTRALIA	*O*	*M*	*R*	*W*
Hogg	11	2	42	1
Lillee	10.5	2	36	3
Alderman	11	1	46	1
Lawson	11	2	42	3
Chappell	11	0	69	1

Umpires: D.J. Constant and A.G.T. Whitehead.

Match No. 121/23

ENGLAND v AUSTRALIA 1981 (3rd Match)

Prudential Trophy

At Headingley, Leeds on 8 June 1981.
Toss: England. Result: AUSTRALIA won by 71 runs.
55 overs match. Award: G.M. Wood.
No débuts.

Marsh became the first to hold five catches in a limited-overs international.

AUSTRALIA		
G.M. Wood	run out	108
J. Dyson	c Gooch b Hendrick	22
G.N. Yallop	run out	48
K.J. Hughes*	c Gatting b Jackman	0
A.R. Border	c Jackman b Willis	5
R.W. Marsh†	c Humpage b Botham	1
T.M. Chappell	c Gooch b Willis	14
G.F. Lawson	run out	8
D.K. Lillee	not out	0
R.M. Hogg		
T.M. Alderman		
Extras	(LB 27, W 1, NB 2)	30
Total	(55 overs – 8 wickets)	**236**

Fall of wickets: 1-43, 2-173, 3-173, 4-187, 5-189, 6-216, 7-236, 8-236.

ENGLAND	*O*	*M*	*R*	*W*
Willis	11	1	35	2
Botham	11	2	42	1
Hendrick	11	3	31	1
Gooch	11	0	50	0
Jackman	11	1	48	1

ENGLAND		
G.A. Gooch	c Marsh b Lawson	37
G. Boycott	c Marsh b Hogg	4
M.W. Gatting	c Marsh b Hogg	32
D.I. Gower	b Alderman	5
J.D. Love	b Chappell	3
P. Willey	c Marsh b Hogg	42
I.T. Botham*	c Hughes b Chappell	5
G.W. Humpage†	c Border b Alderman	6
R.D. Jackman	b Chappell	14
R.G.D. Willis	not out	2
M. Hendrick	c Marsh b Hogg	0
Extras	(B 10, W 1, NB 4)	15
Total	(46.5 overs)	**165**

Fall of wickets: 1-5, 2-71, 3-80, 4-89, 5-95, 6-106, 7-133, 8-160, 9-164, 10-165.

AUSTRALIA	*O*	*M*	*R*	*W*
Hogg	8.5	1	29	4
Lillee	7	0	37	0
Lawson	11	3	34	1
Alderman	11	3	19	2
Chappell	9	0	31	3

Umpires: B.J. Meyer and K.E. Palmer.

PAKISTAN v WEST INDIES 1981-82

Benson and Hedges World Series Cup – 1st Match

At Melbourne Cricket Ground on 21 November 1981.
Toss: Pakistan. Result: WEST INDIES won by 18 runs.
50 overs match. Award: C.G. Greenidge.
Début: Pakistan – Rizwan-uz-Zaman.

WEST INDIES		
C.G. Greenidge	c Rizwan b Sarfraz	103
D.L. Haynes	b Mudassar	84
I.V.A. Richards	b Imran	17
S.F.A.F. Bacchus	c Rizwan b Sarfraz	8
C.H. Lloyd*	b Sarfraz	10
A.M.E. Roberts	c Mansoor b Imran	0
J. Garner	c Ashraf b Imran	0
M.D. Marshall	not out	9
H.A. Gomes	c and b Sarfraz	0
D.A. Murray†	not out	1
C.E.H. Croft		
Extras	(LB 13)	13
Total	(50 overs – 8 wickets)	**245**

Fall of wickets: 1-182, 2-203, 3-222, 4-223, 5-223, 6-224, 7-244, 8-244.

PAKISTAN	*O*	*M*	*R*	*W*
Sarfraz Nawaz	9	2	37	4
Imran Khan	10	2	23	3
Sikander Bakht	9	0	46	0
Iqbal Qasim	10	0	49	0
Majid Khan	5	0	34	0
Mudassar Nazar	7	0	43	1

PAKISTAN		
Mudassar Nazar	b Marshall	51
Rizwan-uz-Zaman	c Roberts b Garner	14
Javed Miandad*	c Murray b Roberts	74
Mansoor Akhtar	b Marshall	2
Majid Khan	c Bacchus b Roberts	56
Imran Khan	c Murray b Roberts	0
Wasim Raja	not out	10
Ashraf Ali†	not out	1
Sarfraz Nawaz		
Iqbal Qasim		
Sikander Bakht		
Extras	(B 2, LB 7, W 4, NB 6)	19
Total	(50 overs – 6 wickets)	**227**

Fall of wickets: 1-53, 2-120, 3-124, 4-212, 5-212, 6-221.

WEST INDIES	*O*	*M*	*R*	*W*
Roberts	10	1	42	3
Marshall	10	1	27	2
Garner	10	0	30	1
Croft	10	1	57	0
Richards	10	0	52	0

Umpires: R.C. Bailhache and R.A. French.

Match No. 123/3

AUSTRALIA v PAKISTAN 1981-82

Benson and Hedges World Series Cup – 2nd Match

At Melbourne Cricket Ground on 22 November 1981.

Toss: Pakistan.	Result: PAKISTAN won by 4 wickets.
50 overs match.	Award: Javed Miandad.

No débuts.

AUSTRALIA		
G.M. Wood	run out	23
W.M. Darling	c Sarfraz b Sikander	41
G.S. Chappell*	c Wasim Raja b Sikander	3
A.R. Border	b Sikander	6
K.J. Hughes	c Mudassar b Sikander	67
R.W. Marsh†	b Sarfraz	15
B. Yardley	b Imran	28
S.F. Graf	run out	8
G.F. Lawson	not out	4
J.R. Thomson	run out	3
T.M. Alderman		
Extras	(B 2, LB 3, W 3, NB 3)	11
Total	(50 overs – 9 wickets)	**209**

Fall of wickets: 1-48, 2-51, 3-71, 4-80, 5-102, 6-188, 7-197, 8-204, 9-209.

PAKISTAN	*O*	*M*	*R*	*W*
Imran Khan	10	1	42	1
Sarfraz Nawaz	10	0	44	1
Tahir Naqqash	10	0	46	0
Sikander Bakht	10	1	34	4
Ijaz Faqih	10	1	32	0

PAKISTAN		
Mudassar Nazar	c Marsh b Chappell	44
Mansoor Akhtar	c Yardley b Alderman	12
Zaheer Abbas	c Marsh b Alderman	2
Javed Miandad*	c Lawson b Chappell	72
Wasim Raja	c Darling b Chappell	8
Imran Khan	not out	28
Ijaz Faqih	b Thomson	17
Ashraf Ali†	not out	15
Sarfraz Nawaz		
Tahir Naqqash		
Sikander Bakht		
Extras	(LB 7, W 3, NB 2)	12
Total	(49.2 overs – 6 wickets)	**210**

Fall of wickets: 1-19, 2-21, 3-126, 4-139, 5-151, 6-184.

AUSTRALIA	*O*	*M*	*R*	*W*
Thomson	9.2	0	47	1
Alderman	10	0	20	2
Graf	10	0	34	0
Lawson	8	1	43	0
Yardley	3	0	21	0
Chappell	9	1	33	3

Umpires: B.E. Martin and R.V. Whitehead.

AUSTRALIA v WEST INDIES 1981-82

Benson and Hedges World Series Cup – 3rd Match

At Sydney Cricket Ground on 24 November 1981.
Toss: West Indies. Result: AUSTRALIA won by 7 wickets.
49 overs match (floodlit). Award: B.M. Laird.
No débuts.

WEST INDIES		
C.G. Greenidge	b Thomson	39
D.L. Haynes	c and b Thomson	30
I.V.A. Richards	run out	47
S.F.A.F. Bacchus	c Hughes b Thomson	4
C.H. Lloyd*	c Thomson b Lawson	63
D.A. Murray†	c Graf b Lawson	5
M.D. Marshall	not out	16
A.M.E. Roberts	run out	15
J. Garner	lbw b Alderman	1
M.A. Holding	not out	2
C.E.H. Croft		
Extras	(LB 7, W 5, NB 2)	14
Total	(49 overs – 8 wickets)	**236**

Fall of wickets 1-64, 2-89, 3-98, 4-170, 5-197, 6-197, 7-229, 8-232.

AUSTRALIA	*O*	*M*	*R*	*W*
Lawson	10	2	28	2
Alderman	10	0	35	1
Thomson	10	0	55	3
Graf	9	0	56	0
Chappell	10	0	48	0

AUSTRALIA		
B.M. Laird	not out	117
W.M. Darling	c Murray b Holding	5
G.S. Chappell*	lbw b Roberts	1
A.R. Border	run out	29
K.J. Hughes	not out	62
G.M. Wood		
R.W. Marsh†		
S.F. Graf		
G.F. Lawson		
J.R. Thomson		
T.M. Alderman		
Extras	(B 1, LB 13, W 4, NB 5)	23
Total	(47 overs – 3 wickets)	**237**

Fall of wickets 1-7, 2-8, 3-90.

WEST INDIES	*O*	*M*	*R*	*W*
Holding	10	0	34	1
Roberts	9	0	44	1
Marshall	10	0	45	0
Garner	9	0	43	0
Croft	9	0	48	0

Umpires: A.R. Crafter and M.W. Johnson.

Match No. 125/8

PAKISTAN v WEST INDIES 1981-82

Benson and Hedges World Series Cup – 4th Match

At Adelaide Oval on 5 December 1981.
Toss: West Indies. Result: PAKISTAN won by 8 runs.
49 overs match. Award: Wasim Raja.
Début: West Indies – P.J.L. Dujon.

PAKISTAN		
Mudassar Nazar	c Greenidge b Holding	11
Mohsin Khan	run out	11
Zaheer Abbas	c Murray b Roberts	46
Javed Miandad*	lbw b Marshall	1
Wasim Raja	b Garner	1
Imran Khan	c Murray b Marshall	1
Ijaz Faqih	c Lloyd b Holding	20
Ashraf Ali†	c Bacchus b Richards	3
Sarfraz Nawaz	not out	34
Tahir Naqqash	run out	1
Sikander Bakht	run out	3
Extras	(B 1, LB 4, W 2, NB 1)	8
Total	(49 overs)	**140**

Fall of wickets: 1-16, 2-27, 3-31, 4-34, 5-35, 6-63, 7-68, 8-125, 9-127, 10-140.

WEST INDIES	*O*	*M*	*R*	*W*
Roberts	10	3	19	1
Holding	10	1	28	2
Garner	10	3	32	1
Marshall	9	0	18	2
Richards	10	1	35	1

WEST INDIES		
C.G. Greenidge	b Sarfraz	4
D.L. Haynes	c Ashraf b Tahir	7
I.V.A. Richards	c Ashraf b Sarfraz	9
S.F.A.F. Bacchus	b Wasim Raja	37
C.H. Lloyd*	c Tahir b Ijaz	28
P.J.L. Dujon	b Wasim Raja	0
M.D. Marshall	b Wasim Raja	20
D.A. Murray†	lbw b Wasim Raja	0
A.M.E. Roberts	b Imran	4
M.A. Holding	c Wasim Raja b Imran	8
J. Garner	not out	1
Extras	(LB 7, W 2, NB 5)	14
Total	(38.5 overs)	**132**

Fall of wickets: 1-7, 2-19, 3-38, 4-85, 5-88, 6-107, 7-107, 8-120, 9-120, 10-132.

PAKISTAN	*O*	*M*	*R*	*W*
Imran Khan	9.5	0	13	2
Sarfraz Nawaz	6	0	24	2
Sikander Bakht	4	0	11	0
Tahir Naqqash	6	0	25	1
Ijaz Faqih	6	0	20	1
Wasim Raja	7	0	25	4

Umpires: A.R. Crafter and B.E. Martin.

AUSTRALIA v PAKISTAN 1981-82

Benson and Hedges World Series Cup – 5th Match

At Adelaide Oval on 6 December 1981.
Toss: Australia. Result: AUSTRALIA won by 38 runs.
50 overs match. Award: G.S. Chappell.
No débuts.

AUSTRALIA		
B.M. Laird	lbw b Sikander	20
W.M. Darling	run out	35
G.S. Chappell*	c Wasim Raja b Ijaz	38
A.R. Border	c Wasim Raja b Mudassar	25
K.J. Hughes	c Mudassar b Sarfraz	14
G.M. Wood	not out	43
R.W. Marsh†	c Ashraf b Mudassar	10
G.F. Lawson	b Sarfraz	2
D.K. Lillee	c Sarfraz b Imran	7
J.R. Thomson	b Imran	6
T.M. Alderman	c Ashraf b Imran	1
Extras	(LB 2, W 3, NB 2)	7
Total	(48.3 overs)	**208**

Fall of wickets: 1-43, 2-84, 3-103, 4-136, 5-136, 6-169, 7-176, 8-187, 9-199, 10-208.

PAKISTAN	*O*	*M*	*R*	*W*
Imran Khan	9.3	3	19	3
Sarfraz Nawaz	10	0	44	2
Sikander Bakht	9	0	29	1
Ijaz Faqih	7	0	43	1
Tahir Naqqash	6	0	41	0
Mudassar Nazar	7	0	25	2

PAKISTAN		
Mudassar Nazar	run out	14
Mohsin Khan	c Marsh b Chappell	27
Zaheer Abbas	c Alderman b Lawson	38
Javed Miandad*	c Alderman b Chappell	4
Wasim Raja	c Darling b Lawson	2
Imran Khan	c Darling b Alderman	18
Ijaz Faqih	c Marsh b Thomson	18
Sarfraz Nawaz	c Darling b Chappell	5
Tahir Naqqash	not out	21
Ashraf Ali†	not out	11
Sikander Bakht		
Extras	(LB 8, W 1, NB 3)	12
Total	(50 overs – 8 wickets)	**170**

Fall of wickets: 1-41, 2-57, 3-79, 4-84, 5-91, 6-121, 7-134, 8-138.

AUSTRALIA	*O*	*M*	*R*	*W*
Alderman	10	1	26	1
Lawson	10	1	33	2
Chappell	10	1	31	3
Lillee	10	0	23	0
Thomson	10	0	45	1

Umpires: R.C. Bailhache and R.A. French.

Match No. 127/5

AUSTRALIA v PAKISTAN 1981-82

Benson and Hedges World Series Cup – 6th Match

At Sydney Cricket Ground on 17 December 1981.
Toss: Pakistan. Result: PAKISTAN won by 6 wickets.
50 overs match. Award: Mudassar Nazar.
Début: Australia – D.M. Wellham.

AUSTRALIA		
W.M. Darling	run out	74
B.M. Laird	b Sikander	12
G.M. Wood	b Mudassar	25
A.R. Border	c Ashraf b Mudassar	2
D.M. Wellham	run out	42
G.S. Chappell*	c Miandad b Mudassar	0
R.W. Marsh†	not out	54
D.K. Lillee		
G.F. Lawson		
J.R. Thomson		
T.M. Alderman		
Extras	(B 2, LB 7, W 1, NB 3)	13
Total	(50 overs – 6 wickets)	**222**

Fall of wickets: 1-40, 2-106, 3-110, 4-132, 5-132, 6-222.

PAKISTAN	*O*	*M*	*R*	*W*
Imran Khan	10	0	47	0
Sikander Bakht	8	0	48	1
Sarfraz Nawaz	9	0	38	0
Tahir Naqqash	3	0	21	0
Majid Khan	10	0	35	0
Mudassar Nazar	10	4	20	3

PAKISTAN		
Mudassar Nazar	c Alderman b Thomson	50
Mohsin Khan	b Lawson	2
Zaheer Abbas	b Chappell	108
Javed Miandad*	lbw b Chappell	22
Majid Khan	not out	20
Wasim Raja	not out	9
Imran Khan		
Ashraf Ali†		
Sarfraz Nawaz		
Tahir Naqqash		
Sikander Bakht		
Extras	(B 2, LB 5, W 4, NB 1)	12
Total	(43.2 overs – 4 wickets)	**223**

Fall of wickets: 1-15, 2-120, 3-174, 4-205.

AUSTRALIA	*O*	*M*	*R*	*W*
Lawson	9	0	43	1
Alderman	10	1	41	0
Lillee	8	1	38	0
Thomson	7	0	27	1
Border	3	0	24	0
Chappell	6.2	0	38	2

Umpires: R.A. French and M.W. Johnson.

PAKISTAN v WEST INDIES 1981-82

Benson and Hedges World Series Cup – 7th Match

At WACA Ground, Perth on 19 December 1981.
Toss: Pakistan. Result: WEST INDIES won by 7 wickets.
50 overs match. Award: D.L. Haynes.
Début: West Indies – A.L. Logie.

PAKISTAN		
Mudassar Nazar	c Richards b Marshall	30
Mohsin Khan	c Lloyd b Garner	6
Zaheer Abbas	c Dujon b Richards	35
Javed Miandad*	c Bacchus b Richards	21
Wasim Raja	c Haynes b Richards	17
Imran Khan	not out	29
Ijaz Faqih	c Haynes b Garner	2
Sarfraz Nawaz	c Roberts b Garner	0
Wasim Bari†	run out	4
Sikander Bakht	c Dujon b Marshall	0
Majid Khan	absent hurt	
Extras	(B 4, LB 3, W 2, NB 7)	16
Total	(44.4 overs)	**160**

Fall of wickets 1-29, 2-61, 3-106, 4-107, 5-148, 6-151, 7-152, 8-156, 9-160.

WEST INDIES	*O*	*M*	*R*	*W*
Holding	8	1	15	0
Roberts	8	1	21	0
Garner	9	1	23	3
Marshall	9.4	0	33	2
Richards	10	0	52	3

WEST INDIES		
D.L. Haynes	not out	82
S.F.A.F. Bacchus	c Wasim Bari b Imran	4
I.V.A. Richards	c Wasim Bari b Sarfraz	8
C.H. Lloyd*	c and b Wasim Raja	32
H.A. Gomes	not out	26
P.J.L. Dujon†		
A.L. Logie		
M.D. Marshall		
M.A. Holding		
J. Garner		
A.M.E. Roberts		
Extras	(B 1, LB 3, W 2, NB 3)	9
Total	(42.2 overs – 3 wickets)	**161**

Fall of wickets 1-5, 2-21, 3-95.

PAKISTAN	*O*	*M*	*R*	*W*
Imran Khan	8.2	0	38	1
Sarfraz Nawaz	10	1	29	1
Sikander Bakht	6	0	27	0
Mudassar Nazar	1	0	1	0
Ijaz Faqih	6	0	30	0
Wasim Raja	10	1	26	1
Javed Miandad	1	0	1	0

Umpires: B.E. Martin and R.V. Whitehead.

Match No. 129/11

AUSTRALIA v WEST INDIES 1981-82

Benson and Hedges World Series Cup – 8th Match

At WACA Ground, Perth on 20 December 1981.

Toss: West Indies.	Result: WEST INDIES won by 8 wickets.
50 overs match.	Award: C.H. Lloyd.

No débuts.

AUSTRALIA		
W.M. Darling	b Holding	7
B.M. Laird	lbw b Marshall	7
G.S. Chappell*	c Haynes b Holding	0
A.R. Border	c Bacchus b Marshall	27
K.J. Hughes	c Holding b Marshall	18
G.M. Wood	run out	54
R.W. Marsh†	c Logie b Richards	0
D.K. Lillee	not out	42
G.F. Lawson	b Garner	0
J.R. Thomson	run out	5
T.M. Alderman	not out	9
Extras	(LB 12, W 5, NB 2)	19
Total	(50 overs – 9 wickets)	**188**

Fall of wickets: 1-10, 2-20, 3-30, 4-62, 5-78, 6-80, 7-150, 8-150, 9-166.

WEST INDIES	*O*	*M*	*R*	*W*
Holding	10	0	37	2
Roberts	10	1	26	0
Garner	10	1	32	1
Marshall	10	0	31	3
Richards	10	0	43	1

WEST INDIES		
D.L. Haynes	c Chappell b Lillee	9
S.F.A.F. Bacchus	c Thomson b Alderman	21
I.V.A. Richards	not out	72
C.H. Lloyd*	not out	80
H.A. Gomes		
P.J.L. Dujon†		
A.L. Logie		
M.D. Marshall		
A.M.E. Roberts		
M.A. Holding		
J. Garner		
Extras	(W 4, NB 4)	8
Total	(30 overs – 2 wickets)	**190**

Fall of wickets: 1-23, 2-37.

AUSTRALIA	*O*	*M*	*R*	*W*
Lillee	6	1	36	1
Alderman	8	1	41	1
Thomson	5	0	24	0
Lawson	6	0	46	0
Chappell	5	0	35	0

Umpires: R.C. Bailhache and A.R. Crafter.

AUSTRALIA v PAKISTAN 1981-82

Benson and Hedges World Series Cup – 9th Match

At Melbourne Cricket Ground on 9 January 1982.
Toss: Australia. Result: PAKISTAN won by 25 runs.
50 overs match. Award: Zaheer Abbas.
No débuts.

PAKISTAN		
Mansoor Akhtar	c Marsh b Alderman	5
Mudassar Nazar	lbw b Thomson	40
Zaheer Abbas	c Laird b Thomson	84
Javed Miandad*	c Darling b Lillee	37
Imran Khan	run out	3
Wasim Raja	not out	19
Ijaz Faqih	run out	1
Sarfraz Nawaz	not out	14
Wasim Bari†		
Tahir Naqqash		
Sikander Bakht		
Extras	(LB 10, W 1, NB 4)	15
Total	(50 overs – 6 wickets)	**218**

Fall of wickets 1-10, 2-79, 3-169, 4-172, 5-193, 6-199.

AUSTRALIA	*O*	*M*	*R*	*W*
Lawson	10	0	36	0
Alderman	10	0	37	1
Lillee	10	1	37	1
Thomson	10	0	55	2
Chappell	10	0	38	0

AUSTRALIA		
G.M. Wood	c Wasim Raja b Mudassar	38
B.M. Laird	run out	4
J. Dyson	lbw b Sikander	11
G.S. Chappell*	b Ijaz	35
A.R. Border	not out	75
W.M. Darling	run out	5
R.W. Marsh†	c Miandad b Ijaz	2
D.K. Lillee	run out	8
G.F. Lawson	run out	1
J.R. Thomson	b Imran	2
T.M. Alderman	b Sikander	0
Extras	(B 4, LB 8)	12
Total	(49 overs)	**193**

Fall of wickets 1-5, 2-41, 3-74, 4-135, 5-147, 6-153, 7-175, 8-181, 9-190, 10-193.

PAKISTAN	*O*	*M*	*R*	*W*
Imran Khan	9	2	21	1
Sarfraz Nawaz	8	0	34	0
Tahir Naqqash	8	0	35	0
Sikander Bakht	8	0	33	2
Mudassar Nazar	6	0	24	1
Ijaz Faqih	10	0	34	2

Umpires: A.R. Crafter and R.V. Whitehead.

Match No. 131/12

AUSTRALIA v WEST INDIES 1981-82

Benson and Hedges World Series Cup – 10th Match

At Melbourne Cricket Ground on 10 January 1982.
Toss: Australia. Result: WEST INDIES won by 5 wickets.
50 overs match. Award: P.J.L. Dujon.
No débuts.

The attendance of 78,142 was the record until *Match No. 174* was played on the same ground a year later.

AUSTRALIA		
B.M. Laird	hit wicket b Holding	4
G.M. Wood	c Greenidge b Holding	3
R.B. McCosker	run out	20
G.S. Chappell*	c Logie b Roberts	59
A.R. Border	b Marshall	6
W.M. Darling	c Holding b Gomes	20
R.W. Marsh†	c Logie b Gomes	0
B. Yardley	c Logie b Holding	23
D.K. Lillee	c Holding b Roberts	1
G.F. Lawson	not out	0
M.F. Malone	b Holding	1
Extras	(LB 4, W 1, NB 4)	9
Total	(42.5 overs)	**146**

Fall of wickets: 1-7, 2-16, 3-33, 4-41, 5-99, 6-101, 7-140, 8-144, 9-145, 10-146.

WEST INDIES	*O*	*M*	*R*	*W*
Holding	7.5	1	32	4
Roberts	7	0	23	2
Garner	6	0	13	0
Marshall	5	0	12	1
Richards	10	1	31	0
Gomes	7	1	26	2

WEST INDIES		
C.G. Greenidge	c Border b Malone	9
D.L. Haynes	lbw b Lawson	1
I.V.A. Richards	c Lawson b Yardley	32
H.A. Gomes	c Laird b Malone	7
C.H. Lloyd*	lbw b Lawson	37
P.J.L. Dujon†	not out	51
M.D. Marshall	not out	5
A.L. Logie		
A.M.E. Roberts		
M.A. Holding		
J. Garner		
Extras	(LB 3, W 1, NB 1)	5
Total	(47.1 overs – 5 wickets)	**147**

Fall of wickets: 1-7, 2-18, 3-48, 4-52, 5-137.

AUSTRALIA	*O*	*M*	*R*	*W*
Lillee	10	0	34	0
Lawson	9.1	0	31	2
Malone	10	5	9	2
Chappell	9	1	33	0
Yardley	6	0	25	1
Border	3	0	10	0

Umpires: R.C. Bailhache and B.E. Martin.

PAKISTAN v WEST INDIES 1981-82

Benson and Hedges World Series Cup – 11th Match

At Sydney Cricket Ground on 12 January 1982.
Toss: Pakistan. Result: WEST INDIES won by 7 wickets.
50 overs match (floodlit). Award: C.G. Greenidge.
Début: Pakistan – Salim Malik.

PAKISTAN		
Mohsin Khan	b Marshall	12
Mansoor Akhtar	run out	13
Zaheer Abbas	run out	1
Javed Miandad*	c Dujon b Garner	26
Wasim Raja	c Logie b Roberts	33
Salim Malik	b Garner	0
Imran Khan	not out	62
Ijaz Faqih	b Garner	5
Tahir Naqqash	not out	23
Wasim Bari†		
Sikander Bakht		
Extras	(B 1, LB 5, W 7, NB 3)	16
Total	(50 overs – 7 wickets)	**191**

Fall of wickets: 1-26, 2-32, 3-32, 4-75, 5-75, 6-122, 7-144.

WEST INDIES	*O*	*M*	*R*	*W*
Holding	10	1	37	0
Roberts	10	0	47	1
Marshall	10	1	33	1
Garner	10	1	17	3
Richards	10	0	41	0

WEST INDIES		
C.G. Greenidge	lbw b Imran	84
D.L. Haynes	b Imran	2
I.V.A. Richards	b Tahir	41
C.H. Lloyd*	not out	35
H.A. Gomes	not out	15
P.J.L. Dujon†		
A.L. Logie		
M.D. Marshall		
A.M.E. Roberts		
M.A. Holding		
J. Garner		
Extras	(LB 5, W 5, NB 5)	15
Total	(42.1 overs – 3 wickets)	**192**

Fall of wickets: 1-37, 2-107, 3-155.

PAKISTAN	*O*	*M*	*R*	*W*
Imran Khan	10	0	42	2
Sikander Bakht	7	1	40	0
Wasim Raja	9.1	0	37	0
Tahir Naqqash	10	0	31	1
Ijaz Faqih	6	0	27	0

Umpires: M.W. Johnson and B.E. Martin.

Match No. 133/7

AUSTRALIA v PAKISTAN 1981-82

Benson and Hedges World Series Cup – 12th Match

At Sydney Cricket Ground on 14 January 1982.
Toss: Pakistan. Result: AUSTRALIA won by 76 runs.
50 overs match (floodlit). Award: K.J. Hughes.
No débuts.

AUSTRALIA		
G.M. Wood	b Mudassar	42
B.M. Laird	c Wasim Bari b Mudassar	45
R.B. McCosker	lbw b Mudassar	13
G.S. Chappell*	c Wasim Raja b Sikander	36
K.J. Hughes	not out	63
R.W. Marsh†	c Zaheer b Imran	3
A.R. Border	not out	11
D.K. Lillee		
G.F. Lawson		
J.R. Thomson		
M.F. Malone		
Extras	(B 3, LB 8, W 3, NB 3)	17
Total	(50 overs – 5 wickets)	**230**

Fall of wickets 1-80, 2-108, 3-111, 4-198, 5-206.

PAKISTAN	*O*	*M*	*R*	*W*
Imran Khan	10	0	37	1
Sarfraz Nawaz	9	0	45	0
Tahir Naqqash	5	2	20	0
Sikander Bakht	9	0	43	1
Mudassar Nazar	10	1	36	3
Ijaz Faqih	7	0	32	0

PAKISTAN		
Mudassar Nazar	b Lillee	5
Mansoor Akhtar	c Lawson b Chappell	40
Zaheer Abbas	c Border b Lawson	12
Javed Miandad*	lbw b Chappell	8
Wasim Raja	b Malone	16
Imran Khan	b Thomson	39
Ijaz Faqih	c Marsh b Malone	0
Sarfraz Nawaz	c Hughes b Lillee	5
Tahir Naqqash	c Lillee b Lawson	13
Wasim Bari†	retired hurt	9
Sikander Bakht	not out	0
Extras	(LB 6, W 1)	7
Total	(40.3 overs)	**154**

Fall of wickets 1-8, 2-30, 3-66, 4-71, 5-89,
6-89, 7-99, 8-129, 9-150.

AUSTRALIA	*O*	*M*	*R*	*W*
Lillee	7.3	1	23	2
Thomson	7	1	19	1
Lawson	8	0	45	2
Malone	10	2	36	2
Chappell	8	0	24	2

Umpires: R.A. French and R.V. Whitehead.

PAKISTAN v WEST INDIES 1981-82

Benson and Hedges World Series Cup – 13th Match

At Woolloongabba, Brisbane on 16 January 1982.
Toss: West Indies. Result: WEST INDIES won by 1 wicket.
50 overs match. Award: S.F.A.F. Bacchus.
No débuts.

Rain reduced West Indies' innings to 30 overs and their target to 107.

PAKISTAN		
Mudassar Nazar	run out	40
Mansoor Akhtar	c Greenidge b Holding	4
Zaheer Abbas	c Lloyd b Richards	17
Javed Miandad*	c Lloyd b Roberts	25
Wasim Raja	retired hurt	12
Imran Khan	c Dujon b Garner	31
Majid Khan	c Dujon b Holding	10
Ashraf Ali†	run out	3
Sarfraz Nawaz	c Clarke b Garner	10
Iqbal Qasim	c Greenidge b Garner	2
Sikander Bakht	not out	1
Extras	(B 2, LB 12, W 6, NB 2)	22
Total	(50 overs)	**177**

Fall of wickets: 1-16, 2-57, 3-101, 4-111, 5-115, 6-161, 7-165, 8-175, 9-177.

WEST INDIES	*O*	*M*	*R*	*W*
Holding	10	3	23	2
Clarke	10	2	28	0
Roberts	10	1	33	1
Garner	10	1	19	3
Richards	10	0	52	1

WEST INDIES		
C.G. Greenidge	b Sarfraz	7
D.L. Haynes	c sub (Mohsin Khan) b Sarfraz	13
I.V.A. Richards	c Imran b Sarfraz	0
H.A. Gomes	b Sikander	13
C.H. Lloyd*	c Mudassar b Sikander	1
S.F.A.F. Bacchus	not out	36
A.M.E. Roberts	c Sarfraz b Mudassar	1
P.J.L. Dujon†	c and b Sikander	13
S.T. Clarke	c Ashraf b Imran	1
M.A. Holding	c Ashraf b Mudassar	8
J. Garner	not out	1
Extras	(B 4, LB 4, W 5)	13
Total	(28.5 overs – 9 wickets)	**107**

Fall of wickets: 1-12, 2-12, 3-36, 4-38, 5-61, 6-69, 7-83, 8-90, 9-105.

PAKISTAN	*O*	*M*	*R*	*W*
Imran Khan	10	1	23	1
Sarfraz Nawaz	10	1	31	3
Sikander Bakht	6.5	0	29	3
Mudassar Nazar	2	0	11	2

Umpires: R.A. French and R.V. Whitehead.

Match No. 135/13

AUSTRALIA v WEST INDIES 1981-82

Benson and Hedges World Series Cup – 14th Match

At Woolloongabba, Brisbane on 17 January 1982.
Toss: West Indies. Result: WEST INDIES won by 5 wickets.
40 overs match. Award: H.A. Gomes.
No débuts.

AUSTRALIA		
B.M. Laird	b Garner	26
G.M. Wood	c Lloyd b Richards	15
R.B. McCosker	c Bacchus b Clarke	18
G.S. Chappell*	c Greenidge b Garner	61
K.J. Hughes	st Dujon b Richards	2
A.R. Border	c Garner b Holding	20
R.W. Marsh†	c Greenidge b Garner	7
J.R. Thomson	b Holding	0
D.K. Lillee	c Holding b Garner	11
G.F. Lawson	not out	4
M.F. Malone	not out	0
Extras	(B 2, LB 9, W 9, NB 1)	21
Total	(40 overs – 9 wickets)	**185**

Fall of wickets: 1-51, 2-58, 3-97, 4-113, 5-159, 6-161, 7-165, 8-181, 9-181.

WEST INDIES	*O*	*M*	*R*	*W*
Holding	8	1	38	2
Clarke	9	1	22	1
Garner	9	0	45	4
Roberts	5	1	11	0
Richards	7	0	36	2
Gomes	2	0	12	0

WEST INDIES		
C.G. Greenidge	c Wood b Chappell	16
D.L. Haynes	c Marsh b Lillee	11
I.V.A. Richards*	c Lillee b Thomson	34
H.A. Gomes	not out	56
S.F.A.F. Bacchus	run out	20
C.H. Lloyd	c Border b Thomson	30
P.J.L. Dujon†	not out	6
A.M.E. Roberts		
S.T. Clarke		
M.A. Holding		
J. Garner		
Extras	(LB 7, W 4, NB 2)	13
Total	(38.4 overs – 5 wickets)	**186**

Fall of wickets: 1-27, 2-32, 3-94, 4-116, 5-174.

AUSTRALIA	*O*	*M*	*R*	*W*
Lillee	9	2	32	1
Thomson	10	2	40	2
Malone	10	1	34	0
Chappell	4	0	22	1
Lawson	5.4	0	45	0

Umpires: A.R. Crafter and M.W. Johnson.

AUSTRALIA v WEST INDIES 1981-82

Benson and Hedges World Series Cup – 15th Match

At Sydney Cricket Ground on 19 January 1982.
Toss: Australia. Result: AUSTRALIA won on scoring rate.
50 overs match (floodlit). Award: A.M.E. Roberts.
No débuts.

A boundary by Border off the final ball before rain ended play gave Australia victory by 0.11 of a run per over. They qualified for the finals ahead of Pakistan only by virtue of a faster scoring rate in the qualifying matches.

WEST INDIES		
C.G. Greenidge	b Lillee	1
D.L. Haynes	b Malone	5
I.V.A. Richards*	b Thomson	64
H.A. Gomes	c Marsh b Pascoe	3
S.F.A.F. Bacchus	c Hughes b Malone	20
P.J.L. Dujon†	b Thomson	30
M.D. Marshall	not out	32
A.M.E. Roberts	c Wood b Pascoe	9
M.A. Holding	c Marsh b Pascoe	0
S.T. Clarke	b Lillee	16
J. Garner	run out	2
Extras	(LB 5, W 1, NB 1)	7
Total	(50 overs)	**189**

Fall of wickets: 1-2, 2-23, 3-40, 4-79, 5-103, 6-137, 7-155, 8-156, 9-182, 10-189.

AUSTRALIA	*O*	*M*	*R*	*W*
Lillee	10	0	47	2
Thomson	10	1	36	2
Pascoe	10	0	44	3
Malone	10	1	27	2
Chappell	10	0	28	0

AUSTRALIA		
G.M. Wood	c Roberts b Holding	1
W.M. Darling	c Clarke b Roberts	34
J. Dyson	b Garner	37
G.S. Chappell*	lbw b Roberts	0
K.J. Hughes	b Roberts	25
A.R. Border	not out	30
R.W. Marsh†	c Greenidge b Marshall	12
D.K. Lillee	b Holding	6
L.S. Pascoe	not out	0
J.R. Thomson		
M.F. Malone		
Extras	(LB 16, W 5, NB 2)	23
Total	(43.1 overs – 7 wickets)	**168**

Fall of wickets: 1-6, 2-57, 3-61, 4-97, 5-125, 6-144, 7-157.

WEST INDIES	*O*	*M*	*R*	*W*
Holding	6.1	0	34	2
Clarke	10	1	20	0
Marshall	10	0	43	1
Roberts	10	3	15	3
Garner	7	0	33	1

Umpires: R.C. Bailhache and M.W. Johnson.

Match No. 137/15

AUSTRALIA v WEST INDIES 1981-82

Benson and Hedges World Series Cup – 1st Final

At Melbourne Cricket Ground on 23 January 1982.

Toss: Australia. Result: WEST INDIES won by 86 runs.

49 overs match. No award.

No débuts.

WEST INDIES		
C.G. Greenidge	b Lillee	59
D.L. Haynes	c Marsh b Pascoe	13
I.V.A. Richards	c Wood b Chappell	78
C.H. Lloyd*	c Pascoe b Thomson	20
S.F.A.F. Bacchus	c Marsh b Thomson	2
P.J.L. Dujon†	c Hughes b Pascoe	6
H.A. Gomes	run out	6
A.M.E. Roberts	run out	5
M.A. Holding	not out	7
S.T. Clarke	not out	0
J. Garner		
Extras	(LB 5, W 12, NB 3)	20
Total	(49 overs – 8 wickets)	**216**

Fall of wickets: 1-26, 2-138, 3-179, 4-184, 5-197, 6-198, 7-204, 8-210.

AUSTRALIA	*O*	*M*	*R*	*W*
Lillee	10	3	35	1
Thomson	10	1	44	2
Malone	10	2	25	0
Pascoe	9	1	33	2
Chappell	10	0	59	1

AUSTRALIA		
W.M. Darling	c Bacchus b Garner	14
G.M. Wood	run out	19
J. Dyson	b Clarke	0
G.S. Chappell*	lbw b Garner	4
K.J. Hughes	b Richards	4
A.R. Border	c and b Gomes	16
R.W. Marsh†	c Bacchus b Clarke	32
D.K. Lillee	b Clarke	11
J.R. Thomson	b Holding	5
L.S. Pascoe	not out	3
M.F. Malone	st Dujon b Gomes	10
Extras	(B 4, LB 5, W 2, NB 1)	12
Total	(37.4 overs)	**130**

Fall of wickets: 1-30, 2-30, 3-43, 4-43, 5-56, 6-64, 7-107, 8-110, 9-117, 10-130.

WEST INDIES	*O*	*M*	*R*	*W*
Holding	8	1	19	1
Roberts	5	1	16	0
Clarke	9	1	22	3
Garner	6	3	7	2
Richards	5	1	29	1
Gomes	4.4	0	25	2

Umpires: M.W. Johnson and R.V. Whitehead.

AUSTRALIA v WEST INDIES 1981-82

Benson and Hedges World Series Cup – 2nd Final

At Melbourne Cricket Ground on 24 January 1982.
Toss: West Indies. Result: WEST INDIES won by 128 runs.
50 overs match. No award.
No débuts.

WEST INDIES		
C.G. Greenidge	c Marsh b Malone	47
D.L. Haynes	c Dyson b Pascoe	52
I.V.A. Richards	c Dyson b Chappell	60
S.F.A.F. Bacchus	c Malone b Thomson	31
C.H. Lloyd*	not out	22
P.J.L. Dujon†	b Lillee	5
A.M.E. Roberts	b Pascoe	0
S.T. Clarke	b Pascoe	5
M.A. Holding	b Pascoe	0
J. Garner	run out	0
H.A. Gomes		
Extras	(B 2, LB 9, W 2)	13
Total	(50 overs – 9 wickets)	**235**

Fall of wickets: 1-65, 2-150, 3-200, 4-204, 5-220, 6-225, 7-235, 8-235, 9-235.

AUSTRALIA	*O*	*M*	*R*	*W*
Lillee	10	0	53	1
Pascoe	10	1	39	4
Thomson	10	1	31	1
Malone	10	0	37	1
Chappell	10	0	62	1

AUSTRALIA		
G.M. Wood	c Haynes b Clarke	7
B.M. Laird	c Haynes b Roberts	13
A.R. Border	c Dujon b Roberts	13
G.S. Chappell*	b Garner	1
K.J. Hughes	lbw b Garner	0
J. Dyson	b Clarke	18
R.W. Marsh†	b Gomes	15
D.K. Lillee	c Dujon b Gomes	0
J.R. Thomson	b Gomes	15
L.S. Pascoe	lbw b Gomes	0
M.F. Malone	not out	15
Extras	(B 2, LB 3, W 4, NB 1)	10
Total	(32.2 overs)	**107**

Fall of wickets: 1-14, 2-42, 3-43, 4-43, 5-43, 6-65, 7-65, 8-81, 9-81, 10-107.

WEST INDIES	*O*	*M*	*R*	*W*
Holding	10	3	25	0
Clarke	6.2	1	15	2
Garner	5	2	10	2
Roberts	5	1	16	2
Gomes	6	1	31	4

Umpires: R.C. Bailhache and R.A. French.

Match No. 139/17

AUSTRALIA v WEST INDIES 1981-82

Benson and Hedges World Series Cup – 3rd Final

At Sydney Cricket Ground on 26 January 1982.
Toss: West Indies. Result: AUSTRALIA won by 46 runs.
50 overs match (floodlit). No award.
No débuts.

AUSTRALIA		
B.M. Laird	c Richards b Clarke	14
G.M. Wood	c and b Gomes	45
G.S. Chappell*	b Garner	0
K.J. Hughes	b Holding	28
A.R. Border	not out	69
D.W. Hookes	c Dujon b Holding	1
R.W. Marsh†	b Clarke	20
D.K. Lillee	b Clarke	1
J.R. Thomson	c Dujon b Roberts	7
L.S. Pascoe	not out	15
M.F. Malone		
Extras	(LB 13, NB 1)	14
Total	(50 overs – 8 wickets)	**214**

Fall of wickets 1-19, 2-20, 3-94, 4-100, 5-103, 6-145, 7-147, 8-167.

WEST INDIES	*O*	*M*	*R*	*W*
Holding	10	2	32	2
Clarke	10	2	30	3
Garner	10	0	42	1
Roberts	10	1	50	1
Gomes	10	0	46	1

WEST INDIES		
C.G. Greenidge	lbw b Lillee	5
D.L. Haynes	c Chappell b Pascoe	26
I.V.A. Richards	lbw b Lillee	4
H.A. Gomes	c Marsh b Thomson	0
C.H. Lloyd*	not out	63
S.F.A.F. Bacchus	run out	19
P.J.L. Dujon†	c sub (J. Dyson) b Malone	10
A.M.E. Roberts	lbw b Chappell	1
M.A. Holding	c Thomson b Chappell	6
S.T. Clarke	run out	16
J. Garner	c sub (J. Dyson) b Pascoe	3
Extras	(B 1, LB 3, W 9, NB 2)	15
Total	(42.5 overs)	**168**

Fall of wickets 1-20, 2-34, 3-41, 4-41, 5-68, 6-88, 7-95, 8-113, 9-164, 10-168.

AUSTRALIA	*O*	*M*	*R*	*W*
Lillee	10	4	18	2
Thomson	6	0	38	1
Pascoe	6.5	1	21	2
Malone	10	1	33	1
Chappell	10	1	43	2

Umpires: A.R. Crafter and B.E. Martin.

AUSTRALIA v WEST INDIES 1981-82

Benson and Hedges World Series Cup – 4th Final

At Sydney Cricket Ground on 27 January 1982.
Toss: West Indies. Result: WEST INDIES won by 18 runs.
50 overs match (floodlit). Finals award: I.V.A. Richards.
No débuts.

After six defeats, West Indies gained their first victory against Australia in a match involving floodlit play.

WEST INDIES		
C.G. Greenidge	b Malone	64
D.L. Haynes	lbw b Lillee	8
I.V.A. Richards	run out	70
S.F.A.F. Bacchus	b Thomson	17
C.H. Lloyd*	not out	41
P.J.L. Dujon†	b Pascoe	13
A.M.E. Roberts	b Thomson	5
S.T. Clarke	not out	2
H.A. Gomes		
M.A. Holding		
J. Garner		
Extras	(LB 14)	14
Total	(50 overs – 6 wickets)	**234**

Fall of wickets 1-13, 2-151, 3-155, 4-198, 5-224, 6-229.

AUSTRALIA	*O*	*M*	*R*	*W*
Lillee	10	4	30	1
Thomson	10	0	60	2
Pascoe	10	1	46	1
Malone	10	1	50	1
Chappell	10	2	34	0

AUSTRALIA		
G.M. Wood	c Lloyd b Holding	69
B.M. Laird	lbw b Garner	13
G.S. Chappell*	c Richards b Clarke	10
K.J. Hughes	c Lloyd b Richards	27
A.R. Border	b Richards	23
D.W. Hookes	c Greenidge b Garner	17
R.W. Marsh†	c Gomes b Roberts	5
L.S. Pascoe	b Roberts	7
J.R. Thomson	not out	19
D.K. Lillee	b Roberts	4
M.F. Malone	not out	5
Extras	(B 4, LB 10, W 2, NB 1)	17
Total	(50 overs – 9 wickets)	**216**

Fall of wickets 1-37, 2-57, 3-102, 4-135, 5-163, 6-173, 7-176, 8-194, 9-198.

WEST INDIES	*O*	*M*	*R*	*W*
Holding	10	1	36	1
Clarke	10	3	40	1
Garner	10	1	27	2
Roberts	10	0	48	3
Richards	10	0	48	2

Umpires: A.R. Crafter and B.E. Martin.

Match No. 141/4

INDIA v ENGLAND 1981-82 (1st Match)

Wills Series

At Sardar Patel Stadium, Ahmedabad on 25 November 1981.
Toss: England. Result: ENGLAND won by 5 wickets.
46 overs match. Award: M.W. Gatting.

Débuts: India – Randhir Singh, R.J. Shastri, K. Srikkanth; England – G. Cook, C.J. Richards.

India staged its first home one-day international more than a decade after the inaugural match.

INDIA		
S.M. Gavaskar*	c Gooch b Willis	0
K. Srikkanth	b Botham	0
D.B. Vengsarkar	c and b Underwood	46
G.R. Viswanath	c Cook b Gooch	8
K. Azad	b Botham	30
Madan Lal	c Lever b Underwood	6
S.M.H. Kirmani†	not out	18
R.J. Shastri	run out	19
R.M.H. Binny	not out	2
D.R. Doshi		
Randhir Singh		
Extras	(B 4, LB 13, W 7, NB 3)	27
Total	(46 overs – 7 wickets)	**156**

Fall of wickets: 1-2, 2-8, 3-39, 4-91, 5-113, 6-119, 7-154.

ENGLAND	*O*	*M*	*R*	*W*
Willis	9	3	17	1
Botham	10	4	20	2
Lever	10	0	46	0
Gooch	7	0	28	1
Underwood	10	3	18	2

ENGLAND		
G.A. Gooch	c Kirmani b Binny	23
G. Boycott	lbw b Madan Lal	5
G. Cook	c Viswanath b Binny	13
D.I. Gower	c and b Binny	8
K.W.R. Fletcher*	b Doshi	26
M.W. Gatting	not out	47
I.T. Botham	not out	25
C.J. Richards†		
J.K. Lever		
D.L. Underwood		
R.G.D. Willis		
Extras	(LB 7, W 2, NB 4)	13
Total	(43.5 overs – 5 wickets)	**160**

Fall of wickets: 1-5, 2-43, 3-46, 4-61, 5-126.

INDIA	*O*	*M*	*R*	*W*
Madan Lal	10	2	30	1
Randhir Singh	6	0	18	0
Binny	7.5	3	35	3
Shastri	10	1	24	0
Doshi	10	1	40	1

Umpires: M.V. Gothoskar and S.N. Hanumantha Rao.

INDIA v ENGLAND 1981-82 (2nd Match)
Wills Series

At Burlton Park, Jullundur on 20 December 1981.
Toss: India. Result: INDIA won by 6 wickets.
36 overs match. Award: D.B. Vengsarkar.
Début: India – S.V. Nayak.

India gained their first limited-overs victory against England in a match reduced by early-morning mist.

ENGLAND		
G.A. Gooch	b Madan Lal	12
G. Boycott	run out	6
I.T. Botham	lbw b Madan Lal	5
K.W.R. Fletcher*	c Azad b Patil	5
D.I. Gower	run out	53
M.W. Gatting	not out	71
G. Cook	b Kapil Dev	1
C.J. Richards†	lbw b Kapil Dev	0
J.K. Lever		
D.L. Underwood		
R.G.D. Willis		
Extras	(B 2, LB 4, W 1, NB 1)	8
Total	(36 overs – 7 wickets)	**161**

Fall of wickets: 1-18, 2-22, 3-25, 4-48, 5-158, 6-161, 7-161.

INDIA	*O*	*M*	*R*	*W*
Kapil Dev	8	1	26	2
Madan Lal	7	0	33	2
Nayak	7	2	25	0
Patil	7	0	16	1
Shastri	7	0	53	0

INDIA		
K. Srikkanth	lbw b Botham	17
D.B. Vengsarkar	not out	88
K. Azad	c Gower b Gooch	14
S.M. Patil	b Gooch	3
Kapil Dev	c Willis b Underwood	6
Yashpal Sharma	not out	28
S.M. Gavaskar*		
S.V. Nayak		
Madan Lal		
S.M.H. Kirmani†		
R.J. Shastri		
Extras	(B 3, LB 3, NB 2)	8
Total	(35.3 overs – 4 wickets)	**164**

Fall of wickets: 1-41, 2-69, 3-78, 4-89.

ENGLAND	*O*	*M*	*R*	*W*
Willis	7.3	2	41	0
Lever	7	0	31	0
Gooch	7	0	25	2
Botham	7	0	33	1
Underwood	7	1	26	1

Umpires: J.D. Ghosh and Swaroop Kishen.

Match No. 143/6

INDIA v ENGLAND 1981-82 (3rd Match)

Wills Series

At Baribati Stadium, Cuttack on 27 January 1982.

Toss: India. Result: INDIA won by 5 wickets.

42 overs match. Award: S.M. Gavaskar.

Débuts: India – Arun Lal, A. Malhotra.

ENGLAND		
G.A. Gooch	c Arun Lal b Madan Lal	3
G. Cook	c Nayak b Patil	30
C.J. Tavaré	c Madan Lal b Shastri	11
D.I. Gower	c and b Patil	42
I.T. Botham	b Nayak	52
K.W.R. Fletcher*	b Madan Lal	69
M.W. Gatting	not out	8
R.W. Taylor†	not out	2
J.K. Lever		
D.L. Underwood		
R.G.D. Willis		
Extras	(LB 9, W 1, NB 3)	13
Total	(46 overs – 6 wickets)	**230**

Fall of wickets 1-13, 2-33, 3-86, 4-101, 5-181, 6-228.

INDIA	*O*	*M*	*R*	*W*
Kapil Dev	8	3	23	0
Madan Lal	8	0	56	2
Nayak	10	1	51	1
Shastri	10	1	34	1
Patil	10	0	53	2

INDIA		
S.M. Gavaskar*	st Taylor b Underwood	71
Arun Lal	c Gooch b Botham	9
D.B. Vengsarkar	c Willis b Gooch	13
S.M. Patil	b Underwood	64
Yashpal Sharma	not out	34
Kapil Dev	c Gooch b Underwood	0
A. Malhotra	not out	28
S.M.H. Kirmani†		
S.V. Nayak		
Madan Lal		
R.J. Shastri		
Extras	(LB 7, W 2, NB 3)	12
Total	(42 overs – 5 wickets)	**231**

Fall of wickets 1-16, 2-59, 3-135, 4-184, 5-184.

ENGLAND	*O*	*M*	*R*	*W*
Willis	6	1	29	0
Botham	8	0	48	1
Lever	10	0	55	0
Gooch	8	0	39	1
Underwood	10	0	48	3

Umpires: P.R. Punjabi and K.B. Ramaswami.

SRI LANKA v ENGLAND 1981-82 (1st Match)

At Sinhalese Sports Club, Colombo on 13 February 1982.
Toss: Sri Lanka. Result: ENGLAND won by 5 runs.
45 overs match. Award: I.T. Botham.

Débuts: Sri Lanka – A.L.F. De Mel, R.S.A. Jayasekera, S. Wettimuny; England – P.J.W. Allott.

Sri Lanka, having been granted full membership of the ICC in 1981, staged its first home international four days before its inaugural Test.

ENGLAND		
G.A. Gooch	b G.R.A. De Silva	64
G. Cook	c G.R.A. De Silva b Kaluperuma	28
D.I. Gower	run out	15
I.T. Botham	b De Mel	60
K.W.R. Fletcher*	b D.S. De Silva	12
M.W. Gatting	c Mendis b De Mel	3
C.J. Richards†	b G.R.A. De Silva	3
J.E. Emburey	lbw b De Mel	0
P.J.W. Allott	run out	0
D.L. Underwood	b De Mel	4
R.G.D. Willis	not out	2
Extras	(B 6, LB 2, W 2, NB 10)	20
Total	(44.4 overs)	**211**

Fall of wickets: 1-55, 2-83, 3-152, 4-191, 5-197, 6-202, 7-205, 8-205, 9-205, 10-211.

SRI LANKA	*O*	*M*	*R*	*W*
De Mel	8.4	1	34	4
Ranasinghe	8	2	20	0
Kaluperuma	7	0	35	1
D.S. De Silva	9	0	31	1
G.R.A. De Silva	9	0	56	2
Wettimuny	3	0	15	0

SRI LANKA		
B. Warnapura*	c Gower b Allott	10
S. Wettimuny	c Richards b Allott	46
R.S.A. Jayasekera†	c Gooch b Willis	17
R.L. Dias	c and b Underwood	4
L.R.D. Mendis	c Gower b Underwood	2
R.S. Madugalle	b Willis	22
A.N. Ranasinghe	c Cook b Botham	51
D.S. De Silva	b Botham	8
A.L.F. De Mel	not out	13
L.W. Kaluperuma	not out	14
G.R.A. De Silva		
Extras	(B 5, LB 10, W 2, NB 2)	19
Total	(45 overs – 8 wickets)	**206**

Fall of wickets: 1-34, 2-75, 3-84, 4-92, 5-92, 6-160, 7-175, 8-187.

ENGLAND	*O*	*M*	*R*	*W*
Willis	9	1	32	2
Botham	9	0	45	2
Emburey	5	0	18	0
Allott	9	0	40	2
Gooch	6	1	18	0
Underwood	7	0	34	2

Umpires: C.E.B. Anthony and H.C. Felsinger.

Match No. 145/2

SRI LANKA v ENGLAND 1981-82 (2nd Match)

At Sinhalese Sports Club, Colombo on 14 February 1982.
Toss: England. Result: SRI LANKA won by 3 runs.
45 overs match. Award: S. Wettimuny.
Débuts: Sri Lanka – H.M. Goonatillake, A. Ranatunga.

Sri Lanka gained a notable victory after England lost their last five wickets for 9 runs.

SRI LANKA		
B. Warnapura*	c Taylor b Botham	4
S. Wettimuny	not out	86
L.R.D. Mendis	c and b Botham	0
R.L. Dias	hit wicket b Lever	26
A. Ranatunga	run out	42
A.N. Ranasinghe	c Gooch b Underwood	0
R.S. Madugalle	c Taylor b Lever	12
A.L.F. De Mel	run out	14
D.S. De Silva	not out	9
H.M. Goonatillake†		
G.R.A. De Silva		
Extras	(B 2, LB 18, W 1, NB 1)	22
Total	(45 overs – 7 wickets)	**215**

Fall of wickets: 1-5, 2-5, 3-43, 4-130, 5-130, 6-138, 7-186.

ENGLAND	*O*	*M*	*R*	*W*
Willis	9	1	26	0
Botham	9	4	29	2
Lever	9	0	51	2
Gooch	9	0	50	0
Underwood	9	0	37	1

ENGLAND		
G.A. Gooch	st Goonatillake b G.R.A. De Silva	74
G. Cook	st Goonatillake b G.R.A. De Silva	32
D.I. Gower	lbw b De Mel	6
I.T. Botham	c and b Warnapura	13
K.W.R. Fletcher*	run out	38
C.J. Tavaré	b D.S. De Silva	5
M.W. Gatting	run out	18
R.W. Taylor†	run out	3
J.K. Lever	not out	2
D.L. Underwood	run out	0
R.G.D. Willis	c Madugalle b De Mel	0
Extras	(LB 19, W 1, NB 1)	21
Total	(44.5 overs)	**212**

Fall of wickets: 1-109, 2-122, 3-122, 4-147, 5-170, 6-203, 7-206, 8-211, 9-211, 10-212.

SRI LANKA	*O*	*M*	*R*	*W*
De Mel	8.5	0	14	2
Ranasinghe	9	0	37	0
Warnapura	9	0	42	1
D.S. De Silva	9	0	54	1
G.R.A. De Silva	9	1	44	2

Umpires: K.T. Francis and P.W. Vidanagamage.

NEW ZEALAND v AUSTRALIA 1981-82 (1st Match)

Rothmans Cup

At Eden Park, Auckland on 13 February 1982.
Toss: Australia. Result: NEW ZEALAND won by 46 runs.
50 overs match. Award: G.S. Chappell.
Début: New Zealand – M.D. Crowe.

NEW ZEALAND		
J.G. Wright	run out	18
B.A. Edgar	b Pascoe	79
J.F. Reid	c Alderman b Chappell	20
G.P. Howarth*	c Marsh b Lillee	34
J.V. Coney	run out	45
R.J. Hadlee	b Alderman	11
B.L. Cairns	not out	18
M.D. Crowe		
I.D.S. Smith†		
M.C. Snedden		
G.B. Troup		
Extras	(LB 13, W 1, NB 1)	15
Total	(50 overs – 6 wickets)	**240**

Fall of wickets: 1-28, 2-89, 3-148, 4-184, 5-210, 6-240.

AUSTRALIA	*O*	*M*	*R*	*W*
Thomson	10	2	36	0
Alderman	10	3	41	1
Pascoe	10	0	35	1
Chappell	10	0	57	1
Lillee	10	0	56	1

AUSTRALIA		
G.M. Wood	run out	1
B.M. Laird	c Crowe b Cairns	11
J. Dyson	c Crowe b Troup	32
G.S. Chappell*	c Howarth b Troup	108
K.J. Hughes	c Crowe b Coney	16
A.R. Border	b Crowe	6
R.W. Marsh†	b Troup	1
J.R. Thomson	c Snedden b Troup	0
D.K. Lillee	c Wright b Crowe	1
L.S. Pascoe	not out	2
T.M. Alderman	b Snedden	1
Extras	(B 4, LB 9, NB 2)	15
Total	(44.5 overs)	**194**

Fall of wickets: 1-1, 2-21, 3-109, 4-144, 5-182, 6-187, 7-189, 8-190, 9-192, 10-194.

NEW ZEALAND	*O*	*M*	*R*	*W*
Cairns	10	1	31	1
Hadlee	8	3	15	0
Snedden	7.5	1	35	1
Coney	7	0	45	1
Troup	10	1	44	4
Crowe	2	0	9	2

Umpires: B.A. Bricknell and J.B.R. Hastie.

Match No. 147/13

NEW ZEALAND v AUSTRALIA 1981-82 (2nd Match)

Rothmans Cup

At Carisbrook, Dunedin on 17 February 1982.
Toss: Australia. Result: AUSTRALIA won by 6 wickets.
49 overs match. Award: A.R. Border.
Début: New Zealand – B.R. Blair.

NEW ZEALAND		
B.A. Edgar	lbw b Alderman	3
J.G. Wright	b Lillee	5
M.D. Crowe	c Hughes b Alderman	3
G.P. Howarth*	c Chappell b Thomson	12
J.V. Coney	b Alderman	54
B.R. Blair	c Laird b Lillee	29
R.J. Hadlee	b Lillee	7
I.D.S. Smith†	not out	14
B.L. Cairns	c Dyson b Pascoe	3
M.C. Snedden	run out	3
E.J. Chatfield	not out	2
Extras	(LB 11, W 1, NB 12)	24
Total	(49 overs – 9 wickets)	**159**

Fall of wickets: 1-14, 2-26, 3-27, 4-39, 5-124, 6-132, 7-136, 8-143, 9-150.

AUSTRALIA	*O*	*M*	*R*	*W*
Thomson	10	1	30	1
Alderman	10	3	22	3
Lillee	10	3	24	3
Chappell	10	1	30	0
Pascoe	9	0	29	1

AUSTRALIA		
G.M. Wood	b Chatfield	4
B.M. Laird	not out	71
J. Dyson	c Smith b Cairns	18
G.S. Chappell*	c Howarth b Hadlee	0
K.J. Hughes	b Hadlee	5
A.R. Border	not out	53
R.W. Marsh†		
D.K. Lillee		
J.R. Thomson		
L.S. Pascoe		
T.M. Alderman		
Extras	(LB 8, NB 1)	9
Total	(45 overs – 4 wickets)	**160**

Fall of wickets: 1-12, 2-37, 3-39, 4-45.

NEW ZEALAND	*O*	*M*	*R*	*W*
Chatfield	10	1	30	1
Hadlee	9	3	24	2
Snedden	9	1	41	0
Coney	9	1	32	0
Cairns	8	1	24	1

Umpires: F.R. Goodall and D.A. Kinsella.

NEW ZEALAND v AUSTRALIA 1981-82 (3rd Match)

Rothmans Cup

At Basin Reserve, Wellington on 20 February 1982.
Toss: Australia. Result: AUSTRALIA won by 8 wickets.
50 overs match. Award: T.M. Alderman.
No débuts.

New Zealand's total remains their lowest in these matches.

NEW ZEALAND		
J.G. Wright	c Alderman b Thomson	0
B.A. Edgar	b Alderman	11
M.D. Crowe	c Laird b Alderman	7
G.P. Howarth*	b Alderman	7
J.V. Coney	c Hughes b Lillee	3
B.R. Blair	lbw b Alderman	2
I.D.S. Smith†	c Border b Alderman	0
R.J. Hadlee	c Hughes b Lillee	18
B.L. Cairns	c Alderman b Pascoe	14
M.C. Snedden	b Lillee	1
G.B. Troup	not out	2
Extras	(LB 6, W 1, NB 2)	9
Total	(29 overs)	**74**

Fall of wickets: 1-0, 2-20, 3-23, 4-30, 5-32, 6-35, 7-37, 8-71, 9-71, 10-74.

AUSTRALIA	*O*	*M*	*R*	*W*
Thomson	5	1	11	1
Alderman	10	2	17	5
Lillee	10	3	14	3
Pascoe	4	1	23	1

AUSTRALIA		
B.M. Laird	lbw b Hadlee	10
R.W. Marsh†	b Cairns	3
J. Dyson	not out	26
G.S. Chappell*	not out	24
K.J. Hughes		
G.M. Wood		
A.R. Border		
J.R. Thomson		
D.K. Lillee		
L.S. Pascoe		
T.M. Alderman		
Extras	(LB 5, W 2, NB 5)	12
Total	(20.3 overs – 2 wickets)	**75**

Fall of wickets: 1-4, 2-28.

NEW ZEALAND	*O*	*M*	*R*	*W*
Hadlee	8.3	2	25	1
Cairns	4	1	12	1
Troup	6	1	23	0
Snedden	2	1	3	0

Umpires: F.R. Goodall and S.J. Woodward.

Match No. 149/2

PAKISTAN v SRI LANKA 1981-82 (1st Match)

Wills Series

At National Stadium, Karachi on 12 March 1982.

Toss: Pakistan. Result: PAKISTAN won by 8 wickets.

33 overs match. Award: Mohsin Khan.

Débuts: Pakistan – Jalaluddin, Salim Yousuf; Sri Lanka – J.R. Ratnayeke, R.G.C.E. Wijesuriya.

SRI LANKA		
B. Warnapura*	b Iqbal Qasim	77
S. Wettimuny	b Jalaluddin	2
R.L. Dias	c and b Tahir	57
L.R.D. Mendis	not out	5
A. Ranatunga	not out	15
R.S. Madugalle		
D.S. De Silva		
A.L.F. De Mel		
R.S.A. Jayasekera†		
J.R. Ratnayeke		
R.G.C.E. Wijesuriya		
Extras	(B 10, LB 1, W 1, NB 3)	15
Total	(33 overs – 3 wickets)	**171**

Fall of wickets 1-5, 2-144, 3-151.

PAKISTAN	*O*	*M*	*R*	*W*
Tahir Naqqash	6	0	19	1
Rashid Khan	8	0	40	0
Iqbal Qasim	5	0	32	1
Jalaluddin	5	1	14	1
Wasim Raja	5	0	29	0
Javed Miandad	4	0	22	0

PAKISTAN		
Mansoor Akhtar	b Wijesuriya	20
Mohsin Khan	c Mendis b Ratnayeke	85
Javed Miandad*	not out	56
Wasim Raja	not out	0
Salim Malik		
Haroon Rashid		
Tahir Naqqash		
Rashid Khan		
Iqbal Qasim		
Salim Yousuf†		
Jalaluddin		
Extras	(B 3, LB 5, W 2, NB 3)	13
Total	(29.2 overs – 2 wickets)	**174**

Fall of wickets 1-52, 2-157.

SRI LANKA	*O*	*M*	*R*	*W*
De Mel	6	2	28	0
Ratnayeke	6.2	0	40	1
Wijesuriya	8	0	48	1
De Silva	6	0	30	0
Ranatunga	3	0	15	0

Umpires: Shakil Khan and Tariq Atta.

PAKISTAN v SRI LANKA 1981-82 (2nd Match)
Wills Series

At Gaddafi Stadium, Lahore on 29 March 1982.
Toss: Sri Lanka. Result: SRI LANKA won on scoring rate.
40 overs match. Award: R.L. Dias.
No débuts.

Sri Lanka scored 21 runs off the last two overs before bad light ended play to win on average runs per over (6.87 against Pakistan's 5.97).

PAKISTAN		
Mudassar Nazar	b De Silva	27
Mohsin Khan	run out	6
Zaheer Abbas	c Madugalle b Ratnayeke	123
Javed Miandad*	run out	1
Haroon Rashid	not out	63
Imran Khan	not out	9
Mansoor Akhtar		
Ashraf Ali†		
Tahir Naqqash		
Rashid Khan		
Sikander Bakht		
Extras	(LB 2, W 8)	10
Total	(40 overs – 4 wickets)	**239**

Fall of wickets 1-14, 2-86, 3-92, 4-215

SRI LANKA	*O*	*M*	*R*	*W*
De Mel	8	1	31	0
Ratnayeke	8	1	42	1
Ranasinghe	6	0	33	0
Warnapura	2	0	21	0
De Silva	8	0	49	1
Ranatunga	8	0	53	0

SRI LANKA		
B. Warnapura*	c Miandad b Sikander	5
S. Wettimuny	c Ashraf b Mudassar	32
R.L. Dias	c Imran b Mudassar	81
L.R.D. Mendis	b Tahir	52
R.S. Madugalle	not out	36
A. Ranatunga	not out	5
D.S. De Silva		
H.M. Goonatillake†		
A.L.F. De Mel		
J.R. Ratnayeke		
A.N. Ranasinghe		
Extras	(LB 7, W 7, NB 2)	16
Total	(33 overs – 4 wickets)	**227**

Fall of wickets 1-10, 2-87, 3-160, 4-185.

PAKISTAN	*O*	*M*	*R*	*W*
Imran Khan	5	1	20	0
Sikander Bakht	5	1	15	1
Tahir Naqqash	8	0	65	1
Mudassar Nazar	8	0	56	2
Rashid Khan	7	0	55	0

Umpires: Mian Mohammad Aslam and Rab Nawaz.

Match No. 151/4

PAKISTAN v SRI LANKA 1981-82 (3rd Match)

Wills Series

At National Stadium, Karachi on 31 March 1982.
Toss: Pakistan. Result: PAKISTAN won by 5 wickets.
40 overs match. Award: Mudassar Nazar.
Début: Pakistan – Tausif Ahmed.

SRI LANKA		
S. Wettimuny	c Mansoor b Mudassar	27
H.M. Goonatillake†	c Imran b Sikander	5
R.L. Dias	b Mudassar	49
L.R.D. Mendis*	b Tausif	44
R.S. Madugalle	st Salim b Wasim Raja	46
A. Ranatunga	b Imran	6
A.N. Ranasinghe	c and b Imran	24
A.L.F. De Mel	run out	5
D.S. De Silva	run out	2
J.R. Ratnayeke	not out	0
G.R.A. De Silva	b Sikander	1
Extras	(LB 4, W 5)	9
Total	(38.3 overs)	**218**

Fall of wickets: 1-7, 2-54, 3-113, 4-147, 5-170, 6-198, 7-211, 8-213, 9-214, 10-218

PAKISTAN	*O*	*M*	*R*	*W*
Imran Khan	7	1	10	2
Sikander Bakht	5.3	0	34	2
Rashid Khan	4	0	37	0
Mudassar Nazar	8	0	42	2
Tausif Ahmed	8	0	41	1
Wasim Raja	6	0	45	1

PAKISTAN		
Mudassar Nazar	c sub (J.B.N. Perera) b Ranatunga	79
Mohsin Khan	c Madugalle b Ranasinghe	36
Zaheer Abbas*	b G.R.A. De Silva	1
Mansoor Akhtar	st Goonatillake b G.R.A. De Silva	31
Haroon Rashid	c and b G.R.A. De Silva	4
Wasim Raja	not out	41
Imran Khan	not out	15
Salim Yousuf†		
Rashid Khan		
Tausif Ahmed		
Sikander Bakht		
Extras	(LB 10, W 2, NB 3)	15
Total	(38.1 overs – 5 wickets)	**222**

Fall of wickets: 1-90, 2-91, 3-154, 4-162, 5-170.

SRI LANKA	*O*	*M*	*R*	*W*
De Mel	7	0	35	0
Ratnayeke	4.1	0	34	0
Ranasinghe	8	1	27	1
D.S. De Silva	4	0	34	0
Ranatunga	7	0	36	1
G.R.A. De Silva	8	0	41	3

Umpires: Ghafoor Butt and Shakil Khan.

ENGLAND v INDIA 1982 (1st Match)

Prudential Trophy

At Headingley, Leeds on 2 June 1982.
Toss: England. Result: ENGLAND won by 9 wickets.
55 overs match. Award: B. Wood.

Débuts: England – A.J. Lamb; India – G.A. Parkar.

INDIA		
S.M. Gavaskar*	c Botham b Allott	38
G.A. Parkar	c Tavaré b Willis	10
D.B. Vengsarkar	c Taylor b Botham	5
G.R. Viswanath	b Botham	9
S.M. Patil	c Taylor b Botham	0
Yashpal Sharma	c Taylor b Allott	20
R.J. Shastri	run out	18
Kapil Dev	run out	60
S.M.H. Kirmani†	c Taylor b Botham	11
S.V. Nayak	c Tavaré b Willis	3
Madan Lal	not out	1
Extras	(B 4, LB 9, W 1, NB 4)	18
Total	(55 overs)	**193**

Fall of wickets 1-30, 2-54, 3-58, 4-59, 5-68, 6-113, 7-114, 8-154, 9-192, 10-193.

ENGLAND	*O*	*M*	*R*	*W*
Willis	11	0	32	2
Dilley	5	1	20	0
Allott	11	4	21	2
Botham	11	0	56	4
Wood	7	2	17	0
Miller	10	0	29	0

ENGLAND		
B. Wood	not out	78
C.J. Tavaré	lbw b Madan Lal	66
A.J. Lamb	not out	35
D.I. Gower		
I.T. Botham		
D.W. Randall		
G. Miller		
G.R. Dilley		
R.W. Taylor†		
P.J.W. Allott		
R.G.D. Willis*		
Extras	(B 1, LB 7, W 3, NB 4)	15
Total	(50.1 overs – 1 wicket)	**194**

Fall of wicket 1-133.

INDIA	*O*	*M*	*R*	*W*
Kapil Dev	9	2	21	0
Madan Lal	9	3	21	1
Nayak	9	0	37	0
Shastri	11	0	37	0
Patil	7	0	29	0
Yashpal Sharma	5.1	0	34	0

Umpires: D.J. Constant and D.O. Oslear.

Match No. 153/8

ENGLAND v INDIA 1982 (2nd Match)

Prudential Trophy

At Kennington Oval, London on 4 June 1982.
Toss: India. Result: ENGLAND won by 114 runs.
55 overs match. Award: A.J. Lamb.
No débuts.

ENGLAND		
B. Wood	b Patil	15
C.J. Tavaré	b Patil	27
A.J. Lamb	c and b Madan Lal	99
D.I. Gower	c Vengsarkar b Yashpal	76
I.T. Botham	run out	4
D.W. Randall	run out	24
G. Miller	run out	0
G.R. Dilley	c Yashpal b Madan Lal	1
R.W. Taylor†	not out	3
P.J.W. Allott	run out	5
R.G.D. Willis*		
Extras	(B 3, LB 10, W 6, NB 3)	22
Total	(55 overs – 9 wickets)	**276**

Fall of wickets: 1-43, 2-53, 3-212, 4-218, 5-260, 6-260, 7-267, 8-268, 9-276.

INDIA	*O*	*M*	*R*	*W*
Kapil Dev	11	1	39	0
Madan Lal	11	0	50	2
Nayak	11	1	48	0
Patil	11	0	37	2
Yashpal Sharma	3	0	27	1
Shastri	8	0	53	0

INDIA		
S.M. Gavaskar*	c Willis b Miller	15
G.A. Parkar	c Botham b Willis	2
D.B. Vengsarkar	c Taylor b Dilley	15
Yashpal Sharma	lbw b Allott	2
A. Malhotra	b Botham	4
S.M. Patil	b Miller	1
Kapil Dev	c Gower b Wood	47
S.M.H. Kirmani†	c Botham b Miller	8
Madan Lal	not out	53
R.J. Shastri	not out	9
S.V. Nayak		
Extras	(B 1, LB 3, W 2)	6
Total	(55 overs – 8 wickets)	**162**

Fall of wickets: 1-5, 2-28, 3-36, 4-42, 5-42, 6-43, 7-66, 8-131.

ENGLAND	*O*	*M*	*R*	*W*
Willis	7	2	10	1
Dilley	7	1	19	1
Botham	9	2	22	1
Allott	8	3	24	1
Miller	11	3	27	3
Wood	11	0	51	1
Tavaré	2	0	3	0

Umpires: D.G.L. Evans and B.J. Meyer.

ENGLAND v PAKISTAN 1982 (1st Match)
Prudential Trophy

At Trent Bridge, Nottingham on 17 July 1982.
Toss: Pakistan. Result: ENGLAND won by 7 wickets.
55 overs match. Award: A.J. Lamb.
Débuts: England – E.E. Hemmings, D.R. Pringle.

Derek Pringle, son of Donald who represented East Africa in the 1975 Prudential World Cup, provided the first instance of two generations of a family appearing in one-day internationals.

PAKISTAN		
Mudassar Nazar	run out	51
Mohsin Khan	b Botham	47
Zaheer Abbas	lbw b Pringle	53
Javed Miandad	c Willis b Pringle	28
Majid Khan	c Willis b Botham	23
Wasim Raja	c Hemmings b Botham	14
Imran Khan*	not out	16
Sarfraz Nawaz	not out	2
Wasim Bari†		
Iqbal Qasim		
Sikander Bakht		
Extras	(B 4, LB 4, W 6, NB 2)	16
Total	(55 overs – 6 wickets)	**250**

Fall of wickets: 1-102, 2-103, 3-175, 4-208, 5-222, 6-238.

ENGLAND	*O*	*M*	*R*	*W*
Willis	11	1	46	0
Botham	11	0	57	3
Pringle	11	1	50	2
Miller	11	1	36	0
Hemmings	11	1	45	0

ENGLAND		
D.I. Gower	c Wasim Bari b Sikander	17
C.J. Tavaré	b Imran	48
A.J. Lamb	c Wasim Bari b Imran	118
M.W. Gatting	not out	37
I.T. Botham	not out	10
D.W. Randall		
G. Miller		
D.R. Pringle		
E.E. Hemmings		
R.W. Taylor†		
R.G.D. Willis*		
Extras	(LB 12, W 5, NB 5)	22
Total	(47.1 overs – 3 wickets)	**252**

Fall of wickets: 1-25, 2-132, 3-234.

PAKISTAN	*O*	*M*	*R*	*W*
Imran Khan	11	2	35	2
Sarfraz Nawaz	11	3	43	0
Sikander Bakht	7	0	34	1
Iqbal Qasim	7	0	49	0
Mudassar Nazar	5.1	0	26	0
Majid Khan	4	0	25	0
Wasim Raja	2	0	18	0

Umpires: D.G.L. Evans and A.G.T. Whitehead.

Match No. 155/10

ENGLAND v PAKISTAN 1982 (2nd Match)

Prudential Trophy

At Old Trafford, Manchester on 19 July 1982.

Toss: Pakistan.	Result: ENGLAND won by 73 runs.
55 overs match.	Award: M.W. Gatting.

No débuts.

Botham scored 49 off 28 balls, hitting four sixes and adding 84 in 27 minutes off 10.4 overs with Gatting.

ENGLAND		
D.I. Gower	c Wasim Bari b Mudassar	33
C.J. Tavaré	run out	16
A.J. Lamb	c Wasim Bari b Iqbal Qasim	27
M.W. Gatting	run out	76
I.T. Botham	c Wasim Raja b Imran	49
D.W. Randall	run out	6
G. Miller	b Imran	26
D.R. Pringle	not out	34
E.E. Hemmings	c Iqbal Qasim b Tahir	1
R.W. Taylor†	not out	1
R.G.D. Willis*		
Extras	(LB 16, W 10)	26
Total	(55 overs – 8 wickets)	**295**

Fall of wickets: 1-32, 2-54, 3-101, 4-185, 5-217, 6-226, 7-280, 8-284

PAKISTAN	*O*	*M*	*R*	*W*
Imran Khan	11	1	48	2
Tahir Naqqash	10	0	37	1
Sikander Bakht	11	0	42	0
Mudassar Nazar	11	0	50	1
Iqbal Qasim	8	0	76	1
Majid Khan	4	1	16	0

PAKISTAN		
Mudassar Nazar	run out	31
Mohsin Khan	b Pringle	17
Zaheer Abbas	c Randall b Pringle	13
Mansoor Akhtar	run out	28
Majid Khan	b Miller	5
Wasim Raja	c Botham b Willis	60
Imran Khan*	c Gower b Miller	31
Tahir Naqqash	run out	1
Wasim Bari†	b Hemmings	4
Iqbal Qasim	lbw b Botham	13
Sikander Bakht	not out	2
Extras	(LB 14, W 2, NB 1)	17
Total	(49.4 overs)	**222**

Fall of wickets: 1-52, 2-55, 3-82, 4-97, 5-123, 6-183, 7-200, 8-201, 9-213, 10-222.

ENGLAND	*O*	*M*	*R*	*W*
Willis	8	0	36	1
Botham	8.4	0	40	1
Miller	11	1	56	2
Pringle	11	0	43	2
Hemmings	11	3	30	1

Umpires: H.D. Bird and D.J. Constant.

INDIA v SRI LANKA 1982-83 (1st Match)

At Gandhi Ground, Amritsar on 12 September 1982.
Toss: Sri Lanka. Result: INDIA won by 78 runs.
46 overs match. Award: D.R. Doshi.
Début: Sri Lanka – V.B. John.

INDIA		
R.M.H. Binny	lbw b De Mel	16
K. Srikkanth	c John b Warnapura	57
D.B. Vengsarkar	c Ratnayeke b De Silva	23
A. Malhotra	b Warnapura	40
S.M. Patil	lbw b Ranasinghe	15
Kapil Dev*	st Goonatillake b De Silva	49
Yashpal Sharma	not out	37
M. Amarnath	c Wettimuny b John	13
S.M.H. Kirmani†		
Madan Lal		
D.R. Doshi		
Extras	(LB 4, W 11, NB 4)	19
Total	(46 overs – 7 wickets)	**269**

Fall of wickets 1-62, 2-95, 3-129, 4-162, 5-173, 6-241, 7-269.

SRI LANKA	*O*	*M*	*R*	*W*
De Mel	7	0	58	1
John	9	1	44	1
Ratnayeke	7	1	37	0
Warnapura	10	1	41	2
De Silva	10	0	49	2
Ranasinghe	3	0	21	1

SRI LANKA		
B. Warnapura*	b Madan Lal	0
S. Wettimuny	b Amarnath	43
R.L. Dias	c Yashpal b Doshi	39
L.R.D. Mendis	c Kapil Dev b Doshi	33
R.S. Madugalle	c Madan Lal b Doshi	1
A.N. Ranasinghe	c Binny b Amarnath	35
A.L.F. De Mel	c Madan Lal b Doshi	1
D.S. De Silva	b Kapil Dev	9
H.M. Goonatillake†	not out	14
J.R. Ratnayeke	not out	6
V.B. John		
Extras	(B 1, LB 5, W 2, NB 2)	10
Total	(46 overs – 8 wickets)	**191**

Fall of wickets 1-8, 2-67, 3-95, 4-98, 5-155, 6-158, 7-166, 8-175.

INDIA	*O*	*M*	*R*	*W*
Kapil Dev	8	6	9	1
Madan Lal	8	2	24	1
Binny	6	0	33	0
Doshi	10	0	44	4
Amarnath	9	0	50	2
Patil	3	0	17	0
Vengsarkar	1	0	4	0
Malhotra	1	1	0	0

Umpires: R. Mehra and P.R. Punjabi.

Match No. 157/3

INDIA v SRI LANKA 1982-83 (2nd Match)

At Feroz Shah Kotla, Delhi on 15 September 1982.
Toss: Sri Lanka. Result: INDIA won by 6 wickets.
50 overs match. Award: K. Srikkanth.
No débuts.

Dias scored Sri Lanka's first century at this level. His partnership of 170 with Wettimuny remains the national record for any wicket.

SRI LANKA		
B. Warnapura*	lbw b Kapil Dev	4
S. Wettimuny	c Srikkanth b Binny	74
R.L. Dias	c Doshi b Binny	102
L.R.D. Mendis	c Srikkanth b Binny	10
A.N. Ranasinghe	b Kapil Dev	20
J.R. Ratnayeke	st Kirmani b Madan Lal	2
R.S. Madugalle	c Kirmani b Madan Lal	7
A.L.F. De Mel	run out	28
H.M. Goonatillake†	not out	4
G.R.A. De Silva	not out	6
V.B. John		
Extras	(B 2, LB 18)	20
Total	(50 overs – 8 wickets)	**277**

Fall of wickets: 1-10, 2-180, 3-198, 4-218, 5-229, 6-229, 7-240, 8-269.

INDIA	*O*	*M*	*R*	*W*
Kapil Dev	10	0	41	2
Madan Lal	10	0	51	2
Binny	7	0	39	3
Patil	4	0	24	0
Amarnath	10	0	52	0
Doshi	5	0	34	0
Yashpal Sharma	4	0	16	0

INDIA		
R.M.H. Binny	lbw b John	10
K. Srikkanth	c Mendis b Warnapura	95
D.B. Vengsarkar	c Warnapura b Ratnayeke	53
A. Malhotra	not out	44
S.M. Patil	c Dias b De Silva	64
Kapil Dev*	not out	1
M. Amarnath		
Yashpal Sharma		
Madan Lal		
S.M.H. Kirmani†		
D.R. Doshi		
Extras	(B 5, LB 8, NB 1)	14
Total	(40.5 overs – 4 wickets)	**281**

Fall of wickets: 1-26, 2-160, 3-168, 4-278.

SRI LANKA	*O*	*M*	*R*	*W*
De Mel	2	0	23	0
John	5	0	44	1
Ratnayeke	8	0	48	1
De Silva	5.5	0	36	1
Ranasinghe	10	0	78	0
Warnapura	10	1	38	1

Umpires: B. Ganguli and S.N. Hanumantha Rao.

INDIA v SRI LANKA 1982-83 (3rd Match)

At Karnataka State CA Ground, Bangalore on 26 September 1982.
Toss: Sri Lanka. Result: INDIA won by 6 wickets.
50 overs match. Award: K. Srikkanth.
Début: Sri Lanka – R.J. Ratnayake.

Dias completed his second hundred in successive innings in these matches. No other Sri Lankan has reached three figures in one-day internationals.

SRI LANKA		
B. Warnapura*	lbw b Kapil Dev	1
S. Wettimuny	lbw b Binny	18
R.L. Dias	c Doshi b Kapil Dev	121
L.R.D. Mendis	b Doshi	23
R.S. Madugalle	run out	18
A.L.F. De Mel	b Doshi	25
J.R. Ratnayeke	b Madan Lal	1
D.S. De Silva	lbw b Madan Lal	3
H.M. Goonatillake†	not out	8
R.J. Ratnayake	not out	6
V.B. John		
Extras	(B 1, LB 3, NB 5)	9
Total	(50 overs – 8 wickets)	**233**

Fall of wickets 1-2, 2-48, 3-106, 4-157, 5-193, 6-198, 7-208, 8-222.

INDIA	*O*	*M*	*R*	*W*
Kapil Dev	10	2	41	2
Madan Lal	10	0	41	2
Amarnath	10	0	53	0
Binny	10	0	54	1
Doshi	10	0	35	2

INDIA		
R.M.H. Binny	run out	15
K. Srikkanth	b De Silva	92
D.B. Vengsarkar	c Dias b De Mel	42
A. Malhotra	not out	27
Kapil Dev*	c Ratnayeke b De Mel	15
Yashpal Sharma	not out	30
Madan Lal		
M. Amarnath		
S.M. Patil		
S.M.H. Kirmani†		
D.R. Doshi		
Extras	(B 7, LB 1, W 3, NB 2)	13
Total	(39.2 overs – 4 wickets)	**234**

Fall of wickets 1-34, 2-153, 3-160, 4-177.

SRI LANKA	*O*	*M*	*R*	*W*
De Mel	8	1	58	2
John	9	0	33	0
Warnapura	2	0	15	0
Ratnayake	7	0	38	0
Ratnayeke	3	0	25	0
De Silva	10	1	51	1
Dias	0.2	0	1	0

Umpires: D.N. Dotiwalla and K.B. Ramaswami.

Match No. 159/8

PAKISTAN v AUSTRALIA 1982-83 (1st Match)

Wills Series

At Niaz Stadium, Hyderabad on 20 September 1982.
Toss: Australia. Result: PAKISTAN won by 59 runs.
40 overs match. Award: Mohsin Khan.

No débuts.

Jalaluddin took the first hat-trick in one-day internationals when he dismissed Marsh, Yardley and Lawson with the fourth, fifth and sixth balls of his seventh over.

PAKISTAN		
Mudassar Nazar	c Marsh b Alderman	28
Mohsin Khan	c Dyson b Lawson	104
Zaheer Abbas*	c Wood b Yardley	26
Javed Miandad	not out	31
Mansoor Akhtar	c Laird b Thomson	8
Haroon Rashid	b Callen	4
Tahir Naqqash	c and b Alderman	8
Wasim Bari†	not out	5
Sikander Bakht		
Jalaluddin		
Tausif Ahmed		
Extras	(B 1, LB 6, NB 8)	15
Total	(40 overs – 6 wickets)	**229**
Fall of wickets	1-82, 2-160, 3-169, 4-180, 5-191, 6-202.	

AUSTRALIA	*O*	*M*	*R*	*W*
Lawson	8	0	29	1
Alderman	8	0	63	2
Callen	8	0	32	1
Thomson	8	0	48	1
Yardley	8	1	42	1

AUSTRALIA		
B.M. Laird	b Tausif	44
G.M. Wood	c Jalaluddin b Tausif	52
K.J. Hughes*	c Haroon b Tausif	2
A.R. Border	c Wasim Bari b Jalaluddin	24
J. Dyson	not out	30
R.W. Marsh†	b Jalaluddin	1
B. Yardley	c Wasim Bari b Jalaluddin	0
G.F. Lawson	b Jalaluddin	0
I.W. Callen	b Sikander	0
J.R. Thomson	c Zaheer b Mohsin	1
T.M. Alderman	not out	1
Extras	(LB 6, W 8, NB 1)	15
Total	(40 overs – 9 wickets)	**170**
Fall of wickets	1-104, 2-106, 3-109, 4-157, 5-162, 6-162, 7-162, 8-164, 9-169.	

PAKISTAN	*O*	*M*	*R*	*W*
Sikander Bakht	7	0	24	1
Tahir Naqqash	7	0	20	0
Jalaluddin	8	1	32	4
Mudassar Nazar	8	0	38	0
Tausif Ahmed	8	0	38	3
Mohsin Khan	1	0	2	1
Mansoor Akhtar	1	0	1	0

Umpires: Khizer Hayat and Mahboob Shah.

PAKISTAN v AUSTRALIA 1982-83 (2nd Match)
Wills Series

At Gaddafi Stadium, Lahore on 8 October 1982.
Toss: Australia. Result: PAKISTAN won by 28 runs.
40 overs match. Award: Zaheer Abbas.
Début: Australia – G.M. Ritchie.

PAKISTAN		
Mohsin Khan	run out	17
Mudassar Nazar	lbw b Thomson	7
Zaheer Abbas	st Marsh b Border	109
Javed Miandad	not out	61
Imran Khan*	not out	29
Mansoor Akhtar		
Haroon Rashid		
Wasim Bari†		
Tahir Naqqash		
Jalaluddin		
Tausif Ahmed		
Extras	(B 1, LB 6, W 1, NB 3)	11
Total	(40 overs – 3 wickets)	**234**

Fall of wickets 1-17, 2-52, 3-171.

AUSTRALIA	*O*	*M*	*R*	*W*
Thomson	8	0	41	1
Lawson	8	0	47	0
Alderman	8	1	29	0
Callen	8	1	50	0
Border	8	1	56	1

AUSTRALIA		
B.M. Laird	not out	91
G.M. Wood	b Jalaluddin	21
J. Dyson	c Imran b Jalaluddin	11
A.R. Border	b Tausif	0
K.J. Hughes*	c Mudassar b Imran	64
G.M. Ritchie	not out	4
R.W. Marsh†		
T.M. Alderman		
G.F. Lawson		
J.R. Thomson		
I.W. Callen		
Extras	(LB 10, W 4, NB 1)	15
Total	(40 overs – 4 wickets)	**206**

Fall of wickets 1-37, 2-73, 3-73, 4-190.

PAKISTAN	*O*	*M*	*R*	*W*
Imran Khan	8	1	38	1
Tahir Naqqash	8	0	28	0
Jalaluddin	8	1	33	2
Tausif Ahmed	8	0	40	1
Mudassar Nazar	6	0	40	0
Zaheer Abbas	2	0	12	0

Umpires: Amanullah Khan and Shakoor Rana.

Match No. 161/10

PAKISTAN v AUSTRALIA 1982-83 (3rd Match)
Wills Series

At National Stadium, Karachi on 22 October 1982.
Toss: Australia. No result.
40 overs match. No award.
Début: Australia – W.B. Phillips.

The final match of the Australians' tour was abandoned after three of the tourists had been struck by missiles thrown by spectators.

PAKISTAN		
Mohsin Khan	not out	25
Mudassar Nazar	b Alderman	8
Zaheer Abbas	not out	5
Javed Miandad		
Mansoor Akhtar		
Imran Khan*		
Wasim Raja		
Wasim Bari†		
Tahir Naqqash		
Jalaluddin		
Tausif Ahmed		
Extras	(B 1, LB 2, W 2, NB 1)	6
Total	(12 overs – 1 wicket)	**44**

Fall of wicket 1-23.

AUSTRALIA	*O*	*M*	*R*	*W*
Thomson	4	2	9	0
Lawson	2	0	7	0
Alderman	6	2	22	1

AUSTRALIA
W.B. Phillips
G.M. Wood
J. Dyson
A.R. Border
K.J. Hughes*
G.M. Ritchie
R.W. Marsh†
T.M. Alderman
G.F. Lawson
J.R. Thomson
I.W. Callen

Umpires: Amanullah Khan and Shakoor Rana.

PAKISTAN v INDIA 1982-83 (1st Match)
Wills Series

At Municipal Stadium, Gujranwala on 3 December 1982.
Toss: India. Result: PAKISTAN won by 14 runs.
40 overs match. Award: Javed Miandad.
Début: India – B.S. Sandhu.

PAKISTAN		
Mohsin Khan	b Madan Lal	5
Mudassar Nazar	run out	20
Zaheer Abbas	c Kapil Dev b Madan Lal	10
Javed Miandad	not out	106
Imran Khan*	b Kapil Dev	49
Mansoor Akhtar	not out	21
Wasim Raja		
Ijaz Faqih		
Tahir Naqqash		
Wasim Bari†		
Jalaluddin		
Extras	(B 1, LB 6, W 6)	13
Total	(40 overs – 4 wickets)	**224**

Fall of wickets 1-5, 2-25, 3-49, 4-160.

INDIA	*O*	*M*	*R*	*W*
Kapil Dev	8	1	42	1
Madan Lal	8	0	39	2
Amarnath	8	1	20	0
Sandhu	8	0	55	0
Shastri	6	0	41	0
Patil	2	0	14	0

INDIA		
S.M. Gavaskar*	lbw b Imran	1
K. Srikkanth	c Wasim Bari b Imran	6
D.B. Vengsarkar	run out	39
M. Amarnath	c Tahir b Jalaluddin	51
S.M. Patil	c Mohsin b Mudassar	4
Kapil Dev	c Mansoor b Jalaluddin	15
Yashpal Sharma	not out	56
S.M.H. Kirmani†	not out	27
Madan Lal		
R.J. Shastri		
B.S. Sandhu		
Extras	(B 1, LB 3, W 5, NB 2)	11
Total	(40 overs – 6 wickets)	**210**

Fall of wickets 1-2, 2-13, 3-84, 4-100, 5-120, 6-121.

PAKISTAN	*O*	*M*	*R*	*W*
Imran Khan	8	0	38	2
Jalaluddin	8	2	36	2
Tahir Naqqash	8	0	31	0
Ijaz Faqih	8	0	38	0
Mudassar Nazar	7	0	50	1
Zaheer Abbas	1	0	6	0

Umpires: Amanullah Khan and Shakil Khan.

Match No. 163/5

PAKISTAN v INDIA 1982-83 (2nd Match)

Wills Series

At Ibn-e-Qasim Bagh Stadium, Multan on 17 December 1982.
Toss: Pakistan. Result: PAKISTAN won by 37 runs.
40 overs match. Award: Zaheer Abbas.
No débuts.

PAKISTAN		
Mohsin Khan	not out	117
Mudassar Nazar	run out	12
Zaheer Abbas	b Kapil Dev	118
Javed Miandad	not out	3
Mansoor Akhtar		
Imran Khan*		
Wasim Raja		
Ijaz Faqih		
Wasim Bari†		
Sikander Bakht		
Jalaluddin		
Extras	(B 1, LB 10, W 2)	13
Total	(40 overs – 2 wickets)	**263**

Fall of wickets 1-41, 2-246.

INDIA	*O*	*M*	*R*	*W*
Kapil Dev	8	0	42	1
Sandhu	8	0	28	0
Amarnath	6	0	46	0
Doshi	8	1	58	0
Yashpal Sharma	6	0	45	0
Shastri	4	0	31	0

INDIA		
K. Srikkanth	b Jalaluddin	8
Arun Lal	b Jalaluddin	6
D.B. Vengsarkar	c Sikander b Zaheer	37
M. Amarnath	c Mansoor b Ijaz	6
S.M. Patil	c Miandad b Zaheer	84
Kapil Dev*	b Mudassar	35
Yashpal Sharma	c and b Mudassar	16
S.M.H. Kirmani†	not out	16
R.J. Shastri	not out	3
B.S. Sandhu		
D.R. Doshi		
Extras	(LB 10, W 3, NB 2)	15
Total	(40 overs – 7 wickets)	**226**

Fall of wickets 1-14, 2-17, 3-34, 4-143, 5-162, 6-190, 7-205.

PAKISTAN	*O*	*M*	*R*	*W*
Imran Khan	8	4	14	0
Jalaluddin	4	0	21	2
Ijaz Faqih	8	0	50	1
Mudassar Nazar	7	0	40	2
Sikander Bakht	8	1	50	0
Zaheer Abbas	4	0	33	2
Mansoor Akhtar	1	0	3	0

Umpires: Khizer Hayat and Shakoor Rana.

PAKISTAN v INDIA 1982-83 (3rd Match)

Wills Series

At Gaddafi Stadium, Lahore on 31 December 1982.
Toss: Pakistan. Result: INDIA won on scoring rate.
33 overs match. Award: Javed Miandad.
Début: Pakistan – Shahid Mahboob.

Zaheer Abbas became the first batsman to score five hundreds in one-day internationals, beating the record set by D.L. Amiss. India were awarded the match on scoring rate over the first 27 overs (7.14 compared with Pakistan's 6.48) when bad light ended play.

PAKISTAN		
Mohsin Khan	c and b Kapil Dev	0
Mudassar Nazar	c and b Shastri	24
Zaheer Abbas	c Srikkanth b Amarnath	105
Javed Miandad	not out	119
Wasim Raja	not out	1
Mansoor Akhtar		
Imran Khan*		
Ijaz Faqih		
Tahir Naqqash		
Wasim Bari†		
Shahid Mahboob		
Extras	(LB 1, W 2)	3
Total	(33 overs – 3 wickets)	**252**

Fall of wickets 1-1, 2-70, 3-228.

INDIA	*O*	*M*	*R*	*W*
Kapil Dev	7	0	73	1
Madan Lal	7	0	35	0
Sandhu	7	0	52	0
Shastri	7	0	39	1
Amarnath	5	0	50	1

INDIA		
S.M. Gavaskar*	c Mansoor b Tahir	69
K. Srikkanth	c Zaheer b Shahid	39
S.M. Patil	c Wasim Raja b Mudassar	51
Kapil Dev	lbw b Mudassar	8
Yashpal Sharma	not out	4
M. Amarnath	not out	1
D.B. Vengsarkar		
S.M.H. Kirmani†		
R.J. Shastri		
Madan Lal		
B.S. Sandhu		
Extras	(LB 8, W 11, NB 2)	21
Total	(27 overs – 4 wickets)	**193**

Fall of wickets 1-57, 2-172, 3-185, 4-192.

PAKISTAN	*O*	*M*	*R*	*W*
Imran Khan	5	2	23	0
Tahir Naqqash	6	0	42	1
Shahid Mahboob	7	0	55	1
Ijaz Faqih	7	0	39	0
Mudassar Nazar	2	0	13	2

Umpires: Khizer Hayat and Shakoor Rana.

Match No. 165/7

PAKISTAN v INDIA 1982-83 (4th Match)

Wills Series

At National Stadium, Karachi on 21 January 1983.
Toss: India. Result: PAKISTAN won by 8 wickets.
40 overs match. Award: Zaheer Abbas.
Débuts: India – Maninder Singh, T.A.P. Sekar.

Zaheer extended his record to six hundreds and became the first batsman to score three in successive innings.

INDIA

K. Srikkanth	c Tahir b Ijaz	48
Arun Lal	b Sarfraz	16
M. Amarnath	b Sarfraz	8
Yashpal Sharma	c Imran b Sarfraz	27
Kapil Dev	c Mansoor b Imran	20
S.M. Gavaskar*	c Wasim Raja b Imran	23
D.B. Vengsarkar	not out	22
S.M.H. Kirmani†	not out	1
B.S. Sandhu		
Maninder Singh		
T.A.P. Sekar		
Extras	(LB 12, W 16, NB 4)	32
Total	(40 overs – 6 wickets)	**197**

Fall of wickets: 1-41, 2-54, 3-120, 4-124, 5-162, 6-192.

PAKISTAN	*O*	*M*	*R*	*W*
Imran Khan	8	3	15	2
Tahir Naqqash	8	1	38	0
Mudassar Nazar	8	1	30	0
Sarfraz Nawaz	8	1	31	3
Ijaz Faqih	8	0	51	1

PAKISTAN

Mohsin Khan	lbw b Sandhu	5
Mudassar Nazar	not out	61
Zaheer Abbas	c Amarnath b Sandhu	113
Javed Miandad	not out	6
Mansoor Akhtar		
Wasim Raja		
Imran Khan*		
Tahir Naqqash		
Ijaz Faqih		
Wasim Bari†		
Sarfraz Nawaz		
Extras	(LB 10, W 3)	13
Total	(35 overs – 2 wickets)	**198**

Fall of wickets: 1-9, 2-179.

INDIA	*O*	*M*	*R*	*W*
Kapil Dev	5	1	11	0
Sandhu	7	0	38	2
Sekar	4	0	19	0
Srikkanth	2	0	27	0
Yashpal Sharma	8	0	39	0
Maninder Singh	8	0	47	0
Gavaskar	1	0	4	0

Umpires: Khizer Hayat and Mahboob Shah.

AUSTRALIA v NEW ZEALAND 1982-83

Benson and Hedges World Series Cup – 1st Match

At Melbourne Cricket Ground on 9 January 1983.
Toss: Australia. Result: AUSTRALIA won by 8 wickets.
50 overs match. Award: J. Dyson.

Débuts: Australia – C.G. Rackemann, K.C. Wessels; New Zealand – J.J. Crowe, P.N. Webb.

NEW ZEALAND		
J.G. Wright	c Dyson b Rackemann	54
B.A. Edgar	lbw b Rackemann	38
G.P. Howarth*	c and b Rackemann	5
J.J. Crowe	c Lawson b Chappell	7
J.V. Coney	c Marsh b Rackemann	4
J.F.M. Morrison	c Marsh b Thomson	10
P.N. Webb†	b Lawson	9
R.J. Hadlee	run out	24
B.L. Cairns	c Hookes b Lawson	7
M.C. Snedden	c Marsh b Hogg	2
E.J. Chatfield	not out	0
Extras	(LB 9, W 7, NB 5)	21
Total	(44.5 overs)	**181**

Fall of wickets: 1-84, 2-89, 3-98, 4-114, 5-128, 6-134, 7-167, 8-173, 9-181, 10-181.

AUSTRALIA	*O*	*M*	*R*	*W*
Lawson	7.5	1	28	2
Thomson	9	1	39	1
Hogg	8	0	32	1
Rackemann	10	1	39	4
Chappell	10	1	22	1

AUSTRALIA		
K.C. Wessels	b Snedden	79
J. Dyson	not out	78
G.S. Chappell	c and b Snedden	3
K.J. Hughes*	not out	7
D.W. Hookes		
A.R. Border		
R.W. Marsh†		
G.F. Lawson		
R.M. Hogg		
J.R. Thomson		
C.G. Rackemann		
Extras	(B 1, LB 11, W 3)	15
Total	(46.4 overs – 2 wickets)	**182**

Fall of wickets: 1-154, 2-168.

NEW ZEALAND	*O*	*M*	*R*	*W*
Hadlee	9.4	2	36	0
Chatfield	10	4	18	0
Snedden	10	1	47	2
Cairns	8	1	30	0
Coney	9	1	36	0

Umpires: A.R. Crafter and R.V. Whitehead.

Match No. 167/24

AUSTRALIA v ENGLAND 1982-83

Benson and Hedges World Series Cup – 2nd Match

At Sydney Cricket Ground on 11 January 1983.
Toss: England. Result: AUSTRALIA won by 31 runs.
50 overs match (floodlit). Award: C.G. Rackemann.
Débuts: England – N.G. Cowans, T.E. Jesty.

AUSTRALIA		
J. Dyson	c Randall b Marks	49
K.C. Wessels	b Cowans	18
G.S. Chappell	c Marks b Botham	3
K.J. Hughes*	c Taylor b Jesty	0
A.R. Border	b Miller	22
D.W. Hookes	b Marks	11
R.W. Marsh†	c Taylor b Miller	7
G.F. Lawson	not out	33
J.R. Thomson	b Miller	8
R.M. Hogg	c and b Cowans	8
C.G. Rackemann	b Willis	0
Extras	(LB 13, W 8)	21
Total	(46.4 overs)	**180**

Fall of wickets: 1-26, 2-33, 3-36, 4-77, 5-118, 6-124, 7-132, 8-158, 9-175, 10-180.

ENGLAND	*O*	*M*	*R*	*W*
Willis	6.4	1	20	1
Cowans	7	0	20	2
Botham	7	1	41	1
Jesty	6	0	23	1
Marks	10	1	27	2
Miller	10	0	28	3

ENGLAND		
D.I. Gower	c Hookes b Thomson	9
C.J. Tavaré	c Border b Rackemann	6
A.J. Lamb	b Thomson	49
D.W. Randall	b Rackemann	5
I.T. Botham	b Rackemann	18
T.E. Jesty	run out	12
G. Miller	lbw b Hogg	2
V.J. Marks	not out	7
R.W. Taylor†	lbw b Chappell	2
R.G.D. Willis*	c Marsh b Chappell	0
N.G. Cowans	b Chappell	4
Extras	(LB 12, W 17, NB 6)	35
Total	(41.1 overs)	**149**

Fall of wickets: 1-11, 2-44, 3-53, 4-95, 5-131, 6-131, 7-135, 8-142, 9-142, 10-149.

AUSTRALIA	*O*	*M*	*R*	*W*
Lawson	8	1	33	0
Thomson	10	4	21	2
Hogg	10	1	15	1
Rackemann	8	1	28	3
Chappell	5.1	0	17	3

Umpires: R.A. French and M.W. Johnson.

ENGLAND v NEW ZEALAND 1982-83

Benson and Hedges World Series Cup – 3rd Match

At Melbourne Cricket Ground on 13 January 1983.
Toss: England. Result: NEW ZEALAND won by 2 runs.
50 overs match. Award: D.I. Gower.
No débuts.

NEW ZEALAND		
J.G. Wright	run out	55
B.A. Edgar	c Randall b Marks	30
B.L. Cairns	c Miller b Botham	36
G.M. Turner	b Miller	38
G.P. Howarth*	c Willis b Botham	13
J.F.M. Morrison	c Randall b Botham	11
R.J. Hadlee	c Botham b Willis	24
J.V. Coney	not out	13
W.K. Lees†	run out	3
M.C. Snedden		
E.J. Chatfield		
Extras	(B 1, LB 10, W 5)	16
Total	(50 overs – 8 wickets)	**239**

Fall of wickets: 1-87, 2-100, 3-137, 4-164, 5-188, 6-205, 7-231, 8-239.

ENGLAND	*O*	*M*	*R*	*W*
Willis	8	1	29	1
Cowans	10	0	50	0
Jesty	3	0	11	0
Botham	10	0	40	3
Marks	9	0	47	1
Miller	10	0	46	1

ENGLAND		
D.I. Gower	c Turner b Hadlee	122
C.J. Tavaré	run out	16
A.J. Lamb	st Lees b Coney	15
T.E. Jesty	c Wright b Coney	5
I.T. Botham	c Chatfield b Snedden	41
D.W. Randall	c Snedden b Coney	8
G. Miller	c Turner b Chatfield	2
V.J. Marks	b Snedden	5
R.W. Taylor†	not out	5
R.G.D. Willis*		
N.G. Cowans		
Extras	(LB 14, W 3, NB 1)	18
Total	(50 overs – 8 wickets)	**237**

Fall of wickets: 1-42, 2-80, 3-92, 4-190, 5-205, 6-221, 7-223, 8-237.

NEW ZEALAND	*O*	*M*	*R*	*W*
Snedden	10	0	34	2
Chatfield	10	0	38	1
Cairns	10	1	64	0
Hadlee	10	1	37	1
Coney	10	0	46	3

Umpires: M.W. Johnson and B.E. Martin.

Match No. 169/10

ENGLAND v NEW ZEALAND 1982-83

Benson and Hedges World Series Cup – 4th Match

At Woolloongabba, Brisbane on 15 January 1983.
Toss: New Zealand. Result: ENGLAND won by 54 runs.
50 overs match. Award: D.I. Gower.

Début: England – I.J. Gould.

Gower's fourth hundred in these matches remains England's record score in one-day internationals.

ENGLAND		
I.J. Gould†	c Howarth b Troup	15
C.J. Tavaré	b Cairns	24
D.I. Gower	c sub (J.J. Crowe) b Snedden	158
A.J. Lamb	c Cairns b Hadlee	13
I.T. Botham	c Webb b Hadlee	0
D.W. Randall	run out	34
T.E. Jesty	not out	4
G. Miller		
V.J. Marks		
R.G.D. Willis*		
N.G. Cowans		
Extras	(LB 9, W 9, NB 1)	19
Total	(50 overs – 6 wickets)	**267**

Fall of wickets: 1-26, 2-89, 3-114, 4-116, 5-229, 6-267.

NEW ZEALAND	*O*	*M*	*R*	*W*
Hadlee	10	1	44	2
Chatfield	10	3	44	0
Snedden	10	0	76	1
Troup	7	1	38	1
Cairns	10	0	29	1
Coney	3	0	17	0

NEW ZEALAND		
J.G. Wright	c Randall b Cowans	30
B.A. Edgar	c Gould b Botham	40
G.P. Howarth*	c Jesty b Marks	13
B.L. Cairns	c Gould b Marks	12
G.M. Turner	c Jesty b Botham	29
J.V. Coney	st Gould b Marks	13
P.N. Webb†	c Cowans b Botham	4
R.J. Hadlee	b Willis	21
M.C. Snedden	run out	0
G.B. Troup	c Botham b Willis	39
E.J. Chatfield	not out	0
Extras	(LB 6, W 6)	12
Total	(48.2 overs)	**213**

Fall of wickets: 1-43, 2-75, 3-100, 4-100, 5-148, 6-148, 7-150, 8-150, 9-213, 10-213.

ENGLAND	*O*	*M*	*R*	*W*
Willis	9.2	1	30	2
Cowans	10	0	52	1
Botham	9	2	47	3
Marks	10	2	30	3
Miller	10	1	42	0

Umpires: R.A. French and B.E. Martin.

AUSTRALIA v ENGLAND 1982-83

Benson and Hedges World Series Cup – 5th Match

At Woolloongabba, Brisbane on 16 January 1983.
Toss: Australia. Result: AUSTRALIA won by 7 wickets.
50 overs match. Award: D.W. Hookes.
No débuts.

ENGLAND		
G. Cook	c Hookes b Lawson	2
I.J. Gould†	run out	2
D.I. Gower	b Hogg	22
A.J. Lamb	c Marsh b Thomson	19
I.T. Botham	c Hookes b Rackemann	29
D.W. Randall	b Lawson	57
T.E. Jesty	c Marsh b Rackemann	0
G. Miller	run out	4
V.J. Marks	b Thomson	3
R.G.D. Willis*	not out	7
N.G. Cowans	c Lawson b Rackemann	0
Extras	(B 4, LB 12, W 13, NB 8)	37
Total	(46.4 overs)	**182**

Fall of wickets 1-2, 2-10, 3-54, 4-71, 5-128, 6-138, 7-143, 8-165, 9-178, 10-182.

AUSTRALIA	*O*	*M*	*R*	*W*
Lawson	10	2	23	2
Thomson	10	0	32	2
Hogg	9	1	29	1
Rackemann	8.4	1	28	3
Chappell	9	1	33	0

AUSTRALIA		
K.C. Wessels	c Gould b Botham	19
J. Dyson	c Marks b Botham	40
G.S. Chappell	c Jesty b Botham	30
D.W. Hookes	not out	54
A.R. Border	not out	30
K.J. Hughes*		
R.W. Marsh†		
G.F. Lawson		
J.R. Thomson		
R.M. Hogg		
C.G. Rackemann		
Extras	(LB 9, W 2)	11
Total	(41 overs – 3 wickets)	**184**

Fall of wickets 1-41, 2-95, 3-98.

ENGLAND	*O*	*M*	*R*	*W*
Willis	7	1	31	0
Cowans	9	1	35	0
Botham	8	1	29	3
Miller	6	0	25	0
Marks	10	0	46	0
Jesty	1	0	7	0

Umpires: M.W. Johnson and P.J. McConnell.

Match No. 171/16

AUSTRALIA v NEW ZEALAND 1982-83

Benson and Hedges World Series Cup – 6th Match

At Sydney Cricket Ground on 18 January 1983.
Toss: Australia. Result: NEW ZEALAND won by 47 runs.
50 overs match (floodlit). Award: D.W. Hookes.
No débuts.

NEW ZEALAND		
J.G. Wright	c Marsh b Hogg	1
B.A. Edgar	b Chappell	32
G.P. Howarth*	c Marsh b Chappell	29
G.M. Turner	b Thomson	55
J.J. Crowe	run out	56
R.J. Hadlee	c Chappell b Thomson	5
J.V. Coney	c Marsh b Lawson	13
B.L. Cairns	c Border b Hogg	2
P.N. Webb†	not out	10
E.J. Chatfield		
M.C. Snedden		
Extras	(B 7, LB 10, W 6)	23
Total	(50 overs – 8 wickets)	**226**

Fall of wickets: 1-7, 2-65, 3-93, 4-159, 5-167, 6-191, 7-194, 8-226.

AUSTRALIA	*O*	*M*	*R*	*W*
Lawson	10	3	33	1
Hogg	10	2	32	2
Thomson	10	0	42	2
Rackemann	10	0	59	0
Chappell	10	0	37	2

AUSTRALIA		
J. Dyson	run out	11
K.C. Wessels	c Cairns b Snedden	58
G.S. Chappell	c Webb b Snedden	1
K.J. Hughes*	c and b Cairns	1
D.W. Hookes	run out	68
A.R. Border	c Hadlee b Cairns	11
R.W. Marsh†	b Cairns	6
G.F. Lawson	run out	0
J.R. Thomson	b Cairns	0
R.M. Hogg	not out	3
C.G. Rackemann	lbw b Hadlee	2
Extras	(B 4, LB 9, W 5)	18
Total	(45.3 overs)	**179**

Fall of wickets: 1-27, 2-28, 3-29, 4-145, 5-163, 6-169, 7-169, 8-169, 9-176, 10-179.

NEW ZEALAND	*O*	*M*	*R*	*W*
Chatfield	10	1	47	0
Hadlee	8.3	2	19	1
Snedden	8	2	24	2
Cairns	10	4	16	4
Coney	9	0	55	0

Umpires: M.W. Johnson and P.J. McConnell.

ENGLAND v NEW ZEALAND 1982-83

Benson and Hedges World Series Cup – 7th Match

At Sydney Cricket Ground on 20 January 1983.
Toss: New Zealand. Result: ENGLAND won by 8 wickets.
50 overs match (floodlit). Award: A.J. Lamb.
Début: England – G. Fowler.

NEW ZEALAND		
J.G. Wright	c Randall b Willis	9
B.A. Edgar	c Willis b Cowans	74
G.P. Howarth*	c Miller b Willis	1
G.M. Turner	c Gower b Marks	37
B.L. Cairns	c Gower b Miller	11
W.K. Lees†	b Botham	12
J.J. Crowe	run out	12
R.J. Hadlee	c Lamb b Willis	15
J.V. Coney	c Miller b Willis	6
M.C. Snedden	not out	2
E.J. Chatfield	lbw b Botham	0
Extras	(LB 17, W 3)	20
Total	(47.2 overs)	**199**

Fall of wickets 1-14, 2-20, 3-101, 4-118, 5-152, 6-171, 7-178, 8-197, 9-197, 10-199.

ENGLAND	*O*	*M*	*R*	*W*
Willis	9	0	23	4
Cowans	10	1	26	1
Botham	8.2	0	30	2
Marks	10	0	49	1
Miller	10	0	51	1

ENGLAND		
C.J. Tavaré	not out	83
G. Fowler	c sub (P.N. Webb) b Chatfield	0
D.I. Gower	b Hadlee	0
A.J. Lamb	not out	108
I.T. Botham		
D.W. Randall		
G. Miller		
I.J. Gould†		
V.J. Marks		
R.G.D. Willis*		
N.G. Cowans		
Extras	(B 1, LB 5, W 3)	9
Total	(42.4 overs – 2 wickets)	**200**

Fall of wickets 1-9, 2-10.

NEW ZEALAND	*O*	*M*	*R*	*W*
Hadlee	9	2	37	1
Chatfield	10	2	25	1
Cairns	8	2	31	0
Snedden	8.4	0	61	0
Coney	7	0	37	0

Umpires: A.R. Crafter and R.A. French.

Match No. 173/17

AUSTRALIA v NEW ZEALAND 1982-83

Benson and Hedges World Series Cup – 8th Match

At Melbourne Cricket Ground on 22 January 1983.
Toss: Australia. Result: NEW ZEALAND won by 58 runs.
50 overs match. Award: J.G. Wright.
No débuts.

NEW ZEALAND		
J.G. Wright	c Dyson b Rackemann	84
B.A. Edgar	c Marsh b Rackemann	32
G.M. Turner	lbw b Thomson	31
R.J. Hadlee	c Wessels b Rackemann	21
G.P. Howarth*	run out	30
J.J. Crowe	not out	20
B.L. Cairns	c Border b Lawson	0
W.K. Lees†	not out	5
E.J. Chatfield		
M.C. Snedden		
G.B. Troup		
Extras	(B 4, LB 13, W 4, NB 2)	23
Total	(50 overs – 6 wickets)	**246**

Fall of wickets: 1-83, 2-151, 3-184, 4-198, 5-236, 6-236.

AUSTRALIA	*O*	*M*	*R*	*W*
Lawson	10	2	27	1
Hogg	10	1	40	0
Rackemann	10	0	52	3
Thomson	10	0	52	1
Chappell	10	0	52	0

AUSTRALIA		
K.C. Wessels	c sub (J.V. Coney) b Troup	62
J. Dyson	c Wright b Snedden	21
D.W. Hookes	c Hadlee b Cairns	1
K.J. Hughes*	c Hadlee b Troup	12
G.S. Chappell	c Snedden b Troup	37
A.R. Border	c and b Troup	5
R.W. Marsh†	c sub (P.N. Webb) b Snedden	32
G.F. Lawson	lbw b Hadlee	0
R.M. Hogg	retired hurt	0
J.R. Thomson	c Crowe b Chatfield	4
C.G. Rackemann	not out	0
Extras	(LB 11, W 1, NB 2)	14
Total	(44.1 overs)	**188**

Fall of wickets: 1-41, 2-43, 3-66, 4-129, 5-142, 6-151, 7-155, 8-155, 9-188.

NEW ZEALAND	*O*	*M*	*R*	*W*
Hadlee	8	2	21	1
Chatfield	9	1	38	1
Snedden	7.1	1	12	2
Troup	10	0	54	4
Cairns	10	0	49	1

Umpires: R.A. French and R.V. Whitehead.

AUSTRALIA v ENGLAND 1982-83

Benson and Hedges World Series Cup – 9th Match

At Melbourne Cricket Ground on 23 January 1983.
Toss: Australia. Result: AUSTRALIA won by 5 wickets.
37 overs match. Award: A.J. Lamb.
Début: Australia – J.N. Maguire.

The attendance of 84,153 was the record until *Match No. 238* was played on the same ground a year later.

ENGLAND		
C.J. Tavaré	c Lillee b Rackemann	20
I.T. Botham	b Lillee	19
D.I. Gower	c Marsh b Rackemann	6
A.J. Lamb	c sub (K.H. MacLeay) b Lillee	94
D.W. Randall	not out	51
I.J. Gould†	b Hogg	3
T.E. Jesty	not out	1
D.R. Pringle		
G. Miller		
R.G.D. Willis*		
N.G. Cowans		
Extras	(LB 10, W 4, NB 5)	19
Total	(37 overs – 5 wickets)	**213**

Fall of wickets 1-32, 2-50, 3-66, 4-205, 5-209.

AUSTRALIA	*O*	*M*	*R*	*W*
Hogg	7	0	36	1
Lillee	8	2	50	2
Rackemann	8	0	41	2
Chappell	7	0	33	0
Maguire	7	0	34	0

AUSTRALIA		
J. Dyson	run out	54
A.R. Border	run out	54
D.W. Hookes	c Gower b Cowans	50
K.J. Hughes*	c Miller b Cowans	6
G.S. Chappell	not out	32
R.W. Marsh†	run out	8
K.C. Wessels	not out	5
R.M. Hogg		
D.K. Lillee		
J.N. Maguire		
C.G. Rackemann		
Extras	(LB 5, W 2, NB 1)	8
Total	(34.4 overs – 5 wickets)	**217**

Fall of wickets 1-85, 2-157, 3-167, 4-176, 5-190.

ENGLAND	*O*	*M*	*R*	*W*
Willis	6.4	1	29	0
Cowans	6	0	46	2
Botham	7	1	45	0
Pringle	7	0	47	0
Miller	8	0	42	0

Umpires: A.R. Crafter and P.J. McConnell.

Match No. 175/27

AUSTRALIA v ENGLAND 1982-83

Benson and Hedges World Series Cup – 10th Match

At Sydney Cricket Ground on 26 January 1983.
Toss: England. Result: ENGLAND won by 98 runs.
41 overs match (floodlit). Award: R.D. Jackman.
No débuts.

ENGLAND

C.J. Tavaré	c Marsh b Thomson	14
I.T. Botham	c Wessels b Hogg	0
D.I. Gower	b Lillee	25
A.J. Lamb	lbw b Lillee	0
D.W. Randall	run out	47
T.E. Jesty	b Maguire	30
I.J. Gould†	c Wessels b Hogg	42
V.J. Marks	c and b Lillee	22
E.E. Hemmings	run out	3
R.D. Jackman	b Hogg	0
R.G.D. Willis*	not out	5
Extras	(B 2, LB 4, W 9, NB 4)	19
Total	(41 overs)	**207**

Fall of wickets: 1-8, 2-45, 3-47, 4-47, 5-101, 6-157, 7-197, 8-201, 9-201, 10-207.

AUSTRALIA	*O*	*M*	*R*	*W*
Hogg	10	1	44	3
Maguire	8	0	42	1
Lillee	8	0	34	3
Thomson	8	0	40	1
Chappell	7	0	28	0

AUSTRALIA

J. Dyson	c Randall b Botham	23
A.R. Border	c and b Willis	31
D.W. Hookes	b Marks	32
K.J. Hughes*	c Gould b Jackman	0
G.S. Chappell	b Jackman	0
K.C. Wessels	b Jackman	1
R.W. Marsh†	b Hemmings	1
D.K. Lillee	b Hemmings	3
J.R. Thomson	b Marks	7
R.M. Hogg	not out	0
J.N. Maguire	c Lamb b Hemmings	2
Extras	(B 2, LB 2, W 3, NB 2)	9
Total	(27.3 overs)	**109**

Fall of wickets: 1-40, 2-72, 3-73, 4-73, 5-77, 6-96, 7-99, 8-106, 9-106, 10-109.

ENGLAND	*O*	*M*	*R*	*W*
Willis	6	1	23	1
Jackman	10	1	41	3
Botham	2	0	13	1
Marks	6	0	12	2
Hemmings	3.3	0	11	3

Umpires: R.A. French and B.E. Martin.

ENGLAND v NEW ZEALAND 1982-83

Benson and Hedges World Series Cup – 11th Match

At Adelaide Oval on 29 January 1983.
Toss: England. Result: NEW ZEALAND won by 4 wickets.
50 overs match. Award: R.J. Hadlee.
No débuts.

Gower became the first batsman to score five centuries for England in limited-overs internationals. New Zealand recorded the highest total by any team batting second in a limited-overs international.

ENGLAND		
C.J. Tavaré	c Crowe b Chatfield	16
I.T. Botham	b Chatfield	65
D.I. Gower	c Chatfield b Troup	109
A.J. Lamb	run out	19
D.W. Randall	c Wright b Snedden	31
T.E. Jesty	not out	52
I.J. Gould†	not out	1
V.J. Marks		
E.E. Hemmings		
R.D. Jackman		
R.G.D. Willis*		
Extras	(LB 1, W 1, NB 1)	3
Total	(50 overs – 5 wickets)	**296**

Fall of wickets: 1-75, 2-86, 3-121, 4-204, 5-278.

NEW ZEALAND	*O*	*M*	*R*	*W*
Hadlee	10	1	36	0
Cairns	10	1	45	0
Snedden	10	0	72	1
Chatfield	10	2	64	2
Troup	10	0	76	1

NEW ZEALAND		
G.M. Turner	b Willis	23
J.G. Wright	run out	30
G.P. Howarth*	b Jackman	3
J.J. Crowe	c Willis b Botham	50
B.L. Cairns	c Gower b Botham	49
J.V. Coney	not out	47
R.J. Hadlee	c Jesty b Jackman	79
W.K. Lees†	not out	1
M.C. Snedden		
E.J. Chatfield		
G.B. Troup		
Extras	(B 2, LB 7, NB 6)	15
Total	(48.5 overs – 6 wickets)	**297**

Fall of wickets: 1-26, 2-33, 3-96, 4-166, 5-166, 6-287.

ENGLAND	*O*	*M*	*R*	*W*
Willis	9.5	2	43	1
Jackman	10	1	49	2
Jesty	8	0	52	0
Hemmings	6	0	49	0
Botham	8	0	61	2
Marks	7	1	28	0

Umpires: A.R. Crafter and R.A. French.

Match No. 177/28

AUSTRALIA v ENGLAND 1982-83

Benson and Hedges World Series Cup – 12th Match

At Adelaide Oval on 30 January 1983.
Toss: England. Result: ENGLAND won by 14 runs.
47 overs match. Award: D.I. Gower.
No débuts.

ENGLAND		
C.J. Tavaré	b Hogg	18
I.T. Botham	b Lawson	14
D.I. Gower	c Lillee b Thomson	77
A.J. Lamb	b Hogg	2
D.W. Randall	c and b Lawson	49
T.E. Jesty	not out	22
I.J. Gould†	c Lillee b Lawson	9
V.J. Marks	not out	10
E.E. Hemmings		
R.D. Jackman		
R.G.D. Willis*		
Extras	(B 1, LB 14, W 6, NB 6)	27
Total	(47 overs – 6 wickets)	**228**

Fall of wickets 1-25, 2-62, 3-70, 4-176, 5-178, 6-200.

AUSTRALIA	*O*	*M*	*R*	*W*
Lawson	10	0	27	3
Lillee	10	0	50	0
Hogg	9	1	25	2
Thomson	9	0	38	1
Chappell	7	0	45	0
Hookes	2	0	16	0

AUSTRALIA		
A.R. Border	c Randall b Willis	19
J. Dyson	c Lamb b Hemmings	17
K.J. Hughes*	c Gower b Marks	4
D.W. Hookes	c Jesty b Jackman	76
R.W. Marsh†	c Jackman b Botham	7
G.S. Chappell	c Gower b Jackman	33
K.C. Wessels	b Botham	7
G.F. Lawson	not out	28
J.R. Thomson	not out	12
D.K. Lillee		
R.M. Hogg		
Extras	(B 6, LB 5)	11
Total	(47 overs – 7 wickets)	**214**

Fall of wickets 1-27, 2-89, 3-97, 4-149, 5-161, 6-167, 7-189

ENGLAND	*O*	*M*	*R*	*W*
Willis	10	1	40	1
Jackman	10	3	36	2
Botham	7	0	49	2
Hemmings	10	0	40	1
Marks	10	1	38	1

Umpires: M.W. Johnson and P.J. McConnell.

AUSTRALIA v NEW ZEALAND 1982-83

Benson and Hedges World Series Cup – 13th Match

At Adelaide Oval on 31 January 1983.
Toss: New Zealand. Result: NEW ZEALAND won by 46 runs.
50 overs match. Award: G.M. Turner.
Débuts: Australia – T.G. Hogan, K.H. MacLeay.

NEW ZEALAND		
J.G. Wright	c Border b Thomson	15
B.A. Edgar	b MacLeay	18
G.M. Turner	c Hookes b Thomson	84
J.J. Crowe	c and b Hogan	14
B.L. Cairns	c MacLeay b Hogan	0
G.P. Howarth*	c Hughes b Chappell	15
R.J. Hadlee	run out	8
J.V. Coney	c Marsh b Thomson	5
W.K. Lees†	b Hogg	9
M.C. Snedden	not out	16
E.J. Chatfield	not out	2
Extras	(LB 8, W 2, NB 3)	13
Total	(50 overs – 9 wickets)	**199**

Fall of wickets: 1-23, 2-64, 3-95, 4-95, 5-144, 6-156, 7-170, 8-171, 9-195.

AUSTRALIA	*O*	*M*	*R*	*W*
Lawson	10	3	20	0
Hogg	9	0	32	1
Thomson	5	0	27	3
MacLeay	10	0	39	1
Hogan	10	0	42	2
Chappell	6	0	26	1

AUSTRALIA		
J. Dyson	c Coney b Chatfield	24
A.R. Border	c Snedden b Chatfield	41
D.W. Hookes	c Lees b Hadlee	27
K.J. Hughes*	c Wright b Coney	6
G.S. Chappell	c Lees b Cairns	7
K.H. MacLeay	lbw b Hadlee	3
R.W. Marsh†	c Hadlee b Coney	15
G.F. Lawson	b Coney	7
T.G. Hogan	run out	4
J.R. Thomson	b Cairns	3
R.M. Hogg	not out	1
Extras	(LB 13, W 2)	15
Total	(44 overs)	**153**

Fall of wickets: 1-64, 2-76, 3-103, 4-112, 5-116, 6-116, 7-141, 8-148, 9-149, 10-153.

NEW ZEALAND	*O*	*M*	*R*	*W*
Hadlee	7	1	15	2
Cairns	10	0	41	2
Snedden	7	1	16	0
Chatfield	10	1	26	2
Coney	10	0	40	3

Umpires: A.R. Crafter and R.A. French.

Match No. 179/13

ENGLAND v NEW ZEALAND 1982-83

Benson and Hedges World Series Cup – 14th Match

At WACA Ground, Perth on 5 February 1983.
Toss: New Zealand. Result: NEW ZEALAND won by 7 wickets.
23 overs match. Award: R.J. Hadlee.
No débuts.

After reaching 45-3 off 17.3 overs, England found their innings reduced to 23 overs because of heavy rain. A helicopter was used to dry the flooded outfield.

ENGLAND		
C.J. Tavaré	c Lees b Hadlee	0
I.T. Botham	c Lees b Hadlee	19
D.I. Gower	not out	35
A.J. Lamb	c Crowe b Snedden	7
D.W. Randall	c Howarth b Snedden	12
T.E. Jesty	run out	0
I.J. Gould†	b Snedden	0
V.J. Marks	b Hadlee	2
R.D. Jackman	not out	0
R.G.D. Willis*		
N.G. Cowans		
Extras	(B 3, LB 10)	13
Total	(23 overs – 7 wickets)	**88**

Fall of wickets: 1-18, 2-23, 3-37, 4-66, 5-66, 6-82, 7-87.

NEW ZEALAND	*O*	*M*	*R*	*W*
Hadlee	8	2	15	3
Cairns	5	0	21	0
Snedden	6	1	25	3
Chatfield	4	1	14	0

NEW ZEALAND		
J.G. Wright	c Tavaré b Willis	12
G.M. Turner	c Jackman b Willis	0
J.J. Crowe	c Botham b Cowans	18
J.V. Coney	not out	29
G.P. Howarth*	not out	26
J.F.M. Morrison		
W.K. Lees†		
R.J. Hadlee		
B.L. Cairns		
M.C. Snedden		
E.J. Chatfield		
Extras	(LB 1, W 3)	4
Total	(20.3 overs – 3 wickets)	**89**

Fall of wickets: 1-5, 2-20, 3-47.

ENGLAND	*O*	*M*	*R*	*W*
Willis	8.3	1	28	2
Cowans	8	0	32	1
Jackman	2	0	16	0
Botham	2	0	9	0

Umpires: R.A. French and P.J. McConnell.

AUSTRALIA v NEW ZEALAND 1982-83

Benson and Hedges World Series Cup – 15th Match

At WACA Ground, Perth on 6 February 1983.
Toss: New Zealand. Result: AUSTRALIA won by 27 runs.
50 overs match. Award: R.W. Marsh.
Début: Australia – S.B. Smith.

AUSTRALIA		
G.M. Wood	c Wright b Chatfield	25
S.B. Smith	c Webb b Chatfield	28
K.J. Hughes*	b Morrison	21
A.R. Border	c and b Coney	2
D.W. Hookes	b Hadlee	12
G.S. Chappell	b Snedden	24
R.W. Marsh†	c Snedden b Morrison	31
G.F. Lawson	b Snedden	8
J.R. Thomson	b Morrison	4
R.M. Hogg	not out	1
D.K. Lillee	not out	0
Extras	(B 9, LB 19, W 7)	35
Total	(50 overs – 9 wickets)	**191**

Fall of wickets: 1-65, 2-74, 3-77, 4-110, 5-118, 6-159, 7-183, 8-188, 9-191.

NEW ZEALAND	*O*	*M*	*R*	*W*
Hadlee	5	2	7	1
Cairns	6	0	20	0
Snedden	10	1	41	2
Chatfield	10	2	30	2
Coney	10	0	22	1
Morrison	9	0	36	3

NEW ZEALAND		
G.P. Howarth*	b Hogg	8
J.G. Wright	c Marsh b Chappell	33
G.M. Turner	c Marsh b Lillee	30
J.J. Crowe	c Marsh b Lillee	0
J.V. Coney	c Thomson b Chappell	10
P.N. Webb†	c Border b Chappell	7
J.F.M. Morrison	not out	25
R.J. Hadlee	c Marsh b Hogg	5
B.L. Cairns	run out	1
M.C. Snedden	c Thomson b Lawson	25
E.J. Chatfield	b Lawson	0
Extras	(B 2, LB 6, W 8, NB 4)	20
Total	(44.5 overs)	**164**

Fall of wickets: 1-9, 2-61, 3-61, 4-81, 5-92, 6-108, 7-123, 8-125, 9-162, 10-164.

AUSTRALIA	*O*	*M*	*R*	*W*
Lawson	9.5	0	24	2
Hogg	9	0	37	2
Lillee	10	2	24	2
Thomson	8	0	24	0
Chappell	8	0	35	3

Umpires: A.R. Crafter and M.W. Johnson.

Match No. 181/20

AUSTRALIA v NEW ZEALAND 1982-83
Benson and Hedges World Series Cup – 1st Final

At Sydney Cricket Ground on 9 February 1983.
Toss: New Zealand. Result: AUSTRALIA won by 6 wickets.
49 overs match (floodlit). No award.
No débuts.

Rain reduced Australia's innings to 38 overs and their target to 150 runs.

NEW ZEALAND		
J.G. Wright	c Chappell b Lawson	36
B.A. Edgar	b Thomson	12
G.M. Turner	lbw b Lillee	4
G.P. Howarth*	c Marsh b Chappell	9
J.V. Coney	not out	58
J.F.M. Morrison	b Lillee	35
W.K. Lees†	c Marsh b Lawson	1
B.L. Cairns	c Lillee b Hogg	9
M.C. Snedden	not out	2
E.J. Chatfield		
G.B. Troup		
Extras	(LB 15, W 11, NB 1)	27
Total	(49 overs – 7 wickets)	**193**

Fall of wickets: 1-44, 2-57, 3-77, 4-81, 5-166, 6-171, 7-190.

AUSTRALIA	*O*	*M*	*R*	*W*
Lawson	10	4	28	2
Hogg	10	2	24	1
Lillee	10	1	35	2
Thomson	10	0	42	1
Chappell	9	0	37	1

AUSTRALIA		
G.M. Wood	b Chatfield	12
S.B. Smith	b Cairns	10
K.J. Hughes*	c Coney b Chatfield	63
A.R. Border	c sub (J.J. Crowe) b Chatfield	9
D.W. Hookes	not out	20
G.S. Chappell	not out	21
R.W. Marsh†		
G.F. Lawson		
D.K. Lillee		
J.R. Thomson		
R.M. Hogg		
Extras	(B 4, LB 16)	20
Total	(31.1 overs – 4 wickets)	**155**

Fall of wickets: 1-14, 2-59, 3-83, 4-119.

NEW ZEALAND	*O*	*M*	*R*	*W*
Troup	5	0	30	0
Cairns	8.1	0	27	1
Snedden	9	0	45	0
Chatfield	10	1	27	3
Coney	1	0	6	0

Umpires: R.A. French and M.W. Johnson.

AUSTRALIA v NEW ZEALAND 1982-83

Benson and Hedges World Series Cup – 2nd Final

At Melbourne Cricket Ground on 13 February 1983.
Toss: Australia. Result: AUSTRALIA won by 149 runs.
50 overs match. Finals award: K.J. Hughes.
Début: New Zealand – R.J. Webb.

Cairns took only 21 balls to complete his fifty and hit six sixes.

AUSTRALIA		
G.M. Wood	b Coney	91
S.B. Smith	b Webb	117
K.J. Hughes*	c Lees b Chatfield	12
A.R. Border	c and b Chatfield	11
D.W. Hookes	c Wright b Webb	40
G.S. Chappell	c Wright b Cairns	7
K.H. MacLeay	run out	10
R.W. Marsh†	not out	3
G.F. Lawson	run out	3
D.K. Lillee		
R.M. Hogg		
Extras	(B 1, LB 7)	8
Total	(50 overs – 8 wickets)	**302**

Fall of wickets: 1-140, 2-167, 3-205, 4-261, 5-280, 6-285, 7-289, 8-302.

NEW ZEALAND	*O*	*M*	*R*	*W*
Webb	9	1	47	2
Cairns	8	0	56	1
Chatfield	10	0	54	2
Snedden	7	0	47	0
Morrison	7	0	39	0
Coney	9	0	51	1

NEW ZEALAND		
J.G. Wright	c Marsh b Hogg	3
G.M. Turner	c Marsh b Lawson	1
G.P. Howarth*	b Lawson	3
J.J. Crowe	lbw b MacLeay	27
J.V. Coney	b Lillee	2
J.F.M. Morrison	b Lillee	2
W.K. Lees†	run out	3
B.L. Cairns	c Smith b Lawson	52
M.C. Snedden	c Marsh b Hookes	35
E.J. Chatfield	lbw b Chappell	10
R.J. Webb	not out	6
Extras	(LB 6, W 2, NB 1)	9
Total	(39.5 overs)	**153**

Fall of wickets: 1-8, 2-8, 3-13, 4-23, 5-42, 6-44, 7-92, 8-103, 9-144, 10-153.

AUSTRALIA	*O*	*M*	*R*	*W*
Lawson	8	3	11	3
Hogg	10	1	31	1
Lillee	7	3	29	2
MacLeay	8	0	56	1
Chappell	5	1	15	1
Hookes	1.5	0	2	1

Umpires: A.R. Crafter and P.J. McConnell.

Match No. 183/14

NEW ZEALAND v ENGLAND 1982-83 (1st Match)
Rothmans Cup

At Eden Park, Auckland on 19 February 1983.
Toss: England. Result: NEW ZEALAND won by 6 wickets.
50 overs match. Award: G.M. Turner.
No débuts.

ENGLAND

C.J. Tavaré	b Cairns	11
I.T. Botham	c Morrison b Chatfield	12
D.I. Gower	c Morrison b Snedden	84
A.J. Lamb	run out	0
D.W. Randall	b Chatfield	30
T.E. Jesty	c Coney b Chatfield	1
I.J. Gould†	lbw b Cairns	3
G. Miller	lbw b Morrison	3
V.J. Marks	not out	23
R.D. Jackman	b Cairns	4
R.G.D. Willis*	not out	1
Extras	(LB 10, W 2)	12
Total	(50 overs – 9 wickets)	**184**

Fall of wickets: 1-17, 2-40, 3-40, 4-104, 5-106, 6-110, 7-115, 8-168, 9-176.

NEW ZEALAND	*O*	*M*	*R*	*W*
Webb	10	0	30	0
Cairns	10	2	28	3
Snedden	8	1	35	1
Chatfield	10	0	27	3
Coney	2	0	17	0
Morrison	10	1	35	1

NEW ZEALAND

G.M. Turner	c sub (N.G. Cowans) b Willis	88
B.A. Edgar	c Jackman b Miller	35
B.L. Cairns	c Lamb b Botham	19
J.J. Crowe	lbw b Botham	15
J.V. Coney	not out	9
G.P. Howarth*	not out	14
J.F.M. Morrison		
W.K. Lees†		
M.C. Snedden		
E.J. Chatfield		
R.J. Webb		
Extras	(B 1, LB 4, NB 2)	7
Total	(46.3 overs – 4 wickets)	**187**

Fall of wickets: 1-101, 2-129, 3-164, 4-166.

ENGLAND	*O*	*M*	*R*	*W*
Willis	10	1	39	1
Jackman	8.3	0	38	0
Botham	8	0	40	2
Marks	10	1	30	0
Miller	10	0	33	1

Umpires: F.R. Goodall and D.A. Kinsella.

NEW ZEALAND v ENGLAND 1982-83 (2nd Match)

Rothmans Cup

At Basin Reserve, Wellington on 23 February 1983.
Toss: England. Result: NEW ZEALAND won by 103 runs.
50 overs match. Award: G.M. Turner.
No débuts.

NEW ZEALAND		
G.M. Turner	b Willis	94
B.A. Edgar	run out	60
B.L. Cairns	b Willis	44
J.G. Wright	b Miller	30
J.V. Coney	not out	31
G.P. Howarth*	c Botham b Jackman	10
J.F.M. Morrison	b Botham	8
W.K. Lees†	not out	3
M.C. Snedden		
E.J. Chatfield		
R.J. Webb		
Extras	(LB 9, W 4, NB 2)	15
Total	(50 overs – 6 wickets)	**295**

Fall of wickets: 1-152, 2-192, 3-214, 4-250, 5-275, 6-287.

ENGLAND	*O*	*M*	*R*	*W*
Willis	9	0	54	2
Jackman	10	2	38	1
Pringle	7	0	57	0
Miller	10	0	51	1
Marks	7	0	34	0
Botham	7	0	46	1

ENGLAND		
C.J. Tavaré	c Howarth b Chatfield	32
I.T. Botham	c Lees b Cairns	15
D.I. Gower	c and b Chatfield	2
A.J. Lamb	b Coney	7
D.W. Randall	c Howarth b Morrison	16
I.J. Gould†	c Wright b Coney	14
G. Miller	b Cairns	46
V.J. Marks	c Snedden b Webb	27
D.R. Pringle	b Webb	11
R.D. Jackman	b Cairns	9
R.G.D. Willis*	not out	2
Extras	(LB 6, W 5)	11
Total	(44.5 overs)	**192**

Fall of wickets: 1-20, 2-37, 3-52, 4-60, 5-83, 6-106, 7-162, 8-170, 9-182, 10-192.

NEW ZEALAND	*O*	*M*	*R*	*W*
Snedden	10	1	37	0
Cairns	10	0	38	3
Webb	7.5	0	27	2
Chatfield	7	1	28	2
Coney	5	0	17	2
Morrison	5	0	34	1

Umpires: S.C. Cowman and S.J. Woodward.

Match No. 185/16

NEW ZEALAND v ENGLAND 1982-83 (3rd Match)

Rothmans Cup

At Lancaster Park, Christchurch on 26 February 1983.
Toss: New Zealand. Result: NEW ZEALAND won by 84 runs.
50 overs match. Award: M.C. Snedden.
No débuts.

NEW ZEALAND		
G.M. Turner	lbw b Botham	34
B.A. Edgar	b Marks	32
J.G. Wright	st Gould b Marks	2
B.L. Cairns	c Marks b Jackman	21
J.J. Crowe	lbw b Jackman	18
J.V. Coney	run out	30
G.P. Howarth*	lbw b Miller	8
J.F.M. Morrison	not out	24
W.K. Lees†	c Botham b Cowans	2
M.C. Snedden	not out	31
E.J. Chatfield		
Extras	(LB 5, W 3, NB 1)	9
Total	(50 overs – 8 wickets)	**211**

Fall of wickets: 1-64, 2-70, 3-93, 4-103, 5-126, 6-152, 7-153, 8-156.

ENGLAND	*O*	*M*	*R*	*W*
Cowans	10	3	55	1
Willis	10	1	35	0
Botham	5	1	17	1
Marks	10	2	31	2
Miller	7	1	32	1
Jackman	8	1	32	2

ENGLAND		
I.J. Gould†	c Turner b Snedden	0
C.J. Tavaré	b Snedden	4
D.I. Gower	c Wright b Chatfield	53
A.J. Lamb	c Chatfield b Morrison	37
I.T. Botham	c and b Morrison	3
D.W. Randall	b Coney	2
G. Miller	c and b Chatfield	7
V.J. Marks	b Cairns	1
R.D. Jackman	b Cairns	5
R.G.D. Willis*	c Coney b Morrison	6
N.G. Cowans	not out	1
Extras	(LB 6, W 1, NB 1)	8
Total	(40.1 overs)	**127**

Fall of wickets: 1-0, 2-8, 3-94, 4-103, 5-105, 6-114, 7-114, 8-116, 9-125, 10-127.

NEW ZEALAND	*O*	*M*	*R*	*W*
Snedden	7	3	14	2
Cairns	7	0	13	2
Chatfield	8	2	26	2
Coney	10	0	42	1
Morrison	8.1	0	24	3

Umpires: F.R. Goodall and I.C. Higginson.

NEW ZEALAND v SRI LANKA 1982-83 (1st Match)

Rothmans Cup

At Carisbrook, Dunedin on 2 March 1983.
Toss: Sri Lanka. Result: NEW ZEALAND won by 65 runs.
50 overs match. Award: J.G. Wright.
Débuts: Sri Lanka – R.G. de Alwis, E.R.N.S. Fernando, Y. Goonasekera, M. de S. Wettimuny.

NEW ZEALAND		
G.M. Turner	b John	18
B.A. Edgar	c de Alwis b De Mel	3
J.G. Wright	lbw b Ratnayake	45
J.J. Crowe	lbw b Ratnayeke	5
J.V. Coney	b Ratnayake	15
G.P. Howarth*	b Ratnayake	11
B.L. Cairns	b John	37
R.J. Hadlee	b John	11
M.C. Snedden	not out	13
W.K. Lees†	not out	7
E.J. Chatfield		
Extras	(LB 10, W 4, NB 4)	18
Total	(50 overs – 8 wickets)	**183**

Fall of wickets: 1-26, 2-26, 3-50, 4-99, 5-113, 6-124, 7-150, 8-165.

SRI LANKA	*O*	*M*	*R*	*W*
De Mel	9.3	2	36	1
John	10	4	28	3
Ratnayake	10	0	30	3
Ratnayeke	10	0	45	1
De Silva	10	1	20	0
S. Wettimuny	0.3	0	6	0

SRI LANKA		
S. Wettimuny	run out	15
E.R.N.S. Fernando	c Turner b Hadlee	0
M. de S. Wettimuny	b Hadlee	2
Y. Goonasekera	run out	23
R.S. Madugalle	run out	3
D.S. De Silva*	b Chatfield	18
A.L.F. De Mel	lbw b Hadlee	1
J.R. Ratnayeke	c Snedden b Coney	14
R.G. de Alwis†	not out	13
R.J. Ratnayake	c Coney b Howarth	15
V.B. John		
Extras	(B 2, LB 10, W 2)	14
Total	(50 overs – 9 wickets)	**118**

Fall of wickets: 1-1, 2-7, 3-39, 4-46, 5-62, 6-65, 7-85, 8-85, 9-118.

NEW ZEALAND	*O*	*M*	*R*	*W*
Hadlee	8	3	9	3
Cairns	10	6	10	0
Snedden	9	1	25	0
Chatfield	10	4	8	1
Coney	10	1	42	1
Howarth	2	0	10	1
Wright	1	1	0	0

Umpires: S.C. Cowman and I.C. Higginson.

Match No. 187/3

NEW ZEALAND v SRI LANKA 1982-83 (2nd Match)

Rothmans Cup

At McLean Park, Napier on 19 March 1983.
Toss: New Zealand. Result: NEW ZEALAND won by 7 wickets.
50 overs match. Award: M.D. Crowe.
No débuts.

SRI LANKA		
S. Wettimuny	b M.D. Crowe	20
E.R.N.S. Fernando	run out	0
R.G. de Alwis†	b Cairns	12
Y. Goonasekera	c Turner b M.D. Crowe	11
L.R.D. Mendis*	c Hadlee b Chatfield	11
R.S. Madugalle	b Cairns	7
A.L.F. De Mel	c Coney b Chatfield	19
J.R. Ratnayeke	c M.D. Crowe b Snedden	27
D.S. De Silva	not out	37
R.J. Ratnayake	not out	1
V.B. John		
Extras	(B 10, LB 11, NB 1)	22
Total	(50 overs – 8 wickets)	**167**

Fall of wickets: 1-5, 2-35, 3-51, 4-51, 5-63, 6-76, 7-105, 8-161.

NEW ZEALAND	*O*	*M*	*R*	*W*
Hadlee	10	3	22	0
Snedden	10	2	25	1
Cairns	10	2	25	2
Chatfield	10	2	43	2
M.D. Crowe	10	2	30	2

NEW ZEALAND		
G.M. Turner	c Ratnayake b John	25
B.A. Edgar	c Madugalle b Ratnayeke	8
J.G. Wright*	hit wicket b De Silva	31
J.J. Crowe	not out	46
M.D. Crowe	not out	43
B.L. Cairns		
R.J. Hadlee		
J.V. Coney		
M.C. Snedden		
E.J. Chatfield		
W.K. Lees†		
Extras	(B 1, LB 4, W 3, NB 7)	15
Total	(36.4 overs – 3 wickets)	**168**

Fall of wickets: 1-32, 2-56, 3-81.

SRI LANKA	*O*	*M*	*R*	*W*
De Mel	4	0	27	0
John	10	4	31	1
Ratnayake	6.4	0	17	0
Ratnayeke	7	0	39	1
De Silva	6	1	28	1
Goonasekera	3	0	11	0

Umpires: F.R. Goodall and D.A. Kinsella.

NEW ZEALAND v SRI LANKA 1982-83 (3rd Match)

Rothmans Cup

At Eden Park, Auckland on 20 March 1983.
Toss: New Zealand. Result: NEW ZEALAND won by 116 runs.
50 overs match. Award: G.M. Turner.
Début: Sri Lanka – S. Jeganathan.

NEW ZEALAND		
G.M. Turner	c Ratnayeke b Ratnayake	140
B.A. Edgar	c De Mel b Goonasekera	52
B.L. Cairns	b Ratnayake	18
J.G. Wright	b Wettimuny	45
R.J. Hadlee	c Ratnayeke b De Mel	9
J.J. Crowe	not out	17
M.D. Crowe	not out	7
G.P. Howarth*		
M.C. Snedden		
E.J. Chatfield		
W.K. Lees†		
Extras	(B 3, LB 10, W 3)	16
Total	(50 overs – 5 wickets)	**304**

Fall of wickets 1-132, 2-158, 3-230, 4-267, 5-279.

SRI LANKA	*O*	*M*	*R*	*W*
De Mel	10	1	65	1
Ratnayake	10	0	50	2
Ratnayeke	5	0	41	0
De Silva	10	0	46	0
Jeganathan	10	0	49	0
Goonasekera	3	0	24	1
Wettimuny	2	0	13	1

SRI LANKA		
S. Wettimuny	run out	31
E.R.N.S. Fernando	b Cairns	36
Y. Goonasekera	c Turner b Cairns	35
L.R.D. Mendis*	c Wright b Cairns	7
R.S. Madugalle	not out	30
D.S. De Silva	b Cairns	1
A.L.F. De Mel	c Hadlee b M.D. Crowe	16
J.R. Ratnayeke	not out	13
R.J. Ratnayake		
S. Jeganathan		
R.G. de Alwis†		
Extras	(B 4, LB 9, W 5, NB 1)	19
Total	(50 overs – 6 wickets)	**188**

Fall of wickets 1-55, 2-110, 3-111, 4-118, 5-123, 6-165.

NEW ZEALAND	*O*	*M*	*R*	*W*
Hadlee	7	2	18	0
Snedden	7	0	22	0
Cairns	10	2	23	4
M.D. Crowe	10	1	51	1
Chatfield	10	0	47	0
Wright	2	0	2	0
Edgar	2	0	5	0
J.J. Crowe	1	0	1	0
Turner	1	1	0	0

Umpires: I.C. Higginson and S.J. Woodward.

Match No. 189/2

WEST INDIES v INDIA 1982-83 (1st Match)

At Queen's Park Oval, Port-of-Spain, Trinidad on 9 March 1983.
Toss: India. Result: WEST INDIES won by 52 runs.
39 overs match. Award: D.L. Haynes.
No débuts.

WEST INDIES		
C.G. Greenidge	c Madan Lal b Maninder	66
D.L. Haynes	c Yashpal b Kapil Dev	97
I.V.A. Richards	c Gaekwad b Amarnath	32
A.L. Logie	not out	6
C.H. Lloyd*	c Kirmani b Kapil Dev	3
H.A. Gomes		
P.J.L. Dujon†		
M.D. Marshall		
A.M.E. Roberts		
M.A. Holding		
J. Garner		
Extras	(B 4, LB 5, W 1, NB 1)	11
Total	(38.5 overs – 4 wickets)	**215**

Fall of wickets 1-125, 2-198, 3-207, 4-215.

INDIA	*O*	*M*	*R*	*W*
Kapil Dev	6.5	0	21	2
Madan Lal	7	0	34	0
Venkataraghavan	9	0	48	0
Amarnath	7	0	39	1
Maninder	9	0	62	1

INDIA		
S.M. Gavaskar	c Roberts b Garner	25
A.D. Gaekwad	b Gomes	22
M. Amarnath	run out	27
D.B. Vengsarkar	c Logie b Roberts	27
Kapil Dev*	lbw b Roberts	0
Yashpal Sharma	c Haynes b Gomes	2
A. Malhotra	c Holding b Gomes	21
S.M.H. Kirmani†	not out	13
Madan Lal	not out	13
Maninder Singh		
S. Venkataraghavan		
Extras	(B 1, LB 3, W 5, NB 4)	13
Total	(39 overs – 7 wickets)	**163**

Fall of wickets 1-55, 2-59, 3-110, 4-110, 5-115,
6-117, 7-140.

WEST INDIES	*O*	*M*	*R*	*W*
Holding	5	1	8	0
Roberts	7	2	27	2
Marshall	8	0	25	0
Garner	9	1	39	1
Gomes	9	0	50	3
Logie	1	0	1	0

Umpires: D.J. Narine and A. Weekes.

WEST INDIES v INDIA 1982-83 (2nd Match)

At Albion Sports Complex, Berbice, Guyana on 29 March 1983.
Toss: West Indies. Result: INDIA won by 27 runs.
47 overs match. Award: Kapil Dev.
Début: West Indies – W.W. Davis.

INDIA		
S.M. Gavaskar	run out	90
R.J. Shastri	c Dujon b Marshall	30
M. Amarnath	b Richards	30
Kapil Dev*	b Roberts	72
Yashpal Sharma	c Greenidge b Davis	23
D.B. Vengsarkar	not out	18
A. Malhotra	not out	1
Madan Lal		
S.M.H. Kirmani†		
B.S. Sandhu		
S. Venkataraghavan		
Extras	(B 1, LB 9, W 4, NB 4)	18
Total	(47 overs – 5 wickets)	**282**

Fall of wickets 1-93, 2-152, 3-224, 4-246, 5-277.

WEST INDIES	*O*	*M*	*R*	*W*
Holding	7	0	49	0
Roberts	9	0	44	1
Davis	8	0	40	1
Marshall	7	0	23	1
Gomes	10	0	64	0
Richards	6	0	44	1

WEST INDIES		
C.G. Greenidge	c and b Kapil Dev	16
D.L. Haynes	lbw b Sandhu	2
I.V.A. Richards	b Madan Lal	64
C.H. Lloyd*	c Amarnath b Madan Lal	8
S.F.A.F. Bacchus	c Yashpal b Shastri	52
H.A. Gomes	c Kapil Dev b Shastri	26
P.J.L. Dujon†	not out	53
M.D. Marshall	c Sandhu b Shastri	5
A.M.E. Roberts	b Kapil Dev	12
M.A. Holding	c Malhotra b Sandhu	2
W.W. Davis	not out	7
Extras	(LB 6, W 1, NB 1)	8
Total	(47 overs – 9 wickets)	**255**

Fall of wickets 1-6, 2-22, 3-62, 4-98, 5-154,
6-181, 7-192, 8-228, 9-232.

INDIA	*O*	*M*	*R*	*W*
Kapil Dev	10	0	33	2
Sandhu	10	0	38	2
Madan Lal	9	0	65	2
Venkataraghavan	10	0	63	0
Shastri	8	0	48	3

Umpires: D.M. Archer and M. Baksh.

Match No. 191/4

WEST INDIES v INDIA 1982-83 (3rd Match)

At Queen's Park, St George's, Grenada on 7 April 1983.
Toss: West Indies. Result: WEST INDIES won by 7 wickets.
50 overs match. Award: C.G. Greenidge.
No débuts.

INDIA

S.M. Gavaskar	c Richards b Roberts	3
R.J. Shastri	c Dujon b Marshall	17
M. Amarnath	b Gomes	11
D.B. Vengsarkar	c Richards b Gomes	54
A. Malhotra	c Richards b Gomes	7
Yashpal Sharma	b Holding	25
Kapil Dev*	lbw b Roberts	1
Madan Lal	b Gomes	6
S.M.H. Kirmani†	run out	3
B.S. Sandhu	not out	16
S. Venkataraghavan	b Holding	3
Extras	(B 5, LB 7, W 5, NB 3)	20
Total	(44.4 overs)	**166**

Fall of wickets: 1-9, 2-36, 3-47, 4-74, 5-109, 6-114, 7-127, 8-138, 9-153, 10-166.

WEST INDIES	*O*	*M*	*R*	*W*
Holding	8.4	2	15	2
Roberts	9	0	38	2
Garner	10	1	30	0
Marshall	7	2	25	1
Gomes	10	0	38	4

WEST INDIES

C.G. Greenidge	c Sandhu b Shastri	64
D.L. Haynes	c Venkataraghavan b Amarnath	19
I.V.A. Richards	c Shastri b Venkataraghavan	28
S.F.A.F. Bacchus	not out	26
P.J.L. Dujon†	not out	20
C.H. Lloyd*		
H.A. Gomes		
M.D. Marshall		
A.M.E. Roberts		
M.A. Holding		
J. Garner		
Extras	(LB 7, W 3)	10
Total	(40.2 overs – 3 wickets)	**167**

Fall of wickets: 1-61, 2-106, 3-132.

INDIA	*O*	*M*	*R*	*W*
Kapil Dev	6	2	21	0
Sandhu	8	2	30	0
Madan Lal	7	1	37	0
Amarnath	4	0	23	1
Venkataraghavan	8	0	24	1
Shastri	5	1	10	1
Yashpal Sharma	2.2	0	12	0

Umpires: S.E. Parris and P. White.

SRI LANKA v AUSTRALIA 1982-83 (1st Match)

At Saravanamuttu Stadium, Colombo on 13 April 1983.
Toss: Australia. Result: SRI LANKA won by 2 wickets.
45 overs match. Award: R.G. de Alwis.
Début: Australia – R.D. Woolley.

De Alwis equalled the record for one-day internationals by holding five catches.

AUSTRALIA		
G.M. Wood	b De Silva	50
S.B. Smith	c de Alwis b John	1
G.N. Yallop	c de Alwis b Ranatunga	39
G.S. Chappell*	c de Alwis b John	11
D.W. Hookes	c de Alwis b Ranatunga	0
A.R. Border	b De Silva	10
R.D. Woolley†	c de Alwis b De Mel	16
T.G. Hogan	c Ratnayake b De Mel	27
D.K. Lillee	run out	5
R.M. Hogg	not out	0
J.N. Maguire		
Extras	(LB 7, W 2)	9
Total	(45 overs – 9 wickets)	**168**

Fall of wickets: 1-15, 2-87, 3-103, 4-107, 5-109, 6-118, 7-144, 8-167, 9-168.

SRI LANKA	*O*	*M*	*R*	*W*
De Mel	9	2	35	2
John	9	1	33	2
Ratnayakc	9	1	44	0
Ranatunga	9	1	26	2
De Silva	9	0	21	2

SRI LANKA		
S. Wettimuny	b Hogan	37
E.R.N.S. Fernando	st Woolley b Hogan	31
R.L. Dias	lbw b Chappell	5
L.R.D. Mendis*	b Hogan	16
R.S. Madugalle	c Smith b Maguire	9
A. Ranatunga	c Hogan b Hogg	10
A.L.F. De Mel	c Woolley b Maguire	27
D.S. De Silva	not out	15
R.G. de Alwis†	b Hogg	6
R.J. Ratnayake	not out	0
V.B. John		
Extras	(LB 5, W 5, NB 3)	13
Total	(44.1 overs – 8 wickets)	**169**

Fall of wickets: 1-71, 2-82, 3-82, 4-102, 5-112, 6-139, 7-157, 8-168.

AUSTRALIA	*O*	*M*	*R*	*W*
Hogg	9	1	40	2
Maguire	8.1	0	43	2
Lillee	9	0	25	0
Chappell	9	2	21	1
Hogan	9	1	27	3

Umpires: C.E.B. Anthony and P.W. Vidanagamage.

Match No. 193/3

SRI LANKA v AUSTRALIA 1982-83 (2nd Match)

At Saravanamuttu Stadium, Colombo on 16 April 1983.

Toss: Sri Lanka.	Result: SRI LANKA won by 4 wickets.
45 overs match.	Award: A. Ranatunga.

No débuts.

AUSTRALIA		
G.M. Wood	lbw b Ratnayake	9
K.C. Wessels	b Ratnayake	39
G.N. Yallop	c Mendis b Ranatunga	59
G.S. Chappell*	not out	54
D.W. Hookes	run out	27
A.R. Border	c Dias b John	6
R.D. Woolley†	not out	3
B. Yardley		
T.G. Hogan		
D.K. Lillee		
R.M. Hogg		
Extras	(LB 8, NB 2)	10
Total	(45 overs – 5 wickets)	**207**

Fall of wickets 1-34, 2-77, 3-136, 4-195, 5-201.

SRI LANKA	*O*	*M*	*R*	*W*
De Mel	9	1	29	0
John	9	0	33	1
Ratnayake	9	0	38	2
Ranatunga	9	0	45	1
De Silva	9	0	52	0

SRI LANKA		
S. Wettimuny	b Yardley	56
E.R.N.S. Fernando	run out	34
R.L. Dias	c Wood b Yardley	2
L.R.D. Mendis*	b Yardley	2
A. Ranatunga	not out	55
R.S. Madugalle	b Hogan	37
A.L.F. De Mel	c Wood b Border	1
D.S. De Silva	not out	7
R.G. de Alwis†		
R.J. Ratnayake		
V.B. John		
Extras	(B 2, LB 14, NB 3)	19
Total	(43.2 overs – 6 wickets)	**213**

Fall of wickets 1-101, 2-101, 3-107, 4-108, 5-177, 6-178.

AUSTRALIA	*O*	*M*	*R*	*W*
Hogg	7	1	18	0
Lillee	9	0	30	0
Chappell	6.2	0	37	0
Hogan	9	0	62	1
Yardley	9	1	28	3
Border	2	0	10	1
Yallop	1	0	9	0

Umpires: D.P. Buultjens and H.C. Felsinger.

SRI LANKA v AUSTRALIA 1982-83 (3rd Match)

At Sinhalese Sports Club, Colombo on 29 April 1983.
Toss: Sri Lanka. No result – rain.
45 overs match. No award.
No débuts.

AUSTRALIA		
G.M. Wood	b Ranatunga	35
K.C. Wessels	c Dias b De Silva	43
G.N. Yallop	c de Alwis b De Silva	51
D.W. Hookes	c de Alwis b John	23
A.R. Border	b De Mel	10
G.S. Chappell*	not out	9
R.D. Woolley†	not out	12
T.G. Hogan		
B. Yardley		
R.M. Hogg		
J.N. Maguire		
Extras	(LB 8, W 1, NB 2)	11
Total	(39.2 overs – 5 wickets)	**194**

Fall of wickets 1-60, 2-105, 3-151, 4-172, 5-172.

SRI LANKA	*O*	*M*	*R*	*W*
De Mel	9	0	44	1
John	6.2	1	23	1
Ranatunga	9	0	42	1
Ratnayake	6	0	23	0
De Silva	9	0	51	2

SRI LANKA
S. Wettimuny
E.R.N.S. Fernando
R.L. Dias
L.R.D. Mendis*
A. Ranatunga
R.S. Madugalle
A.L.F. De Mel
D.S. De Silva
R.G. de Alwis†
R.J. Ratnayake
V.B. John

Umpires: K.T. Francis and P.W. Vidanagamage.

Match No. 195/5

SRI LANKA v AUSTRALIA 1982-83 (4th Match)

At Sinhalese Sports Club, Colombo on 30 April 1983.
Toss: Australia. No result – rain.
30 overs match. No award.
Débuts: Sri Lanka – G.N. De Silva, D.S.B.P. Kuruppu.

AUSTRALIA		
K.C. Wessels	b De Mel	6
G.M. Wood	b De Mel	2
G.N. Yallop	not out	60
D.W. Hookes	b Ratnayeke	49
S.B. Smith	not out	0
G.S. Chappell*		
A.R. Border		
R.D. Woolley†		
B. Yardley		
R.M. Hogg		
J.N. Maguire		
Extras	(B 2, LB 4, W 1)	7
Total	(19.2 overs – 3 wickets)	**124**

Fall of wickets 1-3, 2-12, 3-124.

SRI LANKA	*O*	*M*	*R*	*W*
De Mel	4	0	9	2
John	5	0	15	0
De Silva	4	0	21	0
Ranatunga	3	0	35	0
Ratnayeke	2.2	0	16	1
Wettimuny	1	0	21	0

SRI LANKA
S. Wettimuny
E.R.N.S. Fernando
R.L. Dias
L.R.D. Mendis*
A. Ranatunga
R.S. Madugalle
A.L.F. De Mel
G.N. De Silva
D.S.B.P. Kuruppu†
J.R. Ratnayeke
V.B. John

Umpires: D.P. Buultjens and S. Ponnadurai.

ENGLAND v NEW ZEALAND 1983

Prudential World Cup – 1st Match

At Kennington Oval, London on 9 June 1983.
Toss: England. Result: ENGLAND won by 106 runs.
60 overs match. Award: A.J. Lamb.
No débuts.

ENGLAND		
G. Fowler	c Coney b Cairns	8
C.J. Tavaré	c Edgar b Chatfield	45
D.I. Gower	c Edgar b Coney	39
A.J. Lamb	b Snedden	102
M.W. Gatting	b Snedden	43
I.T. Botham	c Lees b Hadlee	22
I.J. Gould†	not out	14
G.R. Dilley	not out	31
V.J. Marks		
P.J.W. Allott		
R.G.D. Willis*		
Extras	(LB 12, W 1, NB 5)	18
Total	(60 overs – 6 wickets)	**322**

Fall of wickets 1-13, 2-79, 3-117, 4-232, 5-271, 6-278.

NEW ZEALAND	*O*	*M*	*R*	*W*
Hadlee	12	4	26	1
Cairns	12	4	57	1
Snedden	12	1	105	2
Chatfield	12	1	45	1
Coney	6	1	20	1
Crowe	6	0	51	0

NEW ZEALAND		
G.M. Turner	lbw b Willis	14
B.A. Edgar	c Gould b Willis	3
J.G. Wright	c Botham b Dilley	10
G.P. Howarth*	c Lamb b Marks	18
J.V. Coney	run out	23
M.D. Crowe	run out	97
W.K. Lees†	b Botham	8
R.J. Hadlee	c Lamb b Marks	1
B.L. Cairns	lbw b Botham	1
M.C. Snedden	c Gould b Gatting	21
E.J. Chatfield	not out	9
Extras	(B 2, LB 4, W 4, NB 1)	11
Total	(59 overs)	**216**

Fall of wickets 1-3, 2-28, 3-31, 4-62, 5-85, 6-123, 7-136, 8-138, 9-190, 10-216.

ENGLAND	*O*	*M*	*R*	*W*
Willis	7	2	9	2
Dilley	8	0	33	1
Botham	12	0	42	2
Allott	12	1	47	0
Marks	12	1	39	2
Gatting	8	1	35	1

Umpires: B.J. Meyer and D.O. Oslear.

Match No. 197/5

PAKISTAN v SRI LANKA 1983

Prudential World Cup – 2nd Match

At St Helen's, Swansea on 9 June 1983.

Toss: Sri Lanka. Result: PAKISTAN won by 50 runs.
60 overs match. Award: Mohsin Khan.

Début: Sri Lanka – M.A.R. Samarasekera.

This match produced the highest total, the highest total by a team batting second and losing, and the highest match aggregate in international limited-overs cricket.

PAKISTAN		
Mudassar Nazar	c De Silva b Ratnayake	36
Mohsin Khan	b John	82
Zaheer Abbas	c Kuruppu b De Mel	82
Javed Miandad	lbw b De Mel	72
Imran Khan*	not out	56
Ijaz Faqih	run out	2
Tahir Naqqash	not out	0
Wasim Bari†		
Rashid Khan		
Shahid Mahboob		
Sarfraz Nawaz		
Extras	(B 4, LB 4)	8
Total	(60 overs – 5 wickets)	**338**

Fall of wickets 1-88, 2-156, 3-229, 4-325, 5-332.

SRI LANKA	*O*	*M*	*R*	*W*
De Mel	12	2	69	2
John	12	2	58	1
Ratnayake	12	0	65	1
Ranatunga	9	0	53	0
De Silva	10	0	52	0
Samarasekera	5	0	33	0

SRI LANKA		
S. Wettimuny	c Rashid b Sarfraz	12
D.S.B.P. Kuruppu	run out	72
R.L. Dias	b Rashid	5
L.R.D. Mendis*	b Tahir	16
A. Ranatunga	c and b Mudassar	31
M.A.R. Samarasekera	run out	0
D.S. De Silva	c Wasim Bari b Sarfraz	35
A.L.F. De Mel	c Tahir b Shahid	11
R.G. de Alwis†	not out	59
R.J. Ratnayake	c Mudassar b Sarfraz	13
V.B. John	not out	12
Extras	(LB 8, W 10, NB 4)	22
Total	(60 overs – 9 wickets)	**288**

Fall of wickets 1-34, 2-58, 3-85, 4-142, 5-143, 6-157, 7-180, 8-234, 9-262

PAKISTAN	*O*	*M*	*R*	*W*
Sarfraz Nawaz	12	1	40	3
Shahid Mahboob	11	0	48	1
Tahir Naqqash	8	0	49	1
Rashid Khan	12	1	55	1
Ijaz Faqih	12	1	52	0
Mudassar Nazar	4	0	18	1
Zaheer Abbas	1	0	4	0

Umpires: K.E. Palmer and D.R. Shepherd.

AUSTRALIA v ZIMBABWE 1983

Prudential World Cup – 3rd Match

At Trent Bridge, Nottingham on 9 June 1983.
Toss: Australia. Result: ZIMBABWE won by 13 runs.
60 overs match. Award: D.A.G. Fletcher.

Débuts: Zimbabwe – All.

Fletcher, the only player to have scored a fifty and taken four wickets in the same one-day international, led Zimbabwe to victory in their first official match at this level. Lillee became the first bowler to take 100 wickets in one-day internationals when he dismissed Paterson. Marsh made his 100th dismissal when he caught Heron – a unique feat in these matches.

ZIMBABWE		
A.H. Shah	c Marsh b Lillee	16
G.A. Paterson	c Hookes b Lillee	27
J.G. Heron	c Marsh b Yallop	14
A.J. Pycroft	b Border	21
D.L. Houghton†	c Marsh b Yallop	0
D.A.G. Fletcher*	not out	69
K.M. Curran	c Hookes b Hogg	27
I.P. Butchart	not out	34
P.W.E. Rawson		
A.J. Traicos		
V.R. Hogg		
Extras	(LB 18, W 7, NB 6)	31
Total	(60 overs – 6 wickets)	**239**

Fall of wickets: 1-55, 2-55, 3-86, 4-86, 5-94, 6-164.

AUSTRALIA	*O*	*M*	*R*	*W*
Lawson	11	2	33	0
Hogg	12	3	43	1
Lillee	12	1	47	2
Thomson	11	1	46	0
Yallop	9	0	28	2
Border	5	0	11	1

AUSTRALIA		
G.M. Wood	c Houghton b Fletcher	31
K.C. Wessels	run out	76
K.J. Hughes*	c Shah b Fletcher	0
D.W. Hookes	c Traicos b Fletcher	20
G.N. Yallop	c Pycroft b Fletcher	2
A.R. Border	c Pycroft b Curran	17
R.W. Marsh†	not out	50
G.F. Lawson	b Butchart	0
R.M. Hogg	not out	19
D.K. Lillee		
J.R. Thomson		
Extras	(B 2, LB 7, W 2)	11
Total	(60 overs – 7 wickets)	**226**

Fall of wickets: 1-61, 2-63, 3-114, 4-133, 5-138, 6-168, 7-176.

ZIMBABWE	*O*	*M*	*R*	*W*
Hogg	6	2	15	0
Rawson	12	1	54	0
Butchart	10	0	39	1
Fletcher	11	1	42	4
Traicos	12	2	27	0
Curran	9	0	38	1

Umpires: D.J. Constant and M.J. Kitchen.

Match No. 199/5

INDIA v WEST INDIES 1983

Prudential World Cup – 4th Match

At Old Trafford, Manchester on 9, 10 June 1983.
Toss: West Indies. Result: INDIA won by 34 runs.
60 overs match. Award: Yashpal Sharma.
No débuts.

West Indies were defeated for the first time in Prudential Cup matches.

INDIA		
S.M. Gavaskar	c Dujon b Marshall	19
K. Srikkanth	c Dujon b Holding	14
M. Amarnath	c Dujon b Garner	21
S.M. Patil	b Gomes	36
Yashpal Sharma	b Holding	89
Kapil Dev*	c Richards b Gomes	6
R.M.H. Binny	lbw b Marshall	27
Madan Lal	not out	21
S.M.H. Kirmani†	run out	1
R.J. Shastri	not out	5
B.S. Sandhu		
Extras	(B 4, LB 10, W 1, NB 8)	23
Total	(60 overs – 8 wickets)	**262**

Fall of wickets 1-21, 2-46, 3-76, 4-125, 5-141,
6-214, 7-243, 8-246.

WEST INDIES	*O*	*M*	*R*	*W*
Holding	12	3	32	2
Roberts	12	1	51	0
Marshall	12	1	48	2
Garner	12	1	49	1
Richards	2	0	13	0
Gomes	10	0	46	2

WEST INDIES		
C.G. Greenidge	b Sandhu	24
D.L. Haynes	run out	24
I.V.A. Richards	c Kirmani b Binny	17
S.F.A.F. Bacchus	b Madan Lal	14
C.H. Lloyd*	b Binny	25
P.J.L. Dujon†	c Sandhu b Binny	7
H.A. Gomes	run out	8
M.D. Marshall	st Kirmani b Shastri	2
A.M.E. Roberts	not out	37
M.A. Holding	b Shastri	8
J. Garner	st Kirmani b Shastri	37
Extras	(B 4, LB 17, W 4)	25
Total	(54.1 overs)	**228**

Fall of wickets 1-49, 2-56, 3-76, 4-96, 5-107,
6-124, 7-126, 8-130, 9-157, 10-228.

INDIA	*O*	*M*	*R*	*W*
Kapil Dev	10	0	34	0
Sandhu	12	1	36	1
Madan Lal	12	1	34	1
Binny	12	1	48	3
Shastri	5.1	0	26	3
Patil	3	0	25	0

Umpires: B. Leadbeater and A.G.T. Whitehead.

ENGLAND v SRI LANKA 1983

Prudential World Cup – 5th Match

At County Ground, Taunton on 11 June 1983.
Toss: England. Result: ENGLAND won by 47 runs.
60 overs match. Award: D.I. Gower.
No débuts.

Gower's sixth hundred equalled the record held by Zaheer Abbas.

ENGLAND		
G. Fowler	b John	22
C.J. Tavaré	c de Alwis b Ranatunga	32
D.I. Gower	b De Mel	130
A.J. Lamb	b Ratnayake	53
M.W. Gatting	run out	7
I.T. Botham	run out	0
I.J. Gould†	c Ranatunga b Ratnayake	35
G.R. Dilley	b De Mel	29
V.J. Marks	run out	5
P.J.W. Allott	not out	0
R.G.D. Willis*		
Extras	(LB 11, W 9)	20
Total	(60 overs – 9 wickets)	**333**

Fall of wickets: 1-49, 2-78, 3-174, 4-193, 5-194, 6-292, 7-298, 8-333, 9-333.

SRI LANKA	*O*	*M*	*R*	*W*
De Mel	12	3	62	2
John	12	0	55	1
Ratnayake	12	0	66	2
Ranatunga	12	0	65	1
De Silva	12	0	65	0

SRI LANKA		
S. Wettimuny	lbw b Marks	33
D.S.B.P. Kuruppu	c Gatting b Dilley	4
R.L. Dias	c Botham b Dilley	2
L.R.D. Mendis*	c Willis b Marks	56
R.S. Madugalle	c Tavaré b Marks	12
A. Ranatunga	c Lamb b Marks	34
D.S. De Silva	st Gould b Marks	28
R.G. de Alwis†	not out	58
A.L.F. De Mel	c Dilley b Allott	27
R.J. Ratnayake	c Lamb b Dilley	15
V.B. John	b Dilley	0
Extras	(LB 12, W 2, NB 3)	17
Total	(58 overs)	**286**

Fall of wickets: 1-11, 2-17, 3-92, 4-108, 5-117, 6-168, 7-192, 8-246, 9-281, 10-286.

ENGLAND	*O*	*M*	*R*	*W*
Willis	11	3	43	0
Dilley	11	0	45	4
Allott	12	1	82	1
Botham	12	0	60	0
Marks	12	3	39	5

Umpires: M.J. Kitchen and K.E. Palmer.

Match No. 201/3

NEW ZEALAND v PAKISTAN 1983

Prudential World Cup – 6th Match

At Edgbaston, Birmingham on 11, 12 June 1983.
Toss: Pakistan. Result: NEW ZEALAND won by 52 runs.
60 overs match. Award: Abdul Qadir.
Débuts: New Zealand – J.G. Bracewell; Pakistan – Abdul Qadir.

NEW ZEALAND		
G.M. Turner	c Wasim Bari b Rashid	27
B.A. Edgar	c Imran b Qadir	44
J.G. Wright	c Wasim Bari b Qadir	9
B.L. Cairns	b Qadir	4
G.P. Howarth*	st Wasim Bari b Qadir	16
J.V. Coney	c Ijaz b Shahid	33
M.D. Crowe	c Mohsin b Rashid	34
R.J. Hadlee	c Wasim Bari b Sarfraz	13
J.G. Bracewell	lbw b Rashid	3
W.K. Lees†	not out	24
E.J. Chatfield	not out	6
Extras	(LB 20, W 4, NB 1)	25
Total	(60 overs – 9 wickets)	**238**

Fall of wickets: 1-57, 2-68, 3-80, 4-109, 5-120, 6-166, 7-197, 8-202, 9-223.

PAKISTAN	*O*	*M*	*R*	*W*
Sarfraz Nawaz	11	1	49	1
Shahid Mahboob	10	2	38	1
Rashid Khan	11	0	47	3
Mudassar Nazar	12	1	40	0
Abdul Qadir	12	4	21	4
Ijaz Faqih	1	0	6	0
Zaheer Abbas	3	0	12	0

PAKISTAN		
Mohsin Khan	lbw b Hadlee	0
Mudassar Nazar	c Lees b Cairns	0
Zaheer Abbas	b Hadlee	0
Javed Miandad	lbw b Chatfield	35
Imran Khan*	c Chatfield b Hadlee	9
Ijaz Faqih	c Edgar b Coney	12
Shahid Mahboob	c Wright b Coney	17
Wasim Bari†	c Edgar b Coney	34
Abdul Qadir	not out	41
Sarfraz Nawaz	c Crowe b Chatfield	13
Rashid Khan	c and b Cairns	9
Extras	(B 5, LB 6, W 3, NB 2)	16
Total	(55.2 overs)	**186**

Fall of wickets: 1-0, 2-0, 3-0, 4-22, 5-54, 6-60, 7-102, 8-131, 9-158, 10-186.

NEW ZEALAND	*O*	*M*	*R*	*W*
Hadlee	9	2	20	3
Cairns	9.2	3	21	2
Chatfield	12	0	50	2
Crowe	2	0	12	0
Coney	12	3	28	3
Bracewell	11	2	39	0

Umpires: H.D. Bird and B. Leadbeater.

AUSTRALIA v WEST INDIES 1983

Prudential World Cup – 7th Match

At Headingley, Leeds on 11, 12 June 1983.
Toss: Australia. Result: WEST INDIES won by 101 runs.
60 overs match. Award: W.W. Davis.
No débuts.

Davis remains the only bowler to take seven wickets in a one-day international.

WEST INDIES		
C.G. Greenidge	c Wood b Hogg	4
D.L. Haynes	c Marsh b Lawson	13
I.V.A. Richards	b Lawson	7
H.A. Gomes	c Marsh b Lillee	78
C.H. Lloyd*	lbw b MacLeay	19
S.F.A.F. Bacchus	c Wessels b Yallop	47
P.J.L. Dujon†	lbw b Lawson	12
A.M.E. Roberts	c Marsh b Lillee	5
M.A. Holding	run out	20
W.W. Daniel	not out	16
W.W. Davis		
Extras	(B 1, LB 9, W 10, NB 11)	31
Total	(60 overs – 9 wickets)	**252**

Fall of wickets: 1-7, 2-25, 3-32, 4-78, 5-154, 6-192, 7-208, 8-211, 9-252.

AUSTRALIA	*O*	*M*	*R*	*W*
Lawson	12	3	29	3
Hogg	12	1	49	1
MacLeay	12	1	31	1
Lillee	12	0	55	2
Yallop	5	0	26	1
Border	7	0	31	0

AUSTRALIA		
G.M. Wood	retired hurt	2
K.C. Wessels	b Roberts	11
K.J. Hughes*	c Lloyd b Davis	18
D.W. Hookes	c Dujon b Davis	45
G.N. Yallop	c Holding b Davis	29
A.R. Border	c Lloyd b Davis	17
K.H. MacLeay	c Haynes b Davis	1
R.W. Marsh†	c Haynes b Holding	8
G.F. Lawson	c Dujon b Davis	2
R.M. Hogg	not out	0
D.K. Lillee	b Davis	0
Extras	(B 1, LB 4, W 5, NB 8)	18
Total	(30.3 overs)	**151**

Fall of wickets: 1-18, 2-55, 3-114, 4-116, 5-126, 6-137, 7-141, 8-150, 9-151.

WEST INDIES	*O*	*M*	*R*	*W*
Roberts	7	0	14	1
Holding	8	2	23	1
Davis	10.3	0	51	7
Daniel	3	0	35	0
Gomes	2	0	10	0

Umpires: D.J. Constant and D.G.L. Evans.

Match No. 203/1

INDIA v ZIMBABWE 1983

Prudential World Cup – 8th Match

At Grace Road, Leicester on 11 June 1983.
Toss: India. Result: INDIA won by 5 wickets.
60 overs match. Award: Madan Lal.

Début: Zimbabwe – R.D. Brown.

Kirmani became the third wicket-keeper after R.W. Marsh and R.G. de Alwis to hold five catches in a one-day international.

ZIMBABWE		
A.H. Shah	c Kirmani b Sandhu	8
G.A. Paterson	lbw b Madan Lal	22
J.G. Heron	c Kirmani b Madan Lal	18
A.J. Pycroft	c Shastri b Binny	14
D.L. Houghton†	c Kirmani b Madan Lal	21
D.A.G. Fletcher*	b Kapil Dev	13
K.M. Curran	run out	8
I.P. Butchart	not out	22
R.D. Brown	c Kirmani b Shastri	6
P.W.E. Rawson	c Kirmani b Binny	3
A.J. Traicos	run out	2
Extras	(LB 9, W 9)	18
Total	(51.4 overs)	**155**

Fall of wickets: 1-13, 2-55, 3-56, 4-71, 5-106, 6-114, 7-115, 8-139, 9-148, 10-155.

INDIA	*O*	*M*	*R*	*W*
Kapil Dev	9	3	18	1
Sandhu	9	1	29	1
Madan Lal	10.4	0	27	3
Binny	11	2	25	2
Shastri	12	1	38	1

INDIA		
K. Srikkanth	c Butchart b Rawson	20
S.M. Gavaskar	c Heron b Rawson	4
M. Amarnath	c sub (G.E. Peckover) b Traicos	44
S.M. Patil	b Fletcher	50
R.J. Shastri	c Brown b Shah	17
Yashpal Sharma	not out	18
Kapil Dev*	not out	2
R.M.H. Binny		
Madan Lal		
S.M.H. Kirmani†		
B.S. Sandhu		
Extras	(W 2)	2
Total	(37.3 overs – 5 wickets)	**157**

Fall of wickets: 1-13, 2-32, 3-101, 4-128, 5-148.

ZIMBABWE	*O*	*M*	*R*	*W*
Rawson	5.1	1	11	2
Curran	6.5	1	33	0
Butchart	5	1	21	0
Traicos	11	1	41	1
Fletcher	6	1	32	1
Shah	3.3	0	17	1

Umpires: J. Birkenshaw and R. Palmer.

ENGLAND v PAKISTAN 1983

Prudential World Cup – 9th Match

At Lord's, London on 13 June 1983.
Toss: Pakistan. Result: ENGLAND won by 8 wickets.
60 overs match. Award: Zaheer Abbas.
No débuts.

PAKISTAN		
Mohsin Khan	c Tavaré b Willis	3
Mudassar Nazar	c Gould b Allott	26
Mansoor Akhtar	c Gould b Willis	3
Javed Miandad	c Gould b Botham	14
Zaheer Abbas	not out	83
Imran Khan*	run out	7
Wasim Raja	c Botham b Marks	9
Abdul Qadir	run out	0
Sarfraz Nawaz	c and b Botham	11
Wasim Bari†	not out	18
Rashid Khan		
Extras	(B 5, LB 8, W 3, NB 3)	19
Total	(60 overs – 8 wickets)	**193**

Fall of wickets: 1-29, 2-33, 3-49, 4-67, 5-96, 6-112, 7-118, 8-154.

ENGLAND	*O*	*M*	*R*	*W*
Willis	12	4	24	2
Dilley	12	1	33	0
Allott	12	2	48	1
Botham	12	3	36	2
Marks	12	1	33	1

ENGLAND		
G. Fowler	not out	78
C.J. Tavaré	lbw b Rashid	8
D.I. Gower	c Sarfraz b Mansoor	48
A.J. Lamb	not out	48
M.W. Gatting		
I.T. Botham		
I.J. Gould†		
V.J. Marks		
G.R. Dilley		
P.J.W. Allott		
R.G.D. Willis*		
Extras	(B 1, LB 12, W 2, NB 2)	17
Total	(50.4 overs – 2 wickets)	**199**

Fall of wickets: 1-15, 2-93.

PAKISTAN	*O*	*M*	*R*	*W*
Rashid Khan	7	2	19	1
Sarfraz Nawaz	11	5	22	0
Wasim Raja	3	0	14	0
Mudassar Nazar	8	0	30	0
Abdul Qadir	9.4	0	53	0
Mansoor Akhtar	12	2	44	1

Umpires: B.J. Meyer and A.G.T. Whitehead.

Match No. 205/5

NEW ZEALAND v SRI LANKA 1983

Prudential World Cup – 10th Match

At Phoenix County Ground, Bristol on 13 June 1983.
Toss: New Zealand. Result: NEW ZEALAND won by 5 wickets.
60 overs match. Award: R.J. Hadlee.
No débuts.

Five weeks after this match was played, Mr T. Murugaser, manager of the Sri Lankan team, wrote to the Secretary of the TCCB announcing that Howarth was dismissed off the bowling of De Mel. As no such comment was made by the Sri Lankan captain when handed the bowling figures at the end of New Zealand's innings, and as both scorers were adamant that they had identified the bowler correctly, the original version is believed to be accurate.

SRI LANKA		
S. Wettimuny	lbw b Hadlee	7
D.S.B.P. Kuruppu	c Hadlee b Chatfield	26
R.L. Dias	b Chatfield	25
L.R.D. Mendis*	b Hadlee	43
R.S. Madugalle	c Snedden b Coney	60
A. Ranatunga	lbw b Hadlee	0
D.S. De Silva	b Coney	13
R.G. de Alwis†	c Howarth b Snedden	16
A.L.F. De Mel	c and b Hadlee	1
R.J. Ratnayake	b Hadlee	5
V.B. John	not out	2
Extras	(LB 6, W 1, NB 1)	8
Total	(56.1 overs)	**206**

Fall of wickets 1-16, 2-56, 3-73, 4-144, 5-144, 6-171, 7-196, 8-199, 9-199, 10-206.

NEW ZEALAND	*O*	*M*	*R*	*W*
Hadlee	10.1	4	25	5
Snedden	10	1	38	1
Chatfield	12	4	24	2
Cairns	7	0	35	0
Coney	12	0	44	2
M.D. Crowe	5	0	32	0

NEW ZEALAND		
G.M. Turner	c Mendis b De Silva	50
J.G. Wright	lbw b De Mel	45
G.P. Howarth*	c Madugalle b Ratnayake	76
M.D. Crowe	c de Alwis b De Mel	0
J.J. Crowe	lbw b John	23
J.V. Coney	not out	2
I.D.S. Smith†	not out	4
R.J. Hadlee		
B.L. Cairns		
M.C. Snedden		
E.J. Chatfield		
Extras	(LB 6, W 3)	9
Total	(39.2 overs – 5 wickets)	**209**

Fall of wickets 1-89, 2-99, 3-110, 4-176, 5-205.

SRI LANKA	*O*	*M*	*R*	*W*
De Mel	8	2	30	2
John	8.2	0	49	1
Ratnayake	12	0	60	1
De Silva	9	0	39	1
Ranatunga	2	0	22	0

Umpires: H.D. Bird and D.R. Shepherd.

AUSTRALIA v INDIA 1983

Prudential World Cup – 11th Match

At Trent Bridge, Nottingham on 13 June 1983.
Toss: Australia. Result: AUSTRALIA won by 162 runs.
60 overs match. Award: T.M. Chappell.
No débuts.

AUSTRALIA		
K.C. Wessels	b Kapil Dev	5
T.M. Chappell	c Srikkanth b Amarnath	110
K.J. Hughes*	b Madan Lal	52
D.W. Hookes	c Kapil Dev b Madan Lal	1
G.N. Yallop	not out	66
A.R. Border	c Yashpal b Binny	26
R.W. Marsh†	c Sandhu b Kapil Dev	12
K.H. MacLeay	c and b Kapil Dev	4
T.G. Hogan	b Kapil Dev	11
G.F. Lawson	c Srikkanth b Kapil Dev	6
R.M. Hogg	not out	2
Extras	(B 1, LB 14, W 8, NB 2)	25
Total	(60 overs – 9 wickets)	**320**

Fall of wickets: 1-11, 2-155, 3-159, 4-206, 5-254, 6-277, 7-289, 8-301, 9-307.

INDIA	*O*	*M*	*R*	*W*
Kapil Dev	12	2	43	5
Sandhu	12	1	52	0
Binny	12	0	52	1
Shastri	2	0	16	0
Madan Lal	12	0	69	2
Patil	6	0	36	0
Amarnath	4	0	27	1

INDIA		
R.J. Shastri	lbw b Lawson	11
K. Srikkanth	c Border b Hogan	39
M. Amarnath	run out	2
D.B. Vengsarkar	lbw b MacLeay	5
S.M. Patil	b MacLeay	0
Yashpal Sharma	c and b MacLeay	3
Kapil Dev*	b Hogan	40
Madan Lal	c Hogan b MacLeay	27
R.M.H. Binny	lbw b MacLeay	0
S.M.H. Kirmani†	b MacLeay	12
B.S. Sandhu	not out	9
Extras	(B 1, LB 4, W 3, NB 2)	10
Total	(37.5 overs)	**158**

Fall of wickets: 1-38, 2-43, 3-57, 4-57, 5-64, 6-66, 7-124, 8-126, 9-136, 10-158.

AUSTRALIA	*O*	*M*	*R*	*W*
Lawson	5	1	25	1
Hogg	7	2	23	0
Hogan	12	1	48	2
MacLeay	11.5	3	39	6
Border	2	0	13	0

Umpires: D.O. Oslear and R. Palmer.

Match No. 207/1

WEST INDIES v ZIMBABWE 1983

Prudential World Cup – 12th Match

At New Road, Worcester on 13 June 1983.
Toss: West Indies. Result: WEST INDIES won by 8 wickets.
60 overs match. Award: C.G. Greenidge.
Début: Zimbabwe – G.E. Peckover.

ZIMBABWE		
A.H. Shah	b Roberts	2
G.A. Paterson	c Dujon b Holding	4
J.G. Heron	st Dujon b Gomes	12
A.J. Pycroft	run out	13
D.L. Houghton†	c Dujon b Roberts	54
D.A.G. Fletcher*	not out	71
K.M. Curran	b Roberts	7
I.P. Butchart	lbw b Holding	0
G.E. Peckover	not out	16
P.W.E. Rawson		
A.J. Traicos		
Extras	(B 1, LB 23, W 7, NB 7)	38
Total	(60 overs – 7 wickets)	**217**

Fall of wickets 1-7, 2-7, 3-35, 4-65, 5-157, 6-181, 7-183.

WEST INDIES	*O*	*M*	*R*	*W*
Roberts	12	4	36	3
Holding	12	2	33	2
Daniel	12	4	21	0
Davis	12	2	34	0
Gomes	8	0	42	1
Richards	4	1	13	0

WEST INDIES		
C.G. Greenidge	not out	105
D.L. Haynes	c Houghton b Rawson	2
I.V.A. Richards	lbw b Rawson	16
H.A. Gomes	not out	75
S.F.A.F. Bacchus		
C.H. Lloyd*		
P.J.L. Dujon†		
W.W. Daniel		
A.M.E. Roberts		
M.A. Holding		
W.W. Davis		
Extras	(B 1, LB 8, W 9, NB 2)	20
Total	(48.3 overs – 2 wickets)	**218**

Fall of wickets 1-3, 2-23.

ZIMBABWE	*O*	*M*	*R*	*W*
Rawson	12	1	39	2
Curran	10.3	1	37	0
Butchart	9	1	40	0
Fletcher	4	0	22	0
Traicos	9	0	37	0
Shah	4	0	23	0

Umpires: J. Birkenshaw and D.G.L. Evans.

ENGLAND v NEW ZEALAND 1983

Prudential World Cup – 13th Match

At Edgbaston, Birmingham on 15 June 1983.
Toss: England. Result: NEW ZEALAND won by 2 wickets.
60 overs match. Award: J.V. Coney.
No débuts.

ENGLAND		
G. Fowler	c J.J. Crowe b Chatfield	69
C.J. Tavaré	c Cairns b Coney	18
I.T. Botham	c and b Bracewell	12
D.I. Gower	not out	92
A.J. Lamb	c J.J. Crowe b Cairns	8
M.W. Gatting	b Cairns	1
I.J. Gould†	lbw b Cairns	4
V.J. Marks	b Hadlee	5
G.R. Dilley	b Hadlee	10
P.J.W. Allott	c Smith b Hadlee	0
R.G.D. Willis*	lbw b Chatfield	0
Extras	(B 4, LB 10, W 1)	15
Total	(55.2 overs)	**234**

Fall of wickets: 1-63, 2-77, 3-117, 4-143, 5-154, 6-162, 7-203, 8-233, 9-233, 10-234.

NEW ZEALAND	*O*	*M*	*R*	*W*
Hadlee	10	3	32	3
Cairns	11	0	44	3
Coney	12	2	27	1
Bracewell	12	0	66	1
Chatfield	10.2	0	50	2

NEW ZEALAND		
G.M. Turner	lbw b Willis	2
B.A. Edgar	c Gould b Willis	1
G.P. Howarth*	run out	60
J.J. Crowe	b Allott	17
M.D. Crowe	b Marks	20
J.V. Coney	not out	66
I.D.S. Smith†	b Botham	4
R.J. Hadlee	b Willis	31
B.L. Cairns	lbw b Willis	5
J.G. Bracewell	not out	4
E.J. Chatfield		
Extras	(B 2, LB 22, W 1, NB 3)	28
Total	(59.5 overs – 8 wickets)	**238**

Fall of wickets: 1-2, 2-3, 3-47, 4-75, 5-146, 6-151, 7-221, 8-231.

ENGLAND	*O*	*M*	*R*	*W*
Willis	12	1	42	4
Dilley	12	1	43	0
Botham	12	1	47	1
Allott	11.5	2	44	1
Marks	12	1	34	1

Umpires: J. Birkenshaw and K.E. Palmer.

Match No. 209/6

PAKISTAN v SRI LANKA 1983

Prudential World Cup – 14th Match

At Headingley, Leeds on 16 June 1983.
Toss: Sri Lanka. Result: PAKISTAN won by 11 runs.
60 overs match. Award: Abdul Qadir.
No débuts.

PAKISTAN		
Mohsin Khan	c Ranatunga b De Mel	3
Mansoor Akhtar	c de Alwis b De Mel	6
Zaheer Abbas	c Dias b De Mel	15
Javed Miandad	lbw b Ratnayake	7
Imran Khan*	not out	102
Ijaz Faqih	lbw b Ratnayake	0
Shahid Mahboob	c De Silva b De Mel	77
Sarfraz Nawaz	c Madugalle b De Mel	9
Abdul Qadir	not out	5
Wasim Bari†		
Rashid Khan		
Extras	(B 1, LB 4, W 4, NB 2)	11
Total	(60 overs – 7 wickets)	**235**

Fall of wickets 1-6, 2-25, 3-30, 4-43, 5-43, 6-187, 7-204.

SRI LANKA	*O*	*M*	*R*	*W*
De Mel	12	1	39	5
John	12	1	48	0
Ratnayake	12	2	42	2
Ranatunga	11	0	49	0
De Silva	12	1	42	0
Wettimuny	1	0	4	0

SRI LANKA		
S. Wettimuny	c Shahid b Rashid	50
D.S.B.P. Kuruppu	b Rashid	12
R.L. Dias	st Wasim Bari b Qadir	47
L.R.D. Mendis*	c Wasim Bari b Qadir	33
R.J. Ratnayake	st Wasim Bari b Qadir	1
R.S. Madugalle	c Qadir b Shahid	26
A. Ranatunga	c Zaheer b Qadir	0
D.S. De Silva	run out	1
R.G. de Alwis†	c Miandad b Qadir	4
A.L.F. De Mel	c Imran b Sarfraz	17
V.B. John	not out	6
Extras	(LB 8, W 17, NB 2)	27
Total	(58.3 overs)	**224**

Fall of wickets 1-22, 2-101, 3-162, 4-162, 5-166, 6-166, 7-171, 8-193, 9-199, 10-224.

PAKISTAN	*O*	*M*	*R*	*W*
Rashid Khan	12	4	31	2
Sarfraz Nawaz	11.3	2	25	1
Shahid Mahboob	10	1	62	1
Mansoor Akhtar	1	0	8	0
Ijaz Faqih	12	0	27	0
Abdul Qadir	12	1	44	5

Umpires: D.O. Oslear and A.G.T. Whitehead.

AUSTRALIA v ZIMBABWE 1983

Prudential World Cup – 15th Match

At County Ground, Southampton on 16 June 1983.
Toss: Australia. Result: AUSTRALIA won by 32 runs.
60 overs match. Award: D.L. Houghton.
No débuts.

AUSTRALIA		
G.M. Wood	c Rawson b Traicos	73
T.M. Chappell	c Traicos b Rawson	22
K.J. Hughes*	b Traicos	31
D.W. Hookes	c Brown b Fletcher	10
G.N. Yallop	c Houghton b Curran	20
A.R. Border	b Butchart	43
R.W. Marsh†	not out	35
K.H. MacLeay	c Rawson b Butchart	9
T.G. Hogan	not out	5
D.K. Lillee		
R.M. Hogg		
Extras	(LB 16, W 2, NB 6)	24
Total	(60 overs – 7 wickets)	**272**

Fall of wickets: 1-46, 2-124, 3-150, 4-150, 5-219, 6-231, 7-249.

ZIMBABWE	*O*	*M*	*R*	*W*
Hogg	9	2	34	0
Rawson	9	0	50	1
Fletcher	9	1	27	1
Butchart	10	0	52	2
Traicos	12	1	28	2
Curran	11	0	57	1

ZIMBABWE		
R.D. Brown	c Marsh b Hogan	38
G.A. Paterson	lbw b Hogg	17
J.G. Heron	run out	3
A.J. Pycroft	run out	13
D.L. Houghton†	c Hughes b Chappell	84
D.A.G. Fletcher*	b Hogan	2
K.M. Curran	lbw b Chappell	35
I.P. Butchart	lbw b Hogg	0
P.W.E. Rawson	lbw b Hogg	0
A.J. Traicos	b Chappell	19
V.R. Hogg	not out	7
Extras	(B 1, LB 10, W 1, NB 10)	22
Total	(59.5 overs)	**240**

Fall of wickets: 1-48, 2-53, 3-79, 4-97, 5-109, 6-212, 7-213, 8-213, 9-213, 10-240.

AUSTRALIA	*O*	*M*	*R*	*W*
Hogg	12	0	40	3
Lillee	9	1	23	0
Hogan	12	0	33	2
MacLeay	9	0	45	0
Border	9	1	30	0
Chappell	8.5	0	47	3

Umpires: D.G.L. Evans and R. Palmer.

Match No. 211/6

INDIA v WEST INDIES 1983

Prudential World Cup – 16th Match

At Kennington Oval, London on 15 June 1983.

Toss: West Indies.	Result: WEST INDIES won by 66 runs.
60 overs match.	Award: I.V.A. Richards.

No débuts.

WEST INDIES		
C.G. Greenidge	c Vengsarkar b Kapil Dev	9
D.L. Haynes	c Kapil Dev b Amarnath	38
I.V.A. Richards	c Kirmani b Sandhu	119
C.H. Lloyd*	run out	41
S.F.A.F. Bacchus	b Binny	8
P.J.L. Dujon†	c Shastri b Binny	9
H.A. Gomes	not out	27
A.M.E. Roberts	c Patil b Binny	7
M.D. Marshall	run out	4
M.A. Holding	c sub (K. Azad) b Madan Lal	2
W.W. Davis	not out	0
Extras	(LB 13, W 5)	18
Total	(60 overs – 9 wickets)	**282**

Fall of wickets: 1-17, 2-118, 3-198, 4-213, 5-239, 6-240, 7-257, 8-270, 9-280.

INDIA	*O*	*M*	*R*	*W*
Kapil Dev	12	0	46	1
Sandhu	12	2	42	1
Binny	12	0	71	3
Amarnath	12	0	58	1
Madan Lal	12	0	47	1

INDIA		
K. Srikkanth	c Dujon b Roberts	2
R.J. Shastri	c Dujon b Roberts	6
M. Amarnath	c Lloyd b Holding	80
D.B. Vengsarkar	retired hurt	32
S.M. Patil	c and b Gomes	21
Yashpal Sharma	run out	9
Kapil Dev*	c Haynes b Holding	36
R.M.H. Binny	lbw b Holding	1
Madan Lal	not out	8
S.M.H. Kirmani†	b Marshall	0
B.S. Sandhu	run out	0
Extras	(B 3, LB 13, NB 5)	21
Total	(53.1 overs)	**216**

Fall of wickets: 1-2, 2-21, 3-130, 4-143, 5-193, 6-195, 7-212, 8-214, 9-216.

WEST INDIES	*O*	*M*	*R*	*W*
Roberts	9	1	29	2
Holding	9.1	0	40	3
Marshall	11	3	20	1
Davis	12	2	51	0
Gomes	12	1	55	1

Umpires: B.J. Meyer and D.R. Shepherd.

ENGLAND v PAKISTAN 1983
Prudential World Cup – 17th Match

At Old Trafford, Manchester on 18 June 1983.
Toss: Pakistan. Result: ENGLAND won by 7 wickets.
60 overs match. Award: G. Fowler.
No débuts.

PAKISTAN		
Mohsin Khan	c Marks b Allott	32
Mudassar Nazar	c Gould b Dilley	18
Zaheer Abbas	c Gould b Dilley	0
Javed Miandad	run out	67
Imran Khan*	c Willis b Marks	13
Wasim Raja	c Willis b Marks	15
Ijaz Faqih	not out	42
Sarfraz Nawaz	b Willis	17
Abdul Qadir	run out	6
Wasim Bari†	not out	2
Rashid Khan		
Extras	(B 3, LB 14, W 2, NB 1)	20
Total	(60 overs – 8 wickets)	**232**

Fall of wickets: 1-33, 2-34, 3-87, 4-116, 5-144, 6-169, 7-204, 8-221.

ENGLAND	*O*	*M*	*R*	*W*
Willis	12	3	37	1
Dilley	12	2	46	2
Allott	12	1	33	1
Botham	12	1	51	0
Marks	12	0	45	2

ENGLAND		
G. Fowler	c Miandad b Mudassar	69
C.J. Tavaré	c Wasim Raja b Zaheer	58
D.I. Gower	c Zaheer b Mudassar	31
A.J. Lamb	not out	38
M.W. Gatting	not out	14
I.T. Botham		
I.J. Gould†		
V.J. Marks		
G.R. Dilley		
P.J.W. Allott		
R.G.D. Willis*		
Extras	(B 1, LB 15, W 7)	23
Total	(57.2 overs – 3 wickets)	**233**

Fall of wickets: 1-115, 2-165, 3-181.

PAKISTAN	*O*	*M*	*R*	*W*
Rashid Khan	11	1	58	0
Sarfraz Nawaz	10.2	2	22	0
Abdul Qadir	11	0	51	0
Ijaz Faqih	6	0	19	0
Mudassar Nazar	12	2	34	2
Zaheer Abbas	7	0	26	1

Umpires: H.D. Bird and D.O. Oslear.

Match No. 213/6

NEW ZEALAND v SRI LANKA 1983

Prudential World Cup – 18th Match

At County Ground, Derby on 18 June 1983.
Toss: Sri Lanka. Result: SRI LANKA won by 3 wickets.
60 overs match. Award: A.L.F. De Mel.
No débuts.

NEW ZEALAND		
G.M. Turner	c Dias b De Mel	6
J.G. Wright	c de Alwis b De Mel	0
G.P. Howarth*	b Ratnayake	15
M.D. Crowe	lbw b Ratnayake	8
B.A. Edgar	c Samarasekera b De Silva	27
J.V. Coney	c sub (E.R.N.S. Fernando) b De Silva	22
R.J. Hadlee	c Madugalle b De Mel	15
W.K. Lees†	c Ranatunga b De Mel	2
B.L. Cairns	c Dias b De Mel	6
M.C. Snedden	run out	40
E.J. Chatfield	not out	19
Extras	(B 4, LB 5, W 11, NB 1)	21
Total	(58.2 overs)	**181**

Fall of wickets: 1-8, 2-8, 3-32, 4-47, 5-88, 6-91, 7-105, 8-115, 9-116, 10-181.

SRI LANKA	*O*	*M*	*R*	*W*
De Mel	12	4	32	5
Ratnayake	11	4	18	2
Ranatunga	10	2	50	0
De Silva	12	5	11	2
Samarasekera	11.2	2	38	0
Wettimuny	2	0	11	0

SRI LANKA		
S. Wettimuny	b Cairns	4
D.S.B.P. Kuruppu	c and b Snedden	62
A. Ranatunga	b Crowe	15
R.L. Dias	not out	64
L.R.D. Mendis*	lbw b Chatfield	0
R.S. Madugalle	c Lees b Snedden	6
M.A.R. Samarasekera	c Lees b Hadlee	5
D.S. De Silva	run out	2
R.G. de Alwis†	not out	11
A.L.F. De Mel		
R.J. Ratnayake		
Extras	(B 1, LB 4, W 10)	15
Total	(52.5 overs – 7 wickets)	**186**

Fall of wickets: 1-15, 2-49, 3-129, 4-130, 5-139, 6-151, 7-161.

NEW ZEALAND	*O*	*M*	*R*	*W*
Hadlee	12	3	16	1
Cairns	10	2	35	1
Snedden	10.5	1	58	2
Chatfield	12	3	23	1
Crowe	4	2	15	1
Coney	4	1	22	0

Umpires: D.J. Constant and B. Leadbeater.

AUSTRALIA v WEST INDIES 1983
Prudential World Cup – 19th Match

At Lord's, London on 18 June 1983.
Toss: Australia. Result: WEST INDIES won by 7 wickets.
60 overs match. Award: I.V.A. Richards.
No débuts.

AUSTRALIA		
G.M. Wood	b Marshall	17
T.M. Chappell	c Dujon b Marshall	5
K.J. Hughes*	b Gomes	69
D.W. Hookes	c Greenidge b Davis	56
G.N. Yallop	not out	52
A.R. Border	c and b Gomes	11
R.W. Marsh†	c Haynes b Holding	37
T.G. Hogan	not out	0
J.R. Thomson		
D.K. Lillee		
R.M. Hogg		
Extras	(B 1, LB 18, W 6, NB 1)	26
Total	(60 overs – 6 wickets)	**273**

Fall of wickets: 1-10, 2-37, 3-138, 4-176, 5-202, 6-266.

WEST INDIES	*O*	*M*	*R*	*W*
Roberts	12	0	51	0
Marshall	12	0	36	2
Davis	12	0	57	1
Holding	12	1	56	1
Gomes	12	0	47	2

WEST INDIES		
C.G. Greenidge	c Hughes b Hogg	90
D.L. Haynes	b Hogan	33
I.V.A. Richards	not out	95
H.A. Gomes	b Chappell	15
C.H. Lloyd*	not out	19
S.F.A.F. Bacchus		
P.J.L. Dujon†		
M.D. Marshall		
A.M.E. Roberts		
M.A. Holding		
W.W. Davis		
Extras	(B 3, LB 18, W 1, NB 2)	24
Total	(57.5 overs – 3 wickets)	**276**

Fall of wickets: 1-79, 2-203, 3-228.

AUSTRALIA	*O*	*M*	*R*	*W*
Hogg	12	0	25	1
Thomson	11	0	64	0
Hogan	12	0	60	1
Lillee	12	0	52	0
Chappell	10.5	0	51	1

Umpires: K.E. Palmer and A.G.T. Whitehead.

Match No. 215/2

INDIA v ZIMBABWE 1983

Prudential World Cup – 20th Match

At Nevill Ground, Tunbridge Wells on 18 June 1983.
Toss: India. Result: INDIA won by 31 runs.
60 overs match. Award: Kapil Dev.

No débuts.

Coming to the wicket at 11.25 am with his side desperately placed at 17-5, Kapil Dev played one of the greatest international innings of all time. He completed India's first century in these matches at 2.18 pm and went on to record the highest innings in Prudential Cup matches. Batting for 181 minutes, he hit six sixes and 17 fours, and, with Kirmani, shared the first century partnership for the ninth wicket in limited-overs internationals.

INDIA		
S.M. Gavaskar	lbw b Rawson	0
K. Srikkanth	c Butchart b Curran	0
M. Amarnath	c Houghton b Rawson	5
S.M. Patil	c Houghton b Curran	1
Yashpal Sharma	c Houghton b Rawson	9
Kapil Dev*	not out	175
R.M.H. Binny	lbw b Traicos	22
R.J. Shastri	c Pycroft b Fletcher	1
Madan Lal	c Houghton b Curran	17
S.M.H. Kirmani†	not out	24
B.S. Sandhu		
Extras	(LB 9, W 3)	12
Total	(60 overs – 8 wickets)	**266**

Fall of wickets: 1-0, 2-6, 3-6, 4-9, 5-17, 6-77, 7-78, 8-140.

ZIMBABWE	*O*	*M*	*R*	*W*
Rawson	12	4	47	3
Curran	12	1	65	3
Butchart	12	2	38	0
Fletcher	12	2	59	1
Traicos	12	0	45	1

ZIMBABWE		
R.D. Brown	run out	35
G.A. Paterson	lbw b Binny	23
J.G. Heron	run out	3
A.J. Pycroft	c Kirmani b Sandhu	6
D.L. Houghton†	lbw b Madan Lal	17
D.A.G. Fletcher*	c Kapil Dev b Amarnath	13
K.M. Curran	c Shastri b Madan Lal	73
I.P. Butchart	b Binny	18
G.E. Peckover	c Yashpal b Madan Lal	14
P.W.E. Rawson	not out	2
A.J. Traicos	c and b Kapil Dev	3
Extras	(LB 17, W 7, NB 4)	28
Total	(57 overs)	**235**

Fall of wickets: 1-44, 2-48, 3-61, 4-86, 5-103, 6-113, 7-168, 8-189, 9-230, 10-235.

INDIA	*O*	*M*	*R*	*W*
Kapil Dev	11	1	32	1
Sandhu	11	2	44	1
Binny	11	2	45	2
Madan Lal	11	2	42	3
Amarnath	12	1	37	1
Shastri	1	0	7	0

Umpires: M.J. Kitchen and B.J. Meyer.

ENGLAND v SRI LANKA 1983

Prudential World Cup – 21st Match

At Headingley, Leeds on 20 June 1983.
Toss: England. Result: ENGLAND won by 9 wickets.
60 overs match. Award: R.G.D. Willis.
No débuts.

SRI LANKA		
S. Wettimuny	lbw b Botham	22
D.S.B.P. Kuruppu	c Gatting b Willis	6
A. Ranatunga	c Lamb b Botham	0
R.L. Dias	c Gould b Cowans	7
L.R.D. Mendis*	b Allott	10
R.S. Madugalle	c Gould b Allott	0
D.S. De Silva	c Gower b Marks	15
R.G. de Alwis†	c Marks b Cowans	19
A.L.F. De Mel	c Lamb b Marks	10
R.J. Ratnayake	not out	20
V.B. John	c Cowans b Allott	15
Extras	(B 5, LB 2, W 3, NB 2)	12
Total	(50.4 overs)	**136**

Fall of wickets: 1-25, 2-30, 3-32, 4-40, 5-43, 6-54, 7-81, 8-97, 9-103, 10-136.

ENGLAND	*O*	*M*	*R*	*W*
Willis	9	4	9	1
Cowans	12	3	31	2
Botham	9	4	12	2
Allott	10.4	0	41	3
Gatting	4	2	13	0
Marks	6	2	18	2

ENGLAND		
G. Fowler	not out	81
C.J. Tavaré	c de Alwis b De Mel	19
D.I. Gower	not out	27
A.J. Lamb		
M.W. Gatting		
I.T. Botham		
I.J. Gould†		
V.J. Marks		
P.J.W. Allott		
R.G.D. Willis*		
N.G. Cowans		
Extras	(B 1, LB 3, W 3, NB 3)	10
Total	(24.1 overs – 1 wicket)	**137**

Fall of wicket: 1-68.

SRI LANKA	*O*	*M*	*R*	*W*
De Mel	10	1	33	1
Ratnayake	5	0	23	0
John	6	0	41	0
De Silva	3	0	29	0
Ranatunga	0.1	0	1	0

Umpires: B. Leadbeater and R. Palmer.

Match No. 217/4

NEW ZEALAND v PAKISTAN 1983

Prudential World Cup – 22nd Match

At Trent Bridge, Nottingham on 20 June 1983.
Toss: Pakistan. Result: PAKISTAN won by 11 runs.
60 overs match. Award: Imran Khan.

No débuts.

Zaheer became the first batsman to score seven hundreds in these matches.

PAKISTAN		
Mohsin Khan	c Cairns b Coney	33
Mudassar Nazar	b Coney	15
Javed Miandad	b Hadlee	25
Zaheer Abbas	not out	103
Imran Khan*	not out	79
Ijaz Faqih		
Shahid Mahboob		
Sarfraz Nawaz		
Abdul Qadir		
Wasim Bari†		
Rashid Khan		
Extras	(B 1, LB 2, W 2, NB 1)	6
Total	(60 overs – 3 wickets)	**261**

Fall of wickets 1-48, 2-54, 3-114.

NEW ZEALAND	*O*	*M*	*R*	*W*
Hadlee	12	1	61	1
Cairns	12	1	45	0
Chatfield	12	0	57	0
Coney	12	0	42	2
Bracewell	12	0	50	0

NEW ZEALAND		
G.M. Turner	c Wasim Bari b Sarfraz	4
J.G. Wright	c Imran b Qadir	19
G.P. Howarth*	c Miandad b Zaheer	39
M.D. Crowe	b Mudassar	43
B.A. Edgar	lbw b Shahid	6
J.V. Coney	run out	51
R.J. Hadlee	c Mohsin b Mudassar	11
B.L. Cairns	c Imran b Qadir	0
W.K. Lees†	c sub (Mansoor Akhtar) b Mudassar	26
J.G. Bracewell	c Mohsin b Sarfraz	34
E.J. Chatfield	not out	3
Extras	(LB 8, W 5, NB 1)	14
Total	(59.1 overs)	**250**

Fall of wickets 1-13, 2-44, 3-85, 4-102, 5-130, 6-150, 7-152, 8-187, 9-246, 10-250.

PAKISTAN	*O*	*M*	*R*	*W*
Rashid Khan	6	1	24	0
Sarfraz Nawaz	9.1	1	50	2
Abdul Qadir	12	0	53	2
Ijaz Faqih	6	1	21	0
Shahid Mahboob	10	0	37	1
Mudassar Nazar	12	0	43	3
Zaheer Abbas	4	1	8	1

Umpires: D.G.L. Evans and M.J. Kitchen.

AUSTRALIA v INDIA 1983

Prudential World Cup – 23rd Match

At County Ground, Chelmsford on 20 June 1983.
Toss: India. Result: INDIA won by 118 runs.
60 overs match. Award: R.M.H. Binny.
No débuts.

INDIA		
S.M. Gavaskar	c Chappell b Hogg	9
K. Srikkanth	c Border b Thomson	24
M. Amarnath	c Marsh b Thomson	13
Yashpal Sharma	c Hogg b Hogan	40
S.M. Patil	c Hogan b MacLeay	30
Kapil Dev*	c Hookes b Hogg	28
K. Azad	c Border b Lawson	15
R.M.H. Binny	run out	21
Madan Lal	not out	12
S.M.H. Kirmani†	lbw b Hogg	10
B.S. Sandhu	b Thomson	8
Extras	(LB 13, W 9, NB 15)	37
Total	(55.5 overs)	**247**

Fall of wickets: 1-27, 2-54, 3-65, 4-118, 5-157, 6-174, 7-207, 8-215, 9-232, 10-247.

AUSTRALIA	*O*	*M*	*R*	*W*
Lawson	10	1	40	1
Hogg	12	2	40	3
Hogan	11	1	31	1
Thomson	10.5	0	51	3
MacLeay	12	2	48	1

AUSTRALIA		
T.M. Chappell	c Madan Lal b Sandhu	2
G.M. Wood	c Kirmani b Binny	21
G.N. Yallop	c and b Binny	18
D.W. Hookes*	b Binny	1
A.R. Border	b Madan Lal	36
R.W. Marsh†	lbw b Madan Lal	0
K.H. MacLeay	c Gavaskar b Madan Lal	5
T.G. Hogan	c Srikkanth b Binny	8
G.F. Lawson	b Sandhu	16
R.M. Hogg	not out	8
J.R. Thomson	b Madan Lal	0
Extras	(LB 5, W 5, NB 4)	14
Total	(38.2 overs)	**129**

Fall of wickets: 1-3, 2-46, 3-48, 4-52, 5-52, 6-69, 7-78, 8-115, 9-129, 10-129.

INDIA	*O*	*M*	*R*	*W*
Kapil Dev	8	2	16	0
Sandhu	10	1	26	2
Madan Lal	8.2	3	20	4
Binny	8	2	29	4
Amarnath	2	0	17	0
Azad	2	0	7	0

Umpires: J. Birkenshaw and D.R. Shepherd.

Match No. 219/2

WEST INDIES v ZIMBABWE 1983

Prudential World Cup – 24th Match

At Edgbaston, Birmingham on 20 June 1983.
Toss: Zimbabwe. Result: WEST INDIES won by 10 wickets.
60 overs match. Award: S.F.A.F. Bacchus.
No débuts.

ZIMBABWE		
R.D. Brown	c Lloyd b Marshall	14
G.A. Paterson	c Richards b Garner	6
J.G. Heron	c Dujon b Garner	0
A.J. Pycroft	c Dujon b Marshall	4
D.L. Houghton†	c Lloyd b Daniel	0
D.A.G. Fletcher*	b Richards	23
K.M. Curran	b Daniel	62
I.P. Butchart	c Haynes b Richards	8
G.E. Peckover	c and b Richards	3
P.W.E. Rawson	b Daniel	19
A.J. Traicos	not out	1
Extras	(B 4, LB 13, W 7, NB 7)	31
Total	(60 overs)	**171**

Fall of wickets 1-17, 2-17, 3-41, 4-42, 5-42, 6-79, 7-104, 8-115, 9-170, 10-171.

WEST INDIES	*O*	*M*	*R*	*W*
Marshall	12	3	19	2
Garner	7	4	13	2
Davis	8	2	13	0
Daniel	9	2	28	3
Gomes	12	2	26	0
Richards	12	1	41	3

WEST INDIES		
D.L. Haynes	not out	88
S.F.A.F. Bacchus	not out	80
A.L. Logie		
I.V.A. Richards		
H.A. Gomes		
C.H. Lloyd*		
P.J.L. Dujon†		
J. Garner		
M.D. Marshall		
W.W. Daniel		
W.W. Davis		
Extras	(LB 1, W 3)	4
Total	(45.1 overs – 0 wicket)	**172**

ZIMBABWE	*O*	*M*	*R*	*W*
Rawson	12	3	38	0
Butchart	4	0	23	0
Traicos	12	2	24	0
Curran	9	0	44	0
Fletcher	8.1	0	39	0

Umpires: H.D. Bird and D.J. Constant.

ENGLAND v INDIA 1983

Prudential World Cup – Semi-Final

At Old Trafford, Manchester on 22 June 1983.
Toss: England. Result: INDIA won by 6 wickets.
60 overs match. Award: M. Amarnath.
No débuts.

ENGLAND		
G. Fowler	b Binny	33
C.J. Tavaré	c Kirmani b Binny	32
D.I. Gower	c Kirmani b Amarnath	17
A.J. Lamb	run out	29
M.W. Gatting	b Amarnath	18
I.T. Botham	b Azad	6
I.J. Gould†	run out	13
V.J. Marks	b Kapil Dev	8
G.R. Dilley	not out	20
P.J.W. Allott	c Patil b Kapil Dev	8
R.G.D. Willis*	b Kapil Dev	0
Extras	(B 1, LB 17, W 7, NB 4)	29
Total	(60 overs)	**213**

Fall of wickets: 1-69, 2-84, 3-107, 4-141, 5-150, 6-160, 7-175, 8-177, 9-202, 10-213.

INDIA	*O*	*M*	*R*	*W*
Kapil Dev	11	1	35	3
Sandhu	8	1	36	0
Binny	12	1	43	2
Madan Lal	5	0	15	0
Azad	12	1	28	1
Amarnath	12	1	27	2

INDIA		
S.M. Gavaskar	c Gould b Allott	25
K. Srikkanth	c Willis b Botham	19
M. Amarnath	run out	46
Yashpal Sharma	c Allott b Willis	61
S.M. Patil	not out	51
Kapil Dev*	not out	1
K. Azad		
R.M.H. Binny		
Madan Lal		
S.M.H. Kirmani†		
B.S. Sandhu		
Extras	(B 5, LB 6, W 1, NB 2)	14
Total	(54.4 overs – 4 wickets)	**217**

Fall of wickets: 1-46, 2-50, 3-142, 4-205.

ENGLAND	*O*	*M*	*R*	*W*
Willis	10.4	2	42	1
Dilley	11	0	43	0
Allott	10	3	40	1
Botham	11	4	40	1
Marks	12	1	38	0

Umpires: D.G.L. Evans and D.O. Oslear.

Match No. 221/12

PAKISTAN v WEST INDIES 1983

Prudential World Cup – Semi-Final

At Kennington Oval, London on 22 June 1983.
Toss: West Indies. Result: WEST INDIES won by 8 wickets.
60 overs match. Award: I.V.A. Richards.
No débuts.

PAKISTAN		
Mohsin Khan	b Roberts	70
Mudassar Nazar	c and b Garner	11
Ijaz Faqih	c Dujon b Holding	5
Zaheer Abbas	b Gomes	30
Imran Khan*	c Dujon b Marshall	17
Wasim Raja	lbw b Marshall	0
Shahid Mahboob	c Richards b Marshall	6
Sarfraz Nawaz	c Holding b Roberts	3
Abdul Qadir	not out	10
Wasim Bari†	not out	4
Rashid Khan		
Extras	(B 6, LB 13, W 4, NB 5)	28
Total	(60 overs – 8 wickets)	**184**

Fall of wickets 1-23, 2-34, 3-88, 4-139, 5-139, 6-159, 7-164, 8-171.

WEST INDIES	*O*	*M*	*R*	*W*
Roberts	12	3	25	2
Garner	12	1	31	1
Marshall	12	2	28	3
Holding	12	1	25	1
Gomes	7	0	29	1
Richards	5	0	18	0

WEST INDIES		
C.G. Greenidge	lbw b Rashid	17
D.L. Haynes	b Qadir	29
I.V.A. Richards	not out	80
H.A. Gomes	not out	50
C.H. Lloyd*		
S.F.A.F. Bacchus		
P.J.L. Dujon†		
A.M.E. Roberts		
M.D. Marshall		
J. Garner		
M.A. Holding		
Extras	(B 2, LB 6, W 4)	12
Total	(48.4 overs – 2 wickets)	**188**

Fall of wickets 1-34, 2-56.

PAKISTAN	*O*	*M*	*R*	*W*
Rashid Khan	12	2	32	1
Sarfraz Nawaz	8	0	23	0
Abdul Qadir	11	1	42	1
Shahid Mahboob	11	1	43	0
Wasim Raja	1	0	9	0
Zaheer Abbas	4.4	1	24	0
Mohsin Khan	1	0	3	0

Umpires: D.J. Constant and A.G.T. Whitehead.

INDIA v WEST INDIES 1983

Prudential World Cup – Final

At Lord's, London on 25 June 1983.
Toss: West Indies. Result: INDIA won by 43 runs.
60 overs match. Award: M. Amarnath.

No débuts.

India achieved one of cricket's most surprising results when they prevented West Indies from completing a hat-trick of Prudential Cup victories.

INDIA		
S.M. Gavaskar	c Dujon b Roberts	2
K. Srikkanth	lbw b Marshall	38
M. Amarnath	b Holding	26
Yashpal Sharma	c sub (A.L. Logie) b Gomes	11
S.M. Patil	c Gomes b Garner	27
Kapil Dev*	c Holding b Gomes	15
K. Azad	c Garner b Roberts	0
R.M.H. Binny	c Garner b Roberts	2
Madan Lal	b Marshall	17
S.M.H. Kirmani†	b Holding	14
B.S. Sandhu	not out	11
Extras	(B 5, LB 5, W 9, NB 1)	20
Total	(54.4 overs)	**183**

Fall of wickets: 1-2, 2-59, 3-90, 4-92, 5-110, 6-111, 7-130, 8-153, 9-161, 10-183.

WEST INDIES	*O*	*M*	*R*	*W*
Roberts	10	3	32	3
Garner	12	4	24	1
Marshall	11	1	24	2
Holding	9.4	2	26	2
Gomes	11	1	49	2
Richards	1	0	8	0

WEST INDIES		
C.G. Greenidge	b Sandhu	1
D.L. Haynes	c Binny b Madan Lal	13
I.V.A. Richards	c Kapil Dev b Madan Lal	33
C.H. Lloyd*	c Kapil Dev b Binny	8
H.A. Gomes	c Gavaskar b Madan Lal	5
S.F.A.F. Bacchus	c Kirmani b Sandhu	8
P.J.L. Dujon†	b Amarnath	25
M.D. Marshall	c Gavaskar b Amarnath	18
A.M.E. Roberts	lbw b Kapil Dev	4
J. Garner	not out	5
M.A. Holding	lbw b Amarnath	6
Extras	(LB 4, W 10)	14
Total	(52 overs)	**140**

Fall of wickets: 1-5, 2-50, 3-57, 4-66, 5-66, 6-76, 7-119, 8-124, 9-126, 10-140.

INDIA	*O*	*M*	*R*	*W*
Kapil Dev	11	4	21	1
Sandhu	9	1	32	2
Madan Lal	12	2	31	3
Binny	10	1	23	1
Amarnath	7	0	12	3
Azad	3	0	7	0

Umpires: H.D. Bird and B.J. Meyer.

Match No. 223/8

INDIA v PAKISTAN 1983-84 (1st Match)

At Niaz Stadium, Hyderabad on 11 September 1983.
Toss: India. Result: INDIA won by 4 wickets.
46 overs match. Award: M. Amarnath.
Débuts: Pakistan – Azeem Hafeez, Qasim Omar.

PAKISTAN		
Mohsin Khan	b Sandhu	6
Mudassar Nazar	c Kirmani b Kapil Dev	0
Zaheer Abbas*	c Kirmani b Sandhu	20
Javed Miandad	not out	66
Wasim Raja	c Kapil Dev b Sandhu	0
Qasim Omar	c Kirmani b Binny	5
Wasim Bari†	run out	18
Tahir Naqqash	c Amarnath b Binny	1
Jalaluddin	run out	5
Azeem Hafeez	not out	5
Mohammad Nazir		
Extras	(LB 4, W 18, NB 3)	25
Total	(46 overs – 8 wickets)	**151**

Fall of wickets: 1-1, 2-23, 3-35, 4-36, 5-62, 6-123, 7-129, 8-136.

INDIA	*O*	*M*	*R*	*W*
Kapil Dev	9	3	16	1
Sandhu	9	2	27	3
Madan Lal	10	2	22	0
Binny	8	2	34	2
Amarnath	10	0	27	0

INDIA		
S.M. Gavaskar	c Wasim Bari b Mudassar	33
K. Srikkanth	lbw b Jalaluddin	16
M. Amarnath	not out	60
Yashpal Sharma	b Mudassar	2
S.M. Patil	c Miandad b Mudassar	1
K. Azad	c Wasim Raja b Nazir	7
Kapil Dev*	c Mohsin b Azeem	18
R.M.H. Binny	not out	0
Madan Lal		
S.M.H. Kirmani†		
B.S. Sandhu		
Extras	(B 1, LB 3, W 10, NB 1)	15
Total	(43 overs – 6 wickets)	**152**

Fall of wickets: 1-30, 2-69, 3-77, 4-81, 5-113, 6-151.

PAKISTAN	*O*	*M*	*R*	*W*
Jalaluddin	8	0	34	1
Tahir Naqqash	5	1	16	0
Mudassar Nazar	10	3	17	3
Azeem Hafeez	10	0	43	1
Mohammad Nazir	10	1	27	1

Umpires: P.G. Pandit and M.G. Subramaniam.

INDIA v PAKISTAN 1983-84 (2nd Match)

At Sawai Mansingh Stadium, Jaipur on 2 October 1983.
Toss: India. Result: INDIA won by 4 wickets.
46 overs match. Award: S.M. Patil.
No débuts.

PAKISTAN		
Mudassar Nazar	b Binny	27
Mohsin Khan	c Patil b Madan Lal	22
Zaheer Abbas*	lbw b Kapil Dev	48
Javed Miandad	lbw b Madan Lal	1
Wasim Raja	run out	17
Salim Malik	c Azad b Kapil Dev	27
Wasim Bari†	not out	5
Tahir Naqqash	run out	0
Jalaluddin	c and b Madan Lal	0
Azeem Hafeez	run out	7
Mohammad Nazir	not out	0
Extras	(LB 6, W 4, NB 2)	12
Total	(46 overs – 9 wickets)	**166**

Fall of wickets: 1-55, 2-57, 3-60, 4-100, 5-153, 6-155, 7-155, 8-155, 9-165

INDIA	*O*	*M*	*R*	*W*
Kapil Dev	10	2	33	2
Sandhu	10	1	36	0
Madan Lal	10	1	27	3
Binny	10	0	38	1
Amarnath	6	0	26	0

INDIA		
S.M. Gavaskar	b Nazir	41
K. Srikkanth	b Jalaluddin	17
M. Amarnath	b Tahir	1
S.M. Patil	c Mohsin b Nazir	51
Kapil Dev*	c Wasim Bari b Jalaluddin	9
K. Azad	b Mudassar	4
Yashpal Sharma	not out	23
R.M.H. Binny	not out	11
Madan Lal		
S.M.H. Kirmani†		
B.S. Sandhu		
Extras	(B 4, LB 3, W 4, NB 1)	12
Total	(40.4 overs – 6 wickets)	**169**

Fall of wickets: 1-30, 2-52, 3-108, 4-120, 5-129, 6-135.

PAKISTAN	*O*	*M*	*R*	*W*
Azeem Hafeez	6.4	1	24	0
Jalaluddin	10	2	41	2
Tahir Naqqash	4	0	19	1
Mudassar Nazar	10	0	41	1
Mohammad Nazir	10	1	37	2

Umpires: S.R. Bose and R. Mehra.

No-balls and wides debited to bowlers' analyses.

Match No. 225/8

INDIA v WEST INDIES 1983-84 (1st Match)

Charminar Challenge Cup

At Sher-I-Kashmir Stadium, Srinagar on 13 October 1983.
Toss: West Indies. Result: WEST INDIES won on scoring rate.
45 overs match. Award: D.L. Haynes.

Débuts: West Indies – E.A.E. Baptiste, R.A. Harper.

When a dust storm and failing light ended play just after the halfway mark in the West Indies innings, scores were compared after 22 overs. At that point India had reached 80.

INDIA		
S.M. Gavaskar	c Richards b Marshall	11
K. Srikkanth	c Greenidge b Harper	40
D.B. Vengsarkar	c Marshall b Baptiste	28
Yashpal Sharma	c Haynes b Harper	7
S.M. Patil	b Baptiste	0
Kapil Dev*	c Dujon b Holding	17
K. Azad	c and b Harper	21
R.M.H. Binny	c Dujon b Roberts	10
Madan Lal	run out	13
S.M.H. Kirmani†	not out	8
B.S. Sandhu	c Richards b Marshall	0
Extras	(B 2, LB 5, W 3, NB 11)	21
Total	(41.2 overs)	**176**

Fall of wickets: 1-19, 2-65, 3-80, 4-90, 5-114, 6-143, 7-151, 8-155, 9-176, 10-176.

WEST INDIES	*O*	*M*	*R*	*W*
Roberts	9	0	26	1
Marshall	7.2	2	13	2
Holding	7	0	32	1
Baptiste	9	1	50	2
Harper	9	1	34	3

WEST INDIES		
C.G. Greenidge	not out	44
D.L. Haynes	not out	55
I.V.A. Richards		
H.A. Gomes		
C.H. Lloyd*		
P.J.L. Dujon†		
E.A.E. Baptiste		
R.A. Harper		
M.D. Marshall		
A.M.E. Roberts		
M.A. Holding		
Extras	(LB 4, W 2, NB 3)	9
Total	(22.4 overs – 0 wicket)	**108**

INDIA	*O*	*M*	*R*	*W*
Kapil Dev	5	1	12	0
Sandhu	7	0	10	0
Madan Lal	6.4	0	51	0
Binny	4	0	26	0

Umpires: J.D. Ghosh and Mohammad Ghouse.

INDIA v WEST INDIES 1983-84 (2nd Match)
Charminar Challenge Cup

At Moti Bagh Stadium, Baroda on 9 November 1983.
Toss: India. Result: WEST INDIES won by 4 wickets.
49 overs match. Award: C.G. Greenidge.
No débuts.

INDIA		
A.D. Gaekwad	c Dujon b Daniel	0
K. Srikkanth	b Harper	19
R.J. Shastri	c Richards b Gomes	65
S.M. Patil	c Gomes b Baptiste	31
A. Malhotra	c Haynes b Gomes	29
R.M.H. Binny	not out	22
Kapil Dev*	b Marshall	15
K. Azad	not out	9
Madan Lal		
S.M.H. Kirmani†		
B.S. Sandhu		
Extras	(B 5, LB 12, W 3, NB 4)	24
Total	(49 overs – 6 wickets)	**214**

Fall of wickets 1-7, 2-47, 3-116, 4-157, 5-167, 6-189.

WEST INDIES	*O*	*M*	*R*	*W*
Roberts	9	2	30	0
Daniel	8	1	23	1
Marshall	9	0	34	1
Baptiste	10	2	39	1
Harper	10	0	47	1
Gomes	3	0	17	2

WEST INDIES		
C.G. Greenidge	st Kirmani b Azad	63
D.L. Haynes	b Madan Lal	38
I.V.A. Richards	c Gaekwad b Shastri	18
H.A. Gomes	lbw b Kapil Dev	26
C.H. Lloyd*	c Sandhu b Kapil Dev	31
P.J.L. Dujon†	not out	15
M.D. Marshall	b Madan Lal	3
E.A.E. Baptiste	not out	4
R.A. Harper		
A.M.E. Roberts		
W.W. Daniel		
Extras	(B 7, LB 8, W 4)	19
Total	(47.5 overs – 6 wickets)	**217**

Fall of wickets 1-69, 2-101, 3-156, 4-180, 5-203, 6-212.

INDIA	*O*	*M*	*R*	*W*
Kapil Dev	8.5	1	38	2
Sandhu	8	0	53	0
Madan Lal	9	0	39	2
Binny	2	0	16	0
Shastri	10	2	23	1
Azad	10	1	29	1

Umpires: S. Banerjee and V.K. Ramaswami.

Match No. 227/10

INDIA v WEST INDIES 1983-84 (3rd Match)

Charminar Challenge Cup

At Nehru Stadium, Indore on 1 December 1983.
Toss: India. Result: WEST INDIES won by 8 wickets.
47 overs match. Award: C.G. Greenidge.
No débuts.

INDIA

S.M. Gavaskar	c Dujon b Roberts	15
K. Srikkanth	run out	0
M. Amarnath	run out	55
Arun Lal	c Haynes b Holding	0
A. Malhotra	c Harper b Baptiste	40
Kapil Dev*	c Holding b Harper	28
R.M.H. Binny	c and b Harper	12
R.J. Shastri	not out	41
Madan Lal	not out	19
S.M.H. Kirmani†		
B.S. Sandhu		
Extras	(B 6, LB 8, W 11, NB 5)	30
Total	(47 overs – 7 wickets)	**240**

Fall of wickets 1-3, 2-32, 3-39, 4-123, 5-155, 6-172, 7-180.

WEST INDIES	*O*	*M*	*R*	*W*
Marshall	9	1	27	0
Roberts	8	0	35	1
Holding	7	2	19	1
Baptiste	10	4	44	1
Harper	10	0	55	2
Gomes	3	0	30	0

WEST INDIES

C.G. Greenidge	lbw b Kapil Dev	96
D.L. Haynes	st Kirmani b Shastri	54
I.V.A. Richards	not out	49
C.H. Lloyd*	not out	27
H.A. Gomes		
P.J.L. Dujon†		
E.A.E. Baptiste		
R.A. Harper		
M.D. Marshall		
A.M.E. Roberts		
M.A. Holding		
Extras	(B 1, LB 12, NB 2)	15
Total	(45.2 overs – 2 wickets)	**241**

Fall of wickets 1-149, 2-193.

INDIA	*O*	*M*	*R*	*W*
Kapil Dev	9.2	1	41	1
Sandhu	7	0	26	0
Madan Lal	9	0	36	0
Binny	3	0	26	0
Shastri	8	1	53	1
Amarnath	9	0	44	0

Umpires: M.Y. Gupte and S.V. Ramani.

INDIA v WEST INDIES 1983-84 (4th Match)
Charminar Challenge Cup

At Keenan Stadium, Jamshedpur on 7 December 1983.
Toss: India. Result: WEST INDIES won by 104 runs.
45 overs match. Award: I.V.A. Richards.
Début: India – C. Sharma.

The record West Indies total in one-day internationals was founded upon a partnership of 221 between Greenidge and Richards which remains the highest for the second wicket.

WEST INDIES		
C.G. Greenidge	b Shastri	115
D.L. Haynes	b Sharma	1
I.V.A. Richards	c Amarnath b Kapil Dev	149
P.J.L. Dujon†	lbw b Sharma	49
C.H. Lloyd*	c Amarnath b Kapil Dev	3
E.A.E. Baptiste	st Kirmani b Madan Lal	1
M.D. Marshall	b Kapil Dev	5
A.M.E. Roberts	not out	1
R.A. Harper	b Sharma	0
M.A. Holding	not out	0
H.A. Gomes		
Extras	(LB 4, W 4, NB 1)	9
Total	(45 overs – 8 wickets)	**333**

Fall of wickets: 1-27, 2-248, 3-304, 4-320, 5-324, 6-331, 7-332, 8-332.

INDIA	*O*	*M*	*R*	*W*
Kapil Dev	9	1	44	3
Sharma	9	0	60	3
Binny	1.5	0	17	0
Madan Lal	9	0	47	1
Amarnath	9.1	0	79	0
Shastri	7	0	77	1

INDIA		
S.M. Gavaskar	c Dujon b Roberts	83
K. Srikkanth	c Dujon b Roberts	3
M. Amarnath	b Holding	16
A. Malhotra	st Dujon b Harper	65
Kapil Dev*	not out	44
Arun Lal	lbw b Roberts	0
R.M.H. Binny	not out	12
R.J. Shastri		
Madan Lal		
S.M.H. Kirmani†		
C. Sharma		
Extras	(LB 3, W 2, NB 1)	6
Total	(45 overs – 5 wickets)	**229**

Fall of wickets: 1-23, 2-50, 3-155, 4-181, 5-181.

WEST INDIES	*O*	*M*	*R*	*W*
Marshall	6	0	18	0
Roberts	10	1	54	3
Holding	6	1	15	1
Baptiste	10	0	51	0
Harper	10	0	52	1
Gomes	2	0	25	0
Richards	1	0	8	0

Umpires: P.G. Pandit and S.R. Ramachandra Rao.

Match No. 229/12

INDIA v WEST INDIES 1983-84 (5th Match)
Charminar Challenge Cup

At Nehru Stadium, Gauhati on 17 December 1983.
Toss: West Indies. Result: WEST INDIES won by 6 wickets.
44 overs match. Award: G.A. Parkar.
Débuts: India – R.R. Kulkarni; West Indies – R.B. Richardson.

INDIA		
K. Srikkanth	b Daniel	11
G.A. Parkar	c Daniel b Baptiste	42
D.B. Vengsarkar	c Pydanna b Baptiste	2
A. Malhotra	run out	26
M. Amarnath	c Holding b Richards	23
R.M.H. Binny	c Haynes b Richards	33
R.J. Shastri	run out	18
S.M.H. Kirmani*†	not out	6
R.R. Kulkarni	not out	1
C. Sharma		
Randhir Singh		
Extras	(B 4, LB 7, W 1, NB 4)	16
Total	(44 overs – 7 wickets)	**178**

Fall of wickets: 1-54, 2-62, 3-67, 4-113, 5-117, 6-167, 7-172.

WEST INDIES	*O*	*M*	*R*	*W*
Marshall	5	2	8	0
Holding	7	1	28	0
Baptiste	9	0	31	2
Daniel	4	1	9	1
Harper	9	0	39	0
Richards	8	0	33	2
Gomes	2	0	14	0

WEST INDIES		
C.G. Greenidge	c Parkar b Randhir	35
D.L. Haynes	run out	14
R.B. Richardson	st Kirmani b Shastri	44
I.V.A. Richards*	c Kirmani b Shastri	23
H.A. Gomes	not out	33
M.D. Marshall	not out	10
E.A.E. Baptiste		
R.A. Harper		
M.R. Pydanna†		
M.A. Holding		
W.W. Daniel		
Extras	(B 4, LB 10, W 4, NB 5)	23
Total	(41.4 overs – 4 wickets)	**182**

Fall of wickets: 1-99, 2-119, 3-157, 4-163.

INDIA	*O*	*M*	*R*	*W*
Sharma	9	0	30	0
Binny	6	0	30	0
Randhir	8	0	42	1
Kulkarni	7	1	17	0
Shastri	9	2	19	2
Amarnath	2.4	0	21	0

Umpires: R. Mrithyunjayan and A.L. Narasimhan.

AUSTRALIA v WEST INDIES 1983-84

Benson and Hedges World Series Cup – 1st Match

At Melbourne Cricket Ground on 8 January 1984.
Toss: West Indies. Result: WEST INDIES won by 27 runs.
50 overs match. Award: I.V.A. Richards.

Débuts: Australia – G.R.J. Matthews; West Indies – R.S. Gabriel.

WEST INDIES		
D.L. Haynes	c Hughes b Hogg	17
R.S. Gabriel	c Marsh b Hogg	13
I.V.A. Richards	c Marsh b Maguire	53
C.H. Lloyd*	c Rackemann b Matthews	65
P.J.L. Dujon†	c Wessels b Hogg	5
M.D. Marshall	run out	9
E.A.E. Baptiste	not out	28
H.A. Gomes	b Rackemann	21
M.A. Holding	not out	1
J. Garner		
W.W. Daniel		
Extras	(B 1, LB 6, W 1, NB 1)	9
Total	(50 overs – 7 wickets)	**221**

Fall of wickets 1-28, 2-34, 3-137, 4-153, 5-167, 6-173, 7-220.

AUSTRALIA	*O*	*M*	*R*	*W*
Lawson	10	1	34	0
Rackemann	10	2	39	1
Hogg	10	1	29	3
Maguire	10	1	47	1
Matthews	10	0	65	1

AUSTRALIA		
K.C. Wessels	b Garner	7
W.B. Phillips	c and b Marshall	10
K.J. Hughes*	run out	5
A.R. Border	not out	84
G.R.J. Matthews	c Dujon b Daniel	2
R.W. Marsh†	run out	31
G.F. Lawson	b Baptiste	2
J.N. Maguire	b Richards	0
R.M. Hogg	lbw b Holding	21
G.N. Yallop	c Lloyd b Marshall	13
C.G. Rackemann	run out	2
Extras	(LB 10, W 1, NB 6)	17
Total	(46 overs)	**194**

Fall of wickets 1-12, 2-28, 3-31, 4-44, 5-108, 6-114, 7-115, 8-153, 9-191, 10-194.

WEST INDIES	*O*	*M*	*R*	*W*
Garner	8	2	28	1
Marshall	9	2	25	2
Daniel	6	1	24	1
Holding	10	0	42	1
Baptiste	7	0	41	1
Richards	6	1	24	1

Umpires: A.R. Crafter and R.C. Isherwood.

No-balls and wides debited to bowlers' analyses.

Match No. 231/11

AUSTRALIA v PAKISTAN 1983-84

Benson and Hedges World Series Cup – 2nd Match

At Sydney Cricket Ground on 10 January 1984.
Toss: Pakistan. Result: AUSTRALIA won by 34 runs.
50 overs match (floodlit). Award: K.C. Wessels.
No débuts.

Marsh became the first wicket-keeper to complete the double of 1,000 runs and 100 dismissals when he had scored 31.

AUSTRALIA		
K.C. Wessels	b Sarfraz	92
W.B. Phillips	c Wasim Bari b Sarfraz	2
K.J. Hughes*	c Imran b Sarfraz	5
A.R. Border	c Wasim Bari b Sarfraz	54
D.W. Hookes	b Azeem	25
R.W. Marsh†	b Rashid	66
G.R.J. Matthews	run out	0
G.F. Lawson	not out	3
J.N. Maguire	c Wasim Bari b Azeem	2
R.M. Hogg	not out	2
C.G. Rackemann		
Extras	(LB 9, W 2, NB 2)	13
Total	(50 overs – 8 wickets)	**264**

Fall of wickets 1-3, 2-17, 3-157, 4-162, 5-248, 6-249, 7-256, 8-261.

PAKISTAN	*O*	*M*	*R*	*W*
Sarfraz Nawaz	10	2	27	4
Rashid Khan	10	1	42	1
Mohammad Nazir	9	0	67	0
Azeem Hafeez	10	0	60	2
Mudassar Nazar	9	0	44	0
Mansoor Akhtar	2	0	15	0

PAKISTAN		
Mohsin Khan	lbw b Rackemann	9
Mudassar Nazar	c Marsh b Lawson	17
Qasim Omar	lbw b Rackemann	1
Javed Miandad	run out	67
Imran Khan*	run out	39
Mansoor Akhtar	c Lawson b Matthews	33
Sarfraz Nawaz	b Hogg	6
Wasim Bari†	b Matthews	13
Rashid Khan	c Marsh b Rackemann	10
Mohammad Nazir	not out	2
Azeem Hafeez	not out	7
Extras	(B 5, LB 16, W 2, NB 3)	26
Total	(50 overs – 9 wickets)	**230**

Fall of wickets 1-30, 2-32, 3-33, 4-119, 5-175, 6-193, 7-201, 8-217, 9-221.

AUSTRALIA	*O*	*M*	*R*	*W*
Lawson	10	3	26	1
Rackemann	10	2	35	3
Maguire	10	0	49	0
Hogg	10	0	38	1
Matthews	10	0	61	2

Umpires: P.J. McConnell and S.G. Randell.

No-balls and wides debited to bowlers' analyses.

PAKISTAN v WEST INDIES 1983-84

Benson and Hedges World Series Cup – 3rd Match

At Melbourne Cricket Ground on 12 January 1984.
Toss: Pakistan. Result: PAKISTAN won by 97 runs.
50 overs match. Award: Qasim Omar.
No débuts.

PAKISTAN		
Mudassar Nazar	c Dujon b Holding	31
Mohsin Khan	lbw b Garner	16
Mansoor Akhtar	run out	19
Javed Miandad	b Marshall	41
Imran Khan*	c and b Baptiste	7
Qasim Omar	b Daniel	69
Sarfraz Nawaz	c Richards b Holding	7
Abdul Qadir	not out	6
Rashid Khan	run out	2
Wasim Bari†		
Azeem Hafeez		
Extras	(LB 3, W 5, NB 2)	10
Total	(50 overs – 8 wickets)	**208**

Fall of wickets: 1-27, 2-70, 3-77, 4-87, 5-182, 6-196, 7-206, 8-208.

WEST INDIES	*O*	*M*	*R*	*W*
Garner	10	2	21	1
Marshall	6	0	27	1
Holding	10	0	56	2
Daniel	10	0	46	1
Richards	6	0	26	0
Baptiste	8	0	29	1

WEST INDIES		
D.L. Haynes	b Rashid	2
R.S. Gabriel	run out	0
I.V.A. Richards	c Qadir b Sarfraz	7
H.A. Gomes	c Qadir b Rashid	1
C.H. Lloyd*	c Mansoor b Azeem	12
P.J.L. Dujon†	c Imran b Azeem	30
M.D. Marshall	c Azeem b Sarfraz	20
E.A.E. Baptiste	c Mansoor b Azeem	3
M.A. Holding	c and b Azeem	1
J. Garner	not out	21
W.W. Daniel	c Sarfraz b Mudassar	12
Extras	(LB 1, NB 1)	2
Total	(41.4 overs)	**111**

Fall of wickets: 1-1, 2-9, 3-9, 4-10, 5-45, 6-56, 7-63, 8-65, 9-94, 10-111.

PAKISTAN	*O*	*M*	*R*	*W*
Sarfraz Nawaz	9	2	24	2
Rashid Khan	6	3	10	2
Azeem Hafeez	10	1	22	4
Abdul Qadir	10	0	29	0
Mudassar Nazar	6.4	0	25	1

Umpires: M.W. Johnson and S.G. Randell.

No-balls and wides debited to bowlers' analyses.

Match No. 233/14

PAKISTAN v WEST INDIES 1983-84

Benson and Hedges World Series Cup – 4th Match

At Woolloongabba, Brisbane on 14 January 1984.

Toss: Pakistan.	Result: WEST INDIES won by 5 wickets.
50 overs match.	Award: Mudassar Nazar.

No débuts.

PAKISTAN		
Mudassar Nazar	c and b Richards	68
Mohsin Khan	b Daniel	4
Mansoor Akhtar	b Richards	32
Javed Miandad	run out	9
Qasim Omar	c Logie b Daniel	18
Imran Khan*	c Dujon b Holding	9
Sarfraz Nawaz	c Haynes b Holding	0
Abdul Qadir	c Lloyd b Daniel	2
Rashid Khan	c Dujon b Holding	2
Wasim Bari†	not out	10
Azeem Hafeez	not out	3
Extras	(B 1, LB 6, W 3, NB 7)	17
Total	(50 overs – 9 wickets)	**174**

Fall of wickets: 1-10, 2-97, 3-121, 4-128, 5-144, 6-144, 7-157, 8-159, 9-160.

WEST INDIES	*O*	*M*	*R*	*W*
Holding	10	1	46	3
Daniel	10	1	27	3
Davis	10	2	29	0
Baptiste	10	2	28	0
Richards	10	0	37	2

WEST INDIES		
D.L. Haynes	c Wasim Bari b Mudassar	53
R.S. Gabriel	b Qadir	20
R.B. Richardson	c Wasim Bari b Rashid	25
I.V.A. Richards	b Azeem	37
C.H. Lloyd*	c Wasim Bari b Mudassar	11
P.J.L. Dujon†	not out	10
A.L. Logie	not out	1
E.A.E. Baptiste		
M.A. Holding		
W.W. Daniel		
W.W. Davis		
Extras	(LB 9, W 8, NB 1)	18
Total	(40.2 overs – 5 wickets)	**175**

Fall of wickets: 1-47, 2-102, 3-143, 4-161, 5-161.

PAKISTAN	*O*	*M*	*R*	*W*
Sarfraz Nawaz	6	2	28	0
Rashid Khan	8	3	18	1
Azeem Hafeez	9.2	0	58	1
Abdul Qadir	7	4	16	1
Mudassar Nazar	10	0	46	2

Umpires: A.R. Crafter and R.C. Isherwood.

No-balls and wides debited to bowlers' analyses.

AUSTRALIA v PAKISTAN 1983-84

Benson and Hedges World Series Cup – 5th Match

At Woolloongabba, Brisbane on 15 January 1984.
Toss: Australia. No result – rain.
42 overs match. No award.
No débuts.

PAKISTAN		
Mudassar Nazar	c Hookes b Lawson	2
Mohsin Khan	c Wessels b Hogg	14
Mansoor Akhtar	b Hogg	47
Javed Miandad	c Wessels b Maguire	1
Qasim Omar	run out	40
Imran Khan*	c Marsh b Hogg	26
Tahir Naqqash	not out	13
Rashid Khan	not out	11
Sarfraz Nawaz		
Wasim Bari†		
Azeem Hafeez		
Extras	(LB 23, W 7)	30
Total	(42 overs – 6 wickets)	**184**

Fall of wickets: 1-2, 2-29, 3-30, 4-116, 5-159, 6-160.

AUSTRALIA	*O*	*M*	*R*	*W*
Lawson	9	3	12	1
Rackemann	9	3	45	0
Hogg	8	0	34	3
Maguire	10	0	31	1
MacLeay	6	0	39	0

AUSTRALIA		
G.M. Ritchie	not out	6
K.C. Wessels	not out	5
K.J. Hughes*		
A.R. Border		
D.W. Hookes		
K.H. MacLeay		
R.W. Marsh†		
G.F. Lawson		
J.N. Maguire		
R.M. Hogg		
C.G. Rackemann		
Extras	(LB 1, W 3)	4
Total	(3.5 overs – 0 wicket)	**15**

PAKISTAN	*O*	*M*	*R*	*W*
Sarfraz Nawaz	2	1	8	0
Rashid Khan	1.5	0	6	0

Umpires: R.A. French and M.W. Johnson.

No-balls and wides debited to bowlers' analyses.

Match No. 235/22

AUSTRALIA v WEST INDIES 1983-84

Benson and Hedges World Series Cup – 6th Match

At Sydney Cricket Ground on 17 January 1984.
Toss: West Indies. Result: WEST INDIES won by 28 runs.
49 overs match (floodlit). Award: D.L. Haynes.
No débuts.

WEST INDIES		
D.L. Haynes	not out	108
R.S. Gabriel	lbw b Lawson	0
R.B. Richardson	c Hughes b Rackemann	11
I.V.A. Richards	c Wessels b Hogg	19
C.H. Lloyd*	lbw b Hogg	40
P.J.L. Dujon†	c Wessels b Rackemann	8
A.L. Logie	b Lawson	9
E.A.E. Baptiste	b Lawson	5
M.A. Holding	not out	6
W.W. Daniel		
W.W. Davis		
Extras	(LB 16, W 1)	17
Total	(49 overs – 7 wickets)	**223**

Fall of wickets: 1-1, 2-24, 3-55, 4-135, 5-168, 6-195, 7-207.

AUSTRALIA	*O*	*M*	*R*	*W*
Lawson	10	1	30	3
Rackemann	10	0	33	2
MacLeay	10	0	47	0
Hogg	10	1	59	2
Maguire	9	1	38	0

AUSTRALIA		
G.M. Ritchie	run out	30
K.C. Wessels	lbw b Richards	27
K.J. Hughes*	b Baptiste	19
A.R. Border	c Richards b Baptiste	1
D.W. Hookes	c Logie b Daniel	35
R.W. Marsh†	b Daniel	27
K.H. MacLeay	b Holding	15
G.F. Lawson	run out	3
R.M. Hogg	b Holding	1
C.G. Rackemann	not out	9
J.N. Maguire	not out	2
Extras	(LB 19, W 4, NB 3)	26
Total	(49 overs – 9 wickets)	**195**

Fall of wickets: 1-68, 2-75, 3-76, 4-100, 5-155, 6-164, 7-171, 8-175, 9-192.

WEST INDIES	*O*	*M*	*R*	*W*
Holding	10	0	35	2
Daniel	10	0	29	2
Davis	9	1	39	0
Baptiste	10	1	32	2
Richards	10	0	41	1

Umpires: A.R. Crafter and M.W. Johnson.

No-balls and wides debited to bowlers' analyses.

PAKISTAN v WEST INDIES 1983-84

Benson and Hedges World Series Cup – 7th Match

At Sydney Cricket Ground on 19 January 1984.

Toss: Pakistan.	Result: WEST INDIES won by 5 wickets.
50 overs match (floodlit).	Award: R.B. Richardson.

No débuts.

PAKISTAN		
Mudassar Nazar	lbw b Holding	7
Mohsin Khan	c Dujon b Marshall	13
Mansoor Akhtar	c Dujon b Daniel	4
Javed Miandad	b Baptiste	31
Qasim Omar	not out	67
Imran Khan*	lbw b Holding	17
Rashid Khan	b Holding	1
Abdul Qadir	b Holding	7
Sarfraz Nawaz	b Daniel	0
Wasim Bari†	not out	6
Azeem Hafeez		
Extras	(B 1, LB 13, W 7, NB 10)	31
Total	(50 overs – 8 wickets)	**184**

Fall of wickets: 1-16, 2-28, 3-35, 4-96, 5-137, 6-143, 7-157, 8-161.

WEST INDIES	*O*	*M*	*R*	*W*
Holding	10	2	26	4
Daniel	10	2	60	2
Davis	10	3	30	0
Marshall	6	4	5	1
Richards	5	0	24	0
Baptiste	9	2	25	1

WEST INDIES		
D.L. Haynes	c Mudassar b Qadir	37
R.S. Gabriel	b Azeem	15
R.B. Richardson	st Wasim Bari b Qadir	53
I.V.A. Richards*	c Rashid b Qadir	2
P.J.L. Dujon†	run out	13
A.L. Logie	not out	28
M.D. Marshall	not out	16
E.A.E. Baptiste		
M.A. Holding		
W.W. Daniel		
W.W. Davis		
Extras	(B 4, LB 10, W 7)	21
Total	(48.3 overs – 5 wickets)	**185**

Fall of wickets: 1-30, 2-109, 3-120, 4-138, 5-141.

PAKISTAN	*O*	*M*	*R*	*W*
Sarfraz Nawaz	9	1	31	0
Rashid Khan	9.3	3	26	0
Azeem Hafeez	10	0	53	1
Mudassar Nazar	10	1	34	0
Abdul Qadir	10	1	27	3

Umpires: P.J. McConnell and B.E. Martin.

No-balls and wides debited to bowlers' analyses.

Match No. 237/13

AUSTRALIA v PAKISTAN 1983-84

Benson and Hedges World Series Cup – 8th Match

At Melbourne Cricket Ground on 21 January 1984.
Toss: Australia. Result: AUSTRALIA won by 43 runs.
50 overs match. Award: K.C. Wessels.
No débuts.

AUSTRALIA		
G.M. Ritchie	c and b Ijaz	27
K.C. Wessels	c Imran b Qadir	86
K.J. Hughes*	lbw b Mudassar	0
A.R. Border	b Azeem	12
D.W. Hookes	st Wasim Bari b Qadir	37
S.B. Smith	b Qadir	0
R.W. Marsh†	c Imran b Qadir	11
G.F. Lawson	not out	14
R.M. Hogg	c and b Qadir	0
J.N. Maguire	not out	14
C.G. Rackemann		
Extras	(LB 8)	8
Total	(50 overs – 8 wickets)	**209**

Fall of wickets 1-57, 2-58, 3-123, 4-138, 5-140, 6-172, 7-178, 8-178.

PAKISTAN	*O*	*M*	*R*	*W*
Azeem Hafeez	10	0	44	1
Rashid Khan	10	1	32	0
Mudassar Nazar	10	2	31	1
Ijaz Faqih	10	1	41	1
Abdul Qadir	10	1	53	5

PAKISTAN		
Mudassar Nazar	c Wessels b Hogg	12
Mohsin Khan	c Marsh b Border	22
Mansoor Akhtar	run out	1
Javed Miandad	b Hogg	56
Qasim Omar	c and b Border	2
Imran Khan*	c Marsh b Maguire	17
Ijaz Faqih	b Hogg	17
Abdul Qadir	b Hogg	23
Rashid Khan	not out	2
Wasim Bari†	run out	2
Azeem Hafeez	b Lawson	0
Extras	(B 1, LB 6, W 4, NB 1)	12
Total	(45 overs)	**166**

Fall of wickets 1-33, 2-35, 3-56, 4-61, 5-89, 6-124, 7-161, 8-162, 9-164, 10-166.

AUSTRALIA	*O*	*M*	*R*	*W*
Lawson	8	2	19	1
Rackemann	7	0	23	0
Hogg	10	2	33	4
Wessels	7	0	28	0
Border	7	0	24	2
Maguire	6	0	32	1

Umpires: P.J. McConnell and B.E. Martin.

No-balls and wides debited to bowlers' analyses.

AUSTRALIA v WEST INDIES 1983-84

Benson and Hedges World Series Cup – 9th Match

At Melbourne Cricket Ground on 22 January 1984.
Toss: West Indies. Result: WEST INDIES won by 26 runs.
50 overs match. Award: I.V.A. Richards.

No débuts.

Watched by a record crowd for a one-day international of 86,133, Richards scored 106 off 96 balls in 116 minutes with one six and 13 fours.

WEST INDIES		
D.L. Haynes	b Hogg	64
R.S. Gabriel	c Maguire b Rackemann	8
H.A. Gomes	lbw b Wessels	7
I.V.A. Richards	c Smith b Rackemann	106
C.H. Lloyd*	b Maguire	27
P.J.L. Dujon†	not out	21
M.D. Marshall	b Lawson	1
A.L. Logie	not out	9
E.A.E. Baptiste		
M.A. Holding		
W.W. Daniel		
Extras	(LB 7, W 2)	9
Total	(50 overs – 6 wickets)	**252**

Fall of wickets: 1-24, 2-50, 3-140, 4-199, 5-230, 6-238.

AUSTRALIA	*O*	*M*	*R*	*W*
Lawson	10	2	28	1
Rackemann	9	3	43	2
Hogg	10	0	56	1
Wessels	8	0	32	1
Border	5	0	35	0
Maguire	8	0	51	1

AUSTRALIA		
G.M. Ritchie	c Holding b Baptiste	28
K.C. Wessels	b Richards	60
A.R. Border	b Baptiste	0
K.J. Hughes*	b Daniel	71
D.W. Hookes	c Logie b Richards	6
S.B. Smith	c Gomes b Daniel	26
W.B. Phillips†	not out	18
G.F. Lawson	b Holding	0
J.N. Maguire	b Marshall	3
C.G. Rackemann	b Holding	0
R.M. Hogg	b Holding	2
Extras	(B 3, LB 6, W 3)	12
Total	(49.5 overs)	**226**

Fall of wickets: 1-62, 2-63, 3-119, 4-146, 5-186, 6-203, 7-216, 8-223, 9-224, 10-226.

WEST INDIES	*O*	*M*	*R*	*W*
Holding	9.5	0	35	3
Daniel	10	0	38	2
Baptiste	7	0	24	2
Marshall	10	0	49	1
Richards	10	0	51	2
Gomes	3	0	20	0

Umpires: R.A. French and R.C. Isherwood.

No-balls and wides debited to bowlers' analyses.

Match No. 239/14

AUSTRALIA v PAKISTAN 1983-84

Benson and Hedges World Series Cup – 10th Match

At Sydney Cricket Ground on 25 January 1984.
Toss: Australia. Result: AUSTRALIA won by 87 runs.
50 overs match (floodlit). Award: S.B. Smith.
No débuts.

AUSTRALIA		
S.B. Smith	c Qadir b Rashid	106
K.C. Wessels	c Imran b Tahir	7
G.M. Ritchie	st Ashraf b Qadir	31
K.J. Hughes*	b Qadir	3
A.R. Border	b Mudassar	11
W.B. Phillips	run out	25
R.W. Marsh†	c Ashraf b Tahir	20
G.F. Lawson	st Ashraf b Qadir	2
J.N. Maguire	not out	7
R.M. Hogg	not out	8
C.G. Rackemann		
Extras	(B 8, LB 3, W 10, NB 3)	24
Total	(50 overs – 8 wickets)	**244**

Fall of wickets: 1-18, 2-85, 3-97, 4-122, 5-196, 6-216, 7-221, 8-234.

PAKISTAN	*O*	*M*	*R*	*W*
Rashid Khan	9	0	36	1
Tahir Naqqash	10	3	56	2
Abdul Qadir	9	1	42	3
Mudassar Nazar	10	1	33	1
Ijaz Faqih	7	0	36	0
Wasim Raja	5	0	30	0

PAKISTAN		
Mudassar Nazar	run out	0
Mohsin Khan	b Lawson	1
Imran Khan*	run out	41
Javed Miandad	c Marsh b Maguire	26
Qasim Omar	c Marsh b Hogg	0
Wasim Raja	st Marsh b Wessels	32
Ijaz Faqih	b Hogg	14
Tahir Naqqash	b Hogg	0
Abdul Qadir	c Marsh b Hogg	9
Rashid Khan	b Border	17
Ashraf Ali†	not out	11
Extras	(B 2, LB 3, W 1)	6
Total	(47.2 overs)	**157**

Fall of wickets: 1-0, 2-1, 3-45, 4-46, 5-103, 6-103, 7-104, 8-120, 9-129, 10-157.

AUSTRALIA	*O*	*M*	*R*	*W*
Lawson	6	3	15	1
Rackemann	10	2	16	0
Maguire	9	1	19	1
Hogg	10	0	37	4
Wessels	9	0	50	1
Border	3.2	0	15	1

Umpires: R.A. French and R.C. Isherwood.

No-balls and wides debited to bowlers' analyses.

PAKISTAN v WEST INDIES 1983-84

Benson and Hedges World Series Cup – 11th Match

At Adelaide Oval on 28 January 1984.
Toss: Pakistan. Result: WEST INDIES won by 1 wicket.
50 overs match. Award: M.D. Marshall.
No débuts.

PAKISTAN		
Mudassar Nazar	c Dujon b Baptiste	18
Mansoor Akhtar	c Dujon b Marshall	20
Qasim Omar	run out	26
Javed Miandad*	c Dujon b Marshall	4
Salim Malik	b Marshall	1
Wasim Raja	c Richards b Gomes	46
Ijaz Faqih	not out	23
Abdul Qadir	c Baptiste b Gomes	4
Tahir Naqqash	run out	0
Rashid Khan	not out	16
Wasim Bari†		
Extras	(LB 14, W 2, NB 3)	19
Total	(50 overs – 8 wickets)	**177**

Fall of wickets 1-40, 2-42, 3-54, 4-59, 5-127, 6-127, 7-135, 8-136.

WEST INDIES	*O*	*M*	*R*	*W*
Holding	8	1	21	0
Daniel	10	3	25	0
Marshall	9	1	28	3
Baptiste	10	0	33	1
Richards	6	0	30	0
Gomes	7	0	26	2

WEST INDIES		
D.L. Haynes	c Wasim Bari b Wasim Raja	3
R.S. Gabriel	b Qadir	10
A.L. Logie	c Miandad b Rashid	19
I.V.A. Richards	c Mansoor b Qadir	18
H.A. Gomes	c Wasim Bari b Mudassar	3
C.H. Lloyd*	run out	10
P.J.L. Dujon†	st Wasim Bari b Qadir	10
M.D. Marshall	not out	56
E.A.E. Baptiste	c Rashid b Wasim Raja	24
M.A. Holding	lbw b Wasim Raja	10
W.W. Daniel	not out	7
Extras	(B 1, LB 4, W 4, NB 1)	10
Total	(49.1 overs – 9 wickets)	**180**

Fall of wickets 1-9, 2-28, 3-52, 4-59, 5-61, 6-75, 7-92, 8-145, 9-159.

PAKISTAN	*O*	*M*	*R*	*W*
Rashid Khan	8.1	3	29	1
Tahir Naqqash	7	1	35	0
Wasim Raja	10	1	33	3
Abdul Qadir	10	1	34	3
Mudassar Nazar	10	0	32	1
Ijaz Faqih	4	0	12	0

Umpires: R.A. French and B.E. Martin.

No-balls and wides debited to bowlers' analyses.

Match No. 241/24

AUSTRALIA v WEST INDIES 1983-84

Benson and Hedges World Series Cup – 12th Match

At Adelaide Oval on 29 January 1984.
Toss: Australia. Result: WEST INDIES won by 6 wickets.
50 overs match. Award: A.L. Logie.
No débuts.

AUSTRALIA		
S.B. Smith	b Marshall	55
K.C. Wessels	c Dujon b Daniel	4
G.M. Ritchie	run out	0
K.J. Hughes*	c Dujon b Baptiste	10
A.R. Border	b Richards	17
W.B. Phillips	st Dujon b Richards	2
R.W. Marsh†	not out	34
G.F. Lawson	c and b Daniel	18
J.N. Maguire	not out	9
R.M. Hogg		
C.G. Rackemann		
Extras	(B 7, LB 3, W 2, NB 4)	16
Total	(50 overs – 7 wickets)	**165**

Fall of wickets 1-14, 2-14, 3-34, 4-71, 5-85, 6-115, 7-149.

WEST INDIES	*O*	*M*	*R*	*W*
Holding	7	2	20	0
Daniel	8	0	35	2
Marshall	10	3	21	1
Baptiste	5	2	9	1
Gomes	10	1	42	0
Richards	10	0	28	2

WEST INDIES		
D.L. Haynes	c Marsh b Rackemann	4
R.S. Gabriel	c Lawson b Border	41
H.A. Gomes	run out	27
I.V.A. Richards	b Border	0
C.H. Lloyd*	not out	38
A.L. Logie	not out	49
P.J.L. Dujon†		
E.A.E. Baptiste		
M.D. Marshall		
M.A. Holding		
W.W. Daniel		
Extras	(LB 7, W 1, NB 2)	10
Total	(45.1 overs – 4 wickets)	**169**

Fall of wickets 1-14, 2-67, 3-68, 4-89.

AUSTRALIA	*O*	*M*	*R*	*W*
Lawson	6	1	10	0
Rackemann	10	0	35	1
Hogg	10	0	31	0
Maguire	8	1	44	0
Wessels	3	0	9	0
Border	7	0	25	2
Smith	1	0	4	0
Hughes	0.1	0	4	0

Umpires: A.R. Crafter and M.W. Johnson.

No-balls and wides debited to bowlers' analyses.

AUSTRALIA v PAKISTAN 1983-84

Benson and Hedges World Series Cup – 13th Match

At Adelaide Oval on 30 January 1984.
Toss: Australia. Result: AUSTRALIA won by 70 runs.
50 overs match. Award: K.C. Wessels.
Début: Australia – D.M. Jones.

AUSTRALIA		
S.B. Smith	b Ijaz	36
K.C. Wessels	b Ijaz	61
G.M. Ritchie	b Ijaz	12
K.J. Hughes*	st Wasim Bari b Ijaz	11
A.R. Border	run out	10
W.B. Phillips†	b Mudassar	17
D.M. Jones	not out	40
T.G. Hogan	c Wasim Raja b Mudassar	3
J.N. Maguire	c Mansoor b Rashid	1
R.M. Hogg	not out	6
C.G. Rackemann		
Extras	(LB 9, W 2, NB 2)	13
Total	(50 overs – 8 wickets)	**210**

Fall of wickets: 1-70, 2-115, 3-126, 4-135, 5-145, 6-163, 7-169, 8-179.

PAKISTAN	*O*	*M*	*R*	*W*
Rashid Khan	10	1	33	1
Mudassar Nazar	10	0	50	2
Ijaz Faqih	10	1	43	4
Wasim Raja	10	2	23	0
Abdul Qadir	10	0	52	0

PAKISTAN		
Mansoor Akhtar	b Hogg	22
Javed Miandad*	c Hogan b Rackemann	34
Qasim Omar	c Ritchie b Rackemann	2
Wasim Raja	c Hughes b Wessels	17
Mudassar Nazar	c Phillips b Rackemann	1
Mohsin Khan	lbw b Wessels	19
Salim Malik	lbw b Hogan	14
Ijaz Faqih	c Phillips b Rackemann	13
Abdul Qadir	b Hogg	3
Rashid Khan	c Hogan b Rackemann	1
Wasim Bari†	not out	2
Extras	(B 6, LB 5, W 1)	12
Total	(45.2 overs)	**140**

Fall of wickets: 1-56, 2-56, 3-58, 4-60, 5-98, 6-115, 7-123, 8-137, 9-137, 10-140.

AUSTRALIA	*O*	*M*	*R*	*W*
Hogg	8	2	26	2
Rackemann	8.2	2	16	5
Maguire	10	1	33	0
Hogan	10	2	22	1
Wessels	9	0	32	2

Umpires: P.J. McConnell and S.G. Randell.

No-balls and wides debited to bowlers' analyses.

Match No. 243/17

PAKISTAN v WEST INDIES 1983-84

Benson and Hedges World Series Cup – 14th Match

At WACA Ground, Perth on 4 February 1984.

Toss: Pakistan.	Result: WEST INDIES won by 7 wickets.
50 overs match.	Award: I.V.A. Richards.

No débuts.

PAKISTAN

Mudassar Nazar	c Marshall b Baptiste	54
Mansoor Akhtar	c Garner b Davis	3
Mohsin Khan	b Harper	32
Javed Miandad*	b Harper	26
Qasim Omar	c Richards b Davis	16
Salim Malik	b Garner	14
Ijaz Faqih	b Garner	0
Abdul Qadir	not out	6
Rashid Khan	not out	10
Azeem Hafeez		
Ashraf Ali†		
Extras	(B 7, LB 7, W 6, NB 1)	21
Total	(50 overs – 7 wickets)	**182**

Fall of wickets: 1-13, 2-88, 3-129, 4-135, 5-159, 6-163, 7-164.

WEST INDIES	*O*	*M*	*R*	*W*
Garner	9	3	12	2
Davis	10	0	34	2
Baptiste	10	0	36	1
Marshall	6	0	20	0
Harper	10	0	42	2
Richards	5	0	24	0

WEST INDIES

D.L. Haynes	not out	78
R.S. Gabriel	c Ashraf b Mudassar	29
R.B. Richardson	c and b Mudassar	7
I.V.A. Richards*	c Salim b Ijaz	40
A.L. Logie	not out	14
P.J.L. Dujon†		
M.D. Marshall		
E.A.E. Baptiste		
R.A. Harper		
W.W. Davis		
J. Garner		
Extras	(LB 10, W 5)	15
Total	(45.1 overs – 3 wickets)	**183**

Fall of wickets: 1-38, 2-58, 3-153.

PAKISTAN	*O*	*M*	*R*	*W*
Rashid Khan	10	1	25	0
Azeem Hafeez	6	0	51	0
Mudassar Nazar	10	1	33	2
Abdul Qadir	10	3	19	0
Ijaz Faqih	9	0	44	1
Mansoor Akhtar	0.1	0	1	0

Umpires: R.A. French and S.G. Randell.

No-balls and wides debited to bowlers' analyses.

AUSTRALIA v WEST INDIES 1983-84

Benson and Hedges World Series Cup – 15th Match

At WACA Ground, Perth on 5 February 1984.
Toss: Australia. Result: AUSTRALIA won by 14 runs.
50 overs match. Award: M.A. Holding.
No débuts.

AUSTRALIA		
S.B. Smith	c Dujon b Daniel	12
K.C. Wessels	c Daniel b Marshall	50
G.M. Ritchie	c Gabriel b Holding	3
K.J. Hughes*	c Richardson b Marshall	67
A.R. Border	b Richards	1
D.M. Jones	b Holding	23
R.W. Marsh†	not out	27
G.F. Lawson	run out	3
R.M. Hogg	run out	2
T.M. Alderman	not out	0
C.G. Rackemann		
Extras	(B 3, LB 14, W 3, NB 3)	23
Total	(50 overs – 8 wickets)	**211**

Fall of wickets: 1-15, 2-21, 3-140, 4-142, 5-157, 6-185, 7-192, 8-201.

WEST INDIES	*O*	*M*	*R*	*W*
Holding	10	1	31	2
Daniel	10	1	43	1
Marshall	10	2	27	2
Baptiste	10	0	46	0
Richards	10	0	47	1

WEST INDIES		
D.L. Haynes	c Marsh b Wessels	52
R.B. Richardson	c Wessels b Lawson	2
A.L. Logie	c Hughes b Alderman	3
I.V.A. Richards	b Alderman	7
C.H. Lloyd*	b Hogg	31
P.J.L. Dujon†	b Rackemann	0
M.D. Marshall	c Marsh b Rackemann	2
E.A.E. Baptiste	c Marsh b Lawson	1
M.A. Holding	lbw b Wessels	64
R.S. Gabriel	b Rackemann	12
W.W. Daniel	not out	0
Extras	(B 3, LB 11, W 8, NB 1)	23
Total	(43.3 overs)	**197**

Fall of wickets: 1-17, 2-23, 3-37, 4-92, 5-93, 6-101, 7-102, 8-156, 9-188, 10-197.

AUSTRALIA	*O*	*M*	*R*	*W*
Lawson	8	1	32	2
Alderman	10	3	19	2
Hogg	9	2	36	1
Wessels	8	2	50	2
Rackemann	8.3	0	46	3

Umpires: R.C. Isherwood and P.J. McConnell.

No-balls and wides debited to bowlers' analyses.

Match No. 245/26

AUSTRALIA v WEST INDIES 1983-84

Benson and Hedges World Series Cup – 1st Final

At Sydney Cricket Ground on 8 February 1984.

Toss: West Indies. Result: WEST INDIES won by 9 wickets.

46 overs match (floodlit). No award.

No débuts.

AUSTRALIA		
S.B. Smith	c and b Daniel	50
K.C. Wessels	c Richards b Holding	2
G.M. Ritchie	lbw b Garner	10
K.J. Hughes*	b Marshall	0
A.R. Border	b Daniel	18
D.M. Jones	b Marshall	17
R.W. Marsh†	c Lloyd b Baptiste	15
G.F. Lawson	b Garner	22
R.M. Hogg	c Gomes b Baptiste	2
T.M. Alderman	b Holding	7
C.G. Rackemann	not out	4
Extras	(LB 9, W 1, NB 3)	13
Total	(44.4 overs)	**160**

Fall of wickets: 1-5, 2-23, 3-38, 4-82, 5-93, 6-119, 7-127, 8-133, 9-152, 10-160.

WEST INDIES	*O*	*M*	*R*	*W*
Holding	8.4	0	27	2
Garner	9	2	19	2
Marshall	9	1	24	2
Daniel	9	0	42	2
Richards	5	0	29	0
Baptiste	4	0	10	2

WEST INDIES		
D.L. Haynes	lbw b Rackemann	13
R.B. Richardson	not out	80
H.A. Gomes	not out	46
I.V.A. Richards		
C.H. Lloyd*		
P.J.L. Dujon†		
M.D. Marshall		
E.A.E. Baptiste		
M.A. Holding		
J. Garner		
W.W. Daniel		
Extras	(B 3, LB 14, W 1, NB 4)	22
Total	(43.1 overs – 1 wicket)	**161**

Fall of wicket: 1-29.

AUSTRALIA	*O*	*M*	*R*	*W*
Lawson	9	1	21	0
Alderman	9	2	19	0
Rackemann	9	0	31	1
Hogg	7	0	40	0
Wessels	4	0	15	0
Border	5	0	17	0
Smith	0.1	0	1	0

Umpires: A.R. Crafter and R.A. French.

No-balls and wides debited to bowlers' analyses.

AUSTRALIA v WEST INDIES 1983-84

Benson and Hedges World Series Cup – 2nd Final

At Melbourne Cricket Ground on 11 February 1984.
Toss: West Indies. Result: MATCH TIED.
50 overs match. No award.

No débuts.

The first tie in a limited-overs international.

WEST INDIES		
D.L. Haynes	c Hogan b Border	18
R.S. Gabriel	c Smith b Rackemann	19
R.B. Richardson	c Marsh b Lawson	43
I.V.A. Richards	c Hogan b Wessels	59
C.H. Lloyd*	c Hogg b Wessels	11
H.A. Gomes	not out	25
P.J.L. Dujon†	not out	33
M.D. Marshall		
E.A.E. Baptiste		
M.A. Holding		
J. Garner		
Extras	(LB 10, W 3, NB 1)	14
Total	(50 overs – 5 wickets)	**222**

Fall of wickets 1-33, 2-54, 3-116, 4-137, 5-173.

AUSTRALIA	*O*	*M*	*R*	*W*
Lawson	10	4	26	1
Rackemann	10	4	52	1
Hogg	9	1	40	0
Hogan	10	2	31	0
Border	6	0	34	1
Wessels	5	0	29	2

AUSTRALIA		
K.C. Wessels	c Marshall b Holding	77
D.M. Jones	c Dujon b Holding	12
K.J. Hughes*	lbw b Marshall	53
A.R. Border	c Dujon b Garner	14
G.M. Ritchie	c Dujon b Garner	4
R.W. Marsh†	b Garner	16
G.F. Lawson	not out	21
T.G. Hogan	c sub (A.L. Logie) b Holding	6
R.M. Hogg	run out	3
C.G. Rackemann	run out	1
S.B. Smith		
Extras	(B 2, LB 8, W 1, NB 4)	15
Total	(50 overs – 9 wickets)	**222**

Fall of wickets 1-23, 2-132, 3-161, 4-169, 5-176, 6-192, 7-209, 8-218, 9-222.

WEST INDIES	*O*	*M*	*R*	*W*
Holding	10	0	39	3
Garner	10	1	39	3
Baptiste	10	0	44	0
Marshall	10	1	27	1
Richards	3	0	26	0
Gomes	7	0	37	0

Umpires: R.A. French and M.W. Johnson.

No-balls and wides debited to bowlers' analyses.

Match No. 247/28

AUSTRALIA v WEST INDIES 1983-84

Benson and Hedges World Series Cup – 3rd Final

At Melbourne Cricket Ground on 12 February 1984.
Toss: Australia. Result: WEST INDIES won by 6 wickets.
50 overs match. Finals award: J. Garner.

Début: Australia – D.C. Boon.

Incensed at having to play a third final after gaining a victory and a tie in the previous two, West Indies were only partially appeased by the Australian Board's decision to allocate an extra £18,000 in prize-money. Even had Australia won this match, West Indies would still have gained the trophy by virtue of their superior record in the preliminary matches.

AUSTRALIA		
K.C. Wessels	b Garner	17
A.R. Border	b Garner	4
D.C. Boon	b Davis	39
K.J. Hughes*	c and b Baptiste	65
D.M. Jones	c Garner b Holding	3
W.B. Phillips	c Holding b Garner	22
R.W. Marsh†	c Dujon b Garner	35
G.F. Lawson	b Garner	7
T.G. Hogan	not out	1
R.M. Hogg		
C.G. Rackemann		
Extras	(B 1, LB 14, W 2, NB 2)	19
Total	(50 overs – 8 wickets)	**212**

Fall of wickets: 1-14, 2-25, 3-125, 4-140, 5-140, 6-185, 7-210, 8-212.

WEST INDIES	*O*	*M*	*R*	*W*
Holding	10	1	33	1
Garner	10	1	31	5
Marshall	10	0	44	0
Davis	10	0	45	1
Baptiste	10	0	44	1

WEST INDIES		
D.L. Haynes	b Lawson	1
R.B. Richardson	lbw b Hogg	27
H.A. Gomes	lbw b Lawson	0
A.L. Logie	c Rackemann b Wessels	88
P.J.L. Dujon†	not out	82
M.D. Marshall	not out	6
R.A. Harper		
M.A. Holding*		
E.A.E. Baptiste		
J. Garner		
W.W. Davis		
Extras	(B 4, LB 3, W 2)	9
Total	(45.3 overs – 4 wickets)	**213**

Fall of wickets: 1-3, 2-3, 3-52, 4-176.

AUSTRALIA	*O*	*M*	*R*	*W*
Lawson	9	1	45	2
Rackemann	9.3	2	40	0
Hogg	8	1	22	1
Hogan	10	0	39	0
Border	3	0	13	0
Wessels	6	0	47	1

Umpires: M.W. Johnson and P.J. McConnell.

No-balls and wides debited to bowlers' analyses.

NEW ZEALAND v ENGLAND 1983-84 (1st Match)

Rothmans Cup

At Lancaster Park, Christchurch on 18 February 1984.
Toss: New Zealand. Result: ENGLAND won by 54 runs.
50 overs match. Award: D.W. Randall.
Débuts: England – N.A. Foster, C.L. Smith.

ENGLAND		
D.I. Gower	c J.J. Crowe b Hadlee	3
C.L. Smith	run out	17
A.J. Lamb	c Robertson b Hadlee	43
D.W. Randall	c Cairns b Hadlee	70
I.T. Botham	c Smith b Hadlee	1
M.W. Gatting	b Hadlee	0
V.J. Marks	lbw b Cairns	28
R.W. Taylor†	run out	2
N.A. Foster	c Wright b Cairns	0
N.G. Cowans	not out	4
R.G.D. Willis*		
Extras	(B 8, LB 4, NB 8)	20
Total	(50 overs – 9 wickets)	**188**

Fall of wickets: 1-9, 2-59, 3-107, 4-109, 5-109, 6-177, 7-184, 8-184, 9-188.

NEW ZEALAND	*O*	*M*	*R*	*W*
Hadlee	10	2	32	5
Chatfield	10	4	20	0
Cairns	10	2	41	2
Coney	10	1	30	0
Robertson	10	0	45	0

NEW ZEALAND		
J.G. Wright	c Taylor b Willis	4
B.A. Edgar	c Taylor b Botham	10
G.P. Howarth*	run out	18
M.D. Crowe	run out	0
J.J. Crowe	b Botham	0
J.V. Coney	c Botham b Foster	19
B.L. Cairns	lbw b Marks	23
R.J. Hadlee	c Gower b Marks	23
I.D.S. Smith†	c Gower b Foster	7
G.K. Robertson	lbw b Willis	10
E.J. Chatfield	not out	0
Extras	(LB 9, W 6, NB 5)	20
Total	(42.1 overs)	**134**

Fall of wickets: 1-7, 2-38, 3-38, 4-38, 5-44, 6-76, 7-112, 8-120, 9-124, 10-134.

ENGLAND	*O*	*M*	*R*	*W*
Willis	6.1	1	18	2
Cowans	10	2	37	0
Botham	6	3	7	2
Foster	10	4	19	2
Marks	10	1	33	2

Umpires: F.R. Goodall and I.C. Higginson.

Match No. 249/20

NEW ZEALAND v ENGLAND 1983-84 (2nd Match)

Rothmans Cup

At Basin Reserve, Wellington on 22 February 1984.
Toss: New Zealand. Result: ENGLAND won by 6 wickets.
50 overs match. Award: V.J. Marks.
Début: New Zealand – T.J. Franklin.

Marks recorded England's best analysis in these matches and became the first England bowler to take five wickets twice at this level.

NEW ZEALAND		
B.A. Edgar	b Marks	12
T.J. Franklin	c and b Marks	6
G.P. Howarth*	lbw b Marks	21
M.D. Crowe	c Foster b Marks	8
J.J. Crowe	c Foster b Marks	1
J.V. Coney	b Botham	44
R.J. Hadlee	c Randall b Foster	21
B.L. Cairns	c Gower b Foster	0
I.D.S. Smith†	lbw b Botham	0
G.K. Robertson	run out	11
E.J. Chatfield	not out	0
Extras	(LB 9, W 2)	11
Total	(47.1 overs)	**135**

Fall of wickets: 1-23, 2-34, 3-50, 4-52, 5-63, 6-104, 7-104, 8-104, 9-135, 10-135.

ENGLAND	*O*	*M*	*R*	*W*
Willis	9	4	17	0
Cowans	10	1	33	0
Marks	10	3	20	5
Botham	8.1	1	25	2
Foster	10	3	29	2

ENGLAND		
D.I. Gower	c J.J. Crowe b Chatfield	21
C.L. Smith	b Hadlee	70
A.J. Lamb	c and b Chatfield	6
D.W. Randall	not out	25
I.T. Botham	b Hadlee	15
M.W. Gatting	not out	0
V.J. Marks		
R.W. Taylor†		
N.A. Foster		
N.G. Cowans		
R.G.D. Willis*		
Extras	(LB 2)	2
Total	(45.1 overs – 4 wickets)	**139**

Fall of wickets: 1-36, 2-54, 3-117, 4-135.

NEW ZEALAND	*O*	*M*	*R*	*W*
Hadlee	10	2	31	2
Robertson	6	0	28	0
Coney	10	1	29	0
Chatfield	10	5	16	2
Cairns	9.1	1	33	0

Umpires: G.C. Morris and S.J. Woodward.

NEW ZEALAND v ENGLAND 1983-84 (3rd Match)

Rothmans Cup

At Eden Park, Auckland on 25 February 1984.
Toss: England. Result: NEW ZEALAND won by 7 wickets.
50 overs match. Award: M.D. Crowe.
No débuts.

ENGLAND		
D.I. Gower	lbw b Chatfield	35
C.L. Smith	b Hadlee	5
A.J. Lamb	not out	97
D.W. Randall	b Boock	11
I.T. Botham	c Wright b Coney	18
M.W. Gatting	c Smith b Chatfield	4
V.J. Marks	b Chatfield	3
R.W. Taylor†	run out	8
N.A. Foster	run out	1
N.G. Cowans	run out	0
R.G.D. Willis*	not out	7
Extras	(B 4, LB 11, W 1, NB 4)	20
Total	(50 overs – 9 wickets)	**209**

Fall of wickets: 1-6, 2-73, 3-86, 4-130, 5-140, 6-148, 7-185, 8-192, 9-192.

NEW ZEALAND	*O*	*M*	*R*	*W*
Cairns	10	2	31	0
Hadlee	10	2	51	1
Boock	10	0	40	1
Coney	10	0	38	1
Chatfield	10	2	29	3

NEW ZEALAND		
P.N. Webb	b Willis	8
J.G. Wright	c and b Marks	14
G.P. Howarth*	lbw b Botham	72
M.D. Crowe	not out	105
J.V. Coney	not out	2
J.J. Crowe		
R.J. Hadlee		
B.L. Cairns		
I.D.S. Smith†		
S.L. Boock		
E.J. Chatfield		
Extras	(LB 7, W 2)	9
Total	(45.3 overs – 3 wickets)	**210**

Fall of wickets: 1-22, 2-34, 3-194.

ENGLAND	*O*	*M*	*R*	*W*
Willis	10	1	36	1
Cowans	9.3	0	59	0
Marks	10	1	27	1
Botham	7	1	22	1
Foster	6	0	37	0
Smith	3	0	20	0

Umpires: D.A. Kinsella and G.C. Morris.

Match No. 251/29

WEST INDIES v AUSTRALIA 1983-84 (1st Match)

At Albion Sports Complex, Berbice, Guyana on 29 February 1984.
Toss: Australia. Result: WEST INDIES won by 8 wickets.
50 overs match. Award: D.L. Haynes.
Début: West Indies – M.A. Small.

AUSTRALIA		
K.C. Wessels	c Small b Richards	44
S.B. Smith	b Gomes	60
G.M. Ritchie	run out	46
K.J. Hughes*	b Gomes	2
A.R. Border	b Gomes	2
D.M. Jones	not out	43
W.B. Phillips†	not out	0
G.F. Lawson		
R.M. Hogg		
C.G. Rackemann		
T.M. Alderman		
Extras	(B 7, LB 18, NB 9)	34
Total	(50 overs – 5 wickets)	**231**

Fall of wickets 1-106, 2-137, 3-143, 4-159, 5-222.

WEST INDIES	*O*	*M*	*R*	*W*
Garner	10	1	35	0
Daniel	5	0	19	0
Davis	10	1	66	0
Small	5	0	14	0
Richards	10	0	38	1
Gomes	10	0	34	3

WEST INDIES		
C.G. Greenidge	c Phillips b Rackemann	23
D.L. Haynes	not out	133
R.B. Richardson	c Jones b Alderman	61
I.V.A. Richards*	not out	4
A.L. Logie		
P.J.L. Dujon†		
H.A. Gomes		
J. Garner		
W.W. Daniel		
M.A. Small		
W.W. Davis		
Extras	(LB 5, NB 7)	12
Total	(48 overs – 2 wickets)	**233**

Fall of wickets 1-62, 2-229.

AUSTRALIA	*O*	*M*	*R*	*W*
Lawson	10	3	26	0
Alderman	10	0	62	1
Hogg	8	0	40	0
Rackemann	10	1	54	1
Border	6	1	22	0
Wessels	4	0	24	0

Umpires: C.E. Cumberbatch and D.J. Narine.

No-balls and wides debited to bowlers' analyses.

WEST INDIES v AUSTRALIA 1983-84 (2nd Match)

At Queen's Park Oval, Port-of-Spain, Trinidad on 14 March 1984.
Toss: Australia. Result: AUSTRALIA won by 4 wickets.
37 overs match. Award: K.C. Wessels.
No débuts.

WEST INDIES		
C.G. Greenidge	c Lawson b Wessels	63
D.L. Haynes	b Lawson	1
R.B. Richardson	c Phillips b Lawson	0
I.V.A. Richards	c Alderman b Maguire	67
C.H. Lloyd*	not out	31
P.J.L. Dujon†	c Maguire b Alderman	16
M.D. Marshall	run out	0
J. Garner	not out	0
H.A. Gomes		
W.W. Daniel		
M.A. Small		
Extras	(B 1, LB 8, W 3)	12
Total	(37 overs – 6 wickets)	**190**

Fall of wickets 1-25, 2-25, 3-135, 4-145, 5-173, 6-178.

AUSTRALIA	*O*	*M*	*R*	*W*
Lawson	9	1	40	2
Alderman	9	2	39	1
Hogg	6	0	49	0
Maguire	9	1	28	1
Wessels	4	0	25	1

AUSTRALIA		
K.C. Wessels	c Richards b Daniel	67
D.W. Hookes	b Garner	14
S.B. Smith	c Richards b Small	27
K.J. Hughes*	run out	18
D.M. Jones	run out	3
A.R. Border	not out	26
W.B. Phillips†	run out	10
G.F. Lawson	not out	0
J.N. Maguire		
T.M. Alderman		
R.M. Hogg		
Extras	(B 7, LB 15, W 2, NB 5)	29
Total	(36.4 overs – 6 wickets)	**194**

Fall of wickets 1-30, 2-98, 3-143, 4-157, 5-162, 6-188.

WEST INDIES	*O*	*M*	*R*	*W*
Garner	9.4	2	24	1
Daniel	9	0	56	0
Small	9	0	40	1
Marshall	9	0	52	0

Umpires: L. Barker and S. Mohammed.

No-balls and wides debited to bowlers' analyses.

Match No. 253/31

WEST INDIES v AUSTRALIA 1983-84 (3rd Match)

At Mindoo Phillip Park, Castries, St Lucia on 19 April 1984.
Toss: West Indies. Result: WEST INDIES won by 7 wickets.
45 overs match. Award: D.L. Haynes.
Début: West Indies – T.R.O. Payne.

AUSTRALIA		
S.B. Smith	b Garner	6
W.B. Phillips†	b Marshall	0
G.M. Ritchie	c Dujon b Garner	0
A.R. Border	c Dujon b Garner	90
K.J. Hughes*	b Holding	78
D.W. Hookes	c Dujon b Marshall	22
D.M. Jones	c and b Marshall	0
T.G. Hogan	c and b Marshall	0
G.F. Lawson	run out	2
J.N. Maguire	not out	1
C.G. Rackemann	not out	0
Extras	(B 1, LB 2, W 2, NB 2)	7
Total	(45 overs – 9 wickets)	**206**

Fall of wickets: 1-2, 2-6, 3-8, 4-158, 5-198, 6-199, 7-202, 8-205, 9-205.

WEST INDIES	*O*	*M*	*R*	*W*
Garner	10	0	33	3
Marshall	10	2	34	4
Holding	10	0	57	1
Baptiste	8	0	42	0
Harper	7	0	37	0

WEST INDIES		
C.G. Greenidge	c Lawson b Hogan	42
D.L. Haynes	not out	102
R.B. Richardson	c Hogan b Maguire	6
A.L. Logie	c Phillips b Maguire	28
P.J.L. Dujon†	not out	13
T.R.O. Payne		
E.A.E. Baptiste		
M.D. Marshall		
R.A. Harper		
J. Garner		
M.A. Holding*		
Extras	(B 4, LB 10, W 2, NB 1)	17
Total	(41.4 overs – 3 wickets)	**208**

Fall of wickets: 1-96, 2-119, 3-180.

AUSTRALIA	*O*	*M*	*R*	*W*
Lawson	10	1	43	0
Rackemann	10	0	56	0
Maguire	10	0	57	2
Hogan	10	0	31	1
Border	1	0	3	0
Jones	0.4	0	4	0

Umpires: S. Mohammed and P. White.

No-balls and wides debited to bowlers' analyses.

WEST INDIES v AUSTRALIA 1983-84 (4th Match)

At Sabina Park, Kingston, Jamaica on 26 April 1984.
Toss: West Indies. Result: WEST INDIES won by 9 wickets.
50 overs match. Award: D.L. Haynes.
No débuts.

AUSTRALIA		
S.B. Smith	b Harper	50
W.B. Phillips†	c Logie b Garner	13
G.M. Ritchie	c Haynes b Garner	84
A.R. Border	b Harper	28
K.J. Hughes*	c Greenidge b Garner	8
D.W. Hookes	b Marshall	0
G.R.J. Matthews	b Marshall	10
T.G. Hogan	not out	1
G.F. Lawson		
R.M. Hogg		
J.N. Maguire		
Extras	(B 5, LB 2, W 4, NB 4)	15
Total	(50 overs – 7 wickets)	**209**

Fall of wickets 1-22, 2-111, 3-161, 4-185, 5-187, 6-205, 7-209.

WEST INDIES	*O*	*M*	*R*	*W*
Garner	10	0	47	3
Marshall	10	1	26	2
Baptiste	5	0	19	0
Holding	8	0	44	0
Harper	10	1	41	2
Richards	7	0	25	0

WEST INDIES		
C.G. Greenidge	b Maguire	34
D.L. Haynes	not out	104
R.B. Richardson	not out	51
I.V.A. Richards*		
A.L. Logie		
P.J.L. Dujon†		
M.D. Marshall		
E.A.E. Baptiste		
R.A. Harper		
J. Garner		
M.A. Holding		
Extras	(B 5, LB 8, W 4, NB 5)	22
Total	(47.4 overs – 1 wicket)	**211**

Fall of wicket 1-80.

AUSTRALIA	*O*	*M*	*R*	*W*
Lawson	8	1	39	0
Hogg	8.4	0	51	0
Maguire	6	1	16	1
Hogan	10	2	31	0
Matthews	10	1	42	0
Border	5	0	19	0

Umpires: L. Barker and J. Gayle.

No-balls and wides debited to bowlers' analyses.

Match No. 255/7

SRI LANKA v NEW ZEALAND 1983-84 (1st Match)

At Sinhalese Sports Club, Colombo on 3 March 1984.
Toss: Sri Lanka. Result: NEW ZEALAND won by 104 runs.
42 overs match. Award: J.F. Reid.
No débuts.

NEW ZEALAND		
G.P. Howarth*	c Kuruppu b Ranatunga	33
J.G. Wright	c and b De Mel	20
J.F. Reid	c John b Ratnayeke	80
M.D. Crowe	c De Mel b De Silva	29
J.J. Crowe	not out	39
R.J. Hadlee	c Ranatunga b Ratnayeke	6
B.L. Cairns	b John	1
J.V. Coney	not out	4
I.D.S. Smith†		
S.L. Boock		
E.J. Chatfield		
Extras	(B 1, LB 8, W 3, NB 10)	22
Total	(42 overs – 6 wickets)	**234**

Fall of wickets: 1-58, 2-76, 3-123, 4-220, 5-227, 6-229.

SRI LANKA	*O*	*M*	*R*	*W*
De Mel	7	1	40	1
John	9	1	39	1
Ratnayeke	8	0	37	2
De Silva	9	0	42	1
Ranatunga	9	0	54	1

SRI LANKA		
S. Wettimuny	c Coney b Chatfield	16
D.S.B.P. Kuruppu	c Hadlee b Coney	38
R.L. Dias	c and b Boock	9
L.R.D. Mendis*	b Boock	15
A. Ranatunga	c Coney b Boock	16
J.R. Ratnayeke	run out	1
D.S. De Silva	c J.J. Crowe b Hadlee	8
R.S. Madugalle	b Cairns	5
R.G. de Alwis†	c Smith b Hadlee	8
A.L.F. De Mel	b Hadlee	2
V.B. John	not out	6
Extras	(B 1, LB 4, W 1)	6
Total	(37.3 overs)	**130**

Fall of wickets: 1-54, 2-60, 3-73, 4-98, 5-100, 6-102, 7-111, 8-122, 9-123, 10-130.

NEW ZEALAND	*O*	*M*	*R*	*W*
Cairns	9	0	35	1
Hadlee	8.3	0	22	3
Chatfield	4	0	24	1
Boock	9	0	28	3
Coney	7	2	15	1

Umpires: D.P. Buultjens and H.C. Felsinger.

SRI LANKA v NEW ZEALAND 1983-84 (2nd Match)

At Tyronne Fernando Stadium, Moratuwa on 31 March 1984.
Toss: New Zealand. Result: SRI LANKA won by 41 runs.
40 overs match. Award: U.S.H. Karnain.
Débuts: Sri Lanka – P.A. De Silva, U.S.H. Karnain; New Zealand – D.A. Stirling.

SRI LANKA		
S. Wettimuny	b Chatfield	6
D.S.B.P. Kuruppu	c Wright b Stirling	4
R.S. Madugalle	c Coney b Chatfield	10
A. Ranatunga	not out	50
L.R.D. Mendis*	b Cairns	4
P.A. De Silva	b Hadlee	8
J.R. Ratnayeke	run out	12
U.S.H. Karnain	c Cairns b M.D. Crowe	28
R.G. de Alwis†	run out	1
D.S. De Silva	not out	18
V.B. John		
Extras	(B 1, LB 10, W 1, NB 4)	16
Total	(40 overs – 8 wickets)	**157**

Fall of wickets: 1-11, 2-22, 3-37, 4-48, 5-69, 6-110, 7-110, 8-112.

NEW ZEALAND	*O*	*M*	*R*	*W*
Cairns	8	1	11	1
Hadlee	8	2	27	1
Stirling	5	1	34	1
Chatfield	8	0	29	2
Coney	6	0	21	0
M.D. Crowe	5	0	19	1

NEW ZEALAND		
J.G. Wright	c Wettimuny b John	3
B.A. Edgar	c de Alwis b Karnain	12
G.P. Howarth*	b Karnain	12
B.L. Cairns	b Karnain	5
M.D. Crowe	c de Alwis b Karnain	9
J.J. Crowe	lbw b Karnain	9
J.V. Coney	b Ranatunga	11
R.J. Hadlee	c P.A. De Silva b Ranatunga	13
I.D.S. Smith†	c P.A. De Silva b D.S. De Silva	11
D.A. Stirling	not out	13
E.J. Chatfield	lbw b Ranatunga	5
Extras	(B 1, LB 11, NB 1)	13
Total	(34 overs)	**116**

Fall of wickets: 1-4, 2-31, 3-34, 4-39, 5-49, 6-66, 7-76, 8-88, 9-96, 10-116.

SRI LANKA	*O*	*M*	*R*	*W*
John	7	0	12	1
Ratnayeke	6	0	14	0
Karnain	8	1	26	5
D.S. De Silva	5	0	28	1
Ranatunga	8	1	23	3

Umpires: K.T. Francis and P.W. Vidanagamage.

Match No. 257/9

SRI LANKA v NEW ZEALAND 1983-84 (3rd Match)

At Saravanamuttu Stadium, Colombo on 1 April 1984.
Toss: Sri Lanka. Result: NEW ZEALAND won by 86 runs.
44 overs match. Award: B.L. Cairns.
No débuts.

NEW ZEALAND		
J.G. Wright*	c de Alwis b Ratnayeke	10
B.A. Edgar	b D.S. De Silva	24
M.D. Crowe	run out	68
J.F. Reid	c D.S. De Silva b John	9
J.J. Crowe	b Ranatunga	5
J.V. Coney	c and b Ranatunga	13
R.J. Hadlee	c Madugalle b Ranatunga	9
I.D.S. Smith†	run out	13
B.L. Cairns	not out	40
S.L. Boock	not out	8
E.J. Chatfield		
Extras	(LB 1, W 1)	2
Total	(44 overs – 8 wickets)	**201**

Fall of wickets: 1-16, 2-45, 3-63, 4-77, 5-114, 6-124, 7-153, 8-154.

SRI LANKA	*O*	*M*	*R*	*W*
John	9	1	43	1
Ratnayeke	8	0	32	1
Karnain	9	0	41	0
D.S. De Silva	9	0	34	1
Ranatunga	9	0	49	3

SRI LANKA		
S. Wettimuny	c Smith b Hadlee	33
D.S.B.P. Kuruppu	c Smith b Hadlee	3
R.S. Madugalle	c sub (J.G. Bracewell) b Boock	10
P.A. De Silva	run out	7
A. Ranatunga	c J.J. Crowe b Cairns	13
L.R.D. Mendis*	c Hadlee b Chatfield	7
U.S.H. Karnain	c Boock b Cairns	1
J.R. Ratnayeke	c Reid b Chatfield	7
R.G. de Alwis†	lbw b Hadlee	9
D.S. De Silva	not out	14
V.B. John	c sub (J.G. Bracewell) b Coney	1
Extras	(B 6, LB 4)	10
Total	(38.1 overs)	**115**

Fall of wickets: 1-6, 2-29, 3-39, 4-73, 5-76, 6-79, 7-85, 8-94, 9-114, 10-115.

NEW ZEALAND	*O*	*M*	*R*	*W*
Cairns	7	2	14	2
Hadlee	6	0	19	3
Chatfield	9	2	13	2
Boock	9	1	22	1
Coney	6.1	1	24	1
M.D. Crowe	1	0	13	0

Umpires: H.C. Felsinger and K.T. Francis.

PAKISTAN v ENGLAND 1983-84 (1st Match)
Wills Series

At Gaddafi Stadium, Lahore on 9 March 1984.
Toss: Pakistan. Result: PAKISTAN won by 6 wickets.
40 overs match. Award: Zaheer Abbas.
Début: Pakistan – Saadat Ali.

ENGLAND		
G. Fowler†	b Sarfraz	43
C.J. Tavaré	c Ashraf b Rashid	4
D.I. Gower	c Qasim b Shahid	7
A.J. Lamb	run out	57
D.W. Randall	run out	16
I.T. Botham	not out	18
M.W. Gatting	b Sarfraz	9
G.R. Dilley	lbw b Sarfraz	1
V.J. Marks	b Rashid	2
N.A. Foster	not out	6
R.G.D. Willis*		
Extras	(LB 13, W 6, NB 2)	21
Total	(40 overs – 8 wickets)	**184**

Fall of wickets 1-11, 2-24, 3-94, 4-134, 5-147, 6-160, 7-164, 8-173.

PAKISTAN	*O*	*M*	*R*	*W*
Rashid Khan	8	1	28	2
Shahid Mahboob	8	2	28	1
Mudassar Nazar	8	1	34	0
Sarfraz Nawaz	8	0	33	3
Wasim Raja	8	0	40	0

PAKISTAN		
Mohsin Khan	b Dilley	39
Saadat Ali	run out	44
Qasim Omar	c Fowler b Marks	11
Zaheer Abbas*	not out	59
Salim Malik	c Tavaré b Willis	11
Mudassar Nazar	not out	8
Wasim Raja		
Shahid Mahboob		
Ashraf Ali†		
Sarfraz Nawaz		
Rashid Khan		
Extras	(B 1, LB 5, W 1, NB 8)	15
Total	(38.4 overs – 4 wickets)	**187**

Fall of wickets 1-79, 2-96, 3-120, 4-156.

ENGLAND	*O*	*M*	*R*	*W*
Willis	7.4	1	25	1
Dilley	8	0	38	1
Botham	7	0	43	0
Marks	8	1	32	1
Foster	8	0	34	0

Umpires: Amanullah Khan and Shakil Khan.

Match No. 259/14

PAKISTAN v ENGLAND 1983-84 (2nd Match)

Wills Series

At National Stadium, Karachi on 26 March 1984.
Toss: England. Result: ENGLAND won by 6 wickets.
40 overs match. Award: M.W. Gatting.
Débuts: Pakistan – Anil Dalpat, Naved Anjum; England – N.G.B. Cook.

PAKISTAN		
Mohsin Khan	st Fowler b Cook	37
Saadat Ali	not out	78
Wasim Raja	c Fowler b Gatting	14
Salim Malik	c Foster b Gatting	2
Qasim Omar	c and b Gatting	7
Naved Anjum	st Fowler b Smith	2
Mudassar Nazar	run out	6
Abdul Qadir	c Cook b Smith	3
Sarfraz Nawaz*	c Gower b Cowans	3
Anil Dalpat†	not out	0
Rashid Khan		
Extras	(B 4, LB 4, NB 3)	11
Total	(40 overs – 8 wickets)	**163**

Fall of wickets 1-76, 2-102, 3-107, 4-123, 5-135, 6-146, 7-155, 8-160.

ENGLAND	*O*	*M*	*R*	*W*
Foster	8	0	36	0
Cowans	5	0	20	1
Gatting	8	1	32	3
Marks	8	1	22	0
Cook	8	0	34	1
Smith	3	0	8	2

ENGLAND		
G. Fowler†	c Dalpat b Mudassar	25
C.L. Smith	lbw b Qadir	17
D.I. Gower*	b Mudassar	31
A.J. Lamb	c Salim b Naved	19
M.W. Gatting	not out	38
D.W. Randall	not out	19
C.J. Tavaré		
V.J. Marks		
N.A. Foster		
N.G.B. Cook		
N.G. Cowans		
Extras	(B 1, LB 8, W 3, NB 3)	15
Total	(38.4 overs – 4 wickets)	**164**

Fall of wickets 1-37, 2-79, 3-88, 4-119.

PAKISTAN	*O*	*M*	*R*	*W*
Rashid Khan	8	0	31	0
Sarfraz Nawaz	7.4	1	24	0
Mudassar Nazar	8	0	33	2
Abdul Qadir	8	1	22	1
Wasim Raja	5	0	30	0
Naved Anjum	2	0	9	1

Umpires: Mahboob Shah and Shakil Khan.

PAKISTAN v SRI LANKA 1983-84

Rothmans Asia Cup – 1st Match

At Sharjah CA Stadium, UAE on 6 April 1984.
Toss: Sri Lanka. Result: SRI LANKA won by 5 wickets.
46 overs match. Award: R.L. Dias.
No débuts.

The cricket fanaticism of businessman A.R. Bukhatir brought international cricket to the Middle East. His stadium at Sharjah boasts a flat green outfield and turf pitch.

PAKISTAN		
Mohsin Khan	c Dias b D.S. De Silva	27
Saadat Ali	c Kuruppu b Ranatunga	30
Mudassar Nazar	c Kuruppu b Karnain	1
Zaheer Abbas*	c Ratnayeke b Ranatunga	47
Javed Miandad	b John	9
Salim Malik	run out	17
Abdul Qadir	b D.S. De Silva	7
Shahid Mahboob	not out	18
Sarfraz Nawaz	c John b Ranatunga	5
Anil Dalpat†	c Ranatunga b Ratnayeke	5
Rashid Khan	not out	0
Extras	(B 4, LB 8, W 8, NB 1)	21
Total	(46 overs – 9 wickets)	**187**

Fall of wickets: 1-59, 2-60, 3-84, 4-110, 5-142, 6-154, 7-157, 8-165, 9-185.

SRI LANKA	*O*	*M*	*R*	*W*
John	10	3	26	1
Ratnayeke	9	0	33	1
Karnain	7	1	19	1
D.S. De Silva	10	0	50	2
Ranatunga	10	0	38	3

SRI LANKA		
S. Wettimuny	run out	18
D.S.B.P. Kuruppu†	c Dalpat b Mudassar	25
R.L. Dias	not out	57
L.R.D. Mendis*	b Qadir	20
A. Ranatunga	st Dalpat b Qadir	26
R.S. Madugalle	c Zaheer b Sarfraz	4
P.A. De Silva	not out	14
U.S.H. Karnain		
D.S. De Silva		
J.R. Ratnayeke		
V.B. John		
Extras	(B 4, LB 14, W 6, NB 2)	26
Total	(43.3 overs – 5 wickets)	**190**

Fall of wickets: 1-52, 2-67, 3-105, 4-163, 5-170.

PAKISTAN	*O*	*M*	*R*	*W*
Shahid Mahboob	9	1	30	0
Rashid Khan	8	2	26	0
Mudassar Nazar	7	0	25	1
Sarfraz Nawaz	10	1	36	1
Abdul Qadir	9	0	42	2
Saadat Ali	0.3	0	5	0

Umpires: H.D. Bird and Swaroop Kishen.

Match No. 261/5

INDIA v SRI LANKA 1983-84

Rothmans Asia Cup – 2nd Match

At Sharjah CA Stadium, UAE on 8 April 1984.
Toss: India. Result: INDIA won by 10 wickets.
46 overs match. Award: S.C. Khanna.
Début: India – M. Prabhakar.

SRI LANKA		
S. Wettimuny	c Madan Lal b Prabhakar	12
D.S.B.P. Kuruppu†	c Khanna b Sharma	0
R.L. Dias	c Vengsarkar b Prabhakar	5
L.R.D. Mendis*	c Patil b Sharma	1
R.S. Madugalle	b Madan Lal	38
A. Ranatunga	run out	9
P.A. De Silva	lbw b Madan Lal	11
U.S.H. Karnain	lbw b Madan Lal	0
J.R. Ratnayeke	b Shastri	2
D.S. De Silva	not out	8
V.B. John	c Gavaskar b Sharma	2
Extras	(LB 4, W 3, NB 1)	8
Total	(41 overs)	**96**

Fall of wickets: 1-1, 2-17, 3-20, 4-26, 5-53, 6-79, 7-81, 8-82, 9-86, 10-96.

INDIA	*O*	*M*	*R*	*W*
Sharma	8	1	22	3
Prabhakar	10	3	16	2
Binny	7	0	25	0
Madan Lal	8	2	11	3
Shastri	7	1	13	1
Azad	1	0	1	0

INDIA		
S.C. Khanna†	not out	51
G.A. Parkar	not out	32
D.B. Vengsarkar		
S.M. Gavaskar*		
S.M. Patil		
R.J. Shastri		
K. Azad		
R.M.H. Binny		
Madan Lal		
M. Prabhakar		
C. Sharma		
Extras	(B 1, W 12, NB 1)	14
Total	(21.4 overs – 0 wicket)	**97**

SRI LANKA	*O*	*M*	*R*	*W*
John	9	1	30	0
Ratnayeke	4	0	27	0
Karnain	2	0	4	0
D.S. De Silva	6	0	21	0
Madugalle	0.4	0	1	0

Umpires: H.D. Bird and Shakoor Rana.

INDIA v PAKISTAN 1983-84

Rothmans Asia Cup – 3rd Match

At Sharjah CA Stadium, UAE on 13 April 1984.
Toss: India. Result: INDIA won by 54 runs.
46 overs match. Award: S.C. Khanna.
No débuts.

INDIA		
S.C. Khanna†	c Dalpat b Mudassar	56
G.A. Parkar	run out	22
D.B. Vengsarkar	b Shahid	14
S.M. Patil	c Salim b Sarfraz	43
S.M. Gavaskar*	not out	36
R.J. Shastri		
K. Azad		
R.M.H. Binny		
Madan Lal		
M. Prabhakar		
C. Sharma		
Extras	(B 1, LB 12, W 1, NB 3)	17
Total	(46 overs – 4 wickets)	**188**

Fall of wickets 1-54, 2-88, 3-110, 4-188.

PAKISTAN	*O*	*M*	*R*	*W*
Azeem Hafeez	7	0	41	0
Sarfraz Nawaz	10	1	37	1
Shahid Mahboob	10	1	23	1
Abdul Qadir	10	3	36	0
Mudassar Nazar	9	3	34	1

PAKISTAN		
Mohsin Khan	c Parkar b Shastri	35
Saadat Ali	run out	13
Mudassar Nazar	st Khanna b Shastri	18
Zaheer Abbas*	c Madan Lal b Binny	27
Salim Malik	run out	15
Qasim Omar	c Prabhakar b Binny	16
Shahid Mahboob	run out	0
Abdul Qadir	run out	0
Sarfraz Nawaz	c Patil b Binny	4
Anil Dalpat†	st Khanna b Shastri	1
Azeem Hafeez	not out	0
Extras	(LB 5)	5
Total	(39.4 overs)	**134**

Fall of wickets 1-23, 2-69, 3-70, 4-92, 5-125,
6-125, 7-125, 8-128, 9-133, 10-134.

INDIA	*O*	*M*	*R*	*W*
Sharma	7	0	18	0
Prabhakar	7	0	17	0
Binny	9.4	0	33	3
Madan Lal	6	1	21	0
Shastri	10	0	40	3

Umpires: H.D. Bird and H.C. Felsinger.

Match No. 263/16

ENGLAND v WEST INDIES 1984 (1st Match)

Texaco Trophy

At Old Trafford, Manchester on 31 May 1984.
Toss: West Indies. Result: WEST INDIES won by 104 runs.
55 overs match. Award: I.V.A. Richards.

Début: England – T.A. Lloyd.

The first Texaco Trophy match was dominated by the highest innings in any one-day international. Richards (220 minutes, 170 balls, 5 sixes and 21 fours) became the first batsman to score 3,000 runs at this level and dominated the first century partnership for the tenth wicket – 106* with Holding.

WEST INDIES		
C.G. Greenidge	c Bairstow b Botham	9
D.L. Haynes	run out	1
R.B. Richardson	c and b Willis	6
I.V.A. Richards	not out	189
H.A. Gomes	b Miller	4
C.H. Lloyd*	c Pringle b Miller	8
P.J.L. Dujon†	c Gatting b Miller	0
M.D. Marshall	run out	4
E.A.E. Baptiste	c Bairstow b Botham	26
J. Garner	c and b Foster	3
M.A. Holding	not out	12
Extras	(B 4, LB 2, W 1, NB 3)	10
Total	(55 overs – 9 wickets)	**272**

Fall of wickets: 1-5, 2-11, 3-43, 4-63, 5-89, 6-98, 7-102, 8-161, 9-166.

ENGLAND	*O*	*M*	*R*	*W*
Willis	11	2	38	1
Botham	11	0	67	2
Foster	11	0	61	1
Miller	11	1	32	3
Pringle	11	0	64	0

ENGLAND		
G. Fowler	c Lloyd b Garner	1
T.A. Lloyd	c Dujon b Holding	15
M.W. Gatting	lbw b Garner	0
D.I. Gower*	c Greenidge b Marshall	15
A.J. Lamb	c Richardson b Gomes	75
I.T. Botham	c Richardson b Baptiste	2
D.L. Bairstow†	c Garner b Richards	13
G. Miller	b Richards	7
D.R. Pringle	c Garner b Holding	6
N.A. Foster	b Garner	24
R.G.D. Willis	not out	1
Extras	(LB 6, NB 3)	9
Total	(50 overs)	**168**

Fall of wickets: 1-7, 2-8, 3-33, 4-48, 5-51, 6-80, 7-100, 8-115, 9-162, 10-168.

WEST INDIES	*O*	*M*	*R*	*W*
Garner	8	1	18	3
Holding	11	2	23	2
Baptiste	11	0	38	1
Marshall	6	1	20	1
Richards	11	1	45	2
Gomes	3	0	15	1

Umpires: D.J. Constant and D.R. Shepherd.

ENGLAND v WEST INDIES 1984 (2nd Match)

Texaco Trophy

At Trent Bridge, Nottingham on 2 June 1984.
Toss: England. Result: ENGLAND won by 3 wickets.
50 overs match. Award: D.R. Pringle.
No débuts.

WEST INDIES		
C.G. Greenidge	c Botham b Pringle	20
D.L. Haynes	lbw b Willis	4
R.B. Richardson	c Gower b Pringle	10
I.V.A. Richards	c Pringle b Miller	3
H.A. Gomes	b Pringle	15
C.H. Lloyd*	c Pringle b Miller	52
P.J.L. Dujon†	run out	21
M.D. Marshall	run out	20
E.A.E. Baptiste	lbw b Willis	19
M.A. Holding	b Botham	0
J. Garner	not out	6
Extras	(LB 7, NB 2)	9
Total	(48.3 overs)	**179**

Fall of wickets: 1-24, 2-38, 3-39, 4-43, 5-75, 6-128, 7-148, 8-160, 9-161, 10-179.

ENGLAND	*O*	*M*	*R*	*W*
Willis	9.3	0	26	2
Botham	9	1	33	1
Pringle	10	3	21	3
Miller	10	2	44	2
Foster	10	0	46	0

ENGLAND		
G. Fowler	b Baptiste	25
T.A. Lloyd	c Dujon b Baptiste	49
D.I. Gower*	lbw b Marshall	36
A.J. Lamb	b Gomes	11
I.T. Botham	c Gomes b Holding	15
M.W. Gatting	b Garner	6
D.L. Bairstow†	b Holding	9
G. Miller	not out	3
D.R. Pringle	not out	2
N.A. Foster		
R.G.D. Willis		
Extras	(B 4, LB 14, NB 6)	24
Total	(47.5 overs – 7 wickets)	**180**

Fall of wickets: 1-75, 2-103, 3-131, 4-145, 5-157, 6-173, 7-177.

WEST INDIES	*O*	*M*	*R*	*W*
Garner	9	1	22	1
Holding	8.5	1	29	2
Marshall	10	1	30	1
Baptiste	10	2	31	2
Richards	5	0	23	0
Gomes	5	0	21	1

Umpires: H.D. Bird and D.O. Oslear.

Match No. 265/18

ENGLAND v WEST INDIES 1984 (3rd Match)

Texaco Trophy

At Lord's, London on 4 June 1984.
Toss: West Indies. Result: WEST INDIES won by 8 wickets.
55 overs match. Award: R.A. Harper.
No débuts.

ENGLAND		
G. Fowler	b Holding	34
T.A. Lloyd	b Harper	37
D.I. Gower*	b Marshall	29
A.J. Lamb	run out	0
I.T. Botham	c Harper b Baptiste	22
D.W. Randall	c Dujon b Marshall	8
D.L. Bairstow†	b Marshall	8
G. Miller	b Holding	10
D.R. Pringle	lbw b Garner	8
N.A. Foster	not out	4
R.G.D. Willis	not out	6
Extras	(B 1, LB 17, W 4, NB 8)	30
Total	(55 overs – 9 wickets)	**196**

Fall of wickets: 1-60, 2-91, 3-91, 4-128, 5-144, 6-151, 7-167, 8-177, 9-182.

WEST INDIES	*O*	*M*	*R*	*W*
Garner	11	4	17	1
Holding	11	0	33	2
Marshall	11	0	38	3
Baptiste	11	1	40	1
Harper	11	0	38	1

WEST INDIES		
C.G. Greenidge	c Bairstow b Pringle	32
D.L. Haynes	c Randall b Miller	18
H.A. Gomes	not out	56
I.V.A. Richards	not out	84
C.H. Lloyd*		
P.J.L. Dujon†		
M.D. Marshall		
R.A. Harper		
E.A.E. Baptiste		
M.A. Holding		
J. Garner		
Extras	(B 1, W 1, NB 5)	7
Total	(46.5 overs – 2 wickets)	**197**

Fall of wickets: 1-50, 2-63.

ENGLAND	*O*	*M*	*R*	*W*
Willis	10.5	2	52	0
Botham	8	0	25	0
Miller	9	1	35	1
Pringle	8	0	38	1
Foster	11	1	40	0

Umpires: D.G.L. Evans and B.J. Meyer.

INDIA v AUSTRALIA 1984-85 (1st Match)

At Jawaharlal Nehru Stadium, New Delhi on 28 September 1984.
Toss: Australia. Result: AUSTRALIA won by 48 runs.
48 overs match (floodlit). Award: K.C. Wessels.
Début: India – A. Patel.

AUSTRALIA		
K.C. Wessels	c Parkar b Madan Lal	107
G.M. Wood	c Khanna b Sharma	0
K.J. Hughes*	c Parkar b Patel	72
G.N. Yallop	st Khanna b Azad	22
A.R. Border	st Khanna b Azad	0
W.B. Phillips†	run out	1
T.G. Hogan	lbw b Madan Lal	6
G.F. Lawson	c Vengsarkar b Kapil Dev	2
R.M. Hogg	not out	0
C.G. Rackemann	run out	2
J.N. Maguire		
Extras	(B3, LB4, NB1)	8
Total	(48 overs – 9 wickets)	**220**

Fall of wickets: 1-14, 2-142, 3-200, 4-200, 5-204, 6-213, 7-216, 8-220, 9-220.

INDIA	*O*	*M*	*R*	*W*
Kapil Dev	9	1	43	1
Sharma	9	0	49	1
Madan Lal	7	2	23	2
Patel	10	2	27	1
Shastri	3	0	23	0
Azad	10	1	48	2

INDIA		
S.C. Khanna†	c Phillips b Rackemann	13
G.A. Parkar	c Lawson b Rackemann	16
D.B. Vengsarkar	c Yallop b Maguire	33
S.M. Patil	lbw b Hogg	22
S.M. Gavaskar*	c Wood b Rackemann	25
K. Azad	c Phillips b Maguire	0
Kapil Dev	b Hogan	39
R.J. Shastri	st Phillips b Hogan	5
Madan Lal	c Lawson b Rackemann	1
C. Sharma	not out	9
A. Patel	c Phillips b Hogan	0
Extras	(LB 2, NB 7)	9
Total	(40.5 overs)	**172**

Fall of wickets: 1-17, 2-44, 3-76, 4-96, 5-97, 6-148, 7-160, 8-161, 9-172, 10-172.

AUSTRALIA	*O*	*M*	*R*	*W*
Lawson	5	0	23	0
Rackemann	10	1	41	4
Hogg	6	1	21	1
Maguire	10	1	41	2
Hogan	9.5	1	44	3

Umpires: B. Ganguli and P.D. Reporter.

No-balls and wides debited to bowlers' analyses.

Match No. 267/9

INDIA v AUSTRALIA 1984-85 (2nd Match)

At University Stadium, Trivandrum on 1 October 1984.
Toss: Australia. No result – rain.
40 overs match. No award.
No débuts.

INDIA		
S.C. Khanna†	c Phillips b Rackemann	4
G.A. Parkar	c Phillips b Rackemann	3
D.B. Vengsarkar	b Hogan	77
S.M. Patil	c Yallop b Rackemann	16
Kapil Dev	b Wessels	12
K. Azad	c and b Hogan	6
S.M. Gavaskar*	c Wood b Hogan	14
R.J. Shastri	c Rackemann b Hogan	2
Madan Lal	b Border	9
C. Sharma	not out	13
A. Patel	c Hughes b Border	6
Extras	(B 5, LB 6, NB 2)	13
Total	(37 overs)	**175**

Fall of wickets: 1-7, 2-10, 3-53, 4-80, 5-103, 6-136, 7-146, 8-146, 9-166, 10-175.

AUSTRALIA	*O*	*M*	*R*	*W*
Lawson	7	0	29	0
Rackemann	8	4	7	3
Maguire	5	0	38	0
Wessels	7	0	44	1
Hogan	8	0	33	4
Border	2	0	13	2

AUSTRALIA		
G.M. Wood	not out	7
K.C. Wessels	lbw b Kapil Dev	12
A.R. Border	not out	4
K.J. Hughes*		
G.N. Yallop		
S.B. Smith		
W.B. Phillips†		
T.G. Hogan		
G.F. Lawson		
C.G. Rackemann		
J.N. Maguire		
Extras	(B 1, LB 4, W 1)	6
Total	(7.4 overs – 1 wicket)	**29**

Fall of wicket: 1-24.

INDIA	*O*	*M*	*R*	*W*
Kapil Dev	4	1	14	1
Sharma	3.4	1	10	0

Umpires: V.K. Ramaswami and Swaroop Kishen.

No-balls and wides debited to bowlers' analyses.

INDIA v AUSTRALIA 1984-85 (3rd Match)

At Sardar Patel Stadium, Ahmedabad on 5 October 1984.
Toss: Australia. Result: AUSTRALIA won by 7 wickets.
46 overs match. Award: G.F. Lawson.
No débuts.

INDIA		
R.J. Shastri	st Phillips b Hogan	45
R.M.H. Binny	st Phillips b Hogan	57
D.B. Vengsarkar	b Lawson	14
S.M. Patil	c Hughes b Wessels	3
Kapil Dev	b Lawson	28
S.M. Gavaskar*	b Lawson	4
K. Azad	not out	39
Madan Lal	not out	6
S.M.H. Kirmani†		
C. Sharma		
A. Patel		
Extras	(B 1, LB 5, NB 4)	10
Total	(46 overs – 6 wickets)	**206**

Fall of wickets: 1-104, 2-111, 3-122, 4-133, 5-145, 6-161.

AUSTRALIA	*O*	*M*	*R*	*W*
Lawson	10	2	25	3
Rackemann	8	0	50	0
Maguire	8	0	56	0
Wessels	10	0	29	1
Hogan	10	2	40	2

AUSTRALIA		
K.C. Wessels	c Kirmani b Patel	42
G.M. Wood	run out	32
A.R. Border	not out	62
K.J. Hughes*	lbw b Kapil Dev	29
G.N. Yallop	not out	32
S.B. Smith		
W.B. Phillips†		
T.G. Hogan		
J.N. Maguire		
G.F. Lawson		
C.G. Rackemann		
Extras	(B 1, LB 10, NB 2)	13
Total	(43.5 overs – 3 wickets)	**210**

Fall of wickets: 1-67, 2-89, 3-162.

INDIA	*O*	*M*	*R*	*W*
Kapil Dev	8	1	27	1
Sharma	7	1	21	0
Binny	2	0	21	0
Madan Lal	7.5	0	35	0
Patel	10	0	44	1
Azad	9	0	51	0

Umpires: D.N. Dotiwala and V. Vikramraju.

No-balls and wides debited to bowlers' analyses.

Match No. 269/11

INDIA v AUSTRALIA 1984-85 (4th Match)

At Nehru Stadium, Indore on 6 October 1984.
Toss: Australia. Result: AUSTRALIA won by 6 wickets.
44 overs match. Award: R.J. Shastri.
Début: Australia – M.J. Bennett.

INDIA		
G.A. Parkar	b Rackemann	6
R.J. Shastri	b Maguire	102
R.M.H. Binny	c Ritchie b Maguire	37
S.M. Gavaskar*	b Maguire	40
K. Azad	c Smith b Rackemann	11
Kapil Dev	not out	22
S.C. Khanna†	not out	1
Madan Lal		
M. Prabhakar		
B.S. Sandhu		
A. Patel		
Extras	(B 5, LB 3, W 4, NB 4)	16
Total	(44 overs – 5 wickets)	**235**

Fall of wickets 1-23, 2-83, 3-198, 4-207, 5-217.

AUSTRALIA	*O*	*M*	*R*	*W*
Lawson	10	2	48	0
Rackemann	8	1	37	2
Maguire	10	0	61	3
Bennett	10	0	37	0
Wessels	6	0	44	0

AUSTRALIA		
S.B. Smith	c Kapil Dev b Patel	56
W.B. Phillips†	c Patel b Kapil Dev	33
G.N. Yallop	b Patel	42
G.M. Ritchie	not out	59
K.J. Hughes*	c Prabhakar b Patel	6
K.C. Wessels	not out	35
G.F. Lawson		
M.J. Bennett		
C.G. Rackemann		
J.N. Maguire		
G.M. Wood		
Extras	(LB 4, NB 1)	5
Total	(40.1 overs – 4 wickets)	**236**

Fall of wickets 1-53, 2-122, 3-153, 4-163.

INDIA	*O*	*M*	*R*	*W*
Kapil Dev	8	0	62	1
Prabhakar	2	0	15	0
Sandhu	6	0	38	0
Madan Lal	6	0	19	0
Patel	10	0	43	3
Azad	2	0	16	0
Shastri	6	0	35	0
Gavaskar	0.1	0	4	0

Umpires: S.R. Bose and P.G. Pandit.

No-balls and wides debited to bowlers' analyses.

PAKISTAN v INDIA 1984-85 (1st Match)
Wills Series

At Ayub Stadium, Quetta on 12 October 1984.
Toss: India. Result: PAKISTAN won by 46 runs.
40 overs match. Award: Manzoor Elahi.
Début: Pakistan – Manzoor Elahi.

PAKISTAN		
Mohsin Khan	lbw b Sharma	13
Saadat Ali	c Khanna b Sandhu	12
Zaheer Abbas*	c and b Maninder	55
Javed Miandad	run out	25
Naved Anjum	c Mohinder b Kapil Dev	30
Manzoor Elahi	b Kapil Dev	36
Ashraf Ali†	c Maninder b Kapil Dev	6
Mudassar Nazar	not out	7
Tahir Naqqash	not out	0
Rashid Khan		
Tausif Ahmed		
Extras	(LB 12, W 3)	15
Total	(40 overs – 7 wickets)	**199**

Fall of wickets: 1-27, 2-39, 3-113, 4-122, 5-165, 6-174, 7-199.

INDIA	*O*	*M*	*R*	*W*
Kapil Dev	8	0	36	3
Sharma	7	0	42	1
Sandhu	7	0	35	1
Madan Lal	5	1	20	0
Maninder	5	0	24	1
Shastri	8	0	30	0

INDIA		
R.J. Shastri	lbw b Tahir	6
S.C. Khanna†	lbw b Tahir	31
R.M.H. Binny	c Miandad b Mudassar	19
S.M. Gavaskar*	st Ashraf b Tausif	25
S.M. Patil	c Ashraf b Naved	11
Kapil Dev	b Manzoor	0
M. Amarnath	b Manzoor	5
C. Sharma	not out	20
Madan Lal	run out	6
B.S. Sandhu	b Naved	7
Maninder Singh	b Rashid	4
Extras	(B 2, LB 10, W 5, NB 2)	19
Total	(37.1 overs)	**153**

Fall of wickets: 1-33, 2-42, 3-83, 4-91, 5-92, 6-110, 7-114, 8-123, 9-136, 10-153.

PAKISTAN	*O*	*M*	*R*	*W*
Tahir Naqqash	6	0	35	2
Rashid Khan	6.1	1	20	1
Mudassar Nazar	8	2	14	1
Tausif Ahmed	8	0	27	1
Manzoor Elahi	4	0	18	2
Naved Anjum	5	0	27	2

Umpires: Javed Akhtar and Khizer Hayat.

No-balls and wides debited to bowlers' analyses.

Match No. 271/12

PAKISTAN v INDIA 1984-85 (2nd Match)
Wills Series

At Jinnah Stadium, Sialkot on 31 October 1984.
Toss: Pakistan. No result.
40 overs match. No award.
Début: Pakistan – Sajid Ali.

This match and the remainder of the tour were cancelled immediately that news of the assassination of Mrs Gandhi was received from Delhi.

INDIA		
A.D. Gaekwad	b Mudassar	12
G.A. Parkar	b Mudassar	20
D.B. Vengsarkar	not out	94
S.M. Patil	b Tausif	59
R.J. Shastri	not out	6
M. Amarnath*		
R.M.H. Binny		
S.M.H. Kirmani†		
Madan Lal		
B.S. Sandhu		
Maninder Singh		
Extras	(LB 9, W 6, NB 4)	19
Total	(40 overs – 3 wickets)	**210**

Fall of wickets 1-35, 2-53, 3-196.

PAKISTAN	*O*	*M*	*R*	*W*
Rashid Khan	8	0	43	0
Tahir Naqqash	8	0	55	0
Mudassar Nazar	8	1	27	2
Manzoor Elahi	8	3	24	0
Naved Anjum	1	0	10	0
Tausif Ahmed	7	0	42	1

PAKISTAN
Saadat Ali
Sajid Ali
Zaheer Abbas*
Javed Miandad
Naved Anjum
Manzoor Elahi
Mudassar Nazar
Ashraf Ali†
Tahir Naqqash
Tausif Ahmed
Rashid Khan

Umpires: Mian Mohammad Aslam and Shakoor Rana.

No-balls and wides debited to bowlers' analyses.

SRI LANKA v NEW ZEALAND 1984-85 (1st Match)

At Saravanamuttu Stadium, Colombo on 3 November 1984.
Toss: New Zealand. Result: SRI LANKA won by 4 wickets.
45 overs match. Award: P.A. De Silva.
Début: Sri Lanka – S.A.R. Silva.

NEW ZEALAND		
J.G. Wright	c Silva b John	11
B.A. Edgar	c Silva b Ratnayeke	6
M.D. Crowe	b Ranatunga	23
J.F. Reid	c Ratnayeke b De Mel	21
J.J. Crowe	not out	57
J.V. Coney*	c P.A. De Silva b John	24
B.L. Cairns	c P.A. De Silva b John	4
I.D.S. Smith†	not out	5
S.L. Boock		
M.C. Snedden		
E.J. Chatfield		
Extras	(B 1, LB 14, W 3, NB 2)	20
Total	(45 overs – 6 wickets)	**171**

Fall of wickets 1-20, 2-36, 3-58, 4-84, 5-124, 6-133.

SRI LANKA	*O*	*M*	*R*	*W*
De Mel	9	3	26	1
John	9	2	37	3
Ratnayeke	9	0	40	1
Ranatunga	9	0	23	1
D.S. De Silva	9	1	25	0

SRI LANKA		
S. Wettimuny	c Edgar b Cairns	1
S.A.R. Silva†	c Boock b Chatfield	21
R.S. Madugalle	c Wright b Chatfield	31
A. Ranatunga	c Reid b Coney	9
R.L. Dias	c Wright b Boock	34
L.R.D. Mendis*	c J.J. Crowe b Coney	3
P.A. De Silva	not out	50
A.L.F. De Mel	not out	15
D.S. De Silva		
J.R. Ratnayeke		
V.B. John		
Extras	(B 3, LB 5, NB 2)	10
Total	(39.4 overs – 6 wickets)	**174**

Fall of wickets 1-13, 2-43, 3-62, 4-75, 5-79, 6-144.

NEW ZEALAND	*O*	*M*	*R*	*W*
Snedden	6	1	30	0
Cairns	6.4	2	37	1
Chatfield	9	0	34	2
Boock	9	0	29	1
Coney	4	0	16	2
M.D. Crowe	5	0	18	0

Umpires: D.P. Buultjens and H.C. Felsinger.

Match No. 273/11

SRI LANKA v NEW ZEALAND 1984-85 (2nd Match)

At Tyronne Fernando Stadium, Moratuwa on 4 November 1984.
Toss: New Zealand. Result: NEW ZEALAND won by 7 wickets.
41 overs match. Award: M.D. Crowe.
Début: New Zealand – E.J. Gray.

SRI LANKA		
S. Wettimuny	b M.D. Crowe	3
S.A.R. Silva†	c Smith b M.D. Crowe	9
R.S. Madugalle	run out	0
R.L. Dias	st Smith b Coney	10
L.R.D. Mendis*	c Snedden b Stirling	13
A. Ranatunga	run out	15
P.A. De Silva	run out	15
A.L.F. De Mel	c Reid b Stirling	15
D.S. De Silva	b Chatfield	13
J.R. Ratnayeke	not out	8
V.B. John	not out	0
Extras	(B 3, LB 6, W 1, NB 3)	13
Total	(41 overs – 9 wickets)	**114**

Fall of wickets: 1-12, 2-12, 3-22, 4-35, 5-47, 6-66, 7-91, 8-91, 9-114.

NEW ZEALAND	*O*	*M*	*R*	*W*
Chatfield	9	2	17	1
Snedden	7	2	14	0
M.D. Crowe	9	3	17	2
Stirling	9	1	28	2
Coney	4	0	7	1
McEwan	3	0	18	0

NEW ZEALAND		
J.G. Wright	b De Mel	6
P.E. McEwan	c P.A. De Silva b De Mel	9
J.F. Reid	c Dias b Ranatunga	34
M.D. Crowe	not out	52
J.J. Crowe	not out	7
J.V. Coney*		
E.J. Gray		
I.D.S. Smith†		
D.A. Stirling		
M.C. Snedden		
E.J. Chatfield		
Extras	(LB 3, W 5, NB 2)	10
Total	(31.4 overs – 3 wickets)	**118**

Fall of wickets: 1-15, 2-19, 3-98.

SRI LANKA	*O*	*M*	*R*	*W*
De Mel	7	3	23	2
John	9	2	37	0
Ratnayeke	6	1	9	0
D.S. De Silva	4	1	14	0
Ranatunga	5.4	1	25	1

Umpires: K.T. Francis and P.W. Vidanagamage.

PAKISTAN v NEW ZEALAND 1984-85 (1st Match)
Wills Series

At Shahi Bagh Stadium, Peshawar on 12 November 1984.
Toss: New Zealand. Result: PAKISTAN won by 46 runs.
39 overs match. Award: Zakir Khan.

Début: Pakistan – Zakir Khan.

PAKISTAN		
Saadat Ali	c Cairns b Chatfield	1
Sajid Ali	c J.J. Crowe b Cairns	16
Zaheer Abbas*	lbw b Cairns	13
Javed Miandad	not out	80
Naved Anjum	c M.D. Crowe b Stirling	29
Manzoor Elahi	c Stirling b Snedden	15
Mudassar Nazar	not out	17
Sarfraz Nawaz		
Anil Dalpat†		
Tausif Ahmed		
Zakir Khan		
Extras	(B 2, LB 8, W 8, NB 2)	20
Total	(39 overs – 5 wickets)	**191**

Fall of wickets 1-14, 2-27, 3-38, 4-87, 5-123.

NEW ZEALAND	*O*	*M*	*R*	*W*
Stirling	8	0	32	1
Cairns	8	0	38	2
Chatfield	7	0	38	1
M.D. Crowe	8	0	37	0
Snedden	8	0	36	1

NEW ZEALAND		
J.G. Wright	lbw b Manzoor	8
J.J. Crowe	c Dalpat b Zakir	8
M.D. Crowe	c Dalpat b Zakir	8
P.E. McEwan	lbw b Zakir	3
J.F. Reid	c Miandad b Zakir	14
J.V. Coney*	c and b Mudassar	23
I.D.S. Smith†	c Sajid b Mudassar	59
M.C. Snedden	c Dalpat b Mudassar	1
B.L. Cairns	c Zaheer b Tausif	7
D.A. Stirling	run out	2
E.J. Chatfield	not out	1
Extras	(LB 4, W 7)	11
Total	(36.2 overs)	**145**

Fall of wickets 1-19, 2-19, 3-22, 4-39, 5-44,
6-99 7-103, 8-113, 9-142, 10-145.

PAKISTAN	*O*	*M*	*R*	*W*
Manzoor Elahi	8	1	27	1
Zakir Khan	8	2	19	4
Sarfraz Nawaz	4	1	18	0
Naved Anjum	3	0	13	0
Tausif Ahmed	7	0	30	1
Mudassar Nazar	6.2	0	34	3

Umpires: Adheer Zaadi and Javed Akhtar.

No-balls and wides debited to bowlers' analyses.

Match No. 275/6

PAKISTAN v NEW ZEALAND 1984-85 (2nd Match)

Wills Series

At Iqbal Stadium, Faisalabad on 23 November 1984.
Toss: New Zealand. Result: PAKISTAN won by 5 runs.
20 overs match. Award: Salim Malik.
Débuts: Pakistan – Shoaib Mohammad, Wasim Akram.

PAKISTAN		
Salim Malik	b Snedden	41
Mohsin Khan	b M.D. Crowe	0
Zaheer Abbas*	c Stirling b Snedden	25
Javed Miandad	run out	20
Manzoor Elahi	not out	39
Mudassar Nazar	lbw b M.D. Crowe	10
Shoaib Mohammad	not out	10
Anil Dalpat†		
Zakir Khan		
Wasim Akram		
Tausif Ahmed		
Extras	(LB 7, W 4, NB 1)	12
Total	(20 overs – 5 wickets)	**157**

Fall of wickets 1-3, 2-67, 3-81, 4-105, 5-128.

NEW ZEALAND	*O*	*M*	*R*	*W*
M.D. Crowe	4	0	17	2
Coney	2	0	10	0
Cairns	4	0	25	0
Chatfield	2	0	25	0
Snedden	4	0	41	2
Stirling	4	0	32	0

NEW ZEALAND		
J.G. Wright	b Mudassar	55
J.J. Crowe	lbw b Zakir	7
M.D. Crowe	c Zaheer b Mudassar	19
P.E. McEwan	lbw b Mudassar	7
B.L. Cairns	c Salim b Mudassar	10
J.G. Bracewell	not out	16
I.D.S. Smith†	run out	4
D.A. Stirling	run out	1
J.V. Coney*	not out	17
M.C. Snedden		
E.J. Chatfield		
Extras	(B 2, LB 7, W 7)	16
Total	(20 overs – 7 wickets)	**152**

Fall of wickets 1-20, 2-61, 3-78, 4-106, 5-112,
6-127 7-132.

PAKISTAN	*O*	*M*	*R*	*W*
Wasim Akram	4	0	31	0
Zakir Khan	4	0	28	1
Manzoor Elahi	4	0	31	0
Mudassar Nazar	4	0	27	4
Tausif Ahmed	4	0	26	0

Umpires: Amanullah Khan and Ikram Rabbani.

No-balls and wides debited to bowlers' analyses.

PAKISTAN v NEW ZEALAND 1984-85 (3rd Match)
Wills Series

At Jinnah Park Stadium, Sialkot on 2 December 1984.
Toss: Pakistan. Result: NEW ZEALAND won by 34 runs.
36 overs match. Award: M.D. Crowe.

Début: Pakistan – Mohsin Kamal.

Salim Malik became the first non-substitute fielder to hold four catches in a limited-overs international.

NEW ZEALAND

J.G. Wright	c Salim Malik b Kamal	24
J.G. Bracewell	c Salim Malik b Kamal	1
J.F. Reid	run out	34
M.D. Crowe	b Kamal	67
J.J. Crowe	not out	15
P.E. McEwan	st Salim Yousuf b Tausif	4
B.L. Cairns	b Tausif	0
J.V. Coney*	run out	1
I.D.S. Smith†	c Salim Malik b Tausif	9
D.A. Stirling	c Salim Malik b Tausif	4
M.C. Snedden	not out	0
Extras	(LB 6, W 21, NB 1)	28
Total	(36 overs – 9 wickets)	**187**

Fall of wickets: 1-14, 2-47, 3-128, 4-156, 5-162, 6-166, 7-168, 8-178, 9-187.

PAKISTAN	*O*	*M*	*R*	*W*
Mohsin Kamal	8	0	46	3
Zakir Khan	8	0	22	0
Mudassar Nazar	8	0	58	0
Manzoor Elahi	6	0	17	0
Tausif Ahmed	6	0	38	4

PAKISTAN

Mohsin Khan	lbw b Stirling	2
Shoaib Mohammad	lbw b M.D. Crowe	22
Salim Malik	b M.D. Crowe	6
Javed Miandad	c Wright b Cairns	14
Zaheer Abbas*	c J.J. Crowe b Bracewell	42
Manzoor Elahi	b Cairns	16
Mudassar Nazar	c Stirling b Snedden	3
Salim Yousuf†	lbw b Bracewell	1
Tausif Ahmed	not out	27
Zakir Khan	not out	8
Mohsin Kamal		
Extras	(LB 6, W 3, NB 3)	12
Total	(36 overs – 8 wickets)	**153**

Fall of wickets: 1-2, 2-14, 3-42, 4-52, 5-90, 6-97, 7-100, 8-133.

NEW ZEALAND	*O*	*M*	*R*	*W*
Stirling	8	0	36	1
M.D. Crowe	5	0	21	2
Cairns	6	0	30	2
Snedden	8	0	29	1
Bracewell	8	0	23	2
Coney	1	0	8	0

Umpires: Rab Nawaz and Shakoor Rana.

No-balls and wides debited to bowlers' analyses.

Match No. 277/8

PAKISTAN v NEW ZEALAND 1984-85 (4th Match)

Wills Series

At Ibn-e-Qasim Bagh Stadium, Multan on 7 December 1984.
Toss: New Zealand. Result: PAKISTAN won by 1 wicket.
35 overs match. Award: Zaheer Abbas.

Début: Pakistan – Masood Iqbal.

NEW ZEALAND		
J.G. Wright	b Tausif	11
P.E. McEwan	c Saadat b Kamal	22
J.F. Reid	run out	10
M.D. Crowe	run out	28
J.J. Crowe	run out	13
J.V. Coney*	c Salim b Zaheer	34
I.D.S. Smith†	c Miandad b Saadat	41
B.L. Cairns	c Salim b Saadat	2
J.G. Bracewell	not out	14
D.A. Stirling	not out	1
M.C. Snedden		
Extras	(B 18, LB 8, W 10, NB 1)	37
Total	(35 overs – 8 wickets)	**213**

Fall of wickets: 1-40, 2-47, 3-64, 4-110, 5-114, 6-179, 7-183, 8-211.

PAKISTAN	*O*	*M*	*R*	*W*
Mohsin Kamal	5	0	21	1
Shahid Mahboob	4	0	18	0
Tausif Ahmed	7	0	30	1
Mudassar Nazar	7	0	40	0
Zaheer Abbas	6	0	35	1
Manzoor Elahi	2	0	19	0
Saadat Ali	4	0	24	2

PAKISTAN		
Saadat Ali	c Bracewell b Stirling	6
Shoaib Mohammad	c Bracewell b Coney	35
Zaheer Abbas*	b Bracewell	73
Javed Miandad	c Smith b Snedden	32
Salim Malik	c Cairns b Snedden	28
Manzoor Elahi	c Bracewell b Snedden	8
Mudassar Nazar	run out	1
Tausif Ahmed	not out	15
Shahid Mahboob	lbw b M.D. Crowe	1
Masood Iqbal†	run out	2
Mohsin Kamal	not out	5
Extras	(LB 5, W 1, NB 2)	8
Total	(35 overs – 9 wickets)	**214**

Fall of wickets: 1-8, 2-80, 3-148, 4-154, 5-164, 6-169, 7-199, 8-203, 9-206.

NEW ZEALAND	*O*	*M*	*R*	*W*
M.D. Crowe	5	0	22	1
Stirling	7	0	44	1
Snedden	7	0	38	3
Cairns	5	0	42	0
Coney	4	0	27	1
Bracewell	7	0	36	1

Umpires: Said Shah and B.K. Tahir.

No-balls and wides debited to bowlers' analyses.

INDIA v ENGLAND 1984-85 (1st Match)

At Nehru Stadium, Poona on 5 December 1984.
Toss: England. Result: ENGLAND won by 4 wickets.
45 overs match. Awards: D.B. Vengsarkar and M.W. Gatting.
Débuts: India – R.S. Ghai, K.S. More; England – R.M. Ellison, R.T. Robinson.

INDIA		
K. Srikkanth	b Edmonds	50
S.M. Gavaskar*	b Foster	0
D.B. Vengsarkar	b Ellison	105
S.M. Patil	run out	2
Yashpal Sharma	c Ellison b Foster	37
R.J. Shastri	c Ellison b Foster	11
R.M.H. Binny	not out	0
K.S. More†		
M. Prabhakar		
C. Sharma		
R.S. Ghai		
Extras	(LB 2, W 7)	9
Total	(45 overs – 6 wickets)	**214**

Fall of wickets: 1-1, 2-119, 3-126, 4-189, 5-212, 6-214.

ENGLAND	*O*	*M*	*R*	*W*
Cowans	8	0	32	0
Foster	10	0	44	3
Ellison	7	0	45	1
Marks	10	0	48	0
Edmonds	10	0	43	1

ENGLAND		
G. Fowler	c Yashpal b Sharma	5
R.T. Robinson	lbw b Ghai	15
M.W. Gatting	not out	115
A.J. Lamb	c and b Prabhakar	3
V.J. Marks	run out	31
D.I. Gower*	c Shastri b Binny	3
R.M. Ellison	run out	4
P.R. Downton†	not out	27
P.H. Edmonds		
N.A. Foster		
N.G. Cowans		
Extras	(LB 8, NB 4)	12
Total	(43.2 overs – 6 wickets)	**215**

Fall of wickets: 1-14, 2-43, 3-47, 4-114, 5-117, 6-129.

INDIA	*O*	*M*	*R*	*W*
Sharma	8.2	0	50	1
Prabhakar	10	1	27	1
Ghai	9	0	38	1
Shastri	8	0	49	0
Binny	8	0	43	1

Umpires: S. Banerjee and Mohammad Ghouse.

No-balls and wides debited to bowlers' analyses.

Match No. 279/11

INDIA v ENGLAND 1984-85 (2nd Match)

At Baribati Stadium, Cuttack, on 27 December 1984.
Toss: England. Result: ENGLAND won on scoring rate.
49 overs match. Award: R.J. Shastri.

No débuts.

After Srikkanth and Shastri had shared the highest opening partnership for any one-day international, England opted to continue in appalling light until 20 runs from two overs put them ahead on scoring rate for the first time.

INDIA		
K. Srikkanth	lbw b Gatting	99
R.J. Shastri	b Gatting	102
D.B. Vengsarkar	c Gower b Marks	23
Yashpal Sharma	lbw b Marks	4
M. Amarnath	not out	1
R.M.H. Binny	b Marks	2
S.M. Gavaskar*	not out	6
K.S. More†		
M. Prabhakar		
R.S. Ghai		
A. Patel		
Extras	(B 5, LB 5, W 3, NB 2)	15
Total	(49 overs – 5 wickets)	**252**

Fall of wickets 1-188, 2-235, 3-243, 4-243, 5-246.

ENGLAND	*O*	*M*	*R*	*W*
Foster	5	0	26	0
Cowans	10	0	39	0
Ellison	6	0	31	0
Edmonds	10	0	47	0
Marks	8	0	50	3
Gatting	10	0	49	2

ENGLAND		
G. Fowler	c Shastri b Binny	15
R.T. Robinson	b Prabhakar	1
M.W. Gatting	b Patel	59
D.I. Gower*	c Prabhakar b Binny	21
A.J. Lamb	run out	28
V.J. Marks	run out	44
P.R. Downton†	not out	44
R.M. Ellison	not out	14
P.H. Edmonds		
N.A. Foster		
N.G. Cowans		
Extras	(LB 9, W 1, NB 5)	15
Total	(46 overs – 6 wickets)	**241**

Fall of wickets 1-3, 2-50, 3-93, 4-128, 5-145, 6-203.

INDIA	*O*	*M*	*R*	*W*
Ghai	8	0	40	0
Prabhakar	10	1	34	1
Binny	7	0	48	2
Patel	10	0	53	1
Shastri	10	0	48	0
Amarnath	1	0	9	0

Umpires: J.D. Ghosh and P.G. Pandit.

No-balls and wides debited to bowlers' analyses.

INDIA v ENGLAND 1984-85 (3rd Match)

At Chinnaswamy Stadium, Bangalore on 20 January 1985.
Toss: England. Result: ENGLAND won by 3 wickets.
46 overs match. Award: A.J. Lamb.
Débuts: India – M. Azharuddin, S. Viswanath.

INDIA		
S.M. Gavaskar*	c Gatting b Marks	40
K. Srikkanth	b Cowans	29
D.B. Vengsarkar	st Downton b Marks	23
Kapil Dev	c Gower b Marks	8
Yashpal Sharma	run out	8
R.J. Shastri	b Edmonds	33
M. Azharuddin	not out	47
S. Viswanath†	not out	6
A. Patel		
R.S. Ghai		
T.A.P. Sekar		
Extras	(B 4, LB 6, W 1)	11
Total	(46 overs – 6 wickets)	**205**

Fall of wickets 1-70, 2-70, 3-90, 4-108, 5-119, 6-185.

ENGLAND	*O*	*M*	*R*	*W*
Cowans	10	1	31	1
Foster	6	0	33	0
Ellison	6	0	25	0
Marks	10	1	35	3
Edmonds	10	0	44	1
Gatting	4	0	27	0

ENGLAND		
G. Fowler	run out	45
R.T. Robinson	c Viswanath b Kapil Dev	2
M.W. Gatting	run out	3
D.I. Gower*	b Shastri	38
A.J. Lamb	not out	59
V.J. Marks	c Gavaskar b Patel	17
P.R. Downton†	c Shastri b Kapil Dev	12
P.H. Edmonds	c Viswanath b Kapil Dev	7
R.M. Ellison	not out	1
N.A. Foster		
N.G. Cowans		
Extras	(LB 10, W 7, NB 5)	22
Total	(45 overs – 7 wickets)	**206**

Fall of wickets 1-15, 2-21, 3-91, 4-103, 5-144, 6-186, 7-204.

INDIA	*O*	*M*	*R*	*W*
Kapil Dev	10	0	38	3
Sekar	9	0	36	0
Patel	10	1	42	1
Ghai	4	0	37	0
Shastri	10	2	29	1
Yashpal Sharma	2	0	14	0

Umpires: S.K. Das and S.V. Ramani.

No-balls and wides debited to bowlers' analyses.

Match No. 281/13

INDIA v ENGLAND 1984-85 (4th Match)

At Vidarbha CA Ground, Nagpur on 23 January 1985.
Toss: India. Result: INDIA won by 3 wickets.
50 overs match. Award: Kapil Dev.
Débuts: India – L. Rajput; England – J.P. Agnew, C.S. Cowdrey, M.D. Moxon.

ENGLAND		
G. Fowler	b Shastri	37
M.D. Moxon	c Srikkanth b Kapil Dev	70
M.W. Gatting	b Shastri	1
D.I. Gower*	c and b Shastri	11
A.J. Lamb	st Viswanath b Shastri	30
C.S. Cowdrey	not out	46
V.J. Marks	b Sekar	4
P.R. Downton†	c Rajput b Sekar	13
P.H. Edmonds	not out	8
J.P. Agnew		
N.G. Cowans		
Extras	(B 3, LB 15, W 1, NB 1)	20
Total	(50 overs – 7 wickets)	**240**

Fall of wickets: 1-70, 2-78, 3-100, 4-154, 5-176, 6-199, 7-221.

INDIA	*O*	*M*	*R*	*W*
Kapil Dev	10	1	42	1
Prabhakar	10	1	36	0
Sekar	10	0	50	2
Patel	10	1	54	0
Shastri	10	1	40	4

INDIA		
K. Srikkanth	b Cowans	6
L. Rajput	c Downton b Cowans	0
D.B. Vengsarkar	c Downton b Agnew	11
M. Azharuddin	b Cowdrey	47
S.M. Gavaskar*	b Agnew	52
Kapil Dev	c Gatting b Cowans	54
R.J. Shastri	not out	24
M. Prabhakar	b Agnew	4
S. Viswanath†	not out	23
T.A.P. Sekar		
A. Patel		
Extras	(B 3, LB 14, W 1, NB 2)	20
Total	(47.4 overs – 7 wickets)	**241**

Fall of wickets: 1-5, 2-11, 3-31, 4-90, 5-166, 6-197, 7-204.

ENGLAND	*O*	*M*	*R*	*W*
Cowans	10	0	44	3
Agnew	10	0	38	3
Marks	6	0	32	0
Edmonds	10	0	44	0
Cowdrey	7.4	0	52	1
Gatting	4	0	14	0

Umpires: R. Mrithyunjayan and A.L. Narasimhan.

No-balls and wides debited to bowlers' analyses.

INDIA v ENGLAND 1984-85 (5th Match)

At Sector 16 Stadium, Chandigarh on 27 January 1985.
Toss: India. Result: ENGLAND won by 7 runs.
15 overs match. Award: R.J. Shastri.

Début: England – B.N. French.

An overnight storm flooded the ground and reduced this match to a 15-overs affair in slippery conditions before a crowd of 25,000.

ENGLAND		
G. Fowler	run out	17
M.W. Gatting	c Azharuddin b Sekar	31
D.I. Gower*	b Sekar	19
A.J. Lamb	not out	33
C.S. Cowdrey	c Rajput b Shastri	5
P.H. Edmonds	c Azharuddin b Sekar	5
V.J. Marks	run out	2
R.M. Ellison	not out	4
J.P. Agnew		
N.A. Foster		
B.N. French†		
Extras	(LB 5)	5
Total	(15 overs – 6 wickets)	**121**

Fall of wickets: 1-31, 2-71, 3-74, 4-86, 5-93, 6-104.

INDIA	*O*	*M*	*R*	*W*
Kapil Dev	3	0	17	0
Prabhakar	3	0	26	0
Sharma	3	0	20	0
Sekar	3	0	23	3
Shastri	3	0	30	1

INDIA		
R.J. Shastri	run out	53
K. Srikkanth	run out	9
Kapil Dev	c Agnew b Edmonds	17
M. Azharuddin	c Gatting b Edmonds	10
Yashpal Sharma	b Cowdrey	6
S.M. Gavaskar*	not out	2
L. Rajput	not out	1
S. Viswanath†		
T.A.P. Sekar		
M. Prabhakar		
C. Sharma		
Extras	(LB 4, W 12)	16
Total	(15 overs – 5 wickets)	**114**

Fall of wickets: 1-22, 2-49, 3-83, 4-111, 5-112.

ENGLAND	*O*	*M*	*R*	*W*
Agnew	3	0	23	0
Foster	3	0	17	0
Ellison	3	0	20	0
Edmonds	3	0	20	2
Gatting	2	0	27	0
Cowdrey	1	0	3	1

Umpires: R.B. Gupta and B. Nagaraja Rao.

No-balls and wides debited to bowlers' analyses.

Match No. 283/33

AUSTRALIA v WEST INDIES 1984-85

Benson and Hedges World Series Cup – 1st Match

At Melbourne Cricket Ground on 6 January 1985.
Toss: West Indies. Result: WEST INDIES won by 7 wickets.
50 overs match. Award: D.L. Haynes.
Débuts: Australia – C.J. McDermott, S.P. O'Donnell.

AUSTRALIA		
G.M. Wood	c Holding b Garner	0
A.M.J. Hilditch	c Holding b Baptiste	27
K.C. Wessels	run out	33
A.R. Border*	c Baptiste b Garner	73
D.C. Boon	b Marshall	55
W.B. Phillips†	c Greenidge b Garner	23
S.P. O'Donnell	not out	7
G.F. Lawson	not out	8
M.J. Bennett		
C.J. McDermott		
R.M. Hogg		
Extras	(LB 7, W 4, NB 3)	14
Total	(50 overs – 6 wickets)	**240**

Fall of wickets: 1-0, 2-48, 3-78, 4-193, 5-220, 6-224.

WEST INDIES	*O*	*M*	*R*	*W*
Garner	10	2	41	3
Marshall	10	0	32	1
Baptiste	9	0	73	1
Holding	10	1	41	0
Richards	10	1	37	0
Gomes	1	0	9	0

WEST INDIES		
C.G. Greenidge	b Bennett	12
D.L. Haynes	not out	123
R.B. Richardson	c Boon b Lawson	34
I.V.A. Richards	c Phillips b McDermott	47
H.A. Gomes	not out	2
C.H. Lloyd*		
P.J.L. Dujon†		
M.D. Marshall		
E.A.E. Baptiste		
M.A. Holding		
J. Garner		
Extras	(B 1, LB 17, W 5)	23
Total	(44.5 overs – 3 wickets)	**241**

Fall of wickets: 1-69, 2-140, 3-234.

AUSTRALIA	*O*	*M*	*R*	*W*
Lawson	10	0	45	1
McDermott	9.5	0	52	1
Hogg	8	0	43	0
O'Donnell	3	0	24	0
Bennett	10	2	23	1
Wessels	2	0	18	0
Border	2	0	18	0

Umpires: A.R. Crafter and P.J. McConnell.

No-balls and wides debited to bowlers' analyses.

AUSTRALIA v SRI LANKA 1984-85

Benson and Hedges World Series Cup – 2nd Match

At Sydney Cricket Ground on 8 January 1985.

Toss: Sri Lanka. Result: AUSTRALIA won by 6 wickets.

49 overs match (floodlit). Award: A.R. Border.

No débuts.

SRI LANKA		
S. Wettimuny	c Phillips b Rackemann	20
S.A.R. Silva†	c Bennett b Hogg	68
D.S.B.P. Kuruppu	c Wood b Bennett	22
R.L. Dias	c Border b O'Donnell	60
L.R.D. Mendis*	b Hogg	16
P.A. De Silva	b Hogg	17
A.L.F. De Mel	b Hogg	0
J.R. Ratnayeke	not out	8
R.J. Ratnayake	not out	4
D.S. De Silva		
V.B. John		
Extras	(B 5, LB 5, W 13, NB 1)	24
Total	(49 overs – 7 wickets)	**239**

Fall of wickets: 1-66, 2-104, 3-160, 4-181, 5-214, 6-214, 7-229.

AUSTRALIA	*O*	*M*	*R*	*W*
Hogg	10	0	47	4
O'Donnell	9	2	39	1
McDermott	10	1	49	0
Bennett	10	1	44	1
Rackemann	10	0	50	1

AUSTRALIA		
A.M.J. Hilditch	run out	23
G.M. Wood	retired hurt	52
K.C. Wessels	c Silva b Ratnayeke	1
A.R. Border*	not out	79
D.C. Boon	c sub (U.S.H. Karnain) b De Mel	44
W.B. Phillips†	c Silva b De Mel	3
S.P. O'Donnell	not out	20
M.J. Bennett		
C.J. McDermott		
R.M. Hogg		
C.G. Rackemann		
Extras	(B 4, LB 4, W 4, NB 6)	18
Total	(46.2 overs – 4 wickets)	**240**

Fall of wickets: 1-69, 2-70, 3-171, 4-176.

SRI LANKA	*O*	*M*	*R*	*W*
De Mel	9.3	9	59	2
John	9	1	40	0
Ratnayake	8.5	0	32	0
Ratnayeke	9	0	69	1
D.S. De Silva	10	1	32	0

Umpires: R.A. French and P.J. McConnell.

No-balls and wides debited to bowlers' analyses.

Match No. 285/2

SRI LANKA v WEST INDIES 1984-85

Benson and Hedges World Series Cup – 3rd Match

At Tasmanian CA Ground, Hobart on 10 January 1985.
Toss: West Indies. Result: WEST INDIES won by 8 wickets.
50 overs match. Award: L.R.D. Mendis.

Début: West Indies – C.A. Walsh.

SRI LANKA		
S. Wettimuny	c Richards b Garner	8
S.A.R. Silva†	c Dujon b Garner	4
D.S.B.P. Kuruppu	c Richardson b Holding	8
R.L. Dias	c Dujon b Walsh	27
L.R.D. Mendis*	run out	56
P.A. De Silva	c sub (R.A. Harper) b Richards	8
J.R. Ratnayeke	b Richards	8
U.S.H. Karnain	not out	20
R.J. Ratnayake	not out	23
D.S. De Silva		
V.B. John		
Extras	(B 12, LB 10, W 12, NB 1)	35
Total	(50 overs – 7 wickets)	**197**

Fall of wickets: 1-19, 2-24, 3-39, 4-115, 5-127, 6-142, 7-145.

WEST INDIES	*O*	*M*	*R*	*W*
Marshall	10	3	37	0
Garner	10	1	19	2
Holding	10	1	25	1
Walsh	10	1	47	1
Richards	10	2	47	2

WEST INDIES		
C.G. Greenidge	c Kuruppu b D.S. De Silva	61
D.L. Haynes	c Silva b Ratnayake	32
R.B. Richardson	not out	52
A.L. Logie	not out	34
I.V.A. Richards*		
H.A. Gomes		
P.J.L. Dujon†		
M.D. Marshall		
M.A. Holding		
J. Garner		
C.A. Walsh		
Extras	(LB 11, W 5, NB 3)	19
Total	(40.4 overs – 2 wickets)	**198**

Fall of wickets: 1-50, 2-144.

SRI LANKA	*O*	*M*	*R*	*W*
John	6.4	2	30	0
Ratnayeke	7	0	41	0
Ratnayake	7	0	31	1
D.S. De Silva	10	3	29	1
Karnain	8	0	41	0
P.A. De Silva	2	0	15	0

Umpires: R.C. Isherwood and S.G. Randell.

No-balls and wides debited to bowlers' analyses.

SRI LANKA v WEST INDIES 1984-85

Benson and Hedges World Series Cup – 4th Match

At Woolloongabba, Brisbane on 12 January 1985.
Toss: Sri Lanka. Result: WEST INDIES won by 90 runs.
50 overs match. Award: I.V.A. Richards.
No débuts.

WEST INDIES		
R.B. Richardson	c Silva b John	1
T.R.O. Payne	c John b Karnain	20
H.A. Gomes	c Silva b Karnain	28
I.V.A. Richards*	c Silva b John	98
A.L. Logie	c P.A. De Silva b D.S. De Silva	10
C.H. Lloyd	not out	89
P.J.L. Dujon†	c Mendis b Ratnayake	11
M.D. Marshall	not out	1
M.A. Holding		
W.W. Davis		
J. Garner		
Extras	(B 1, LB 5, W 4, NB 2)	12
Total	(50 overs – 6 wickets)	**270**

Fall of wickets 1-7, 2-45, 3-73, 4-92, 5-244, 6-269.

SRI LANKA	*O*	*M*	*R*	*W*
G.N. De Silva	10	0	42	0
John	10	2	52	2
Ratnayake	10	0	39	1
Karnain	10	0	55	2
D.S. De Silva	8	0	57	1
Dias	2	0	19	0

SRI LANKA		
S. Wettimuny	c Dujon b Garner	2
S.A.R. Silva†	b Davis	20
D.S.B.P. Kuruppu	c Payne b Holding	4
R.L. Dias	c Dujon b Holding	80
L.R.D. Mendis*	b Holding	14
P.A. De Silva	c Richards b Davis	13
U.S.H. Karnain	st Dujon b Richards	9
R.J. Ratnayake	st Dujon b Richards	19
D.S. De Silva	b Lloyd	9
V.B. John	c Logie b Gomes	0
G.N. De Silva	not out	2
Extras	(LB 3, W 3, NB 2)	8
Total	(48.1 overs)	**180**

Fall of wickets 1-4, 2-29, 3-35, 4-59, 5-88, 6-114, 7-144, 8-176, 9-177, 10-180.

WEST INDIES	*O*	*M*	*R*	*W*
Marshall	5	2	9	0
Garner	5	2	14	1
Holding	10	0	38	3
Davis	10	0	29	2
Richards	10	0	45	2
Gomes	8	0	42	1
Lloyd	0.1	0	0	1

Umpires: R.A. French and M.W. Johnson.

No-balls and wides debited to bowlers' analyses.

Match No. 287/34

AUSTRALIA v WEST INDIES 1984-85

Benson and Hedges World Series Cup – 5th Match

At Woolloongabba, Brisbane on 13 January 1985.

Toss: West Indies.	Result: WEST INDIES won by 5 wickets.
50 overs match.	Award: C.H. Lloyd.

No débuts.

AUSTRALIA		
G.M. Wood	c Dujon b Richards	38
A.M.J. Hilditch	c Garner b Davis	19
K.C. Wessels	c Logie b Richards	47
A.R. Border*	run out	7
D.C. Boon	lbw b Richards	4
S.P. O'Donnell	run out	25
S.J. Rixon†	run out	3
M.J. Bennett	c Logie b Marshall	3
G.F. Lawson	c Dujon b Garner	7
C.J. McDermott	run out	13
R.M. Hogg	not out	6
Extras	(LB 10, W 4, NB 5)	19
Total	(50 overs)	**191**

Fall of wickets: 1-49, 2-77, 3-97, 4-107, 5-153, 6-160, 7-162, 8-171, 9-173, 10-191.

WEST INDIES	*O*	*M*	*R*	*W*
Marshall	10	2	42	1
Garner	10	1	33	1
Holding	10	0	31	0
Davis	10	0	37	1
Richards	10	0	38	3

WEST INDIES		
D.L. Haynes	c Hogg b O'Donnell	46
R.B. Richardson	b McDermott	16
H.A. Gomes	b McDermott	0
I.V.A. Richards	c Border b Hogg	49
C.H. Lloyd*	not out	52
A.L. Logie	c Rixon b O'Donnell	7
P.J.L. Dujon†	not out	6
M.D. Marshall		
M.A. Holding		
W.W. Davis		
J. Garner		
Extras	(B 5, LB 8, W 5, NB 1)	19
Total	(37.4 overs – 5 wickets)	**195**

Fall of wickets: 1-50, 2-50, 3-74, 4-172, 5-188.

AUSTRALIA	*O*	*M*	*R*	*W*
Lawson	10	1	35	0
Hogg	8	1	41	1
O'Donnell	9	0	47	2
McDermott	7	1	33	2
Bennett	3	0	21	0
Boon	0.4	0	5	0

Umpires: M.W. Johnson and S.G. Randell.

No-balls and wides debited to bowlers' analyses.

AUSTRALIA v WEST INDIES 1984-85

Benson and Hedges World Series Cup – 6th Match

At Sydney Cricket Ground on 15 January 1985.
Toss: Australia. Result: WEST INDIES won by 5 wickets.
50 overs match (floodlit). Award: I.V.A. Richards.
Début: Australia – R.G. Holland.

Richards became the first batsman to score eight hundreds in limited-overs internationals. His record was equalled by Haynes in *Match No. 322.*

AUSTRALIA		
G.M. Wood	c Holding b Davis	21
K.C. Wessels	st Dujon b Richards	63
D.C. Boon	run out	20
A.R. Border*	run out	24
G.M. Ritchie	not out	30
S.P. O'Donnell	b Marshall	17
S.J. Rixon†	not out	2
G.F. Lawson		
M.J. Bennett		
C.J. McDermott		
R.G. Holland		
Extras	(LB 10, W 3, NB 10)	23
Total	(50 overs – 5 wickets)	**200**

Fall of wickets 1-42, 2-103, 3-137, 4-161, 5-197.

WEST INDIES	*O*	*M*	*R*	*W*
Marshall	10	0	38	1
Garner	10	1	44	0
Holding	10	1	36	0
Davis	10	2	31	1
Richards	10	0	41	1

WEST INDIES		
D.L. Haynes	c O'Donnell b McDermott	13
R.B. Richardson	lbw b Lawson	9
H.A. Gomes	c Wessels b McDermott	0
I.V.A. Richards	not out	103
C.H. Lloyd*	c Rixon b McDermott	38
A.L. Logie	c Rixon b Lawson	12
P.J.L. Dujon†	not out	15
M.D. Marshall		
M.A. Holding		
W.W. Davis		
J. Garner		
Extras	(B 1, LB 5, W 2, NB 3)	11
Total	(43.3 overs – 5 wickets)	**201**

Fall of wickets 1-23, 2-23, 3-25, 4-115, 5-138.

AUSTRALIA	*O*	*M*	*R*	*W*
Lawson	10	1	32	2
McDermott	10	0	30	3
Bennett	6	0	40	0
O'Donnell	7.3	0	43	0
Holland	10	0	50	0

Umpires: R.C. Isherwood and S.G. Randell.

No-balls and wides debited to bowlers' analyses.

Match No. 289/4

SRI LANKA v WEST INDIES 1984-85

Benson and Hedges World Series Cup – 7th Match

At Sydney Cricket Ground on 17 January 1985.
Toss: West Indies. Result: WEST INDIES won by 65 runs.
50 overs match (floodlit). Award: C.G. Greenidge.
No débuts.

WEST INDIES		
C.G. Greenidge	b D.S. De Silva	67
D.L. Haynes	run out	54
R.B. Richardson	not out	57
I.V.A. Richards*	b De Mel	30
A.L. Logie	not out	47
P.J.L. Dujon†		
M.D. Marshall		
R.A. Harper		
M.A. Holding		
W.W. Davis		
C.A. Walsh		
Extras	(LB 5, W 5, NB 2)	12
Total	(50 overs – 3 wickets)	**267**

Fall of wickets 1-128, 2-128, 3-186.

SRI LANKA	*O*	*M*	*R*	*W*
De Mel	10	1	50	1
John	10	0	53	0
Ratnayeke	3	0	19	0
Ratnayake	10	0	58	0
D.S. De Silva	10	1	48	1
Karnain	7	1	34	0

SRI LANKA		
S.A.R. Silva†	c Greenidge b Marshall	5
J.R. Ratnayeke	c Dujon b Davis	17
P.A. De Silva	c Dujon b Holding	21
L.R.D. Mendis*	c Dujon b Holding	2
R.L.D. Dias	not out	65
R.S. Madugalle	b Harper	25
U.S.H. Karnain	not out	41
R.J. Ratnayake		
A.L.F. De Mel		
D.S. De Silva		
V.B. John		
Extras	(B 2, LB 7, W 4, NB 13)	26
Total	(50 overs – 5 wickets)	**202**

Fall of wickets 1-12, 2-54, 3-54, 4-64, 5-124.

WEST INDIES	*O*	*M*	*R*	*W*
Marshall	10	1	33	1
Walsh	10	1	45	0
Davis	10	0	52	1
Holding	10	2	32	2
Harper	10	0	31	1

Umpires: M.W. Johnson and B.E. Martin.

No-balls and wides debited to bowlers' analyses.

AUSTRALIA v SRI LANKA 1984-85

Benson and Hedges World Series Cup – 8th Match

At Melbourne Cricket Ground on 19 January 1985.
Toss: Sri Lanka. Result: SRI LANKA won by 4 wickets.
50 overs match. Award: R.J. Ratnayake.
No débuts.

AUSTRALIA		
G.M. Wood	b Ratnayake	42
K.C. Wessels	b Ratnayake	28
G.M. Ritchie	c Madugalle b Karnain	13
A.R. Border*	st Silva b D.S. De Silva	1
D.C. Boon	c Wettimuny b Dias	34
W.B. Phillips†	c De Mel b Dias	67
S.P. O'Donnell	b Ratnayake	7
G.F. Lawson	c Madugalle b Dias	11
M.J. Bennett	not out	6
C.J. McDermott	b Ratnayake	0
R.M. Hogg	not out	5
Extras	(LB 9, W 3)	12
Total	(50 overs – 9 wickets)	**226**

Fall of wickets: 1-68, 2-73, 3-74, 4-88, 5-160, 6-191, 7-204, 8-220, 9-220.

SRI LANKA	*O*	*M*	*R*	*W*
De Mel	7	1	45	0
John	10	1	32	0
Ratnayake	10	3	37	4
D.S. De Silva	10	0	33	1
Karnain	9	0	45	1
Dias	4	0	25	3

SRI LANKA		
S. Wettimuny	lbw b Hogg	17
S.A.R. Silva†	c Hogg b O'Donnell	23
R.S. Madugalle	c Border b O'Donnell	24
R.L. Dias	run out	48
L.R.D. Mendis*	c Wessels b Hogg	35
P.A. De Silva	not out	46
U.S.H. Karnain	b Lawson	16
R.J. Ratnayake	not out	5
A.L.F. De Mel		
D.S. De Silva		
V.B. John		
Extras	(B 1, LB 14, NB 1)	16
Total	(49.2 overs – 6 wickets)	**230**

Fall of wickets: 1-38, 2-52, 3-86, 4-150, 5-161, 6-196.

AUSTRALIA	*O*	*M*	*R*	*W*
Lawson	10	0	51	1
McDermott	9.2	1	36	0
Hogg	10	1	31	2
O'Donnell	10	1	43	2
Bennett	9	1	48	0
Wessels	1	0	6	0

Umpires: R.A. French and M.W. Johnson.

No-balls and wides debited to bowlers' analyses.

Match No. 291/36

AUSTRALIA v WEST INDIES 1984-85

Benson and Hedges World Series Cup – 9th Match

At Melbourne Cricket Ground on 20 January 1985.
Toss: Australia. Result: WEST INDIES won by 65 runs.
50 overs match. Award: I.V.A. Richards.
No débuts.

WEST INDIES		
C.G. Greenidge	c Phillips b Hogg	33
D.L. Haynes	c and b O'Donnell	23
R.B. Richardson	c Phillips b O'Donnell	21
I.V.A. Richards	c Boon b McDermott	74
C.H. Lloyd*	run out	16
A.L. Logie	c Border b Wessels	72
P.J.L. Dujon†	c Phillips b Hogg	23
M.A. Holding	not out	2
M.D. Marshall	not out	2
J. Garner		
W.W. Davis		
Extras	(B 1, LB 3, W 1)	5
Total	(50 overs – 7 wickets)	**271**

Fall of wickets: 1-56, 2-58, 3-103, 4-138, 5-201, 6-252, 7-268.

AUSTRALIA	*O*	*M*	*R*	*W*
Lawson	10	0	47	0
McDermott	10	0	50	1
Hogg	10	1	56	2
O'Donnell	10	0	40	2
Wessels	8	0	58	1
Border	2	0	16	0

AUSTRALIA		
G.M. Wood	c Dujon b Marshall	9
W.B. Phillips†	c Greenidge b Garner	4
D.M. Jones	c Haynes b Marshall	0
S.P. O'Donnell	run out	11
A.R. Border*	c Richards b Holding	61
D.C. Boon	b Richards	34
G.M. Ritchie	b Davis	6
K.C. Wessels	b Richards	21
G.F. Lawson	not out	18
C.J. McDermott	run out	19
R.M. Hogg		
Extras	(B 6, LB 12, W 1, NB 4)	23
Total	(50 overs – 9 wickets)	**206**

Fall of wickets: 1-14, 2-15, 3-21, 4-34, 5-115, 6-126, 7-163, 8-169, 9-206.

WEST INDIES	*O*	*M*	*R*	*W*
Marshall	9	1	29	2
Garner	9	2	17	1
Holding	10	1	36	1
Davis	10	1	52	1
Richards	10	0	43	2
Logie	1	0	10	0
Richardson	1	0	1	0

Umpires: R.C. Isherwood and P.G. McConnell.

No-balls and wides debited to bowlers' analyses.

AUSTRALIA v SRI LANKA 1984-85

Benson and Hedges World Series Cup – 10th Match

At Sydney Cricket Ground on 23 January 1985.
Toss: Australia. Result: AUSTRALIA won by 3 wickets.
50 overs match. Award: K.C. Wessels.
No débuts.

SRI LANKA		
S.A.R. Silva†	run out	2
S. Wettimuny	b Wessels	21
R.S. Madugalle	c Phillips b Hogg	7
R.L. Dias	c Phillips b Wessels	19
L.R.D. Mendis*	c Phillips b Lawson	80
P.A. De Silva	not out	81
R.J. Ratnayake	b McDermott	7
U.S.H. Karnain	not out	10
A.L.F. De Mel		
D.S. De Silva		
V.B. John		
Extras	(LB 9, W 1, NB 3)	13
Total	(50 overs – 6 wickets)	**240**

Fall of wickets 1-3, 2-23, 3-54, 4-55, 5-194, 6-204.

AUSTRALIA	*O*	*M*	*R*	*W*
Lawson	10	2	32	1
McDermott	10	1	59	1
Hogg	10	2	33	1
O'Donnell	10	0	46	0
Wessels	10	0	61	2

AUSTRALIA		
G.M. Wood	c Ratnayake b De Mel	0
S.B. Smith	c Silva b John	4
K.C. Wessels	c Mendis b Karnain	82
A.R. Border*	st Silva b D.S. De Silva	57
D.M. Jones	not out	62
D.C. Boon	lbw b John	3
W.B. Phillips†	b Ratnayake	19
S.P. O'Donnell	c Karnain b De Mel	2
G.F. Lawson	not out	0
C.J. McDermott		
R.M. Hogg		
Extras	(LB 10, W 3)	13
Total	(47.1 overs – 7 wickets)	**242**

Fall of wickets 1-0, 2-29, 3-119, 4-187, 5-195, 6-231, 7-238.

SRI LANKA	*O*	*M*	*R*	*W*
De Mel	8	0	53	2
John	10	1	35	2
D.S. De Silva	10	0	62	1
Karnain	10	0	38	1
Ratnayake	8.1	0	37	1
Dias	1	0	7	0

Umpires: A.R. Crafter and S.G. Randell.

No-balls and wides debited to bowlers' analyses.

Match No. 293/5

SRI LANKA v WEST INDIES 1984-85

Benson and Hedges World Series Cup – 11th Match

At Adelaide Oval on 26 January 1985.
Toss: West Indies. Result: WEST INDIES won by 8 wickets.
50 overs match. Award: C.G. Greenidge.
No débuts.

SRI LANKA		
S.A.R. Silva†	c Garner b Davis	5
D.S.B.P. Kuruppu	c Dujon b Walsh	7
R.S. Madugalle	b Davis	1
R.L. Dias	b Holding	66
L.R.D. Mendis*	c Richards b Davis	45
A. Ranatunga	c sub (R.B. Richardson) b Holding	31
U.S.H. Karnain	not out	20
R.J. Ratnayake	not out	12
A.L.F. De Mel		
D.S. De Silva		
G.N. De Silva		
Extras	(B 2, LB 9, W 2, NB 4)	17
Total	(50 overs – 6 wickets)	**204**

Fall of wickets 1-5, 2-13, 3-22, 4-115, 5-164, 6-181.

WEST INDIES	*O*	*M*	*R*	*W*
Garner	10	2	27	0
Davis	10	5	21	3
Walsh	10	0	54	1
Holding	10	0	46	2
Richards	10	0	45	0

WEST INDIES		
C.G. Greenidge	not out	110
D.L. Haynes	b D.S. De Silva	51
H.A. Gomes	c and b Ranatunga	24
A.L. Logie	not out	7
I.V.A. Richards*		
C.H. Lloyd		
P.J.L. Dujon†		
M.A. Holding		
J. Garner		
W.W. Davis		
C.A. Walsh		
Extras	(LB 4, W 1, NB 8)	13
Total	(37.2 overs – 2 wickets)	**205**

Fall of wickets 1-133, 2-178.

SRI LANKA	*O*	*M*	*R*	*W*
De Mel	4	0	34	0
G.N. De Silva	8.2	1	56	0
Ratnayake	10	0	41	0
D.S. De Silva	7	0	36	1
Ranatunga	8	1	34	1

Umpires: R.A. French and B.E. Martin.

No-balls and wides debited to bowlers' analyses.

AUSTRALIA v WEST INDIES 1984-85

Benson and Hedges World Series Cup – 12th Match

At Adelaide Oval on 27 January 1985.
Toss: West Indies. Result: WEST INDIES won by 6 wickets.
50 overs match. Award: J. Garner.
Début: Australia – R.J. McCurdy.

AUSTRALIA		
K.C. Wessels	run out	1
G.M. Wood	not out	104
A.R. Border*	lbw b Marshall	0
D.M. Jones	b Garner	11
S.B. Smith	c Dujon b Davis	21
W.B. Phillips†	run out	36
S.P. O'Donnell	c Dujon b Garner	9
G.F. Lawson	hit wicket b Marshall	4
C.J. McDermott	c Logie b Garner	2
R.J. McCurdy	run out	1
R.M. Hogg	not out	3
Extras	(LB 5, NB 3)	8
Total	(50 overs – 9 wickets)	**200**

Fall of wickets: 1-4, 2-4, 3-19, 4-72, 5-154, 6-167, 7-178, 8-181, 9-184.

WEST INDIES	*O*	*M*	*R*	*W*
Garner	10	3	17	3
Marshall	10	1	35	2
Davis	10	0	53	1
Holding	10	0	51	0
Richards	10	0	39	0

WEST INDIES		
C.G. Greenidge	lbw b McDermott	39
D.L. Haynes	b McCurdy	14
R.B. Richardson	c Smith b McDermott	34
I.V.A. Richards	c Border b McCurdy	51
C.H. Lloyd*	not out	47
A.L. Logie	not out	2
P.J.L. Dujon†		
M.D. Marshall		
W.W. Davis		
M.A. Holding		
J. Garner		
Extras	(B 2, LB 8, W 1, NB 3)	14
Total	(43.4 overs – 4 wickets)	**201**

Fall of wickets: 1-31, 2-93, 3-103, 4-199.

AUSTRALIA	*O*	*M*	*R*	*W*
Lawson	9	0	32	0
McCurdy	9.4	2	38	2
McDermott	7	0	37	2
Hogg	8	0	46	0
O'Donnell	10	1	38	0

Umpires: A.R. Crafter and M.W. Johnson.

No-balls and wides debited to bowlers' analyses.

Match No. 295/9

AUSTRALIA v SRI LANKA 1984-85

Benson and Hedges World Series Cup – 13th Match

At Adelaide Oval on 28 January 1985.
Toss: Sri Lanka. Result: AUSTRALIA won by 232 runs.
50 overs match. Award: A.R. Border.

No débuts.

An unbroken third-wicket partnership of 224 between Jones and Border, the highest for any wicket in limited-overs internationals, carried Australia to the highest total at this level in Australia. The margin of victory is the largest in these matches.

AUSTRALIA		
G.M. Wood	c D.S. De Silva b Karnain	30
S.B. Smith	c Silva b Karnain	55
D.M. Jones	not out	99
A.R. Border*	not out	118
D.C. Boon		
K.C. Wessels		
W.B. Phillips†		
G.F. Lawson		
S.P. O'Donnell		
R.J. McCurdy		
R.M. Hogg		
Extras	(B 6, LB 8, W 4, NB 3)	21
Total	(50 overs – 2 wickets)	**323**
Fall of wickets	1-94, 2-99.	

SRI LANKA	*O*	*M*	*R*	*W*
Ratnayake	10	1	51	0
John	10	1	64	0
G.N. De Silva	10	0	50	0
D.S. De Silva	5	0	42	0
Karnain	8	0	56	2
Ranatunga	6	0	36	0
Dias	1	0	10	0

SRI LANKA		
S.A.R. Silva†	lbw b McCurdy	0
A. Ranatunga	c Phillips b McCurdy	5
P.A. De Silva	lbw b Lawson	6
R.L. Dias	c Smith b Lawson	3
L.R.D. Mendis*	c Boon b McCurdy	7
R.S. Madugalle	lbw b O'Donnell	8
U.S.H. Karnain	c Wessels b O'Donnell	21
R.J. Ratnayake	c Jones b Hogg	2
D.S. De Silva	not out	15
V.B. John	c Hogg b Wessels	8
G.N. De Silva	st Phillips b Wessels	7
Extras	(B 1, LB 5, W 3)	9
Total	(35.5 overs)	**91**
Fall of wickets	1-3, 2-12, 3-14, 4-23, 5-25, 6-45, 7-52, 8-66, 9-75, 10-91.	

AUSTRALIA	*O*	*M*	*R*	*W*
Lawson	7	5	5	2
McCurdy	5	1	19	3
Hogg	8	1	18	1
O'Donnell	9	1	19	2
Wessels	4.5	0	16	2
Boon	2	0	8	0

Umpires: R.C. Isherwood and B.E. Martin.

No-balls and wides debited to bowlers' analyses.

SRI LANKA v WEST INDIES 1984-85

Benson and Hedges World Series Cup – 14th Match

At WACA Ground, Perth on 2 February 1985.
Toss: Sri Lanka. Result: WEST INDIES won by 82 runs.
50 overs match. Award: H.A. Gomes.
No débuts.

WEST INDIES		
C.G. Greenidge	b Ratnayake	42
D.L. Haynes	c Silva b John	27
H.A. Gomes	c Dias b De Mel	101
I.V.A. Richards*	b John	46
A.L. Logie	run out	6
C.H. Lloyd	not out	54
P.J.L. Dujon†	c De Silva b De Mel	13
M.D. Marshall	not out	2
W.W. Davis		
J. Garner		
C.A. Walsh		
Extras	(LB 10, W 6, NB 2)	18
Total	(50 overs – 6 wickets)	**309**

Fall of wickets: 1-47, 2-99, 3-216, 4-223, 5-241, 6-280.

SRI LANKA	*O*	*M*	*R*	*W*
De Mel	10	0	67	2
John	10	0	44	2
Ratnayake	10	0	58	1
Ratnayeke	10	0	48	0
Karnain	6	0	35	0
Ranatunga	3	0	39	0
Dias	1	0	8	0

SRI LANKA		
S. Wettimuny	run out	0
S.A.R. Silva†	c Dujon b Walsh	85
J.R. Ratnayeke	b Richards	24
R.L. Dias	run out	1
L.R.D. Mendis*	c Dujon b Walsh	8
P.A. De Silva	c Dujon b Richards	5
A. Ranatunga	not out	63
U.S.H. Karnain	not out	28
R.J. Ratnayake		
A.L.F. De Mel		
V.B. John		
Extras	(LB 6, W 5, NB 2)	13
Total	(50 overs – 6 wickets)	**227**

Fall of wickets: 1-0, 2-100, 3-102, 4-120, 5-133, 6-137.

WEST INDIES	*O*	*M*	*R*	*W*
Garner	6	3	6	0
Davis	6	1	34	0
Marshall	6	0	17	0
Walsh	10	0	52	2
Richards	10	0	47	2
Gomes	7	0	41	0
Haynes	5	0	24	0

Umpires: A.R. Crafter and S.G. Randell.

No-balls and wides debited to bowlers' analyses.

Match No. 297/10

AUSTRALIA v SRI LANKA 1984-85

Benson and Hedges World Series Cup – 15th Match

At WACA Ground, Perth on 3 February 1985.
Toss: Sri Lanka. Result: AUSTRALIA won by 9 wickets.
50 overs match. Award: S.B. Smith.
Début: Sri Lanka – D.M. Vonhagt.

SRI LANKA		
S.A.R. Silva†	c Phillips b O'Donnell	51
D.M. Vonhagt	c Wessels b Alderman	8
L.R.D. Mendis*	c Wood b Lawson	2
R.L. Dias	c Alderman b Lawson	4
P.A. De Silva	st Phillips b Wessels	52
A. Ranatunga	c Phillips b Hogg	10
U.S.H. Karnain	c Border b Hogg	8
J.R. Ratnayeke	run out	1
R.J. Ratnayake	c Phillips b O'Donnell	16
A.L.F. De Mel	not out	11
V.B. John	b McCurdy	0
Extras	(LB 2, W 5, NB 1)	8
Total	(44.3 overs)	**171**

Fall of wickets: 1-16, 2-19, 3-26, 4-94, 5-110, 6-123, 7-126, 8-147, 9-166, 10-171.

AUSTRALIA	*O*	*M*	*R*	*W*
Lawson	7	1	24	2
Alderman	10	0	41	1
McCurdy	5.3	0	15	1
O'Donnell	10	0	42	2
Hogg	10	1	40	2
Wessels	2	0	7	1

AUSTRALIA		
K.C. Wessels	c Silva b John	8
S.B. Smith	not out	73
W.B. Phillips†	not out	75
S.P. O'Donnell		
A.R. Border*		
G.M. Wood		
D.M. Jones		
G.F. Lawson		
R.J. McCurdy		
R.M. Hogg		
T.M. Alderman		
Extras	(LB 8, W 6, NB 2)	16
Total	(23.5 overs – 1 wicket)	**172**

Fall of wicket: 1-15.

SRI LANKA	*O*	*M*	*R*	*W*
De Mel	8	0	45	0
John	6.5	0	43	1
Ratnayake	5	0	40	0
Ratnayeke	4	0	36	0

Umpires: P.J. McConnell and B.E. Martin.

No-balls and wides debited to bowlers' analyses.

AUSTRALIA v WEST INDIES 1984-85

Benson and Hedges World Series Cup – 1st Final

At Sydney Cricket Ground on 6 February 1985.
Toss: West Indies. Result: AUSTRALIA won by 26 runs.
50 overs match (floodlit). No award.
No débuts.

AUSTRALIA		
S.B. Smith	c Richardson b Garner	6
G.M. Wood	c Richards b Garner	0
K.C. Wessels	c Dujon b Marshall	11
A.R. Border*	not out	127
D.M. Jones	b Davis	3
W.B. Phillips†	c Garner b Holding	50
S.P. O'Donnell	lbw b Garner	17
G.F. Lawson	not out	14
C.J. McDermott		
R.J. McCurdy		
R.M. Hogg		
Extras	(B 2, LB 6, NB 11)	19
Total	(50 overs – 6 wickets)	**247**

Fall of wickets: 1-3, 2-7, 3-58, 4-64, 5-169, 6-205.

WEST INDIES	*O*	*M*	*R*	*W*
Garner	10	3	29	3
Holding	10	0	40	1
Marshall	10	0	55	1
Davis	10	0	57	1
Richards	10	0	58	0

WEST INDIES		
D.L. Haynes	b Lawson	11
R.B. Richardson	lbw b McCurdy	0
H.A. Gomes	lbw b McCurdy	9
I.V.A. Richards	b McDermott	68
C.H. Lloyd*	c Wessels b McDermott	20
A.L. Logie	c Wood b Hogg	12
P.J.L. Dujon†	b McDermott	14
M.D. Marshall	b McCurdy	43
M.A. Holding	b O'Donnell	1
J. Garner	run out	27
W.W. Davis	not out	8
Extras	(LB 7, NB 1)	8
Total	(47.3 overs)	**221**

Fall of wickets: 1-10, 2-20, 3-20, 4-82, 5-107, 6-137, 7-140, 8-147, 9-210, 10-221.

AUSTRALIA	*O*	*M*	*R*	*W*
Lawson	9	1	41	1
McCurdy	9.3	1	40	3
Hogg	10	0	35	1
McDermott	10	0	44	3
O'Donnell	9	0	54	1

Umpires: A.R. Crafter and M.W. Johnson.

No-balls and wides debited to bowlers' analyses.

Match No. 299/39

AUSTRALIA v WEST INDIES 1984-85

Benson and Hedges World Series Cup – 2nd Final

At Melbourne Cricket Ground on 10 February 1985.
Toss: West Indies. Result: WEST INDIES won by 4 wickets.
50 overs match. No award.
No débuts.

AUSTRALIA		
S.B. Smith	b Davis	54
G.M. Wood	c Richards b Holding	81
A.R. Border*	c Dujon b Marshall	39
W.B. Phillips†	not out	56
D.M. Jones	not out	13
K.C. Wessels		
S.P. O'Donnell		
G.F. Lawson		
C.J. McDermott		
R.J. McCurdy		
R.M. Hogg		
Extras	(B 2, LB 10, W 7, NB 9)	28
Total	(50 overs – 3 wickets)	**271**

Fall of wickets 1-135, 2-186, 3-203.

WEST INDIES	*O*	*M*	*R*	*W*
Garner	10	0	60	0
Marshall	10	0	64	1
Holding	10	1	41	1
Davis	10	0	43	1
Richards	10	0	51	0

WEST INDIES		
D.L. Haynes	c Wessels b Hogg	44
R.B. Richardson	c Wessels b O'Donnell	50
H.A. Gomes	b O'Donnell	47
I.V.A. Richards	lbw b Lawson	9
C.H. Lloyd*	c O'Donnell b Lawson	13
A.L. Logie	hit wicket b McCurdy	60
P.J.L. Dujon†	not out	39
M.D. Marshall	not out	0
M.A. Holding		
W.W. Davis		
J. Garner		
Extras	(B 2, LB 8, NB 1)	11
Total	(49.2 overs – 6 wickets)	**273**

Fall of wickets 1-78, 2-137, 2-154, 3-158, 5-179, 6-265.

AUSTRALIA	*O*	*M*	*R*	*W*
Lawson	10	0	34	2
McCurdy	10	0	69	1
McDermott	10	0	56	0
Hogg	9.2	0	58	1
O'Donnell	10	0	46	2

Umpires: R.C. Isherwood and P.J. McConnell.

No-balls and wides debited to bowlers' analyses.

AUSTRALIA v WEST INDIES 1984-85

Benson and Hedges World Series Cup – 3rd Final

At Sydney Cricket Ground on 12 February 1985.
Toss: West Indies. Result: WEST INDIES won by 7 wickets.
50 overs match (floodlit). Finals awards: A.R. Border and M.A. Holding.
Début: Australia – R.B. Kerr.

AUSTRALIA		
G.M. Wood	not out	36
K.C. Wessels	c Richards b Holding	17
R.B. Kerr	c Logie b Davis	4
A.R. Border*	c Garner b Holding	4
D.M. Jones	b Richards	16
W.B. Phillips†	c Dujon b Holding	3
S.P. O'Donnell	c and b Garner	69
G.F. Lawson	c Richards b Holding	4
C.J. McDermott	c Dujon b Holding	0
R.J. McCurdy	run out	12
R.M. Hogg	c Richards b Garner	1
Extras	(B 2, LB 4, W 4, NB 2)	12
Total	(50 overs)	**178**

Fall of wickets: 1-47, 2-51, 3-57, 4-64, 5-80, 6-89, 7-89, 8-124, 9-176, 10-178.

WEST INDIES	*O*	*M*	*R*	*W*
Garner	10	4	34	2
Marshall	10	0	37	0
Davis	10	1	23	1
Holding	10	1	26	5
Richards	10	0	52	1

WEST INDIES		
D.L. Haynes	not out	76
R.B. Richardson	run out	3
H.A. Gomes	c Border b McDermott	3
I.V.A. Richards	c sub (P.H. Marks) b McDermott	76
A.L. Logie	not out	11
C.H. Lloyd*		
P.J.L. Dujon†		
M.D. Marshall		
M.A. Holding		
W.W. Davis		
J. Garner		
Extras	(B 4, LB 2, NB 4)	10
Total	(47 overs – 3 wickets)	**179**

Fall of wickets: 1-14, 2-34, 3-162.

AUSTRALIA	*O*	*M*	*R*	*W*
Lawson	10	1	22	0
McCurdy	10	2	31	0
McDermott	10	2	36	2
Hogg	9	0	42	0
O'Donnell	8	0	42	0

Umpires: R.A. French and P.J. McConnell.

No-balls and wides debited to bowlers' analyses.

Match No. 301/9

NEW ZEALAND v PAKISTAN 1984-85 (1st Match)

Rothmans Cup

At McLean Park, Napier on 12 January 1985.
Toss: New Zealand. Result: NEW ZEALAND won by 110 runs.
50 overs match. Award: R.J. Hadlee.
No débuts.

NEW ZEALAND		
J.G. Wright	c Kamal b Tahir	24
G.P. Howarth*	st Dalpat b Qasim	68
J.F. Reid	b Mudassar	11
M.D. Crowe	c Omar b Tahir	32
I.D.S. Smith†	run out	14
J.J. Crowe	run out	35
J.V. Coney	not out	24
R.J. Hadlee	not out	34
B.L. Cairns		
E.J. Chatfield		
J.G. Bracewell		
Extras	(B 4, LB 17, W 14)	35
Total	(50 overs – 6 wickets)	**277**

Fall of wickets: 1-62, 2-103, 3-157, 4-160, 5-189, 6-225.

PAKISTAN	*O*	*M*	*R*	*W*
Azeem Hafeez	10	0	47	0
Mohsin Kamal	10	0	61	0
Tahir Naqqash	10	0	60	2
Mudassar Nazar	10	0	51	1
Iqbal Qasim	10	1	37	1

PAKISTAN		
Mohsin Khan	b Cairns	4
Mudassar Nazar	c Smith b Hadlee	17
Qasim Omar	c Smith b Hadlee	0
Javed Miandad*	run out	38
Salim Malik	run out	11
Wasim Raja	c Smith b Chatfield	30
Tahir Naqqash	lbw b Cairns	11
Iqbal Qasim	b Chatfield	9
Anil Dalpat†	not out	21
Azeem Hafeez	c Hadlee b Howarth	15
Mohsin Kamal	not out	0
Extras	(B 4, LB 3, W 4)	11
Total	(50 overs – 9 wickets)	**167**

Fall of wickets: 1-24, 2-24, 3-26, 4-46, 5-91, 6-106, 7-125, 8-132, 9-161.

NEW ZEALAND	*O*	*M*	*R*	*W*
Hadlee	8	0	30	2
Cairns	10	0	27	2
Chatfield	10	2	20	2
Coney	10	0	45	0
Bracewell	10	1	28	0
Howarth	1	0	4	1
Wright	1	0	6	0

Umpires: D.A. Kinsella and S.J. Woodward.

No-balls and wides debited to bowlers' analyses.

NEW ZEALAND v PAKISTAN 1984-85 (2nd Match).
Rothmans Cup

At Seddon Park, Hamilton on 15 January 1985.
Toss: Pakistan. Result: NEW ZEALAND won by 4 wickets.
50 overs match. Award: Javed Miandad.
No débuts.

PAKISTAN		
Mohsin Khan	c Smith b Chatfield	49
Wasim Raja	c Reid b Coney	15
Qasim Omar	b Coney	15
Javed Miandad*	not out	90
Salim Malik	run out	14
Mudassar Nazar	not out	22
Shoaib Mohammad		
Tahir Naqqash		
Anil Dalpat†		
Iqbal Qasim		
Azeem Hafeez		
Extras	(B 1, LB 10, W 3, NB 2)	16
Total	(50 overs – 4 wickets)	**221**

Fall of wickets 1-32, 2-62, 3-131, 4-160.

NEW ZEALAND	*O*	*M*	*R*	*W*
Cairns	10	2	58	0
Hadlee	10	3	46	0
Coney	10	1	16	2
Bracewell	10	0	51	0
Chatfield	10	0	39	1

NEW ZEALAND		
G.P. Howarth*	c Dalpat b Wasim	5
J.G. Wright	c Miandad b Salim	39
J.F. Reid	b Wasim	17
M.D. Crowe	c Tahir b Qasim	59
J.J. Crowe	b Qasim	35
J.V. Coney	not out	31
I.D.S. Smith†	c Azeem b Tahir	13
R.J. Hadlee	not out	13
B.L. Cairns		
E.J. Chatfield		
J.G. Bracewell		
Extras	(LB 5, W 5)	10
Total	(48.5 overs – 6 wickets)	**222**

Fall of wickets 1-9, 2-36, 3-90, 4-154, 5-164, 6-191.

PAKISTAN	*O*	*M*	*R*	*W*
Wasim Raja	10	0	29	2
Salim Malik	10	1	34	1
Iqbal Qasim	10	0	58	2
Azeem Hafeez	7.5	0	36	0
Mudassar Nazar	7	0	41	0
Tahir Naqqash	4	0	19	1

Umpires: D.A. Kinsella and T.A. McCall.

No-balls and wides debited to bowlers' analyses.

Match No. 303/11

NEW ZEALAND v PAKISTAN 1984-85 (3rd Match)

Rothmans Cup

At Lancaster Park, Christchurch on 6 February 1985.
Toss: New Zealand. Result: NEW ZEALAND won by 13 runs.
50 overs match. Award: J.F. Reid.

Début: Pakistan – Ramiz Raja.

NEW ZEALAND		
G.P. Howarth*	c Dalpat b Azeem	12
J.G. Wright	c Salim b Tahir	65
J.F. Reid	c Salim b Azeem	88
M.D. Crowe	run out	20
B.L. Cairns	c and b Mudassar	8
R.J. Hadlee	c Dalpat b Tahir	9
J.V. Coney	c Iqbal Qasim b Azeem	12
J.J. Crowe	c Wasim b Tahir	13
I.D.S. Smith†	not out	5
J.G. Bracewell	not out	20
E.J. Chatfield		
Extras	(B 3, LB 5, W 4)	12
Total	(50 overs – 8 wickets)	**264**

Fall of wickets: 1-29, 2-121, 3-166, 4-177, 5-192, 6-216, 7-237, 8-241.

PAKISTAN	*O*	*M*	*R*	*W*
Wasim Raja	10	1	34	0
Azeem Hafeez	10	0	56	3
Iqbal Qasim	5	0	33	0
Mudassar Nazar	10	0	56	1
Tahir Naqqash	8	0	40	3
Salim Malik	3	0	16	0
Zaheer Abbas	4	0	21	0

PAKISTAN		
Mudassar Nazar	c J.J. Crowe b Cairns	8
Qasim Omar	run out	1
Salim Malik	b Cairns	0
Zaheer Abbas	st Smith b Bracewell	58
Javed Miandad*	c M.D. Crowe b Cairns	30
Ramiz Raja	run out	75
Wasim Raja	c Howarth b Chatfield	12
Anil Dalpat†	c M.D. Crowe b Hadlee	37
Tahir Naqqash	c Howarth b Hadlee	11
Azeem Hafeez	not out	1
Iqbal Qasim	b Hadlee	0
Extras	(B 4, LB 6, W 4, NB 4)	18
Total	(49.4 overs)	**251**

Fall of wickets: 1-1, 2-1, 3-22, 4-105, 5-105, 6-129, 7-237, 8-250, 9-250, 10-251.

NEW ZEALAND	*O*	*M*	*R*	*W*
Cairns	10	4	39	3
Hadlee	9.4	1	32	3
Chatfield	10	0	75	1
Coney	10	0	44	0
Bracewell	10	1	51	1

Umpires: F.R. Goodall and G.C. Morris.

No-balls and wides debited to bowlers' analyses.

NEW ZEALAND v PAKISTAN 1984-85 (4th Match)

Rothmans Cup

At Eden Park, Auckland on 16 (no play), 17 February 1985.

Toss: Pakistan.	No result – rain.
50 overs match.	No award.

No débuts.

PAKISTAN

Mudassar Nazar	c M.D. Crowe b Chatfield	10
Qasim Omar	c Smith b Snedden	6
Zaheer Abbas	c Smith b Chatfield	4
Javed Miandad*	run out	9
Ramiz Raja	st Smith b Bracewell	59
Salim Malik	lbw b Chatfield	7
Wasim Raja	c Howarth b Bracewell	0
Anil Dalpat†	c Bracewell b McEwan	3
Tahir Naqqash	c Wright b Snedden	61
Rashid Khan	not out	8
Wasim Akram	b Hadlee	2
Extras	(B 3, LB 9, W 8)	20
Total	(49.1 overs)	**189**

Fall of wickets: 1-17, 2-25, 3-25, 4-61, 5-70, 6-73, 7-92, 8-156, 9-182, 10-189.

NEW ZEALAND	*O*	*M*	*R*	*W*
Chatfield	10	2	20	3
Hadlee	9.1	3	24	1
Snedden	10	3	36	2
McEwan	10	0	54	1
Bracewell	10	1	43	2

NEW ZEALAND

G.P. Howarth*
J.G. Wright
J.F. Reid
M.D. Crowe
J.V. Coney
P.E. McEwan
R.J. Hadlee
I.D.S. Smith†
M.C. Snedden
J.G. Bracewell
E.J. Chatfield

Umpires: T.A. McCall and S.J. Woodward.

No-balls and wides debited to bowlers' analyses.

Match No. 305/29

AUSTRALIA v ENGLAND 1984-85

Benson and Hedges World Championship – 1st Match

At Melbourne Cricket Ground on 17 February 1985.
Toss: England. Result: AUSTRALIA won by 7 wickets.
49 overs match (floodlit). Award: R.B. Kerr.
No débuts.

Australia's first World Championship of Cricket celebrated the 150th anniversary of the founding of the state of Victoria. Its opening match was the first to be played under floodlights at the MCG.

ENGLAND		
G. Fowler	c and b McDermott	26
P.R. Downton†	c McCurdy b McDermott	27
D.I. Gower*	c Alderman b McCurdy	6
A.J. Lamb	c Kerr b Lawson	53
M.W. Gatting	c Alderman b O'Donnell	34
C.S. Cowdrey	lbw b McDermott	0
V.J. Marks	b Lawson	24
P.H. Edmonds	b Lawson	20
R.M. Ellison	not out	2
J.P. Agnew	not out	2
N.G. Cowans		
Extras	(B 3, LB 12, NB 5)	20
Total	(49 overs – 8 wickets)	**214**

Fall of wickets: 1-61, 2-66, 3-76, 4-159, 5-159, 6-166, 7-200, 8-211.

AUSTRALIA	*O*	*M*	*R*	*W*
Lawson	10	3	31	3
Alderman	10	0	48	0
McDermott	10	0	39	3
McCurdy	10	1	42	1
O'Donnell	9	0	39	1

AUSTRALIA		
K.C. Wessels	c Gatting b Ellison	39
R.B. Kerr	not out	87
K.J. Hughes	run out	0
A.R. Border*	c Cowans b Marks	1
D.M. Jones	not out	78
W.B. Phillips†		
S.P. O'Donnell		
G.F. Lawson		
C.J. McDermott		
R.J. McCurdy		
T.M. Alderman		
Extras	(B 1, LB 3, NB 6)	10
Total	(45.2 overs – 3 wickets)	**215**

Fall of wickets: 1-57, 2-57, 3-58.

ENGLAND	*O*	*M*	*R*	*W*
Cowans	10	0	52	0
Ellison	10	4	34	1
Agnew	8	0	59	0
Marks	7.2	0	33	1
Edmonds	10	0	33	0

Umpires: A.R. Crafter and R.C. Isherwood.

No-balls and wides debited to bowlers' analyses.

INDIA v PAKISTAN 1984-85

Benson and Hedges World Championship – 2nd Match

At Melbourne Cricket Ground on 20 February 1985.
Toss: Pakistan. Result: INDIA won by 6 wickets.
50 overs match (floodlit). Award: M. Azharuddin.
Début: India – L. Sivaramakrishnan.

PAKISTAN		
Mohsin Khan	c Viswanath b Binny	3
Qasim Omar	c and b Sivaramakrishnan	57
Zaheer Abbas	c and b Sivaramakrishnan	25
Javed Miandad*	c Sivaramakrishnan b Binny	17
Ramiz Raja	c Shastri b Kapil Dev	29
Imran Khan	c Madan Lal b Kapil Dev	14
Mudassar Nazar	run out	6
Tahir Naqqash	c Amarnath b Madan Lal	0
Rashid Khan	c Shastri b Binny	17
Anil Dalpat†	c Kapil Dev b Binny	9
Wasim Akram	not out	0
Extras	(LB 3, W 2, NB 1)	6
Total	(49.2 overs)	**183**

Fall of wickets: 1-8, 2-73, 3-98, 4-119, 5-144, 6-151, 7-155, 8-156, 9-183, 10-183.

INDIA	*O*	*M*	*R*	*W*
Kapil Dev	9	1	31	2
Binny	8.2	3	35	4
Madan Lal	9	2	27	1
Amarnath	3	0	11	0
Sivaramakrishnan	10	0	49	2
Shastri	10	1	27	0

INDIA		
R.J. Shastri	c Miandad b Imran	2
K. Srikkanth	c Mohsin b Imran	12
M. Azharuddin	not out	93
D.B. Vengsarkar	c Mudassar b Imran	0
S.M. Gavaskar*	lbw b Mudassar	54
M. Amarnath	not out	11
R.M.H. Binny		
Madan Lal		
Kapil Dev		
L. Sivaramakrishnan		
S. Viswanath†		
Extras	(LB 9, W 3)	12
Total	(45.5 overs – 4 wickets)	**184**

Fall of wickets: 1-2, 2-27, 3-27, 4-159.

PAKISTAN	*O*	*M*	*R*	*W*
Imran Khan	10	1	27	3
Wasim Akram	8.5	0	38	0
Rashid Khan	7	0	38	0
Tahir Naqqash	10	0	34	0
Mudassar Nazar	10	0	38	1

Umpires: R.A. French and P.J. McConnell.

No-balls and wides debited to bowlers' analyses.

Match No. 307/4

NEW ZEALAND v WEST INDIES 1984-85

Benson and Hedges World Championship – 3rd Match

At Sydney Cricket Ground on 21 February 1985.
Toss: New Zealand. No result – rain.
50 overs match (floodlit). No award.
No débuts.

This match was originally scheduled for 19 February when rain prevented any play. Because the television coverage was already booked for the match at Melbourne on 20 February between India and Pakistan, it was rescheduled for 21 February, when rain again intervened. The sides shared the two points.

NEW ZEALAND		
G.P. Howarth*	c Dujon b Garner	8
J.G. Wright	c Logie b Davis	22
J.F. Reid	not out	22
M.D. Crowe		
J.J. Crowe		
J.V. Coney		
R.J. Hadlee		
I.D.S. Smith†		
B.L. Cairns		
M.C. Snedden		
E.J. Chatfield		
Extras	(B 1, NB 4)	5
Total	(18.4 overs – 2 wickets)	**57**

Fall of wickets 1-21, 2-57.

WEST INDIES	*O*	*M*	*R*	*W*
Garner	6	3	11	1
Marshall	6	1	13	0
Davis	3.4	0	23	1
Holding	3	0	9	0

WEST INDIES
R.B. Richardson
D.L. Haynes
H.A. Gomes
I.V.A. Richards
C.H. Lloyd*
A.L. Logie
P.J.L. Dujon†
M.D. Marshall
M.A. Holding
W.W. Davis
J. Garner

Umpires: M.W. Johnson and S.G. Randell.

No-balls and wides debited to bowlers' analyses.

NEW ZEALAND v SRI LANKA 1984-85

Benson and Hedges World Championship – 4th Match

At Melbourne Cricket Ground on 23 February 1985.
Toss: Sri Lanka. Result: NEW ZEALAND won by 51 runs.
50 overs match (floodlit). Award: J.F. Reid.
No débuts.

NEW ZEALAND		
G.P. Howarth*	c Madugalle b John	11
J.G. Wright	b John	4
J.F. Reid	c Dias b Karnain	62
M.D. Crowe	run out	22
P.E. McEwan	b John	27
J.V. Coney	c De Silva b Karnain	21
R.J. Hadlee	c De Mel b Ranatunga	9
I.D.S. Smith†	b Ratnayake	22
B.L. Cairns	c De Mel b Ratnayake	25
M.C. Snedden	b Ratnayake	7
E.J. Chatfield	not out	2
Extras	(LB 6, W 5)	11
Total	(49.4 overs)	**223**

Fall of wickets: 1-11, 2-21, 3-64, 4-100, 5-145, 6-161, 7-170, 8-213, 9-216, 10-223.

SRI LANKA	*O*	*M*	*R*	*W*
John	10	1	29	3
De Mel	10	0	48	0
Ratnayake	8.5	1	40	3
De Silva	5	0	25	0
Karnain	9.5	0	50	2
Ranatunga	6	0	25	1

SRI LANKA		
S.A.R. Silva†	c Crowe b Chatfield	33
J.R. Ratnayeke	run out	8
R.S. Madugalle	lbw b Coney	8
R.L. Dias	c Smith b Coney	9
L.R.D. Mendis*	c and b Hadlee	7
A. Ranatunga	c Wright b Coney	34
U.S.H. Karnain	lbw b Hadlee	0
A.L.F. De Mel	run out	27
R.J. Ratnayake	c Hadlee b Coney	1
D.S. De Silva	not out	24
V.B. John	c Chatfield b Cairns	11
Extras	(LB 9, NB 1)	10
Total	(42.4 overs)	**172**

Fall of wickets: 1-26, 2-48, 3-60, 4-67, 5-75, 6-75, 7-118, 8-125, 9-143, 10-172.

NEW ZEALAND	*O*	*M*	*R*	*W*
Cairns	8.4	1	25	1
Hadlee	6	1	23	2
Chatfield	10	3	25	1
Snedden	8	0	44	0
Coney	10	0	46	4

Umpires: P.J. McConnell and B.E. Martin.

No-balls and wides debited to bowlers' analyses.

Match No. 309/16

AUSTRALIA v PAKISTAN 1984-85

Benson and Hedges World Championship – 5th Match

At Melbourne Cricket Ground on 24 February 1985.

Toss: Australia.	Result: PAKISTAN won by 62 runs.
50 overs match.	Award: Wasim Akram.

No débuts.

PAKISTAN		
Mudassar Nazar	c McDermott b O'Donnell	69
Mohsin Khan	b Alderman	81
Qasim Omar	b O'Donnell	31
Javed Miandad	b McCurdy	19
Zaheer Abbas*	b Lawson	3
Imran Khan	not out	32
Ramiz Raja	c Alderman b Lawson	3
Tahir Naqqash	not out	5
Anil Dalpat†		
Rashid Khan		
Wasim Akram		
Extras	(LB 8, W 9, NB 2)	19
Total	(50 overs – 6 wickets)	**262**

Fall of wickets: 1-141, 2-190, 3-190, 4-196, 5-224, 6-229.

AUSTRALIA	*O*	*M*	*R*	*W*
Lawson	10	2	45	2
Alderman	10	0	42	1
McDermott	8	0	51	0
McCurdy	10	0	58	1
O'Donnell	10	1	42	2
Wessels	2	0	16	0

AUSTRALIA		
K.C. Wessels	b Wasim	10
R.B. Kerr	b Wasim	2
D.M. Jones	b Wasim	11
A.R. Border*	hit wicket b Wasim	11
K.J. Hughes	c Tahir b Wasim	1
W.B. Phillips†	c Miandad b Tahir	44
S.P. O'Donnell	not out	74
G.F. Lawson	c Ramiz b Mudassar	27
C.J. McDermott	run out	4
R.J. McCurdy	run out	1
T.M. Alderman	b Imran	2
Extras	(B 2, LB 9, W 2)	13
Total	(42.3 overs)	**200**

Fall of wickets: 1-4, 2-15, 3-30, 4-37, 5-42, 6-121, 7-128, 8-184, 9-187, 10-200.

PAKISTAN	*O*	*M*	*R*	*W*
Imran Khan	6.3	0	24	1
Wasim Akram	8	1	21	5
Rashid Khan	10	0	51	0
Zaheer Abbas	3	0	16	0
Tahir Naqqash	7	0	37	1
Mudassar Nazar	8	0	40	1

Umpires: R.C. Isherwood and M.W. Johnson.

No-balls and wides debited to bowlers' analyses.

ENGLAND v INDIA 1984-85

Benson and Hedges World Championship – 6th Match

At Sydney Cricket Ground on 26 February 1985.
Toss: England. Result: INDIA won by 86 runs.
50 overs match (floodlit). Award: K. Srikkanth.

No débuts.

Viswanath became the fourth wicket-keeper to make five dismissals in an innings in limited-overs internationals.

INDIA		
R.J. Shastri	c Fowler b Ellison	13
K. Srikkanth	run out	57
M. Azharuddin	c and b Cowans	45
D.B. Vengsarkar	run out	43
Kapil Dev	c Downton b Cowans	29
S.M. Gavaskar*	not out	30
M. Amarnath	c Lamb b Cowans	6
R.M.H. Binny	c Marks b Foster	2
Madan Lal	c Downton b Foster	0
S. Viswanath†	run out	8
L. Sivaramakrishnan		
Extras	(LB 2)	2
Total	(50 overs – 9 wickets)	**235**

Fall of wickets 1-67, 2-74, 3-147, 4-183, 5-197, 6-216, 7-220, 8-220, 9-235.

ENGLAND	*O*	*M*	*R*	*W*
Cowans	10	0	59	3
Ellison	10	1	46	1
Foster	10	0	33	2
Edmonds	10	1	38	0
Marks	10	0	57	0

ENGLAND		
G. Fowler	c Viswanath b Binny	26
M.D. Moxon	c and b Sivaramakrishnan	48
D.I. Gower*	c Vengsarkar b Sivaramakrishnan	25
A.J. Lamb	b Sivaramakrishnan	13
M.W. Gatting	c Viswanath b Shastri	7
P.R. Downton†	c Shastri b Kapil Dev	9
V.J. Marks	st Viswanath b Shastri	2
P.H. Edmonds	st Viswanath b Shastri	5
R.M. Ellison	c Viswanath b Madan Lal	1
N.A. Foster	c Srikkanth b Madan Lal	1
N.G. Cowans	not out	3
Extras	(B 3, LB 4, W 1, NB 1)	9
Total	(41.4 overs)	**149**

Fall of wickets 1-41, 2-94, 3-113, 4-126, 5-126, 6-130, 7-142, 8-144, 9-146, 10-149.

INDIA	*O*	*M*	*R*	*W*
Kapil Dev	7	0	21	1
Binny	8	0	33	1
Madan Lal	6.4	0	19	2
Sivaramakrishnan	10	0	39	3
Shastri	10	2	30	3

Umpires: R.A. French and B.E. Martin.

No-balls and wides debited to bowlers' analyses.

Match No. 311/7

SRI LANKA v WEST INDIES 1984-85

Benson and Hedges World Championship – 7th Match

At Melbourne Cricket Ground on 27 February 1985.
Toss: Sri Lanka. Result: WEST INDIES won by 8 wickets.
47 overs match (floodlit). Award: J.R. Ratnayeke.
No débuts.

SRI LANKA		
S.A.R. Silva†	c Haynes b Garner	4
J.R. Ratnayeke	c Haynes b Holding	50
R.L. Dias	c Dujon b Davis	16
A. Ranatunga	b Richards	1
L.R.D. Mendis*	run out	1
R.S. Madugalle	not out	36
D.S. De Silva	c and b Richards	5
U.S.H. Karnain	c and b Richards	1
A.L.F. De Mel	not out	15
R.J. Ratnayake		
V.B. John		
Extras	(B 1, LB 4, W 1)	6
Total	(47 overs – 7 wickets)	**135**

Fall of wickets 1-7, 2-52, 3-53, 4-57, 5-86, 6-102, 7-106.

WEST INDIES	*O*	*M*	*R*	*W*
Marshall	10	1	26	0
Garner	10	3	16	1
Davis	9	0	35	1
Holding	9	1	26	1
Richards	9	0	27	3

WEST INDIES		
D.L. Haynes	b De Mel	36
R.B. Richardson	retired hurt	11
H.A. Gomes	retired hurt	20
I.V.A. Richards	c De Mel b Ratnayake	12
C.H. Lloyd*	not out	14
A.L. Logie	not out	29
P.J.L. Dujon†		
M.D. Marshall		
M.A. Holding		
W.W. Davis		
J. Garner		
Extras	(B 1, LB 7, W 2, NB 4)	14
Total	(23.1 overs – 2 wickets)	**136**

Fall of wickets 1-86, 2-90.

SRI LANKA	*O*	*M*	*R*	*W*
De Mel	8	0	47	1
John	7	0	39	0
Ratnayake	7	0	29	1
Ranatunga	1.1	0	13	0

Umpires: A.R. Crafter and S.G. Randell.

No-balls and wides debited to bowlers' analyses.

ENGLAND v PAKISTAN 1984-85

Benson and Hedges World Championship – 8th Match

At Melbourne Cricket Ground on 2 March 1985.
Toss: Pakistan. Result: PAKISTAN won by 67 runs.
50 overs match (floodlit). Award: A.J. Lamb.
No débuts.

PAKISTAN		
Mudassar Nazar	c Foster b Edmonds	77
Mohsin Khan	c Moxon b Ellison	9
Ramiz Raja	c Moxon b Marks	21
Javed Miandad*	c Downton b Foster	11
Imran Khan	b Ellison	35
Salim Malik	c Gatting b Foster	8
Qasim Omar	b Cowans	12
Tahir Naqqash	not out	21
Anil Dalpat†	b Ellison	8
Azeem Hafeez	not out	0
Wasim Akram		
Extras	(B 5, LB 4, W 2)	11
Total	(50 overs – 8 wickets)	**213**

Fall of wickets: 1-37, 2-93, 3-114, 4-126, 5-144, 6-181, 7-183, 8-212.

ENGLAND	*O*	*M*	*R*	*W*
Cowans	10	0	52	1
Ellison	10	0	42	3
Foster	10	0	56	2
Marks	10	2	25	1
Edmonds	10	1	29	1

ENGLAND		
G. Fowler	c Dalpat b Imran	0
D.I. Gower*	c Tahir b Imran	27
A.J. Lamb	c Wasim b Azeem	81
M.W. Gatting	c Mudassar b Tahir	11
P.R. Downton†	run out	6
R.M. Ellison	c Dalpat b Tahir	6
V.J. Marks	run out	1
M.D. Moxon	c Imran b Azeem	3
P.H. Edmonds	not out	0
N.A. Foster	run out	1
N.G. Cowans	b Tahir	0
Extras	(B 1, LB 7, W 1, NB 1)	10
Total	(24.2 overs)	**146**

Fall of wickets: 1-0, 2-56, 3-102, 4-125, 5-138, 6-139, 7-141, 8-145, 9-146, 10-146.

PAKISTAN	*O*	*M*	*R*	*W*
Imran Khan	7	0	33	2
Wasim Akram	10	0	59	0
Azeem Hafeez	3	0	22	2
Tahir Naqqash	4.2	0	24	3

Umpires: R.C. Isherwood and M.W. Johnson.

No-balls and wides debited to bowlers' analyses.

Match No. 313/12

AUSTRALIA v INDIA 1984-85

Benson and Hedges World Championship – 9th Match

At Melbourne Cricket Ground on 3 March 1985.
Toss: India. Result: INDIA won by 8 wickets.
50 overs match. Award: R.J. Shastri.
No débuts.

AUSTRALIA		
G.M. Wood	b Binny	1
R.B. Kerr	b Kapil Dev	4
K.C. Wessels	c Madan Lal b Kapil Dev	6
A.R. Border*	b Binny	4
D.M. Jones	c Viswanath b Amarnath	12
W.B. Phillips†	c Amarnath b Sivaramakrishnan	60
S.P. O'Donnell	c Amarnath b Shastri	17
G.F. Lawson	c and b Sivaramakrishnan	0
R.M. Hogg	run out	22
R.J. McCurdy	not out	13
T.M. Alderman	b Binny	6
Extras	(B 2, LB 9, W 5, NB 2)	18
Total	(49.3 overs)	**163**

Fall of wickets 1-5, 2-5, 3-17, 4-17, 5-37, 6-85, 7-85, 8-134, 9-147, 10-163.

INDIA	*O*	*M*	*R*	*W*
Kapil Dev	10	2	25	2
Binny	7.3	0	27	3
Madan Lal	5	0	18	0
Amarnath	7	1	16	1
Sivaramakrishnan	10	0	32	2
Shastri	10	1	34	1

INDIA		
R.J. Shastri	c Phillips b O'Donnell	51
K. Srikkanth	not out	93
M. Azharuddin	lbw b Alderman	0
D.B. Vengsarkar	not out	11
S.M. Gavaskar*		
M. Amarnath		
Kapil Dev		
Madan Lal		
R.M.H. Binny		
S. Viswanath†		
L. Sivaramakrishnan		
Extras	(LB 1, W 3, NB 6)	10
Total	(36.1 overs – 2 wickets)	**165**

Fall of wickets 1-124, 2-125.

AUSTRALIA	*O*	*M*	*R*	*W*
Lawson	8	1	35	0
Hogg	6	2	16	0
McCurdy	1.1	0	30	0
Alderman	8	0	38	1
O'Donnell	7	0	45	1

Umpires: A.R. Crafter and P.J. McConnell.

No-balls and wides debited to bowlers' analyses.

INDIA v NEW ZEALAND 1984-85

Benson and Hedges World Championship – Semi-Final

At Sydney Cricket Ground on 5 March 1985.
Toss: India. Result: INDIA won by 7 wickets.
50 overs match (floodlit). Award: R.J. Shastri.
No débuts.

NEW ZEALAND		
J.G. Wright	c Viswanath b Kapil Dev	0
P.E. McEwan	c Viswanath b Binny	9
J.F. Reid	c Kapil Dev b Shastri	55
M.D. Crowe	c Azharuddin b Shastri	9
G.P. Howarth*	run out	7
J.V. Coney	b Shastri	33
I.D.S. Smith†	c Amarnath b Madan Lal	19
R.J. Hadlee	c Madan Lal b Shastri	3
B.L. Cairns	c Srikkanth b Madan Lal	39
M.C. Snedden	c Azharuddin b Madan Lal	7
Extras	(LB 21, W 1, NB 3)	25
Total	(50 overs)	206

Fall of wickets 1-0, 2-14, 3-52, 4-69, 5-119, 6-145, 7-151, 8-188, 9-206, 10-206.

INDIA	*O*	*M*	*R*	*W*
Kapil Dev	10	1	34	1
Binny	6	0	28	1
Madan Lal	8	1	37	4
Amarnath	7	0	24	0
Sivaramakrishnan	9	1	31	0
Shastri	10	1	31	3

INDIA		
R.J. Shastri	c McEwan b Hadlee	53
K. Srikkanth	c Reid b Chatfield	9
M. Azharuddin	c Coney b Cairns	24
D.B. Vengsarkar	not out	63
Kapil Dev	not out	54
S.M. Gavaskar*		
M. Amarnath		
R.M.H. Binny		
Madan Lal		
S. Viswanath†		
L. Sivaramakrishnan		
Extras	(B 1, LB 2, NB 1)	4
Total	(46 overs – 3 wickets)	**207**

Fall of wickets 1-28, 2-73, 3-102.

NEW ZEALAND	*O*	*M*	*R*	*W*
Cairns	9	0	35	1
Hadlee	8.3	3	50	1
Chatfield	10	0	38	1
Snedden	8	1	37	0
Coney	8	0	44	0

Umpires: R.A. French and P.J. McConnell.

No-balls and wides debited to bowlers' analyses.

Match No. 315/18

PAKISTAN v WEST INDIES 1984-85

Benson and Hedges World Championship – Semi-Final

At Melbourne Cricket Ground on 6 March 1985.
Toss: West Indies. Result: PAKISTAN won by 7 wickets.
50 overs match (floodlit). Award: Ramiz Raja.
No débuts.

WEST INDIES		
D.L. Haynes	c Mudassar b Tahir	18
R.B. Richardson	b Tahir	13
P.J.L. Dujon†	c Dalpat b Wasim Raja	22
I.V.A. Richards	c Dalpat b Tahir	1
C.H. Lloyd*	c Miandad b Mudassar	25
A.L. Logie	c Omar b Mudassar	8
M.D. Marshall	c Miandad b Mudassar	10
R.A. Harper	not out	25
M.A. Holding	b Wasim Akram	5
J. Garner	c Wasim Raja b Mudassar	13
W.W. Davis	c Miandad b Mudassar	3
Extras	(B 4, LB 7, W 4, NB 1)	16
Total	(44.3 overs)	**159**

Fall of wickets: 1-29, 2-44, 3-45, 4-61, 5-75, 6-96, 7-103, 8-122, 9-152, 10-159.

PAKISTAN	*O*	*M*	*R*	*W*
Imran Khan	9	1	39	0
Wasim Akram	10	2	26	1
Tahir Naqqash	8	3	23	3
Wasim Raja	10	0	32	1
Mudassar Nazar	7.3	0	28	5

PAKISTAN		
Mudassar Nazar	c Logie b Marshall	6
Mohsin Khan	c Dujon b Garner	23
Ramiz Raja	c and b Harper	60
Qasim Omar	not out	42
Javed Miandad*	not out	10
Salim Malik		
Wasim Raja		
Imran Khan		
Tahir Naqqash		
Anil Dalpat†		
Wasim Akram		
Extras	(B 3, LB 7, W 6, NB 3)	19
Total	(46 overs – 3 wickets)	**160**

Fall of wickets: 1-8, 2-97, 3-116.

WEST INDIES	*O*	*M*	*R*	*W*
Marshall	9	2	25	1
Garner	8	3	19	1
Holding	8	3	19	0
Davis	7	0	35	0
Harper	10	1	38	1
Richards	4	0	14	0

Umpires: R.C. Isherwood and S.G. Randell.

No-balls and wides debited to bowlers' analyses.

NEW ZEALAND v WEST INDIES 1984-85

Benson and Hedges World Championship – Plate-Winner's Final

At Sydney Cricket Ground on 9 March 1985.
Toss: West Indies. Result: WEST INDIES won by 6 wickets.
50 overs match. Award: I.V.A. Richards.
No débuts.

NEW ZEALAND		
G.P. Howarth*	lbw b Garner	11
J.G. Wright	c Logie b Garner	5
J.F. Reid	c Dujon b Davis	18
M.D. Crowe	c Harper b Holding	8
J.J. Crowe	b Harper	1
J.V. Coney	c Payne b Garner	35
I.D.S. Smith†	c Payne b Harper	15
B.L. Cairns	b Holding	5
R.J. Hadlee	b Marshall	11
J.G. Bracewell	not out	11
E.J. Chatfield	not out	2
Extras	(B 1, LB 8, W 2, NB 5)	16
Total	(50 overs – 9 wickets)	**138**

Fall of wickets: 1-14, 2-24, 3-45, 4-51, 5-52, 6-78, 7-83, 8-116, 9-127.

WEST INDIES	*O*	*M*	*R*	*W*
Garner	10	2	29	3
Marshall	10	1	32	1
Davis	10	0	23	1
Holding	10	1	23	2
Harper	10	2	22	2

WEST INDIES		
D.L. Haynes	c Coney b Hadlee	1
R.B. Richardson	c Smith b Hadlee	8
T.R.O. Payne	b Chatfield	28
A.L. Logie	not out	34
I.V.A. Richards*	b Hadlee	51
P.J.L. Dujon†	not out	9
M.D. Marshall		
R.A. Harper		
M.A. Holding		
J. Garner		
W.W. Davis		
Extras	(LB 3, W 2, NB 3)	8
Total	(37.2 overs – 4 wickets)	**139**

Fall of wickets: 1-4, 2-24, 3-54, 4-126.

NEW ZEALAND	*O*	*M*	*R*	*W*
Hadlee	10	4	23	3
Bracewell	8	2	42	0
Chatfield	9	0	25	1
Cairns	8	0	39	0
Coney	2.2	0	7	0

Umpires: R.A. French and M.W. Johnson.

No-balls and wides debited to bowlers' analyses.

Match No. 317/14

INDIA v PAKISTAN 1984-85

Benson and Hedges World Championship – Final

At Melbourne Cricket Ground on 10 March 1985.
Toss: Pakistan. Result: INDIA won by 8 wickets.
50 overs match (floodlit). Award: K. Srikkanth.
No débuts.

PAKISTAN		
Mudassar Nazar	c Viswanath b Kapil Dev	14
Mohsin Khan	c Azharuddin b Kapil Dev	5
Ramiz Raja	c Srikkanth b Sharma	4
Qasim Omar	b Kapil Dev	0
Javed Miandad*	st Viswanath b Sivaramakrishnan	48
Imran Khan	run out	35
Salim Malik	c Sharma b Sivaramakrishnan	14
Wasim Raja	not out	21
Tahir Naqqash	c Viswanath b Shastri	10
Anil Dalpat†	c Shastri b Sivaramakrishnan	0
Azeem Hafeez	not out	7
Extras	(B 7, LB 8, W 1, NB 2)	18
Total	(50 overs – 9 wickets)	**176**

Fall of wickets 1-17, 2-29, 3-29, 4-33, 5-101, 6-131, 7-131, 8-142, 9-145.

INDIA	*O*	*M*	*R*	*W*
Kapil Dev	9	1	23	3
Sharma	7	1	17	1
Madan Lal	6	1	15	0
Amarnath	9	0	27	0
Shastri	10	0	44	1
Sivaramakrishnan	9	0	35	3

INDIA		
R.J. Shastri	not out	63
K. Srikkanth	c Wasim b Imran	67
M. Azharuddin	b Tahir	25
D.B. Vengsarkar	not out	18
S.M. Gavaskar*		
M. Amarnath		
Kapil Dev		
Madan Lal		
C. Sharma		
S. Viswanath†		
L. Sivaramakrishnan		
Extras	(LB 2, W 2)	4
Total	(47.1 overs – 2 wickets)	**177**

Fall of wickets 1-103, 2-142.

PAKISTAN	*O*	*M*	*R*	*W*
Imran Khan	10	3	28	1
Azeem Hafeez	10	1	29	0
Tahir Naqqash	10	2	35	1
Wasim Raja	7.1	0	42	0
Mudassar Nazar	8	0	26	0
Salim Malik	2	0	15	0

Umpires: A.R. Crafter and R.C. Isherwood.

No-balls and wides debited to bowlers' analyses.

WEST INDIES v NEW ZEALAND 1984-85 (1st Match)

At Recreation Ground, St John's, Antigua on 20 March 1985.
Toss: New Zealand. Result: WEST INDIES won by 23 runs.
46 overs match. Award: R.A. Harper.
Début: New Zealand – R.T. Hart.

WEST INDIES		
C.G. Greenidge	c Smith b Troup	3
D.L. Haynes	b Troup	54
R.B. Richardson	b Hadlee	3
I.V.A. Richards*	c Coney	70
A.L. Logie	c Cairns b Coney	11
P.J.L. Dujon†	st Smith b Coney	14
R.A. Harper	not out	45
E.A.E. Baptiste	b Cairns	8
M.A. Holding	b Hadlee	9
J. Garner	not out	1
W.W. Davis		
Extras	(B 1, LB 6, W 3, NB 3)	13
Total	(46 overs – 8 wickets)	**231**

Fall of wickets: 1-4, 2-7, 3-134, 4-141, 5-160, 6-191, 7-208, 8-226.

NEW ZEALAND	*O*	*M*	*R*	*W*
Troup	10	0	52	2
Hadlee	10	0	29	2
Chatfield	8	0	38	0
Cairns	8	0	42	1
Coney	10	0	63	3

NEW ZEALAND		
J.G. Wright	b Holding	0
R.T. Hart	c Dujon b Garner	3
J.J. Crowe	b Harper	53
M.D. Crowe	lbw b Harper	41
B.L. Cairns	c Richards b Holding	20
J.V. Coney	run out	18
R.J. Hadlee	c Harper b Holding	2
I.D.S. Smith†	c Holding b Garner	12
G.P. Howarth*	not out	12
G.B. Troup	not out	16
E.J. Chatfield		
Extras	(B 2, LB 18, W 5, NB 6)	31
Total	(46 overs – 8 wickets)	**208**

Fall of wickets: 1-5, 2-20, 3-111, 4-124, 5-151, 6-158, 7-173, 8-180.

WEST INDIES	*O*	*M*	*R*	*W*
Garner	10	4	26	2
Holding	10	2	33	3
Baptiste	10	1	49	0
Davis	8	0	46	0
Harper	8	0	34	2

Umpires: A. Weekes and P. White.

No-balls and wides debited to bowlers' analyses.

Match No. 319/17

WEST INDIES v NEW ZEALAND 1984-85 (2nd Match)

At Queen's Park Oval, Port-of-Spain on 27 March 1985.
Toss: West Indies. Result: WEST INDIES won by 6 wickets.
22 overs match. Award: W.W. Davis.
Début: New Zealand – K.R. Rutherford.

NEW ZEALAND		
J.G. Wright	c Dujon b Davis	5
K.R. Rutherford	c Dujon b Davis	2
J.J. Crowe	c Richards b Davis	0
M.D. Crowe	not out	20
J.V. Coney	not out	19
G.P. Howarth*		
I.D.S. Smith†		
R.J. Hadlee		
B.L. Cairns		
G.B. Troup		
E.J. Chatfield		
Extras	(LB 1, W 1, NB 3)	5
Total	(22 overs – 3 wickets)	**51**

Fall of wickets 1-6, 2-9, 3-9.

WEST INDIES	*O*	*M*	*R*	*W*
Garner	6	2	6	0
Davis	6	2	7	3
Holding	5	0	16	0
Baptiste	5	0	21	0

WEST INDIES		
D.L. Haynes	b Chatfield	4
R.B. Richardson	c Smith b Troup	3
H.A. Gomes	c Smith b Troup	4
I.V.A. Richards*	c Cairns b Rutherford	27
A.L. Logie	not out	8
P.J.L. Dujon†	not out	4
R.A. Harper		
E.A.E. Baptiste		
M.A. Holding		
J. Garner		
W.W. Davis		
Extras	(LB 2, W 1, NB 2)	5
Total	(17 overs – 4 wickets)	**55**

Fall of wickets 1-4, 2-11, 3-21, 4-51.

NEW ZEALAND	*O*	*M*	*R*	*W*
Chatfield	6	0	15	1
Troup	5	1	22	2
Coney	3	1	4	0
Rutherford	3	0	12	1

Umpires: C.E. Cumberbatch and S. Mohammed.

No-balls and wides debited to bowlers' analyses.

WEST INDIES v NEW ZEALAND 1984-85 (3rd Match)

At Albion Sports Complex, Berbice, Guyana on 14 April 1985.
Toss: New Zealand. Result: WEST INDIES won by 130 runs.
50 overs match. Award: D.L. Haynes.

No débuts.

Richards became the first batsman to score 4,000 runs when his score reached 13.

WEST INDIES		
D.L. Haynes	not out	146
R.B. Richardson	c Smith b Hadlee	7
H.A. Gomes	c Smith b Chatfield	13
I.V.A. Richards*	c Wright b Bracewell	51
A.L. Logie	c Troup b Cairns	26
R.A. Harper	c Smith b Troup	1
P.J.L. Dujon†	not out	4
E.A.E. Baptiste		
M.A. Holding		
J. Garner		
W.W. Davis		
Extras	(LB 5, W 1, NB 5)	11
Total	(50 overs – 5 wickets)	**259**

Fall of wickets 1-18, 2-47, 3-172, 4-252, 5-253.

NEW ZEALAND	*O*	*M*	*R*	*W*
Troup	7	0	28	0
Hadlee	10	1	47	1
Chatfield	10	1	36	1
Bracewell	9	0	50	1
Cairns	10	0	68	1
Coney	4	0	25	0

NEW ZEALAND		
G.P. Howarth*	b Garner	3
J.G. Wright	b Garner	0
J.J. Crowe	b Davis	9
M.D. Crowe	b Holding	20
J.V. Coney	b Baptiste	11
I.D.S. Smith†	b Baptiste	1
R.J. Hadlee	b Harper	16
J.G. Bracewell	c Richards b Gomes	15
B.L. Cairns	c Davis b Harper	33
G.B. Troup	not out	6
E.J. Chatfield	b Gomes	6
Extras	(B 2, LB 4, W 1, NB 2)	9
Total	(48.1 overs)	**129**

Fall of wickets 1-4, 2-8, 3-24, 4-41, 5-48,
6-55, 7-75, 8-115, 9-121, 10-129.

WEST INDIES	*O*	*M*	*R*	*W*
Garner	6	1	16	2
Davis	6	3	7	1
Holding	6	0	12	1
Baptiste	7	2	18	2
Harper	10	1	35	2
Richards	10	4	20	0
Gomes	2.1	0	6	2
Logie	1	0	8	0

Umpires: L.H. Barker and D.J. Narine.

No-balls and wides debited to bowlers' analyses.

Match No. 321/9

WEST INDIES v NEW ZEALAND 1984-85 (4th Match)

At Queen's Park Oval, Port-of-Spain, Trinidad on 17 April 1985.

Toss: West Indies.	Result: WEST INDIES won by 10 wickets.
50 overs match.	Award: J. Garner.

No débuts.

NEW ZEALAND		
G.P. Howarth*	c Dujon b Garner	6
J.G. Wright	c Dujon b Garner	1
J.J. Crowe	c Richardson b Garner	4
M.D. Crowe	b Garner	1
J.V. Coney	c Dujon b Richards	33
I.D.S. Smith†	c and b Holding	3
R.J. Hadlee	c Richards b Davis	41
B.L. Cairns	b Harper	12
J.G. Bracewell	run out	1
G.B. Troup	run out	4
E.J. Chatfield	not out	1
Extras	(LB 3, W 2, NB 4)	9
Total	(42.2 overs)	**116**

Fall of wickets: 1-6, 2-10, 3-14, 4-18, 5-25, 6-83, 7-100, 8-104, 9-114, 10-116.

WEST INDIES	*O*	*M*	*R*	*W*
Garner	6	1	10	4
Davis	6.2	1	10	1
Baptiste	5	0	31	0
Holding	7	1	24	1
Harper	10	2	18	1
Richards	8	1	20	1

WEST INDIES		
D.L. Haynes	not out	85
R.B. Richardson	not out	28
H.A. Gomes		
I.V.A. Richards*		
A.L. Logie		
P.J.L. Dujon†		
E.A.E. Baptiste		
R.A. Harper		
M.A. Holding		
W.W. Davis		
J. Garner		
Extras	(LB 2, NB 2)	4
Total	(25.2 overs – 0 wicket)	**117**

NEW ZEALAND	*O*	*M*	*R*	*W*
Hadlee	6	1	18	0
Troup	8	2	30	0
Cairns	7	0	50	0
Chatfield	4	0	14	0
Bracewell	0.2	0	3	0

Umpires: C.E. Cumberbatch and S. Mohammed.

No-balls and wides debited to bowlers' analyses.

WEST INDIES v NEW ZEALAND 1984-85 (5th Match)

At Kensington Oval, Bridgetown, Barbados on 23 April 1985.
Toss: New Zealand. Result: WEST INDIES won by 112 runs.
50 overs match. Award: D.L. Haynes.

No débuts.

Haynes equalled the world record held by Richards when he completed his eighth hundred in limited-overs internationals.

WEST INDIES		
D.L. Haynes	c Coney b Chatfield	116
R.B. Richardson	c Coney b Chatfield	21
H.A. Gomes	c J.J. Crowe b Cairns	78
I.V.A. Richards*	not out	33
A.L. Logie	not out	11
P.J.L. Dujon†		
R.A. Harper		
E.A.E. Baptiste		
M.A. Holding		
J. Garner		
W.W. Davis		
Extras	(LB 5, W 1)	6
Total	(49 overs – 3 wickets)	**265**

Fall of wickets 1-31, 2-215, 3-223.

NEW ZEALAND	*O*	*M*	*R*	*W*
Troup	10	0	57	0
Hadlee	9	1	26	0
Chatfield	10	1	61	2
Cairns	10	1	63	1
Coney	10	0	53	0

NEW ZEALAND		
G.P. Howarth*	c Dujon b Davis	6
J.G. Wright	c Richards b Garner	22
K.R. Rutherford	c Holding b Harper	18
M.D. Crowe	c Logie b Davis	6
J.V. Coney	b Baptiste	5
J.J. Crowe	c Logie b Harper	30
B.L. Cairns	c Logie b Harper	5
I.D.S. Smith†	c Garner b Davis	37
R.J. Hadlee	not out	16
G.B. Troup	not out	0
E.J. Chatfield		
Extras	(B 2, LB 2, W 1, NB 3)	8
Total	(49 overs – 8 wickets)	**153**

Fall of wickets 1-30, 2-30, 3-36, 4-47, 5-83,
6-91, 7-103, 8-152.

WEST INDIES	*O*	*M*	*R*	*W*
Garner	6	2	10	1
Davis	8	0	32	3
Baptiste	7	1	11	1
Holding	6	1	10	0
Harper	10	3	38	3
Richards	8	0	31	0
Gomes	3	1	16	0
Logie	1	0	1	0

Umpires: D.M. Archer and L.H. Barker.

No-balls and wides debited to bowlers' analyses.

Match No. 323/15

INDIA v PAKISTAN 1984-85

Rothmans Four Nations Trophy – Semi-Final

At Sharjah CA Stadium, UAE on 22 March 1985.
Toss: Pakistan. Result: INDIA won by 38 runs.
50 overs match. Award: Imran Khan.
No débuts.

Imran became the first Pakistan bowler to take six wickets in these matches. Gavaskar equalled the non-wicket-keeping record for most catches.

INDIA		
R.J. Shastri	lbw b Imran	0
K. Srikkanth	c Salim b Imran	6
M. Azharuddin	b Tausif	47
D.B. Vengsarkar	c Ashraf b Imran	1
S.M. Gavaskar*	c Ashraf b Imran	2
M. Amarnath	b Imran	5
Kapil Dev	b Tausif	30
R.M.H. Binny	c Miandad b Mudassar	8
Madan Lal	c Ashraf b Imran	11
S. Viswanath†	not out	3
L. Sivaramakrishnan	c Salim b Wasim	1
Extras	(B 5, LB 4, W 2)	11
Total	(42.4 overs)	**125**

Fall of wickets: 1-0, 2-12, 3-20, 4-28, 5-34, 6-80, 7-95, 8-113, 9-121, 10-125.

PAKISTAN	*O*	*M*	*R*	*W*
Imran Khan	10	2	14	6
Wasim Akram	7.4	0	27	1
Tahir Naqqash	5	0	12	0
Mudassar Nazar	10	1	36	1
Tausif Ahmed	10	0	27	2

PAKISTAN		
Mudassar Nazar	c Gavaskar b Binny	18
Mohsin Khan	run out	10
Ramiz Raja	c Gavaskar b Kapil Dev	29
Javed Miandad*	c Gavaskar b Shastri	0
Ashraf Ali†	c Vengsarkar b Sivaramakrishnan	0
Imran Khan	st Viswanath b Sivaramakrishnan	0
Salim Malik	c Gavaskar b Shastri	17
Manzoor Elahi	c and b Madan Lal	9
Tahir Naqqash	c Viswanath b Kapil Dev	1
Tausif Ahmed	b Kapil Dev	0
Wasim Akram	not out	0
Extras	(LB 1, W 1, NB 1)	3
Total	(32.5 overs)	**87**

Fall of wickets: 1-13, 2-35, 3-40, 4-41, 5-41, 6-74, 7-85, 8-87, 9-87, 10-87.

INDIA	*O*	*M*	*R*	*W*
Kapil Dev	6.5	1	17	3
Binny	3	0	24	1
Sivaramakrishnan	7	2	16	2
Shastri	10	5	17	2
Madan Lal	6	2	12	1

Umpires: H.D. Bird and M.W. Johnson.

No-balls and wides debited to bowlers' analyses.

AUSTRALIA v ENGLAND 1984-85

Rothmans Four Nations Trophy – Semi-Final

At Sharjah CA Stadium, UAE on 24 March 1985.
Toss: Australia. Result: AUSTRALIA won by 2 wickets.
50 overs match. Award: G.R.J. Matthews.

Débuts: England – N. Gifford, C.M. Wells.

ENGLAND		
G. Fowler	c Hughes b Alderman	26
R.T. Robinson	c Rixon b Matthews	37
M.D. Moxon	lbw b O'Donnell	0
D.W. Randall	st Rixon b Bennett	19
C.M. Wells	lbw b Bennett	17
D.R. Pringle	st Rixon b Border	4
P.H. Edmonds	not out	15
B.N. French†	c Rixon b Border	4
R.M. Ellison	c Wessels b Border	24
N.A. Foster	not out	5
N. Gifford*		
Extras	(B 9, LB 5, W 6, NB 6)	26
Total	(50 overs – 8 wickets)	**177**

Fall of wickets: 1-47, 2-53, 3-95, 4-109, 5-123, 6-128, 7-134, 8-169.

AUSTRALIA	*O*	*M*	*R*	*W*
Alderman	7	1	36	1
McCurdy	5	0	23	0
O'Donnell	8	2	26	1
Bennett	10	2	27	2
Matthews	10	3	15	1
Border	7	0	21	3
Wessels	3	0	15	0

AUSTRALIA		
K.C. Wessels	b Edmonds	16
G.M. Wood	c French b Pringle	35
D.M. Jones	c Moxon b Edmonds	27
A.R. Border*	c and b Pringle	9
K.J. Hughes	c French b Foster	14
G.R.J. Matthews	c Foster b Ellison	24
S.P. O'Donnell	c Moxon b Ellison	19
S.J. Rixon†	not out	11
M.J. Bennett	run out	0
R.J. McCurdy	not out	6
T.M. Alderman		
Extras	(LB 9, W 8)	17
Total	(50 overs – 8 wickets)	**178**

Fall of wickets: 1-54, 2-64, 3-82, 4-100, 5-120, 6-151, 7-168, 8-168.

ENGLAND	*O*	*M*	*R*	*W*
Foster	10	1	34	1
Ellison	10	1	28	2
Pringle	10	0	49	2
Edmonds	10	2	31	2
Gifford	10	1	27	0

Umpires: Khizer Hayat and Swaroop Kishen.

No-balls and wides debited to bowlers' analyses.

Match No. 325/16

ENGLAND v PAKISTAN 1984-85

Rothmans Four Nations Trophy – Plate-Winner's Final

At Sharjah CA Stadium, UAE on 26 March 1985.
Toss: England. Result: PAKISTAN won by 43 runs.
50 overs match. Award: Javed Miandad.

Débuts: England – R.J. Bailey, P.I. Pocock.

PAKISTAN		
Mudassar Nazar	c French b Gifford	36
Mohsin Khan	c Robinson b Pringle	13
Ramiz Raja	c Robinson b Pringle	16
Javed Miandad*	c Gifford b Edmonds	71
Salim Malik	lbw b Gifford	2
Imran Khan	c Pringle b Gifford	0
Shoaib Mohammad	st French b Gifford	3
Ashraf Ali†	not out	19
Tahir Naqqash	not out	2
Tausif Ahmed		
Wasim Akram		
Extras	(B 1, LB 9, W 2, NB 1)	13
Total	(50 overs – 7 wickets)	**175**

Fall of wickets: 1-24, 2-43, 3-107, 4-113, 5-113, 6-125, 7-172.

ENGLAND	*O*	*M*	*R*	*W*
Ellison	7	1	18	0
Pringle	7	1	32	2
Edmonds	10	0	47	1
Pocock	10	1	20	0
Gifford	10	0	23	4
Bailey	6	0	25	0

ENGLAND		
G. Fowler	c Miandad b Tausif	19
R.T. Robinson	b Tahir	9
M.D. Moxon	b Shoaib	11
C.M. Wells	b Shoaib	5
R.J. Bailey	not out	41
D.R. Pringle	b Wasim	13
P.H. Edmonds	c and b Shoaib	3
R.M. Ellison	b Wasim	3
B.N. French†	c Shoaib b Tahir	7
N. Gifford*	c Miandad b Imran	0
P.I. Pocock	run out	4
Extras	(B 1, LB 12, NB 4)	17
Total	(48.2 overs)	**132**

Fall of wickets: 1-19, 2-35, 3-48, 4-49, 5-76, 6-89, 7-98, 8-117, 9-132, 10-132.

PAKISTAN	*O*	*M*	*R*	*W*
Imran Khan	9	2	26	1
Wasim Akram	10	0	28	2
Tahir Naqqash	9.2	1	20	2
Tausif Ahmed	10	1	25	1
Shoaib Mohammad	10	1	20	3

Umpires: M.W. Johnson and Swaroop Kishen.

No-balls and wides debited to bowlers' analyses.

AUSTRALIA v INDIA 1984-85

Rothmans Four Nations Trophy – Final

At Sharjah CA Stadium, UAE on 29 March 1985.
Toss: India. Result: INDIA won by 3 wickets.
50 overs match. Award: M. Amarnath.
No débuts.

AUSTRALIA		
G.M. Wood	run out	27
K.C. Wessels	c Gavaskar b Madan Lal	30
D.M. Jones	c Viswanath b Madan Lal	8
A.R. Border*	c and b Amarnath	27
K.J. Hughes	c and b Amarnath	11
G.R.J. Matthews	lbw b Kapil Dev	11
S.P. O'Donnell	run out	3
S.J. Rixon†	run out	4
M.J. Bennett	lbw b Shastri	0
R.J. McCurdy	c Vengsarkar b Shastri	0
C.J. McDermott	not out	0
Extras	(LB 13, W 5)	18
Total	(42.3 overs)	**139**

Fall of wickets: 1-60, 2-71, 3-78, 4-114, 5-115, 6-131, 7-138, 8-139, 9-139, 10-139.

INDIA	*O*	*M*	*R*	*W*
Kapil Dev	6	3	9	1
Binny	5	0	25	0
Madan Lal	7	0	30	2
Sivaramakrishnan	8	1	29	0
Shastri	9.3	1	14	2
Amarnath	7	1	19	2

INDIA		
R.J. Shastri	c Rixon b O'Donnell	9
K. Srikkanth	lbw b McDermott	0
M. Azharuddin	c Jones b McDermott	22
D.B. Vengsarkar	b McDermott	35
S.M. Gavaskar	run out	20
M. Amarnath	not out	24
Kapil Dev*	b Matthews	1
R.M.H. Binny	b Matthews	2
Madan Lal	not out	7
S. Viswanath†		
L. Sivaramakrishnan		
Extras	(LB 9, W 7, NB 4)	20
Total	(39.2 overs – 7 wickets)	**140**

Fall of wickets: 1-2, 2-37, 3-41, 4-98, 5-103, 6-117, 7-120.

AUSTRALIA	*O*	*M*	*R*	*W*
McDermott	10	0	36	3
McCurdy	4	1	10	0
O'Donnell	4	1	11	1
Bennett	10	0	35	0
Matthews	10	1	33	2
Border	1.2	0	6	0

Umpires: H.D. Bird and Khizer Hayat.

No-balls and wides debited to bowlers' analyses.

Match No. 327/31

ENGLAND v AUSTRALIA 1985 (1st Match)

Texaco Trophy

At Old Trafford, Manchester on 30 May 1985.
Toss: England. Result: AUSTRALIA won by 3 wickets.
55 overs match. Award: I.T. Botham.
No débuts.

ENGLAND		
G.A. Gooch	c O'Donnell b Holland	57
G. Fowler	c Phillips b McDermott	10
D.I. Gower*	b Lawson	3
A.J. Lamb	c Phillips b Lawson	0
I.T. Botham	b Matthews	72
M.W. Gatting	not out	31
P. Willey	b Holland	12
P.R. Downton†	c Matthews b Lawson	11
P.H. Edmonds	c Border b Lawson	0
P.J.W. Allott	b McDermott	2
N.G. Cowans	c and b McDermott	1
Extras	(B 2, LB 7, W 2, NB 9)	20
Total	(54 overs)	**219**

Fall of wickets 1-21, 2-27, 3-27, 4-143, 5-160, 6-181, 7-203, 8-203, 9-213, 10-219.

AUSTRALIA	*O*	*M*	*R*	*W*
Lawson	10	1	26	4
McDermott	11	0	46	3
O'Donnell	11	0	44	0
Matthews	11	1	45	1
Holland	11	2	49	2

AUSTRALIA		
K.C. Wessels	c Botham b Willey	39
G.M. Wood	c Downton b Cowans	8
D.M. Wellham	c and b Edmonds	12
A.R. Border*	c and b Allott	59
D.C. Boon	c Botham b Gooch	12
W.B. Phillips†	c Gatting b Cowans	28
S.P. O'Donnell	b Botham	1
G.R.J. Matthews	not out	29
G.F. Lawson	not out	14
C.J. McDermott		
R.G. Holland		
Extras	(B 2, LB 12, W 4)	18
Total	(54.1 overs – 7 wickets)	**220**

Fall of wickets 1-15, 2-52, 3-74, 4-118, 5-156, 6-157, 7-186.

ENGLAND	*O*	*M*	*R*	*W*
Cowans	10.1	1	44	2
Botham	11	2	41	1
Allott	11	0	47	1
Edmonds	11	2	33	1
Willey	9	1	31	1
Gooch	2	0	10	1

Umpires: D.G.L. Evans and K.E. Palmer.

No-balls and wides debited to bowlers' analyses.

ENGLAND v AUSTRALIA 1985 (2nd Match)
Texaco Trophy

At Edgbaston, Birmingham on 1 June 1985.
Toss: Australia. Result: AUSTRALIA won by 4 wickets.
55 overs match. Award: A.R. Border.
No débuts.

ENGLAND		
G.A. Gooch	b McDermott	115
R.T. Robinson	c and b O'Donnell	26
D.I. Gower*	c Phillips b O'Donnell	0
A.J. Lamb	b Thomson	25
I.T. Botham	c Wellham b Lawson	29
M.W. Gatting	c Lawson b McDermott	6
P. Willey	c Phillips b Lawson	0
P.R. Downton†	not out	16
P.H. Edmonds	not out	6
P.J.W. Allott		
N.G. Cowans		
Extras	(LB 2, W 2, NB 4)	8
Total	(55 overs – 7 wickets)	**231**

Fall of wickets 1-63, 2-69, 3-134, 4-193, 5-206, 6-208, 7-216.

AUSTRALIA	*O*	*M*	*R*	*W*
Lawson	11	0	53	2
McDermott	11	0	56	2
O'Donnell	11	2	32	2
Thomson	11	0	47	1
Matthews	10	0	38	0
Border	1	0	3	0

AUSTRALIA		
K.C. Wessels	c and b Willey	57
G.M. Wood	lbw b Cowans	5
D.M. Wellham	lbw b Botham	7
A.R. Border*	not out	85
D.C. Boon	b Allott	13
W.B. Phillips†	c Gatting b Cowans	14
S.P. O'Donnell	b Botham	28
G.R.J. Matthews	not out	8
G.F. Lawson		
C.J. McDermott		
J.R. Thomson		
Extras	(LB 13, W 2, NB 1)	16
Total	(54 overs – 6 wickets)	**233**

Fall of wickets 1-10, 2-19, 3-116, 4-137, 5-157, 6-222.

ENGLAND	*O*	*M*	*R*	*W*
Botham	10	2	38	2
Cowans	11	2	42	2
Allott	10	1	40	1
Willey	11	1	38	1
Edmonds	10	0	48	0
Gooch	2	0	14	0

Umpires: D.J. Constant and D.R. Shepherd.

No-balls and wides debited to bowlers' analyses.

Match No. 329/33

ENGLAND v AUSTRALIA 1985 (3rd Match)

Texaco Trophy

At Lord's, London on 3 June 1985.
Toss: England. Result: ENGLAND won by 8 wickets.
55 overs match. Award: D.I. Gower.

No débuts.

Botham became the first player to complete the double of 1,000 runs and 100 wickets in one-day internationals when he dismissed Ritchie. Gower extended his England record number of hundreds to seven and shared with Gooch a national record partnership for any wicket (202).

AUSTRALIA		
G.M. Wood	not out	114
A.M.J. Hilditch	lbw b Foster	4
G.M. Ritchie	c Gooch b Botham	15
A.R. Border*	b Gooch	44
D.C. Boon	c Gower b Willey	45
W.B. Phillips†	run out	10
S.P. O'Donnell	not out	0
G.R.J. Matthews		
G.F. Lawson		
C.J. McDermott		
J.R. Thomson		
Extras	(B 2, LB 13, W 6, NB 1)	22
Total	(55 overs – 5 wickets)	**254**

Fall of wickets 1-6, 2-47, 3-143, 4-228, 5-252.

ENGLAND	*O*	*M*	*R*	*W*
Cowans	8	2	22	0
Foster	11	0	55	1
Botham	8	1	27	1
Allott	7	1	45	0
Gooch	11	0	46	1
Willey	10	1	44	1

ENGLAND		
G.A. Gooch	not out	117
R.T. Robinson	lbw b McDermott	7
D.I. Gower*	c Border b McDermott	102
A.J. Lamb	not out	9
I.T. Botham		
M.W. Gatting		
P. Willey		
P.R. Downton†		
N.A. Foster		
P.J.W. Allott		
N.G. Cowans		
Extras	(B 2, LB 9, W 2, NB 9)	22
Total	(49 overs – 2 wickets)	**257**

Fall of wickets 1-25, 2-227.

AUSTRALIA	*O*	*M*	*R*	*W*
Lawson	9	0	37	0
McDermott	10	0	51	2
Thomson	8	1	50	0
O'Donnell	11	0	54	0
Matthews	10	0	49	0
Border	1	0	5	0

Umpires: H.D. Bird and B.J. Meyer.

No-balls and wides debited to bowlers' analyses.

ONE-DAY INTERNATIONAL RECORDS 1970-71 to 1985

RESULTS SUMMARY

RESULTS OF ONE-DAY INTERNATIONAL MATCHES 1970-71 to 1985

(*329 MATCHES*)

		Matches	*E*	*A*	*I*	*NZ*	*P*	*SL*	*WI*	*C*	*EA*	*Z*	*Tied*	*NR*
England	v Australia	33	17	15	–	–	–	–	–	–	–	–	–	1
	v India	15	10	–	5	–	–	–	–	–	–	–	–	–
	v New Zealand	21	10	–	–	8	–	–	–	–	–	–	–	3
	v Pakistan	16	10	–	–	–	6	–	–	–	–	–	–	–
	v Sri Lanka	4	3	–	–	–	–	1	–	–	–	–	–	–
	v West Indies	18	4	–	–	–	–	–	14	–	–	–	–	–
	v Canada	1	1	–	–	–	–	–	–	–	–	–	–	–
	v East Africa	1	1	–	–	–	–	–	–	–	–	–	–	–
Australia	v India	13	–	8	4	–	–	–	–	–	–	–	–	1
	v New Zealand	21	–	13	–	7	–	–	–	–	–	–	–	1
	v Pakistan	16	–	7	–	–	7	–	–	–	–	–	–	2
	v Sri Lanka	10	–	5	–	–	–	3	–	–	–	–	–	2
	v West Indies	40	–	11	–	–	–	–	28	–	–	–	1	–
	v Canada	1	–	1	–	–	–	–	–	–	–	–	–	–
	v Zimbabwe	2	–	1	–	–	–	–	–	–	–	1	–	–
India	v New Zealand	12	–	–	3	9	–	–	–	–	–	–	–	–
	v Pakistan	15	–	–	8	–	6	–	–	–	–	–	–	1
	v Sri Lanka	5	–	–	4	–	–	1	–	–	–	–	–	–
	v West Indies	12	–	–	3	–	–	–	9	–	–	–	–	–
	v East Africa	1	–	–	1	–	–	–	–	–	–	–	–	–
	v Zimbabwe	2	–	–	2	–	–	–	–	–	–	–	–	–
New Zealand	v Pakistan	12	–	–	–	7	4	–	–	–	–	–	–	1
	v Sri Lanka	12	–	–	–	9	–	3	–	–	–	–	–	–
	v West Indies	10	–	–	–	1	–	–	8	–	–	–	–	1
	v East Africa	1	–	–	–	1	–	–	–	–	–	–	–	–
Pakistan	v Sri Lanka	7	–	–	–	–	5	2	–	–	–	–	–	–
	v West Indies	18	–	–	–	–	3	–	15	–	–	–	–	–
	v Canada	1	–	–	–	–	1	–	–	–	–	–	–	–
Sri Lanka	v West Indies	7	–	–	–	–	–	–	7	–	–	–	–	–
West Indies	v Zimbabwe	2	–	–	–	–	–	–	2	–	–	–	–	–
		329	56	61	30	42	32	10	83	–	–	1	1	13

	Matches	*Won*	*Lost*	*Tied*	*No Result*
England	109	56	49	–	4
Australia	136	61	67	1	7
India	75	30	43	–	2
New Zealand	89	42	41	–	6
Pakistan	85	32	49	–	4
Sri Lanka	45	10	33	–	2
West Indies	107	83	22	1	1
Canada	3	–	3	–	–
East Africa	3	–	3	–	–
Zimbabwe	6	1	5	–	–

TEAM RECORDS

HIGHEST INNINGS TOTALS

338-5	(60 overs)	Pakistan v Sri Lanka	Swansea	1983
334-4	(60 overs)	England v India	Lord's	1975
333-9	(60 overs)	England v Sri Lanka	Taunton	1983
333-8	(45 overs)	West Indies v India	Jamshedpur	1983-84
330-6	(60 overs)	Pakistan v Sri Lanka	Nottingham	1975
328-5	(60 overs)	Australia v Sri Lanka	The Oval	1975
323-2	(50 overs)	Australia v Sri Lanka	Adelaide	1984-85
322-6	(60 overs)	England v New Zealand	The Oval	1983
320-8	(55 overs)	England v Australia	Birmingham	1980
320-9	(60 overs)	Australia v India	Nottingham	1983
313-9	(50 overs)	West Indies v Australia	St John's	1977-78
309-5	(60 overs)	New Zealand v East Africa	Birmingham	1975
309-6	(50 overs)	West Indies v Sri Lanka	Perth	1984-85
304-5	(50 overs)	New Zealand v Sri Lanka	Auckland	1982-83
302-8	(50 overs)	Australia v New Zealand	Melbourne	1982-83

HIGHEST TOTAL BATTING SECOND

297-6	(48.5 overs)	New Zealand v England	Adelaide	1982-83

HIGHEST TOTAL BATTING SECOND AND LOSING

288-9	(60 overs)	Sri Lanka v Pakistan	Swansea	1983

HIGHEST MATCH AGGREGATES

626-14	(120 overs)	Pakistan v Sri Lanka	Swansea	1983
619-19	(118 overs)	England v Sri Lanka	Taunton	1983
604-9	(120 overs)	Australia v Sri Lanka	The Oval	1975
593-13	(110 overs)	England v Australia	Birmingham	1980
593-11	(98.5 overs)	England v New Zealand	Adelaide	1982-83

LOWEST INNINGS TOTALS

(Excluding abbreviated matches)

45	(40.3 overs)	Canada v England	Manchester	1979
63	(25.5 overs)	India v Australia	Sydney	1980-81
70	(25.2 overs)	Australia v England	Birmingham	1977
74	(29 overs)	New Zealand v Australia	Wellington	1981-82
79	(34.2 overs)	India v Pakistan	Sialkot	1978-79
5	(47 overs)	Pakistan v England	Manchester	1978
6	(37.2 overs)	Sri Lanka v West Indies	Manchester	1975
7	(32.5 overs)	Pakistan v India	Sharjah	1984-85
1	(35.5 overs)	Sri Lanka v Australia	Adelaide	1984-85
3	(36.2 overs)	England v Australia	Leeds	1975
4	(31.7 overs)	England v Australia	Melbourne	1978-79
4	(52.3 overs)	East Africa v England	Birmingham	1975
6	(41 overs)	Sri Lanka v India	Sharjah	1983-84

LOWEST MATCH AGGREGATES

91-12	(54.2 overs)	England v Canada	Manchester	1979
127-11	(46.5 overs)	Australia v India	Sydney	1980-81
149-12	(49.3 overs)	New Zealand v Australia	Wellington	1981-82
162-12	(51.1 overs)	Pakistan v India	Sialkot	1978-79

LARGEST MARGINS OF VICTORY

Runs

232 runs	Australia beat Sri Lanka	Adelaide	1984-85
202 runs	England beat India	Lord's	1975
196 runs	England beat East Africa	Birmingham	1975
192 runs	Pakistan beat Sri Lanka	Nottingham	1975

Wickets

10 wickets	India beat East Africa	Leeds	1975
10 wickets	New Zealand beat India	Melbourne	1980-81
10 wickets	West Indies beat Zimbabwe	Birmingham	1983
10 wickets	India beat Sri Lanka	Sharjah	1983-84
10 wickets	West Indies beat New Zealand	Port-of-Spain	1984-85

TIED MATCH

Australia	222-9	West Indies	222-5	Melbourne	1984

SMALLEST MARGINS OF VICTORY

(*Excluding abbreviated matches*)

Runs

1 run	New Zealand beat Pakistan	Sialkot	1976-77
1 run	New Zealand beat Australia	Sydney	1980-81
2 runs	West Indies beat England	Melbourne	1979-80
2 runs	West Indies beat England	Arnos Vale	1980-81
2 runs	Australia beat England	Birmingham	1981
2 runs	New Zealand beat England	Melbourne	1982-83

Wickets

1 wicket	England beat West Indies	Leeds	1973
1 wicket	West Indies beat Pakistan	Birmingham	1975
1 wicket	New Zealand beat West Indies	Christchurch	1979-80
1 wicket	West Indies beat Pakistan	Adelaide	1983-84
1 wicket	Pakistan beat New Zealand	Multan	1984-85

PLAYERS' RECORDS – BATTING

HUNDREDS IN ONE-DAY INTERNATIONALS

189*	I.V.A. Richards	West Indies v England	Manchester	1984
175*	Kapil Dev	India v Zimbabwe	Tunbridge Wells	1983
171*	G.M. Turner	New Zealand v East Africa	Birmingham	1975
158	D.I. Gower	England v New Zealand	Brisbane	1982-83
153*	I.V.A. Richards	West Indies v Australia	Melbourne	1979-80
149	I.V.A. Richards	West Indies v India	Jamshedpur	1983-84
148	D.L. Haynes	West Indies v Australia	St John's	1977-78
145*	D.L. Haynes	West Indies v New Zealand	Berbice	1984-8
140	G.M. Turner	New Zealand v Sri Lanka	Auckland	1982-8
138*	I.V.A. Richards	West Indies v England	Lord's	197
138*	G.S. Chappell	Australia v New Zealand	Sydney	1980-8
137	D.L. Amiss	England v India	Lord's	197

133*	D.L. Haynes	West Indies v Australia	Berbice	1983-84
131	K.W.R. Fletcher	England v New Zealand	Nottingham	1975
130	D.I. Gower	England v Sri Lanka	Taunton	1983
127*	A.R. Border	Australia v West Indies	Sydney	1984-85
125*	G.S. Chappell	Australia v England	The Oval	1977
123	Zaheer Abbas	Pakistan v Sri Lanka	Lahore	1981-82
123*	D.L. Haynes	West Indies v Australia	Melbourne	1984-85
122	D.I. Gower	England v New Zealand	Melbourne	1982-83
121	R.L. Dias	Sri Lanka v India	Bangalore	1982-83
119*	I.V.A. Richards	West Indies v England	Scarborough	1976
119*	Javed Miandad	Pakistan v India	Lahore	1982-83
119	I.V.A. Richards	West Indies v India	The Oval	1983
118	A.J. Lamb	England v Pakistan	Nottingham	1982
118	Zaheer Abbas	Pakistan v India	Multan	1982-83
118*	A.R. Border	Australia v Sri Lanka	Adelaide	1984-85
117*	C.T. Radley	England v New Zealand	Manchester	1978
117*	B.M. Laird	Australia v West Indies	Sydney	1981-82
117*	Mohsin Khan	Pakistan v India	Multan	1982-83
117	S.B. Smith	Australia v New Zealand	Melbourne	1982-83
117*	G.A. Gooch	England v Australia	Lord's	1985
116*	D. Lloyd	England v Pakistan	Nottingham	1974
116	D.L. Haynes	West Indies v New Zealand	Bridgetown	1984-85
115	C.G. Greenidge	West Indies v India	Jamshedpur	1983-84
115*	M.W. Gatting	England v India	Poona	1984-85
115	G.A. Gooch	England v Australia	Birmingham	1985
114*	G.M. Turner	New Zealand v India	Manchester	1975
114*	D.I. Gower	England v Pakistan	The Oval	1978
114*	G.M. Wood	Australia v England	Lord's	1985
113	Zaheer Abbas	Pakistan v India	Karachi	1982-83
110	T.M. Chappell	Australia v India	Nottingham	1983
110*	C.G. Greenidge	West Indies v Sri Lanka	Adelaide	1984-85
109	Majid Khan	Pakistan v England	Nottingham	1974
109	Zaheer Abbas	Pakistan v Australia	Lahore	1982-83
109	D.I. Gower	England v New Zealand	Adelaide	1982-83
108	D.L. Amiss	England v Australia	The Oval	1977
108	G.A. Gooch	England v Australia	Birmingham	1980
108	G.M. Wood	Australia v England	Leeds	1981
108	Zaheer Abbas	Pakistan v Australia	Sydney	1981-82
108	G.S. Chappell	Australia v New Zealand	Auckland	1981-82
108*	A.J. Lamb	England v New Zealand	Sydney	1982-83
108*	D.L. Haynes	West Indies v Australia	Sydney	1983-84
107	K.C. Wessels	Australia v India	New Delhi	1984-85
106*	C.G. Greenidge	West Indies v India	Birmingham	1979
106*	Javed Miandad	Pakistan v India	Gujranwala	1982-83
106	I.V.A. Richards	West Indies v Australia	Melbourne	1983-84
106	S.B. Smith	Australia v Pakistan	Sydney	1983-84
105	R.C. Fredericks	West Indies v England	The Oval	1973
105	G. Boycott	England v Australia	Sydney	1979-80
105*	A.R. Border	Australia v India	Sydney	1980-81
105	Zaheer Abbas	Pakistan v India	Lahore	1982-83
105*	C.G. Greenidge	West Indies v Zimbabwe	Worcester	1983
105*	M.D. Crowe	New Zealand v England	Auckland	1983-84
105	D.B. Vengsarkar	India v England	Poona	1984
104	K.J. Wadsworth	New Zealand v Australia	Christchurch	1973-74
104	Mohsin Khan	Pakistan v Australia	Hyderabad	1982-83
104*	D.L. Haynes	West Indies v Australia	Kingston	1983-84
104*	G.M. Wood	Australia v West Indies	Adelaide	1984-85
103	D.L. Amiss	England v Australia	Manchester	1972
103	C.G. Greenidge	West Indies v New Zealand	Christchurch	1979-80
103	C.G. Greenidge	West Indies v Pakistan	Melbourne	1981-82
103*	Zaheer Abbas	Pakistan v New Zealand	Nottingham	1983
103*	I.V.A. Richards	West Indies v Australia	Sydney	1984-85
02	C.H. Lloyd	West Indies v Australia	Lord's	1975
02*	B.A. Edgar	New Zealand v Australia	Melbourne	1980-81
02	R.L. Dias	Sri Lanka v India	Delhi	1982-83
02	A.J. Lamb	England v New Zealand	The Oval	1983
02*	Imran Khan	Pakistan v Sri Lanka	Leeds	1983

102*	D.L. Haynes	West Indies v Australia	Castries	1983-84
102	R.J. Shastri	India v Australia	Indore	1984-85
102	R.J. Shastri	India v England	Cuttack	1984-85
102	D.I. Gower	England v Australia	Lord's	1985
101	B.E. Congdon	New Zealand v England	Wellington	1974-75
101	A. Turner	Australia v Sri Lanka	The Oval	1975
101*	D.I. Gower	England v Australia	Melbourne	1978-79
101	H.A. Gomes	West Indies v Sri Lanka	Perth	1984-85
100	D.L. Amiss	England v New Zealand	Swansea	1973

MOST HUNDREDS

8 I.V.A. Richards (West Indies) and D.L. Haynes (West Indies)
7 Zaheer Abbas (Pakistan) and D.I. Gower (England)
6 C.G. Greenidge (West Indies).

HUNDRED ON DÉBUT

D.L. Amiss	103	England v Australia	Manchester	1972
D.L. Haynes	148	West Indies v Australia	St John's	1977-78

HUNDRED PARTNERSHIPS

First Wicket

188	K. Srikkanth/R.J. Shastri	India v England	Cuttack	1984-85
182	R.B. McCosker/A. Turner	Australia v Sri Lanka	The Oval	1975
182	C.G. Greenidge/D.L. Haynes	West Indies v Pakistan	Melbourne	1981-82
172*	D.L. Haynes/S.F.A.F. Bacchus	West Indies v Zimbabwe	Birmingham	1983
161	D.L. Amiss/J.M. Brearley	England v Australia	The Oval	1977
159	Sadiq Mohammad/Majid Khan	Pakistan v Sri Lanka	Nottingham	1975
158	B. Wood/D.L. Amiss	England v East Africa	Birmingham	1975
154	G.A. Gooch/G. Boycott	England v Australia	Birmingham	1980
154	K.C. Wessels/J. Dyson	Australia v New Zealand	Melbourne	1982-83
152	G.M. Turner/B.A. Edgar	New Zealand v England	Wellington	1982-83
149	C.G. Greenidge/D.L. Haynes	West Indies v India	Indore	1983-84
141	Mudassar Nazar/Mohsin Khan	Pakistan v Australia	Melbourne	1984-85
140	G.M. Wood/S.B. Smith	Australia v New Zealand	Melbourne	1982-83
138	C.G. Greenidge/D.L. Haynes	West Indies v India	Birmingham	1979
135	P. Willey/G. Boycott	England v West Indies	Lord's	1980
135	S.B. Smith/G.M. Wood	Australia v West Indies	Melbourne	1984-85
133	B. Wood/C.J. Tavaré	England v India	Leeds	1982
133	C.G. Greenidge/D.L. Haynes	West Indies v Sri Lanka	Adelaide	1984-85
132	C.G. Greenidge/D.L. Haynes	West Indies v Pakistan	The Oval	1979
132	G.M. Turner/B.A. Edgar	New Zealand v Sri Lanka	Auckland	1982-83
129	J.M. Brearley/G. Boycott	England v West Indies	Lord's	1979
128	C.G. Greenidge/D.L. Haynes	West Indies v Sri Lanka	Sydney	1984-85
125	C.G. Greenidge/D.L. Haynes	West Indies v India	Port-of-Spain	1982-83
124	R.J. Shastri/K. Srikkanth	India v Australia	Melbourne	1984-85
123*	S.M. Gavaskar/F.M. Engineer	India v East Africa	Leeds	1975
117*	D.L. Haynes/R.B. Richardson	West Indies v New Zealand	Port-of-Spain	1984-85
115	G. Fowler/C.J. Tavaré	England v Pakistan	Manchester	1983
113	Sadiq Mohammad/Majid Khan	Pakistan v England	Nottingham	1974
113*	J.G. Wright/B.A. Edgar	New Zealand v India	Melbourne	1980-81
109	C.G. Greenidge/D.L. Haynes	West Indies v England	Brisbane	1979-80
109	G.A. Gooch/G. Cook	England v Sri Lanka	Colombo	1981-82
108	G.A. Gooch/G. Boycott	England v Australia	The Oval	1980
108*	C.G. Greenidge/D.L. Haynes	West Indies v India	Srinagar	1983-84
106	K.C. Wessels/S.B. Smith	Australia v West Indies	Berbice	1983-84
104	B.M. Laird/G.M. Wood	Australia v Pakistan	Hyderabad	1982-83
104	R.J. Shastri/R.M.H. Binny	India v Australia	Ahmedabad	1984-85
103	J.M. Wiener/R.B. McCosker	Australia v West Indies	Sydney	1979-80
103	R.J. Shastri/K. Srikkanth	India v Pakistan	Melbourne	1984-85
102	Mudassar Nazar/Mohsin Khan	Pakistan v England	Nottingham	1982

101	G.M. Turner/B.A. Edgar	New Zealand v England	Auckland	1982-83
101	S. Wettimuny/E.R.N.S. Fernando	Sri Lanka v Australia	Colombo	1982-83
100	J.G. Wright/B.A. Edgar	New Zealand v India	Leeds	1979

Second Wicket

221	C.G. Greenidge/I.V.A. Richards	West Indies v India	Jamshedpur	1983-84
205	D.L. Haynes/I.V.A. Richards	West Indies v Australia	Melbourne	1979-80
205	Mohsin Khan/Zaheer Abbas	Pakistan v India	Multan	1982-83
202	G.A. Gooch/D.I. Gower	England v Australia	Lord's	1985
184	D.L. Haynes/H.A. Gomes	West Indies v New Zealand	Bridgetown	1984-85
176	D.L. Amiss/K.W.R. Fletcher	England v India	Lord's	1975
176	S.F.A.F. Bacchus/I.V.A. Richards	West Indies v Pakistan	Sialkot	1980-81
170	S. Wettimuny/R.L. Dias	Sri Lanka v India	Delhi	1982-83
170	Mudassar Nazar/Zaheer Abbas	Pakistan v India	Karachi	1982-83
167	D.L. Haynes/R.B. Richardson	West Indies v Australia	Berbice	1983-84
166	Majid Khan/Zaheer Abbas	Pakistan v West Indies	The Oval	1979
157*	S.B. Smith/W.B. Phillips	Australia v Sri Lanka	Perth	1984-85
151	J. Dyson/G.S. Chappell	Australia v New Zealand	Sydney	1980-81
148	R.D. Robinson/G.S. Chappell	Australia v England	The Oval	1977
145	G.M. Wood/G.S. Chappell	Australia v New Zealand	Melbourne	1980-81
144	T.M. Chappell/K.J. Hughes	Australia v India	Nottingham	1983
143	R.C. Fredericks/A.I. Kallicharran	West Indies v England	The Oval	1973
139	B. Warnapura/R.L. Dias	Sri Lanka v Pakistan	Karachi	1981-82
138	C.G. Greenidge/I.V.A. Richards	West Indies v Australia	Sydney	1981-82
136	K.R. Stackpole/I.M. Chappell	Australia v New Zealand	Dunedin	1973-74
134	K. Srikkanth/D.B. Vengsarkar	India v Sri Lanka	Delhi	1982-83
132*	R.B. Richardson/H.A. Gomes	West Indies v Australia	Sydney	1983-84
131*	D.L. Haynes/R.B. Richardson	West Indies v Australia	Kingston	1983-84
130	G.M. Wood/G.N. Yallop	Australia v England	Leeds	1981
128	K.C. Wessels/K.J. Hughes	Australia v India	New Delhi	1984-85
127*	A.R. Border/G.S. Chappell	Australia v India	Sydney	1980-81
126*	G.M. Turner/G.P. Howarth	New Zealand v Sri Lanka	Nottingham	1979
125	D.L. Amiss/K.W.R. Fletcher	England v Australia	Manchester	1972
125	C.G. Greenidge/A.I. Kallicharran	West Indies v New Zealand	The Oval	1975
124	R.C. Fredericks/A.I. Kallicharran	West Indies v Australia	The Oval	1975
124	C.G. Greenidge/I.V.A. Richards	West Indies v Australia	Lord's	1983
119	A.D. Gaekwad/S. Amarnath	India v Pakistan	Sahiwal	1978-79
119	C.G. Greenidge/I.V.A. Richards	West Indies v England	Sydney	1979-80
119	K. Srikkanth/D.B. Vengsarkar	India v Sri Lanka	Bangalore	1982-83
118	G. Boycott/P. Willey	England v Australia	Sydney	1979-80
118	K. Srikkanth/D.B. Vengsarkar	India v England	Poona	1984-85
115	S.M. Gavaskar/S.M. Patil	India v Pakistan	Lahore	1982-83
112	C.G. Greenidge/I.V.A. Richards	West Indies v Australia	Melbourne	1981-82
111	G.A. Gooch/C.T. Radley	England v New Zealand	Scarborough	1978
111	G. Boycott/P. Willey	England v Australia	Sydney	1979-80
109*	C.G. Greenidge/I.V.A. Richards	West Indies v England	Brisbane	1979-80
109	K.C. Wessels/K.J. Hughes	Australia v West Indies	Melbourne	1983-84
107	C.J. Tavaré/A.J. Lamb	England v Pakistan	Nottingham	1982
105	Mudassar Nazar/Zaheer Abbas	Pakistan v Australia	Sydney	1981-82
105	Mohsin Khan/Javed Miandad	Pakistan v Sri Lanka	Karachi	1981-82
103	J.G. Wright/G.P. Howarth	New Zealand v Australia	Sydney	1980-81
101	S.M. Gavaskar/D.B. Vengsarkar	India v Australia	Melbourne	1980-81
101	D.L. Haynes/I.V.A. Richards	West Indies v India	The Oval	1983
100	S.A.R. Silva/J.R. Ratnayeke	Sri Lanka v West Indies	Perth	1984-85

Third Wicket

224*	D.M. Jones/A.R. Border	Australia v Sri Lanka	Adelaide	1984-85
195*	C.G. Greenidge/H.A. Gomes	West Indies v Zimbabwe	Worcester	1983
190*	C.J. Tavaré/A.J. Lamb	England v New Zealand	Sydney	1982-83
160	G.P. Howarth/M.D. Crowe	New Zealand v England	Auckland	1983-84
159	A.J. Lamb/D.I. Gower	England v India	The Oval	1982
158	Zaheer Abbas/Javed Miandad	Pakistan v India	Lahore	1982-83
153*	I.V.A. Richards/C.H. Lloyd	West Indies v Australia	Perth	1981-82
149	G.M. Turner/J.M. Parker	New Zealand v East Africa	Birmingham	1975
143	D.B. Vengsarkar/S.M. Patil	India v Pakistan	Sialkot	1984-85
140	K.C. Wessels/A.R. Border	Australia v Pakistan	Sydney	1983-84
134*	H.A. Gomes/I.V.A. Richards	West Indies v England	Lord's	1984

132*	I.V.A. Richards/H.A. Gomes	West Indies v Pakistan	The Oval	1983
128	D.L. Haynes/I.V.A. Richards	West Indies v Australia	Sydney	1984-85
127	D.L. Haynes/I.V.A. Richards	West Indies v New Zealand	St John's	1984-85
125	D.L. Haynes/I.V.A. Richards	West Indies v New Zealand	Berbice	1984-85
119	Zaheer Abbas/Javed Miandad	Pakistan v Australia	Lahore	1982-83
119	K.C. Wessels/K.J. Hughes	Australia v West Indies	Perth	1983-84
117	H.A. Gomes/I.V.A. Richards	West Indies v Sri Lanka	Perth	1984-85
115	R.J. Shastri/S.M. Gavaskar	India v Australia	Indore	1984-85
112	G.N. Yallop/D.W. Hookes	Australia v Sri Lanka	Colombo	1982-83
110	C.G. Greenidge/I.V.A. Richards	West Indies v Australia	Port-of-Spain	1983-84
109	I.V.A. Richards/A.I. Kallicharran	West Indies v England	Adelaide	1979-80
108	J.M. Brearley/G.A. Gooch	England v Australia	Lord's	1979
106*	G. Fowler/A.J. Lamb	England v Pakistan	Lord's	1983
105	C.T. Radley/D.I. Gower	England v New Zealand	Manchester	1978
105	Mudassar Nazar/Javed Miandad	Pakistan v Australia	Melbourne	1981-82
105	S.M. Gavaskar/A. Malhotra	India v West Indies	Jamshedpur	1983-84
103	D. Lloyd/M.H. Denness	England v Pakistan	Nottingham	1974
103	I.V.A. Richards/C.H. Lloyd	West Indies v Australia	Melbourne	1983-84
102	A.J. Lamb/M.W. Gatting	England v Pakistan	Nottingham	1982
101	K.J. Hughes/D.W. Hookes	Australia v West Indies	Lord's	1983
100	A.R. Border/K.J. Hughes	Australia v India	Sydney	1980-81
100	D.C. Boon/K.J. Hughes	Australia v West Indies	Melbourne	1983-84

Fourth Wicket

157*	R.B. Kerr/D.M. Jones	Australia v England	Melbourne	1984-85
150	A.R. Border/K.J. Hughes	Australia v West Indies	Castries	1983-84
149	R.B. Kanhai/C.H. Lloyd	West Indies v Australia	Lord's	1975
147*	B.M. Laird/K.J. Hughes	Australia v West Indies	Sydney	1981-82
147*	Zaheer Abbas/Imran Khan	Pakistan v New Zealand	Nottingham	1983
139	A.J. Lamb/D.W. Randall	England v Australia	Melbourne	1982-83
132	M. Azharuddin/S.M. Gavaskar	India v Pakistan	Melbourne	1984-85
124	A.L. Logie/P.J.L. Dujon	West Indies v Australia	Melbourne	1983-84
123	Zaheer Abbas/Haroon Rashid	Pakistan v Sri Lanka	Lahore	1981-82
117	G.S. Chappell/K.D. Walters	Australia v Sri Lanka	The Oval	1975
117	B.M. Laird/K.J. Hughes	Australia v Pakistan	Lahore	1982-83
116	K.C. Wessels/D.W. Hookes	Australia v New Zealand	Sydney	1982-83
116	G.A. Gooch/I.T. Botham	England v Australia	Manchester	1985
115	A.J. Lamb/M.W. Gatting	England v New Zealand	The Oval	1983
115	A.R. Border/D.C. Boon	Australia v West Indies	Melbourne	1984-85
111	Javed Miandad/Imran Khan	Pakistan v India	Gujranwala	1982-83
110	A. Malhotra/S.M. Patil	India v Sri Lanka	Delhi	1982-83
109	D.B. Vengsarkar/S.M. Patil	India v Pakistan	Multan	1982-83
106	D.I. Gower/D.W. Randall	England v Australia	Adelaide	1982-83
105	D.I. Gower/G.R.J. Roope	England v Pakistan	The Oval	1978
105*	D.B. Vengsarkar/Kapil Dev	India v New Zealand	Sydney	1984-85
103	G.S. Chappell/A.P. Sheahan	Australia v England	Lord's	197
103	K.J. Hughes/G.N. Yallop	Australia v England	Birmingham	198

Fifth Wicket

152	I.V.A. Richards/C.H. Lloyd	West Indies v Sri Lanka	Brisbane	1984-8
139	I.V.A. Richards/C.L. King	West Indies v England	Lord's	197
139	L.R.D. Mendis/P.A. De Silva	Sri Lanka v Australia	Sydney	1984-8
115*	B.M. Laird/A.R. Border	Australia v New Zealand	Dunedin	1981-8
113	D.I. Gower/D.W. Randall	England v New Zealand	Brisbane	1982-8
110	D.I. Gower/M.W. Gatting	England v India	Jullundur	1981-8
105	A.R. Border/W.B. Phillips	Australia v West Indies	Sydney	1984-8

Sixth Wicket

144	Imran Khan/Shahid Mahboob	Pakistan v Sri Lanka	Leeds	198
130	K.J. Wadsworth/B.E. Congdon	New Zealand v Australia	Christchurch	1973-7
126	D.L. Haynes/D.L. Murray	West Indies v Australia	St John's	1977-7
121	J.V. Coney/R.J. Hadlee	New Zealand v England	Adelaide	1982-8
103	D.L. Houghton/K.M. Curran	Zimbabwe v Australia	Southampton	198

Seventh Wicket

108	Ramiz Raja/Anil Dalpat	Pakistan v New Zealand	Christchurch	1984-85

Eighth Wicket

No century partnership: highest

68	B.E. Congdon/B.L. Cairns	New Zealand v England	Scarborough	1978

Ninth Wicket

126*	Kapil Dev/S.M.H. Kirmani	India v Zimbabwe	Tunbridge Wells	1983

Tenth Wicket

106*	I.V.A. Richards/M.A. Holding	West Indies v England	Manchester	1984

CAREER RECORDS – 1500 RUNS

4071	I.V.A. Richards	West Indies
3348	D.L. Haynes	West Indies
2912	C.G. Greenidge	West Indies
2898	A.R. Border	Australia
2464	Zaheer Abbas	Pakistan
2427	D.I. Gower	England
2329	G.S. Chappell	Australia
2155	Javed Miandad	Pakistan
2129	G.M. Wood	Australia
1977	C.H. Lloyd	West Indies
1955	K.J. Hughes	Australia
1767	J.G. Wright	New Zealand
1740	K.C. Wessels	Australia
1598	G.M. Turner	New Zealand
1569	A.J. Lamb	England
1516	D.B. Vengsarkar	India

PLAYERS' RECORDS – BOWLING

FIVE WICKETS IN AN INNINGS

7–51	W.W. Davis	West Indies v Australia	Leeds	1983
6–14	G.J. Gilmour	Australia v England	Leeds	1975
6–14	Imran Khan	Pakistan v India	Sharjah	1984-85
6–15	C.E.H. Croft	West Indies v England	Arnos Vale	1980-81
6–39	K.H. MacLeay	Australia v India	Nottingham	1983
5–15	G.S. Chappell	Australia v India	Sydney	1980-81
5–16	C.G. Rackemann	Australia v Pakistan	Adelaide	1983-84
5–17	T.M. Alderman	Australia v New Zealand	Wellington	1981-82
5–18	G.J. Cosier	Australia v England	Birmingham	1977
5–20	G.S. Chappell	Australia v England	Birmingham	1977
5–20	V.J. Marks	England v New Zealand	Wellington	1983-84
5–21	A.G. Hurst	Australia v Canada	Birmingham	1979
5–21	Wasim Akram	Pakistan v Australia	Melbourne	1984-85
5–22	A.M.E. Roberts	West Indies v England	Adelaide	1979-80
5–23	R.O. Collinge	New Zealand v India	Christchurch	1975-76
5–25	R.J. Hadlee	New Zealand v Sri Lanka	Bristol	1983
5–26	R.J. Hadlee	New Zealand v Australia	Sydney	1980-81
5–26	U.S.H. Karnain	Sri Lanka v New Zealand	Moratuwa	1983-84
5–26	M.A. Holding	West Indies v Australia	Sydney	1984-85
5–28	B.L. Cairns	New Zealand v England	Scarborough	1978
5–28	Mudassar Nazar	Pakistan v West Indies	Melbourne	1984-85
5–30	L.S. Pascoe	Australia v New Zealand	Sydney	1980-81
5–31	M. Hendrick	England v Australia	The Oval	1980
5–31	J. Garner	West Indies v Australia	Melbourne	1983-84
5–32	R.J. Hadlee	New Zealand v India	Perth	1980-81
5–32	A.L.F. De Mel	Sri Lanka v New Zealand	Derby	1983
5–32	R.J. Hadlee	New Zealand v England	Christchurch	1983-84

5-34	D.K. Lillee	Australia v Pakistan	Leeds	1975
5-34	E.J. Chatfield	New Zealand v Australia	Adelaide	1980-81
5-38	J. Garner	West Indies v England	Lord's	1979
5-39	V.J. Marks	England v Sri Lanka	Taunton	1983
5-39	A.L.F. De Mel	Sri Lanka v Pakistan	Leeds	1983
5-43	Kapil Dev	India v Australia	Nottingham	1983
5-44	Abdul Qadir	Pakistan v Sri Lanka	Leeds	1983
5-48	G.J. Gilmour	Australia v West Indies	Lord's	1975
5-50	V.A. Holder	West Indies v England	Birmingham	1976
5-53	Abdul Qadir	Pakistan v Australia	Melbourne	1983-84

HAT-TRICK

Jalaluddin	Pakistan v Australia	Hyderabad	1982-83

CAREER RECORDS - 75 WICKETS

122	M.A. Holding	West Indies
116	J. Garner	West Indies
103	D.K. Lillee	Australia
100	I.T. Botham	England
100	R.J. Hadlee	New Zealand
89	B.L. Cairns	New Zealand
87	A.M.E. Roberts	West Indies
85	R.M. Hogg	Australia
81	E.J. Chatfield	New Zealand
80	R.G.D. Willis	England
79	G.F. Lawson	Australia
79	Kapil Dev	India

PLAYERS' RECORDS - WICKET-KEEPING

MOST DISMISSALS IN AN INNINGS

5 (all ct)	R.G. de Alwis	Sri Lanka v Australia	Colombo	1982-8
5 (all ct)	S.M.H. Kirmani	India v Zimbabwe	Leicester	198
5 (all ct)	R.W. Marsh	Australia v England	Leeds	198
5 (3 ct 2 st)	S. Viswanath	India v England	Sydney	1984-8

CAREER RECORDS - MOST DISMISSALS

123 (119 ct 4 st)	R.W. Marsh	Australia
93 (85 ct 8 st)	P.J.L. Dujon	West Indies
62 (52 ct 10 st)	Wasim Bari	Pakistan

PLAYERS' RECORDS - FIELDING

MOST CATCHES IN AN INNINGS

4	Salim Malik	Pakistan v New Zealand	Sialkot	1984-
4	S.M. Gavaskar	India v Pakistan	Sharjah	1984-

J.G. Bracewell held 4 catches while fielding as substitute for New Zealand v Australia at Adelai in 1980-81.

CAREER RECORDS – MOST CATCHES

44	I.V.A. Richards	West Indies
40	C.H. Lloyd	West Indies
32	J.V. Coney	New Zealand
31	A.R. Border	Australia
30	D.I. Gower	England

PLAYERS' RECORDS – ALL-ROUND

50 RUNS AND FOUR WICKETS IN A MATCH

D.A.G. Fletcher	69* and 4–42	Zimbabwe v Australia	Nottingham	1984

CAREER RECORDS – 1000 RUNS AND 50 WICKETS

I.T. Botham	England	1248 runs	100 wickets
G.S. Chappell	Australia	2329 runs	71 wickets
Imran Khan	Pakistan	1023 runs	56 wickets
Kapil Dev	India	1336 runs	79 wickets
Mudassar Nazar	Pakistan	1497 runs	73 wickets
I.V.A. Richards	West Indies	4071 runs	62 wickets

1000 RUNS AND 100 DISMISSALS

R.W. Marsh	Australia	1220 runs	119 catches, 4 stumpings

PRUDENTIAL WORLD CUP RECORDS

Highest total	338-5	Pakistan v Sri Lanka	Swansea	1983
Highest total batting second	288-9	Sri Lanka v Pakistan	Swansea	1983
Lowest total	45	Canada v England	Manchester	1979
Highest match aggregate	626	Pakistan (338-5) v Sri Lanka (288-9)	Swansea	1983
Lowest match aggregate	91	Canada (45) v England (46-1)	Manchester	1979
Biggest victories	10 wickets	India beat East Africa	Leeds	1975
	10 wickets	West Indies beat Zimbabwe	Birmingham	1983
	202 runs	England beat India	Lord's	1975
Narrowest victories	1 wicket	West Indies beat Pakistan (*with 2 balls to spare*)	Birmingham	1975
	9 runs	England beat New Zealand	Manchester	1979

Highest individual score	175*	Kapil Dev, India v Zimbabwe	Tunbridge Wells	1983
Hundred before lunch	101	A. Turner, Australia v Sri Lanka	The Oval	1975

Highest partnerships for each wicket

Wkt	*Runs*				
1st	182	R.B. McCosker/A. Turner	Australia v Sri Lanka	The Oval	1975
2nd	176	D.L. Amiss/K.W.R. Fletcher	England v India	Lord's	1975
3rd	195*	C.G. Greenidge/H.A. Gomes	West Indies v Zimbabwe	Worcester	1983
4th	149	R.B. Kanhai/C.H. Lloyd	West Indies v Australia	Lord's	1975
5th	139	I.V.A. Richards/C.L. King	West Indies v England	Lord's	1979
6th	144	Imran Khan/Shahid Mahboob	Pakistan v Sri Lanka	Leeds	1983
7th	75*	D.A.G. Fletcher/I.P. Butchart	Zimbabwe v Australia	Nottingham	1983
8th	62	Kapil Dev/Madan Lal	India v Zimbabwe	Tunbridge Wells	1983
9th	126*	Kapil Dev/S.M.H. Kirmani	India v Zimbabwe	Tunbridge Wells	1983
10th	71	A.M.E. Roberts/J. Garner	West Indies v India	Manchester	1983

Best bowling	7–51	W.W. Davis, West Indies v Australia	Leeds	1983
Most economical analysis	12–8–6–1	B.S. Bedi, India v East Africa	Leeds	1975
Most expensive analysis	12–1–105–2	M.C. Snedden, New Zealand v England	The Oval	1983

Wicket-keeping – most dismissals	5	S.M.H. Kirmani, India v Zimbabwe	Leicester	1983
Fielding – most catches	3	C.H. Lloyd, West Indies v Sri Lanka	Manchester	1975

PRUDENTIAL WORLD CUP NATIONAL RECORDS

ENGLAND			*Opponents*		
Highest total	334–4		India	Lord's	197
Lowest total	93		Australia	Leeds	197
Highest score	137	D.L. Amiss	India	Lord's	197
Best bowling	5–39	V.J. Marks	Sri Lanka	Taunton	198

AUSTRALIA			*Opponents*		
Highest total	328–5		Sri Lanka	The Oval	197
Lowest total	129		India	Chelmsford	198
Highest score	110	T.M. Chappell	India	Nottingham	198
Best bowling	6–14	G.J. Gilmour	England	Leeds	197

INDIA			*Opponents*		
Highest total	262–8		West Indies	Manchester	198
Lowest total	132–3		England	Lord's	197
Highest score	175*	Kapil Dev	Zimbabwe	Tunbridge Wells	198
Best bowling	5–43	Kapil Dev	Australia	Nottingham	198

NEW ZEALAND			*Opponents*		
Highest total	309–5		East Africa	Birmingham	1975
Lowest total	158		West Indies	The Oval	1975
Highest score	171*	G.M. Turner	East Africa	Birmingham	1975
Best bowling	5–25	R.J. Hadlee	Sri Lanka	Bristol	1983

PAKISTAN			*Opponents*		
Highest total	338–5		Sri Lanka	Swansea	1983
Lowest total	151		England	Leeds	1979
Highest score	103*	Zaheer Abbas	New Zealand	Nottingham	1983
Best bowling	5–44	Abdul Qadir	Sri Lanka	Leeds	1983

SRI LANKA			*Opponents*		
Highest total	288–9		Pakistan	Swansea	1983
Lowest total	86		West Indies	Manchester	1975
Highest score	72	D.S.B.P. Kuruppu	Pakistan	Swansea	1983
Best bowling	5–32	A.L.F. De Mel	New Zealand	Derby	1983

WEST INDIES			*Opponents*		
Highest total	293–6		Pakistan	The Oval	1979
Lowest total	140		India	Lord's	1983
Highest score	138*	I.V.A. Richards	England	Lord's	1979
Best bowling	7–51	W.W. Davis	Australia	Leeds	1983

ZIMBABWE			*Opponents*		
Highest total	240		Australia	Southampton	1983
Lowest total	155		India	Leicester	1983
Highest score	84	D.L. Houghton	Australia	Southampton	1983
Best bowling	4–42	D.A.G. Fletcher	Australia	Nottingham	1983

INDIVIDUAL CAREER RECORDS

ENGLAND (*84 players*)

	BATTING AND FIELDING									BOWLING					
	M	*I*	*NO*	*HS*	*Runs*	*Avge*	*100*	*50*	*Ct/St*	*Balls*	*Runs*	*Wkts*	*Avge*	*Best*	*4W*
Agnew, J.P.	3	1	1	2*	2	–	–	–	1	126	120	3	40.00	3–38	–
Allott, P.J.W.	13	6	1	8	15	3.00	–	–	2	819	552	15	36.80	3–41	–
Amiss, D.L.	18	18	0	137	859	47.72	4	1	2						
Arnold, G.G.	14	6	3	18*	48	16.00	–	–	2	714	339	19	17.84	4–27	1
Athey, C.W.J.	2	2	0	51	83	41.50	–	1	1						
Bailey, R.J.	1	1	1	41*	41	–	–	–	–	36	25	0	–	–	–
Bairstow, D.L.	21	20	6	23*	206	14.71	–	–	17/4						
Barlow, G.D.	6	6	1	80*	149	29.80	–	1	4						
Botham, I.T.	75	66	8	72	1248	21.51	–	5	27	3936	2639	100	26.39	4–56	1
Boycott, G.	36	34	4	105	1082	36.06	1	9	5	168	105	5	21.00	2–14	–
Brearley, J.M.	25	24	3	78	510	24.28	–	3	12						
Butcher, A.R.	1	1	0	14	14	14.00	–	–	–						
Butcher, R.O.	3	3	0	52	58	19.33	–	1	–						
Close, D.B.	3	3	0	43	49	16.33	–	–	1	18	21	0	–	–	–
Cook, G.	6	6	0	32	106	17.66	–	–	2						
Cook, N.G.B.	1	–	–	–	–	–	–	–	1	48	34	1	34.00	1–34	–
Cope, G.A.	2	1	1	1*	1	–	–	–	–	112	35	2	17.50	1–16	–
Cowans, N.G.	23	8	3	4*	13	2.60	–	–	5	1282	913	23	39.66	3–44	–
Cowdrey, C.S.	3	3	1	46*	51	25.50	–	–	–	52	55	2	27.50	1–3	–
Cowdrey, M.C.	1	1	0	1	1	1.00	–	–	–						
Denness, M.H.	12	11	2	66	264	29.33	–	1	1						
Dilley, G.R.	18	11	3	31*	96	12.00	–	–	1	972	595	18	33.05	4–45	1
D'Oliveira, B.L.	4	4	1	17	30	10.00	–	–	1	204	140	3	46.66	1–19	–
Downton, P.R.	11	9	3	44*	165	27.50	–	–	7/1						
Edmonds, P.H.	23	16	6	20	100	10.00	–	–	3	1168	687	20	34.35	3–39	–
Edrich, J.H.	7	6	0	90	223	37.16	–	2	–						
Ellison, R.M.	9	9	4	24	59	11.80	–	–	2	414	289	8	36.12	3–42	–
Emburey, J.E.	8	7	1	18	31	5.16	–	–	3	435	262	5	52.40	2–22	–
Fletcher, K.W.R.	24	22	3	131	757	39.84	1	5	4						
Foster, N.A.	16	8	3	24	42	8.40	–	–	6	834	600	14	42.85	3–44	–
Fowler, G.	24	24	2	81*	714	32.45	–	4	3/2						
French, B.N.	3	2	0	7	11	5.50	–	–	3/1						
Gatting, M.W.	42	39	10	115*	902	31.10	1	4	12	248	212	6	35.33	3–32	–
Gifford, N.	2	1	0	0	0	0.00	–	–	1	120	50	4	12.50	4–23	1
Gooch, G.A.	40	39	2	117*	1335	36.08	3	9	16	889	682	18	37.88	2–12	–
Gould, I.J.	18	14	2	42	155	12.91	–	–	15/3						
Gower, D.I.	77	74	7	158	2427	36.22	7	8	30	3	5	0	–	–	–

ENGLAND – *continued*

		BATTING AND FIELDING								*BOWLING*					
	M	*I*	*NO*	*HS*	*Runs*	*Avge*	*100*	*50*	*Ct/St*	*Balls*	*Runs*	*Wkts*	*Avge*	*Best*	*4W*
Greig, A.W.	22	19	3	48	269	16.81	–	–	7	916	619	19	32.57	4–45	1
Hampshire, J.H.	3	3	1	25*	48	24.00	–	–	–						
Hayes, F.C.	6	6	1	52	128	25.60	–	1	–						
Hemmings, E.E.	5	2	0	3	4	2.00	–	–	1	249	175	5	35.00	3–11	–
Hendrick, M.	22	10	5	2*	6	1.20	–	–	5	1248	681	35	19.45	5–31	3
Humpage, G.W.	3	2	0	6	11	5.50	–	–	2						
Illingworth, R.	3	2	0	4	5	2.50	–	–	1	130	84	4	21.00	3–50	–
Jackman, R.D.	15	9	1	14	54	6.75	–	–	4	873	598	19	31.47	3–41	–
Jameson, J.A.	3	3	0	28	60	20.00	–	–	–	12	3	0	–	–	–
Jesty, T.E.	10	10	4	52*	127	21.16	–	1	5	108	93	1	93.00	1–23	–
Knott, A.P.E.	20	14	4	50	200	20.00	–	1	15/1						
Lamb, A.J.	43	42	8	118	1569	46.14	3	9	11						
Larkins, W.	6	6	0	34	84	14.00	–	–	2	12	21	0	–	–	–
Lever, J.K.	22	11	4	27*	56	8.00	–	–	6	1152	713	24	29.70	4–29	1
Lever, P.	10	3	2	8*	17	17.00	–	–	2	440	261	11	23.72	4–35	1
Lloyd, D.	8	8	1	116*	285	40.71	1	–	3	12	3	1	3.00	1–3	–
Lloyd, T.A.	3	3	0	49	101	33.66	–	–	–						
Love, J.D.	3	3	0	43	61	20.33	–	–	1						
Luckhurst, B.W.	3	3	0	14	15	5.00	–	–	–						
Marks, V.J.	33	24	3	44	285	13.57	–	–	8	1772	1076	44	24.45	5–20	2
Miller, G.	25	18	2	46	136	8.50	–	–	4	1268	813	25	32.52	3–27	–
Moxon, M.D.	5	5	0	70	132	26.40	–	1	4						
Old, C.M.	32	25	7	51*	338	18.77	–	1	8	1755	999	45	22.20	4–8	2
Pocock, P.I.	1	1	0	4	4	4.00	–	–	–	60	20	0	–	–	–
Pringle, D.R.	9	7	2	34*	78	15.60	–	–	5	492	401	12	33.41	3–21	–
Radley, C.T.	4	4	1	117*	250	83.33	1	1	–						
Randall, D.W.	49	45	5	88	1067	26.67	–	5	25	2	2	1	2.00	1–2	–
Richards, C.J.	3	2	0	3	3	1.50	–	–	1						
Robinson, R.T.	7	7	0	37	97	13.85	–	–	1						
Roope, G.R.J.	8	8	0	44	173	21.62	–	–	2						
Rose, B.C.	2	2	0	54	99	49.50	–	1	1						
Shuttleworth, K.	1	1	0	7	7	7.00	–	–	1	56	29	1	29.00	1–29	–
Smith, C.L.	4	4	0	70	109	27.25	–	1	–	36	28	2	14.00	2–8	–
Smith, M.J.	5	5	0	31	70	14.00	–	–	1						
Snow, J.A.	9	4	2	5*	9	4.50	–	–	1	538	232	14	16.57	4–11	2
Steele, D.S.	1	1	0	8	8	8.00	–	–	–	6	9	0	–	–	–
Stevenson, G.B.	4	4	3	28*	43	43.00	–	–	2	192	125	7	17.85	4–33	1

INDIVIDUAL CAREER RECORDS – *continued*

ENGLAND – *continued*

		BATTING AND FIELDING								*BOWLING*					
	M	*I*	*NO*	*HS*	*Runs*	*Avge*	*100*	*50*	*Ct/St*	*Balls*	*Runs*	*Wkts*	*Avge*	*Best*	*4W*
Tavaré, C.J.	29	28	2	83*	720	27.69	–	4	7	12	3	0	–	–	–
Taylor, R.W.	27	17	7	26*	130	13.00	–	–	26/6						
Titmus, F.J.	2	1	0	11	11	11.00	–	–	1	56	53	3	17.66	3–53	–
Tolchard, R.W.	1	–	–	–	–	–	–	–	1						
Underwood, D.L.	26	13	4	17	53	5.88	–	–	6	1278	734	32	22.93	4–44	1
Wells, C.M.	2	2	0	17	22	11.00	–	–	–						
Willey, P.	22	20	1	64	487	25.63	–	5	4	936	594	12	49.50	3–33	–
Willis, R.G.D.	64	22	14	24	83	10.37	–	–	22	3595	1968	80	24.60	4–11	4
Wood, B.	13	12	2	78*	314	31.40	–	2	6	420	224	9	24.88	2–14	–
Woolmer, R.A.	6	4	0	9	21	5.25	–	–	3	321	260	9	28.88	3–33	–
Extras, subs & run outs.					*1608*				*2*		*1365* *(61)*	*98*			
TOTALS	1199	951	171	158	21304	27.31	22	87	397/18	30545	20485	779	26.29	5–20	22

Figures in brackets relate to wides and no-balls debited to bowlers.

AUSTRALIA (*85 players*)

		BATTING AND FIELDING								*BOWLING*					
	M	*I*	*NO*	*HS*	*Runs*	*Avge*	*100*	*50*	*Ct/St*	*Balls*	*Runs*	*Wkts*	*Avge*	*Best*	*4W*
Alderman, T.M.	23	9	3	9*	27	4.50	–	–	12	1290	803	29	27.69	5–17	1
Beard, G.R.	2	–	–	–	–	–	–	–	–	112	70	4	17.50	2–20	–
Bennett, M.J.	8	4	1	6*	9	3.00	–	–	1	408	275	4	68.75	2–27	–
Boon, D.C.	12	11	0	55	303	27.54	–	1	2	16	13	0	–	–	–
Border, A.R.	114	106	16	127*	2898	32.20	3	18	31	900	717	20	35.85	3–21	–
Bright, R.J.	8	6	3	19*	60	20.00	–	–	2	366	291	2	145.50	1–40	–
Callen, I.W.	5	3	2	3*	6	6.00	–	–	2	180	148	5	29.60	3–24	–
Carlson, P.H.	4	2	0	11	11	5.50	–	–	–	168	70	2	35.00	1–21	–
Chappell, G.S.	73	71	14	138*	2329	40.85	3	14	23	3066	2060	71	29.01	5–15	2
Chappell, I.M.	16	16	2	86	673	48.07	–	8	5	42	23	2	11.50	2–14	–
Chappell, T.M.	20	13	0	110	229	17.61	1	–	8	736	538	19	28.31	3–31	–
Clark, W.M.	2	–	–	–	–	–	–	–	–	100	61	3	20.33	2–39	–
Colley, D.J.	1	–	–	–	–	–	–	–	–	66	72	0	–	–	–
Connolly, A.N.	1	–	–	–	–	–	–	–	–	64	62	0	–	–	–
Cosier, G.J.	9	7	2	84	154	30.80	–	1	4	409	248	14	17.71	5–18	1

AUSTRALIA – *continued*

		BATTING AND FIELDING								BOWLING					
	M	*I*	*NO*	*HS*	*Runs*	*Avge*	*100*	*50*	*Ct/St*	*Balls*	*Runs*	*Wkts*	*Avge*	*Best*	*4W*
Darling, W.M.	18	18	1	74	363	21.35	–	1	6						
Davis, I.C.	3	3	1	11*	12	6.00	–	–	–						
Dymock, G.	15	7	4	14*	35	11.66	–	–	1	806	412	15	27.46	2–21	–
Dyson, J.	29	27	4	79	755	32.82	–	4	12						
Edwards, R.	9	8	1	80*	255	36.42	–	3	–						
Edwards, W.J.	1	1	0	2	2	2.00	–	–	–	1	0	0	–	–	–
Gilmour, G.J.	5	2	1	28*	42	42.00	–	–	2	320	165	16	10.31	6–14	2
Graf, S.F.	11	6	0	8	24	4.00	–	–	1	522	345	8	43.12	2–23	–
Hammond, J.R.	1	1	1	15*	15	–	–	–	–	54	41	1	41.00	1–41	–
Hilditch, A.M.J.	8	8	0	72	226	28.25	–	1	1						
Hogan, T.G.	16	12	4	27	72	9.00	–	–	10	917	574	23	24.95	4–33	1
Hogg, R.M.	70	35	20	22	137	9.13	–	–	8	3677	2418	85	28.44	4–29	5
Holland, R.G.	2	–	–	–	–	–	–	–	–	126	99	2	49.50	2–49	–
Hookes, D.W.	36	34	2	76	803	25.09	–	5	10	29	28	1	28.00	1–2	–
Hughes, K.J.	95	87	6	98	1955	24.13	–	17	26	1	4	0	–	–	–
Hurst, A.G.	8	4	4	3*	7	–	–	–	1	402	203	12	16.91	5–21	1
Jenner, T.J.	1	1	0	12	12	12.00	–	–	–	64	28	0	–	–	–
Jones, D.M.	21	20	6	99*	481	34.35	–	3	3	4	4	0	–	–	–
Kent, M.F.	5	5	1	33	78	19.50	–	–	4						
Kerr, R.B.	4	4	1	87*	97	32.33	–	1	1						
Laird, B.M.	23	23	3	117*	594	29.70	1	2	5						
Laughlin, T.J.	6	5	1	74	105	26.25	–	1	–	308	224	8	28.00	3–54	–
Lawry, W.M.	1	1	0	27	27	27.00	–	–	1						
Lawson, G.F.	70	48	17	33*	373	12.03	–	–	17	3772	2270	79	28.73	4–26	1
Lillee, D.K.	63	34	8	42*	240	9.23	–	–	10	3593	2145	103	20.82	5–34	6
Maclean, J.A.	2	1	0	11	11	11.00	–	–	–						
MacLeay, K.H.	8	7	0	15	47	6.71	–	–	2	473	344	10	34.40	6–39	1
McCosker, R.B.	14	14	0	95	320	22.85	–	2	3						
McCurdy, R.J.	11	6	2	13*	33	8.25	–	–	1	515	375	12	31.25	3–19	–
McDermott, C.J.	17	7	1	19	38	6.33	–	–	4	1039	776	29	26.75	3–30	–
McKenzie, G.D.	1	–	–	–	–	–	–	–	1	60	22	2	11.00	2–22	–
Maguire, J.N.	21	10	5	14*	41	8.20	–	–	2	967	760	17	44.70	3–61	–
Mallett, A.A.	9	3	1	8	14	7.00	–	–	4	502	341	11	31.00	3–34	–
Malone, M.F.	10	7	3	15*	36	9.00	–	–	1	612	315	11	28.63	2–9	–
Marsh, R.W.	91	75	15	66	1220	20.33	–	4	119/4						
Massie, R.A.L.	3	1	1	16*	16	–	–	–	1	183	129	3	43.00	2–25	–
Matthews, G.R.J.	8	7	2	29*	84	16.80	–	–	1	426	333	6	55.50	2–33	–
Moss, J.K.	1	1	0	7	7	7.00	–	–	2						

INDIVIDUAL CAREER RECORDS – *continued*

AUSTRALIA – *continued*

		BATTING AND FIELDING								*BOWLING*					
	M	*I*	*NO*	*HS*	*Runs*	*Avge*	*100*	*50*	*Ct/St*	*Balls*	*Runs*	*Wkts*	*Avge*	*Best*	*4W*
O'Donnell, S.P.	21	17	4	74*	326	25.07	–	2	4	1113	816	22	37.09	2–19	–
O'Keeffe, K.J.	2	2	1	16*	16	16.00	–	–	–	132	79	2	39.50	1–36	–
Pascoe, L.S.	29	11	7	15*	39	9.75	–	–	6	1568	1066	53	20.11	5–30	5
Phillips, W.B.	33	28	4	75*	645	26.87	–	5	26/5						
Porter, G.D.	2	1	0	3	3	3.00	–	–	1	108	33	3	11.00	2–13	–
Rackemann, C.G.	26	10	4	9*	20	3.33	–	–	4	1434	996	45	22.13	5–16	3
Redpath, I.R.	5	5	0	24	46	9.20	–	–	2						
Ritchie, G.M.	20	19	4	84	408	27.20	–	2	2						
Rixon, S.J.	6	6	3	20*	40	13.33	–	–	9/2						
Robinson, R.D.	2	2	0	70	82	41.00	–	1	3/1						
Serjeant, C.S.	3	3	0	46	73	24.33	–	–	1						
Sheahan, A.P.	3	3	0	50	75	25.00	–	1	–						
Simpson, R.B.	2	2	0	23	36	18.00	–	–	4	102	95	2	47.50	2–30	–
Smith, S.B.	26	23	2	117	853	40.61	2	8	7	7	5	0	–	–	–
Stackpole, K.R.	6	6	0	61	224	37.33	–	3	1	77	54	3	18.00	3–40	–
Thomson, A.L.	1	–	–	–	–	–	–	–	–	64	22	1	22.00	1–22	–
Thomson, J.R.	50	30	6	21	181	7.54	–	–	9	2696	1942	55	35.30	4–67	1
Toohey, P.M.	5	4	2	54*	105	52.50	–	1	–						
Turner, A.	6	6	0	101	247	41.16	1	–	3						
Walker, M.H.N.	17	11	3	20	79	9.87	–	–	6	1006	546	20	27.30	4–19	1
Walters, K.D.	28	24	6	59	513	28.50	–	2	10	314	273	4	68.25	2–24	–
Watson, G.D.	2	2	1	11*	11	11.00	–	–	–	48	28	2	14.00	2–28	–
Wiener, J.M.	7	7	0	50	140	20.00	–	1	2	24	34	0	–	–	–
Wellham, D.M.	3	3	0	42	61	20.33	–	–	1						
Wessels, K.C.	53	51	3	107	1740	36.25	1	14	19	737	655	18	36.38	2–16	–
Whatmore, D.F.	1	1	0	2	2	2.00	–	–	–						
Wood, G.M.	76	71	9	114*	2129	34.33	3	11	17						
Woodcock, A.J.	1	1	0	53	53	53.00	–	1	–						
Woolley, R.D.	4	3	2	16	31	31.00	–	–	1/1						
Wright, K.J.	5	2	0	23	29	14.50	–	–	8						
Yallop, G.N.	29	27	6	66*	823	39.19	–	7	5	138	119	3	39.66	2–28	–
Yardley, B.	7	4	0	28	58	14.50	–	–	1	198	130	7	18.57	3–28	–
Extras, subs & run outs.					*1909*				*7*		*2040* (*221*)	*81*			
TOTALS	1496	1166	226	138*	26273	27.95	15	145	509/13	37062	26518	950	27.91	6–14	31

Figures in brackets relate to wides and no-balls debited to bowlers.

INDIVIDUAL CAREER RECORDS – *continued*

INDIA (*54 players*)

		BATTING AND FIELDING								*BOWLING*					
	M	*I*	*NO*	*HS*	*Runs*	*Avge*	*100*	*50*	*Ct/St*	*Balls*	*Runs*	*Wkts*	*Avge*	*Best*	*4W*
Abid Ali, S.	5	3	0	70	93	31.00	–	1	–	336	187	7	26.71	2–22	–
Amarnath, M.	44	35	6	90	722	24.89	–	5	14	1661	1239	29	42.72	3–12	–
Amarnath, S.	3	3	0	62	100	33.33	–	1	1						
Arun Lal	5	5	0	16	31	6.20	–	–	1						
Azad, K.	21	18	2	39*	238	14.87	–	–	6	312	213	5	42.60	2–48	–
Azharuddin, M.	10	10	2	93*	360	45.00	–	1	3						
Bedi, B.S.	10	7	2	13	31	6.20	–	–	4	590	340	7	48.57	2–44	–
Binny, R.M.H.	44	36	7	57	533	18.37	–	1	7	1827	1383	52	26.59	4–29	3
Bose, G.	1	1	0	13	13	13.00	–	–	–	66	39	1	39.00	1–39	–
Chandrasekhar, B.S.	1	1	1	11*	11	–	–	–	–	56	36	3	12.00	3–36	–
Chauhan, C.P.S.	7	7	0	46	153	21.85	–	–	3						
Doshi, D.R.	15	5	2	5*	9	3.00	–	–	3	792	524	22	23.81	4–30	2
Engineer, F.M.	5	4	1	54*	114	38.00	–	1	3/1						
Gaekwad, A.D.	13	12	1	78*	257	23.36	–	1	5						
Gavaskar, S.M.	61	56	6	90	1338	26.76	–	9	12	20	25	1	25.00	1–10	–
Ghai, R.S.	3	–	–	–	–	–	–	–	–	126	115	1	115.00	1–38	–
Ghavri, K.D.	19	16	6	20	114	11.40	–	–	2	1033	708	15	47.20	3–40	–
Kapil Dev	61	57	8	175*	1336	27.26	1	6	21	3200	1929	79	24.41	5–43	1
Khanna, S.C.	9	9	2	56	173	24.71	–	2	4/4						
Kirmani, S.M.H.	45	29	12	48*	341	20.05	–	–	25/9						
Krishnamurthy, P.	1	1	0	6	6	6.00	–	–	1/1						
Kulkarni, R.R.	1	1	1	1*	1	–	–	–	–	54	26	0	–	–	–
Madan Lal	49	25	10	53*	299	19.93	–	1	14	2423	1576	62	25.41	4–20	2
Malhotra, A.	12	12	4	65	332	41.50	–	1	1	6	0	0	–	–	–
Maninder Singh	4	1	0	4	4	4.00	–	–	2	132	133	2	66.50	1–24	–
Mankad, A.V.	1	1	0	44	44	44.00	–	–	–	35	47	1	47.00	1–47	–
More, K.S.	2	–	–	–	–	–	–	–	–						
Naik, S.S.	2	2	0	20	38	19.00	–	–	–						
Nayak, S.V.	4	1	0	3	3	3.00	–	–	1	222	161	1	161.00	1–51	–
Parkar, G.A.	9	9	1	42	153	19.12	–	–	4						
Patel, A.	7	2	0	6	6	3.00	–	–	1	360	263	7	37.57	3–43	–
Patel, B.P.	10	9	1	82	243	30.37	–	1	1						
Patil, S.M.	41	39	1	84	976	25.68	–	9	8	864	589	15	39.26	2–28	–
Prabhakar, M.	7	1	0	4	4	4.00	–	–	4	312	171	4	42.75	2–16	–
Rajput, L.	2	2	1	1*	1	1.00	–	–	1						
Randhir Singh	2	–	–	–	–	–	–	–	–	72	48	1	48.00	1–30	–
Reddy, B.	3	2	2	8*	11	–	–	–	2						
Sandhu, B.S.	22	7	3	16*	51	12.75	–	–	5	1110	763	16	47.68	3–27	–

INDIVIDUAL CAREER RECORDS – *continued*

INDIA – *continued*

		BATTING AND FIELDING								*BOWLING*					
	M	*I*	*NO*	*HS*	*Runs*	*Avge*	*100*	*50*	*Ct/St*	*Balls*	*Runs*	*Wkts*	*Avge*	*Best*	*4W*
Sekar, T.A.P.	4	–	–	–	–	–	–	–	–	156	128	5	25.60	3–24	–
Sharma, C.	11	3	3	20*	42	–	–	–	1	468	340	10	34.00	3–22	–
Sharma, P.	2	2	0	14	20	10.00	–	–	–						
Shastri, R.J.	39	32	7	102	840	33.60	2	5	13	1648	1163	37	31.43	4–40	1
Sivaramakrishnan, L.	7	1	0	1	1	1.00	–	–	5	378	231	12	19.25	3–25	–
Solkar, E.D.	7	6	0	13	27	4.50	–	–	2	252	169	4	42.25	2–31	–
Srikkanth, K.	36	36	1	99	1061	30.31	–	8	10	12	27	0	–	–	–
Srinivasan, T.E.	2	2	0	6	10	5.00	–	–	–						
Sudhakar Rao	1	1	0	4	4	4.00	–	–	1						
Vengsarkar, D.B.	55	53	8	105	1516	33.68	1	8	17	6	4	0	–	–	–
Venkataraghavan, S.	15	9	4	26*	54	10.80	–	–	4	868	542	5	108.40	2–34	–
Viswanath, G.R.	25	23	1	75	439	19.95	–	2	3						
Wiswanath, S.	10	4	3	23*	40	40.00	–	–	13/5						
Wadekar, A.L.	2	2	0	67	73	36.50	–	1	1						
Yashpal Sharma	42	40	9	89	883	28.48	–	4	10	201	199	1	199.00	1–27	–
Yograj Singh	6	4	2	1	1	0.50	–	–	2	244	186	4	46.50	2–44	–
Extras, subs & run outs.					*1041*				*5*		*984* *(64)*	*67*			
TOTALS	825	647	120	175*	14191	26.92	4	68	246/20	19842	14424	476	30.30	5–43	9

Figures in brackets relate to wides and no-balls debited to bowlers.

NEW ZEALAND (*50 players*)

		BATTING AND FIELDING								*BOWLING*					
	M	*I*	*NO*	*HS*	*Runs*	*Avge*	*100*	*50*	*Ct/St*	*Balls*	*Runs*	*Wkts*	*Avge*	*Best*	*4W*
Anderson, R.W.	2	2	1	12	16	16.00	–	–	1						
Blair, B.R.	2	2	0	29	31	15.50	–	–	–						
Boock, S.L.	6	2	1	8*	10	10.00	–	–	3	336	206	9	22.88	3–28	–
Bracewell, B.P.	1	1	1	0*	0	–	–	–	–	66	41	1	41.00	1–41	–
Bracewell, J.G.	13	10	5	34	119	23.80	–	–	4	644	482	8	60.25	2–23	–
Burgess, M.G.	26	20	0	47	336	16.80	–	–	8	74	69	1	69.00	1–10	–
Cairns, B.L.	77	64	6	60	986	17.00	–	2	18	3985	2689	89	30.21	5–28	3
Chatfield, E.J.	63	27	21	19*	83	13.83	–	–	9	3447	2042	81	25.20	5–34	1
Collinge, R.O.	15	9	3	9	34	5.66	–	–	1	859	479	18	26.61	5–23	1

INDIVIDUAL CAREER RECORDS – *continued*

NEW ZEALAND – *continued*

		BATTING AND FIELDING								*BOWLING*					
	M	*I*	*NO*	*HS*	*Runs*	*Avge*	*100*	*50*	*Ct/St*	*Balls*	*Runs*	*Wkts*	*Avge*	*Best*	*4W*
Coman, P.G.	3	3	0	38	62	20.66	–	–	2						
Coney, J.V.	68	60	17	66*	1357	31.55	–	5	32	2463	1661	48	34.60	4–46	1
Congdon, B.E.	11	9	3	101	338	56.33	1	2	–	437	287	7	41.00	2–17	–
Crowe, J.J.	37	36	7	57*	686	23.65	–	4	14	6	1	0	–	–	–
Crowe, M.D.	36	33	5	105*	916	32.71	1	5	9	486	364	14	26.00	2–9	–
Edgar, B.A.	47	47	5	102*	1392	33.14	1	7	11	12	5	0	–	–	–
Edwards, G.N.	6	6	0	41	138	23.00	–	–	5	6	5	1	5.00	1–5	–
Franklin, T. J.	1	1	0	6	6	6.00	–	–	–						
Gray, E.J.	1	–	–	–	–	–	–	–	–						
Hadlee, B.G.	2	2	1	19	26	26.00	–	–	–						
Hadlee, D.R.	11	7	2	20	40	8.00	–	–	2	628	364	20	18.20	4–34	1
Hadlee, R.J.	75	61	7	79	952	17.62	–	1	22	4017	2148	100	21.48	5–25	4
Hart, R.T.	1	1	0	3	3	3.00	–	–	–						
Hastings, B.F.	11	9	1	37	151	18.87	–	–	4						
Howarth, G.P.	69	64	5	76	1378	23.35	–	6	14	90	68	3	22.66	1–4	–
Howarth, H.J.	9	5	2	11	18	6.00	–	–	3	492	280	11	25.45	3–29	–
Lees, W.K.	30	23	5	26	211	11.72	–	–	24/2						
McEwan, P.E.	18	15	0	41	204	13.60	–	–	1	420	353	6	58.83	2–29	–
McKechnie, B.J.	14	8	4	27	54	13.50	–	–	2	818	495	19	26.05	3–23	–
Morrison, J.F.M.	17	14	2	55	237	19.75	–	1	6	283	199	8	24.87	3–24	–
O'Sullivan, D.R.	3	2	1	1*	2	2.00	–	–	–	168	123	2	61.50	1–38	–
Parker, J.M.	24	20	0	66	248	12.40	–	1	11/1	16	10	1	10.00	1–10	–
Parker, N.M.	1	1	0	0	0	0.00	–	–	1						
Pollard, V.	3	2	0	55	67	33.50	–	1	1						
Redmond, R.E.	2	1	0	3	3	3.00	–	–	–						
Reid, J.F.	17	16	1	88	500	33.33	–	4	5						
Roberts, A.D.G.	1	1	0	16	16	16.00	–	–	1	56	30	1	30.00	1–30	–
Robertson, G.K.	3	3	0	17	38	12.66	–	–	1	156	102	2	51.00	2–29	–
Rutherford, K.R.	2	2	0	18	20	10.00	–	–	–	18	12	1	12.00	1–12	–
Smith, I.D.S.	40	31	6	59	377	15.08	–	1	32/4						
Snedden, M.C.	46	22	9	40	238	18.30	–	–	12	2253	1677	54	31.05	3–25	–
Stirling, D.A.	6	5	2	14*	22	7.33	–	–	3	246	206	6	34.33	2–28	–
Stott, L.W.	1	–	–	–	–	–	–	–	1	72	48	3	16.00	3–48	–
Taylor, B.R.	2	1	0	22	22	22.00	–	–	1	114	62	4	15.50	3–25	–
Troup, G.B.	22	12	8	39	101	25.25	–	–	2	1180	791	32	24.71	4–19	3
Turner, G.M.	41	40	6	171*	1598	47.00	3	9	14	6	0	0	–	–	–
Vivian, G.E.	1	1	0	14	14	14.00	–	–	–						
Wadsworth, K.J.	13	10	1	104	258	28.66	1	–	13/2						

INDIVIDUAL CAREER RECORDS – *continued*

NEW ZEALAND – *continued*

	M	I	NO	HS	Runs	Avge	100	50	Ct/St	Balls	Runs	Wkts	Avge	Best	4W
		BATTING AND FIELDING								*BOWLING*					
Webb, P.N.	5	5	1	10*	38	9.50	–	–	3						
Webb, R.J.	3	1	1	6*	6	–	–	–	–	161	104	4	26.00	2–27	–
Wright, J.G.	71	70	1	84	1767	25.60	–	11	28	24	8	0	–	–	–
Extras, subs & run outs.					*1311*				*11*		*1071* *(69)*	*76*			
TOTALS	979	787	141	171*	16430	25.43	7	60	335/9	24039	16408	630	26.04	5–23	14

Figures in brackets relate to wides and no-balls debited to bowlers.

PAKISTAN (*56 players*)

	M	I	NO	HS	Runs	Avge	100	50	Ct/St	Balls	Runs	Wkts	Avge	Best	4W
		BATTING AND FIELDING								*BOWLING*					
Aamer Hameed	2	–	–	–	–	–	–	–	1	88	38	1	38.00	1–32	–
Abdul Qadir	17	16	5	41*	132	12.00	–	–	5	1024	647	30	21.56	5–44	3
Anil Dalpat	14	9	2	37	84	12.00	–	–	13/2						
Arshad Pervez	2	2	0	8	11	5.50	–	–	–						
Ashraf Ali	15	9	5	19*	69	17.25	–	–	16/3						
Asif Iqbal	10	8	2	62	330	55.00	–	5	7	592	378	16	23.62	4–56	1
Asif Masood	7	3	1	6	10	5.00	–	–	1	402	234	5	46.80	2–9	–
Azeem Hafeez	15	10	7	15	45	15.00	–	–	3	719	586	15	39.06	4–22	1
Azmat Rana	2	2	1	22*	42	42.00	–	–	–						
Haroon Rashid	12	10	2	63*	166	20.75	–	1	3						
Hasan Jamil	6	5	0	28	111	22.20	–	–	1	232	154	8	19.25	3–18	–
Ijaz Faqih	23	18	2	42*	191	11.93	–	–	2	1008	727	12	60.58	4–43	1
Imran Khan	55	45	14	102*	1023	33.00	1	3	18	2123	1152	56	20.57	6–14	1
Intikhab Alam	4	2	0	10	17	8.50	–	–	–	158	118	4	29.50	2–36	–
Iqbal Qasim	14	7	1	13	39	6.50	–	–	3	610	487	9	57.44	2–16	–
Jalaluddin	8	2	0	5	5	2.50	–	–	1	306	221	14	15.78	4–32	1
Javed Miandad	75	72	14	119*	2155	37.15	2	13	26	352	209	5	41.80	2–22	–
Liaquat Ali	3	1	0	7	7	7.00	–	–	–	188	111	2	55.50	1–41	–
Majid Khan	23	22	1	109	786	37.42	1	7	3	658	374	13	28.76	3–27	–
Mansoor Akhtar	29	23	1	47	398	18.09	–	–	10	102	72	1	72.00	1–44	–
Manzoor Elahi	7	6	1	39*	123	24.60	–	–	–	192	136	3	45.33	2–18	–
Masood Iqbal	1	1	0	2	2	2.00	–	–	–						
Mohammad Nazir	4	3	3	2*	4	–	–	–	–	222	156	3	52.00	2–37	–
Mohsin Kamal	3	2	2	5*	5	–	–	–	1	138	128	4	32.00	3–46	–

INDIVIDUAL CAREER RECORDS – *continued*

PAKISTAN – *continued*		*BATTING AND FIELDING*								*BOWLING*					
	M	*I*	*NO*	*HS*	*Runs*	*Avge*	*100*	*50*	*Ct/St*	*Balls*	*Runs*	*Wkts*	*Avge*	*Best*	*4W*
Mohsin Khan	55	55	3	117*	1337	25.71	2	5	8	12	5	1	5.00	1–2	–
Mudassar Nazar	71	69	6	79	1497	23.76	–	10	17	2886	2005	73	27.46	5–28	2
Mushtaq Mohammad	10	9	3	55	209	34.83	–	1	3	42	23	0	–	–	–
Naeem Ahmed	1	1	1	0*	0	–	–	–	1	60	43	0	–	–	–
Naseer Malik	3	1	1	0*	0	–	–	–	–	180	98	5	19.60	2–37	–
Nasim-ul-Ghani	1	1	0	1	1	1.00	–	–	–						
Naved Anjum	4	3	0	30	61	20.33	–	–	–	66	59	3	19.66	2–27	–
Parvez Mir	3	3	1	18	26	13.00	–	–	2	122	77	3	25.66	1–17	–
Qasim Omar	23	23	2	69	444	21.14	–	3	3						
Ramiz Raja	9	9	0	75	296	32.88	–	3	1						
Rashid Khan	29	15	7	17	110	13.75	–	–	3	1414	923	20	46.15	3–47	–
Rizwan-uz-Zaman	1	1	0	14	14	14.00	–	–	2						
Saadat Ali	8	7	1	78*	184	30.66	–	1	1	27	29	2	14.50	2–24	–
Sadiq Mohammad	19	19	1	74	383	21.27	–	2	5	38	26	2	13.00	2–20	–
Sajid Ali	2	1	0	16	16	16.00	–	–	1						
Salim Altaf	6	2	1	21	25	25.00	–	–	1	285	151	5	30.20	2–7	–
Salim Malik	22	20	0	41	249	12.45	–	–	14	90	65	1	65.00	1–34	–
Salim Pervez	1	1	0	18	18	18.00	–	–	–						
Salim Yousuf	3	1	0	1	1	1.00	–	–	0/2						
Sarfraz Nawaz	45	31	8	34*	221	9.60	–	–	8	2412	1463	63	23.22	4–27	4
Shafiq Ahmed	3	3	0	29	41	13.66	–	–	1						
Shahid Mahboob	10	6	1	77	119	23.80	–	1	1	540	382	7	54.57	1–23	–
Shoaib Mohammad	5	4	1	35	70	23.33	–	–	2	60	20	3	6.66	3–20	–
Sikander Bakht	26	10	6	16*	25	6.25	–	–	4	1226	817	32	25.53	4–34	1
Tahir Naqqash	36	22	8	61	203	14.50	–	1	8	1444	1105	28	39.46	3–23	–
Taslim Arif	2	2	0	24	28	14.00	–	–	1/1						
Tausif Ahmed	12	3	2	27*	42	42.00	–	–	–	498	364	16	22.75	4–38	1
Wasim Akram	8	3	2	2	2	2.00	–	–	1	351	230	9	25.55	5–21	1
Wasim Bari	51	26	13	34	221	17.00	–	–	52/10						
Wasim Raja	54	45	10	60	782	22.34	–	2	22	1036	687	21	32.71	4–25	1
Zaheer Abbas	58	57	6	123	2464	48.31	7	12	15	238	187	5	37.40	2–23	–
Zakir Khan	3	1	1	8*	8	–	–	–	–	120	69	5	13.80	4–19	1
Extras, subs & run outs.					*1182*				*3*		*1311* *(163)*	*64*			
TOTALS	935	732	149	123	16034	27.50	13	70	294/18	22261	15904	569	27.95	6–14	19

Figures in brackets relate to wides and no-balls debited to bowlers.

INDIVIDUAL CAREER RECORDS – *continued*

SRI LANKA (*40 players*)

		BATTING AND FIELDING								*BOWLING*					
	M	*I*	*NO*	*HS*	*Runs*	*Avge*	*100*	*50*	*Ct/St*	*Balls*	*Runs*	*Wkts*	*Avge*	*Best*	*4W*
de Alwis, R.G.	15	12	4	59*	216	27.00	–	2	16						
De Mel, A.L.F.	33	23	4	28	301	15.84	–	–	7	1647	1333	46	28.97	5–32	2
De Silva, D.L.S.	2	1	0	10	10	10.00	–	–	1	120	54	2	27.00	2–36	–
De Silva, D.S.	41	29	10	37*	371	19.52	–	–	5	2076	1556	32	48.53	3–29	–
De Silva, G.N.	4	2	1	7	9	9.00	–	–	–	194	169	0	–	–	–
De Silva, G.R.A.	6	4	2	6*	9	4.50	–	–	2	305	262	9	29.11	3–41	–
De Silva, P.A.	15	15	4	81*	354	32.18	–	3	7	12	15	0	–	–	–
Dias, R. L.	37	35	3	121	1224	38.25	2	9	13	56	70	3	23.33	3–25	–
Fernando, E.R.	3	3	0	22	47	15.66	–	–	–						
Fernando, E.R.N.S.	7	5	0	36	101	20.20	–	–	–						
Goonasekera, Y.	3	3	0	35	69	23.00	–	–	–	36	35	1	35.00	1–24	–
Goonatillake, F.R.M.	1	–	–	–	–	–	–	–	–	54	34	0	–	–	–
Goonatillake, H.M.	6	4	3	14*	31	31.00	–	–	2/2						
Heyn, P.D.	2	2	0	2	3	1.50	–	–	1						
Jayasekera, R.S.A.	2	1	0	17	17	17.00	–	–	–						
Jayasinghe, S.A.	2	1	0	1	1	1.00	–	–	1						
Jeganathan, S.	1	–	–	–	–	–	–	–	–	60	49	0	–	–	–
John, V.B.	32	13	5	15	63	7.87	–	–	4	1705	1222	30	40.73	3–28	–
Kaluperuma, L.W.	4	3	3	14*	33	–	–	–	–	208	137	2	68.50	1–35	–
Karnain, U.S.H.	15	14	5	41*	203	22.55	–	–	1	563	444	14	31.71	5–26	1
Kuruppu, D.S.B.P.	16	15	0	72	293	19.53	–	2	5						
Madugalle, R.S.	35	32	3	60	543	18.72	–	1	11	4	1	0	–	–	–
Mendis, L.R.D.	43	41	2	80	817	20.94	–	5	8						
Opatha, A.R.M.	5	3	0	18	29	9.66	–	–	3	253	180	5	36.00	3–31	–
Pasqual, S.P.	2	2	1	23*	24	24.00	–	–	–	28	20	0	–	–	–
Pieris, H.S.M.	3	3	1	16	19	9.50	–	–	–	132	135	2	67.50	2–68	–
Ranasinghe, A. N.	9	8	1	51	153	21.85	–	1	–	324	281	2	140.50	1–21	–
Ranatunga, A.	27	25	5	63*	495	24.75	–	3	6	1002	851	20	42.55	3–23	–
Ratnayake, R.J.	25	18	8	23*	165	16.50	–	–	3	1353	1002	26	38.53	4–37	1
Ratnayeke, J.R.	24	19	5	50	209	14.92	–	1	6	863	772	12	64.33	2–37	–
Samarasekera, M.A.R.	2	2	0	5	5	2.50	–	–	1	98	71	0	–	–	–
Silva, S.A.R.	14	14	0	85	330	23.57	–	3	12/2						
Tennekoon, A.P.B.	4	4	0	59	137	34.25	–	1	3						
Tissera, M.H.	3	3	0	52	78	26.00	–	1	–						
Vonhagt, D.M.	1	1	0	8	8	8.00	–	–	–						
Warnapura, B.	12	12	0	77	180	15.00	–	1	5	414	316	8	39.50	3–42	–
Wettimuny, M. de S.	1	1	0	2	2	2.00	–	–	–						

INDIVIDUAL CAREER RECORDS – *continued*

SRI LANKA – *continued*

	M	I	NO	HS	Runs	Avge	100	50	Ct/St	Balls	Runs	Wkts	Avge	Best	4W
		BATTING AND FIELDING								*BOWLING*					
Wettimuny, S.	34	32	1	86*	772	24.90	–	4	3	57	70	1	70.00	1–13	–
Wettimuny, S.R. de S.	3	3	1	67	136	68.00	–	2	–						
Wijesuriya, R.G.C.E.	1	–	–	–	–	–	–	–	–	48	48	1	48.00	1–48	–
Extras, subs & run outs.					*651*				*4*		*637* *(80)*	*24*			
TOTALS	495	408	72	121	8108	24.13	2	39	130/4	11612	9684	240	40.35	5–26	5

Figures in brackets relate to wides and no-balls debited to bowlers.

WEST INDIES (*45 players*)

	M	I	NO	HS	Runs	Avge	100	50	Ct/St	Balls	Runs	Wkts	Avge	Best	4W
		BATTING AND FIELDING								*BOWLING*					
Austin, R.A.	1	1	0	8	8	8.00	–	–	–	6	13	0	–	–	–
Bacchus, S.F.A.F.	29	26	3	80*	612	26.60	–	3	10						
Baptiste, E.A.E.	29	10	2	28*	119	14.87	–	–	4	1476	989	27	36.63	2–10	–
Boyce, K.D.	8	4	0	34	57	14.25	–	–	–	470	313	13	24.07	4–50	1
Clarke, S.T.	10	8	2	20	60	10.00	–	–	4	524	245	13	18.84	3–22	–
Croft, C.E.H.	19	6	4	8	18	9.00	–	–	1	1070	620	30	20.66	6–15	1
Daniel, W.W.	18	5	4	16*	49	49.00	–	–	5	912	595	23	25.86	3–27	–
Davis, W.W.	32	4	3	8*	18	18.00	–	–	1	1749	1139	36	31.63	7–51	1
Dujon, P.J.L.	69	43	16	82*	760	28.14	–	3	85/8						
Foster, M.L.C.	2	1	0	25	25	25.00	–	–	–	30	22	2	11.00	2–22	–
Fredericks, R.C.	12	12	0	105	311	25.91	1	1	4	10	10	2	5.00	2–10	–
Gabriel, R.S.	11	11	0	41	167	15.18	–	–	1						
Garner, J.	76	31	13	37	195	10.83	–	–	17	4184	2102	116	18.12	5–31	4
Gibbs, L.R.	3	1	1	0*	0	–	–	–	–	156	59	2	29.50	1–12	–
Gomes, H.A.	63	48	13	101	1076	30.74	1	6	11	1337	1039	40	25.97	4–31	2
Greenidge, A.E.	1	1	0	23	23	23.00	–	–	–						
Greenidge, C.G.	68	68	7	115	2912	47.73	6	19	23	60	45	1	45.00	1–21	–
Harper, R.A.	18	4	2	45*	71	35.50	–	–	7	924	602	24	25.08	3–34	–
Haynes, D.L.	93	92	12	148	3348	41.85	8	19	26	30	24	0	–	–	–
Headley, R.G.A.	1	1	0	19	19	19.00	–	–	–						
Holder, V.A.	12	6	1	30	64	12.80	–	–	6	681	454	19	23.89	5–50	1

INDIVIDUAL CAREER RECORDS – *continued*

WEST INDIES – *continued*

		BATTING AND FIELDING								*BOWLING*					
	M	*I*	*NO*	*HS*	*Runs*	*Avge*	*100*	*50*	*Ct/St*	*Balls*	*Runs*	*Wkts*	*Avge*	*Best*	*4W*
Holding, M.A.	87	35	9	64	215	8.26	–	1	26	4734	2613	122	21.41	5–26	5
Julien, B.D.	12	8	2	26*	86	14.33	–	–	4	778	463	18	25.72	4–20	2
Kallicharran, A.I.	31	28	4	78	826	34.41	–	6	8	105	64	3	21.33	2–10	–
Kanhai, R.B.	7	5	2	55	164	54.66	–	2	4						
King, C.L.	18	14	2	86	280	23.33	–	1	6	744	529	11	48.09	4–23	1
Lloyd, C.H.	87	69	19	102	1977	39.54	1	11	40	358	210	8	26.25	2–4	–
Logie, A.L.	39	30	15	88	661	44.06	–	3	21	24	18	0	–	–	–
Marshall, M.D.	60	32	12	56*	339	16.95	–	1	8	3252	1783	70	25.47	4–34	1
Mattis, E.H.	2	2	0	62	86	43.00	–	1	2						
Murray, D.A.	10	7	2	35	45	8.80	–	–	16						
Murray, D.L.	26	17	5	61*	294	24.58	–	2	37/1						
Parry, D.R.	6	5	1	32	61	15.25	–	–	8	330	259	11	23.54	3–47	–
Payne, T.R.O.	3	2	0	28	48	24.00	–	–	3						
Phillip, N.	1	1	0	0	0	0.00	–	–	–	42	22	1	22.00	1–22	–
Pydanna, M.R.	3	1	1	2*	2	–	–	–	2/1						
Richards, I.V.A.	98	89	15	189*	4071	55.01	8	27	44	3160	2348	62	37.87	3–27	–
Richardson, R.B.	35	34	6	80*	799	28.53	–	7	6	6	1	0	–	–	–
Roberts, A.M.E.	56	32	9	37*	231	10.04	–	–	6	3123	1771	87	20.35	5–22	3
Rowe, L.G.	11	8	0	60	136	17.00	–	1	2						
Shillingford, I.T.	2	2	0	24	30	15.00	–	–	2						
Shivnarine, S.	1	1	1	20*	20	–	–	–	–	18	16	0	–	–	–
Small, M.A.	2	–	–	–	–	–	–	–	1	84	54	1	54.00	1–40	–
Sobers, G.St A.	1	1	0	0	0	0.00	–	–	1	63	31	1	31.00	1–31	–
Walsh, C.A.	4	–	–	–	–	–	–	–	–	240	198	4	49.50	2–52	–
Extras, subs & run outs.					*1397*				*6*		*1792* *(283)*	*103*			
TOTALS	1177	806	188	189*	21680	35.08	25	114	458/10	30680	20160	850	23.71	7–51	22

Figures in brackets relate to wides and no-balls debited to bowlers.

INDIVIDUAL CAREER RECORDS – *continued*

CANADA (*13 players*)

		BATTING AND FIELDING								*BOWLING*					
	M	*I*	*NO*	*HS*	*Runs*	*Avge*	*100*	*50*	*Ct/St*	*Balls*	*Runs*	*Wkts*	*Avge*	*Best*	*4W*
Baksh, S.	1	1	0	0	0	0.00	–	–	–						
Callender, R.G.	2	2	0	0	0	0.00	–	–	–	54	26	1	26.00	1–14	–
Chappell, C.J.D.	3	3	0	19	38	12.66	–	–	–						
Dennis, F.A.	3	3	0	25	47	15.66	–	–	–						
Henry, C.C.	2	2	1	5	6	6.00	–	–	–	90	53	2	26.50	2–27	–
Marshall, C.A.	2	2	0	8	10	5.00	–	–	–						
Mauricette, B.M.	3	3	0	15	20	6.66	–	–	–						
Patel, J.M.	3	3	0	2	3	1.00	–	–	–	91	47	0	–	–	–
Sealy, G.R.	3	3	0	45	73	24.33	–	–	–	36	21	0	–	–	–
Stead, M.P.	2	2	0	10	10	5.00	–	–	–	29	24	0	–	–	–
Tariq Javed	3	3	0	8	15	5.00	–	–	–						
Valentine, J.N.	3	2	2	3*	3	–	–	–	1	114	66	3	22.00	1–18	–
Vaughan, J.C.B.	3	3	0	29	30	10.00	–	–	–	66	36	0	–	–	–
Extras, subs & run outs.					*34*				–		*19*	*1*			
TOTALS	33	32	3	45	289	9.96	–	–	1	480	292	7	41.71	2–27	–

EAST AFRICA (*14 players*)

		BATTING AND FIELDING								*BOWLING*					
	M	*I*	*NO*	*HS*	*Runs*	*Avge*	*100*	*50*	*Ct/St*	*Balls*	*Runs*	*Wkts*	*Avge*	*Best*	*4W*
Frasat Ali	3	3	0	45	57	19.00	–	–	–	144	107	0	–	–	–
Harilal R. Shah	3	3	0	6	6	2.00	–	–	–						
Jawahir Shah	3	3	0	37	46	15.33	–	–	–						
McLeod, H.	2	2	0	5	5	2.50	–	–	–						
Mehmood Quaraishy	3	3	1	19	41	20.50	–	–	–	108	94	3	31.33	2–55	–
Nagenda, J.	1	–	–	–	–	–	–	–	–	54	50	1	50.00	1–50	–
Nana, P.G.	3	3	2	8*	9	9.00	–	–	2	173	116	1	116.00	1–34	–
Praful Mehta	1	1	0	12	12	12.00	–	–	–						
Pringle, D.	2	2	0	3	5	2.50	–	–	–	90	55	0	–	–	–
Ramesh Sethi	3	3	0	30	54	18.00	–	–	1	120	100	1	100.00	1–51	–
Shiraz Sumar	1	1	0	4	4	4.00	–	–	–						
Walusimba, S.	3	3	0	16	38	12.66	–	–	–						
Yunus Badat	2	2	0	1	1	0.50	–	–	–						
Zulfiqar Ali	3	3	1	30	39	19.50	–	–	1	210	166	4	41.50	3–63	–
Extras, subs & run outs.					*25*				–		*34*	–			
TOTALS	33	32	4	45	342	12.21	–		4	899	722	10	72.20	3–63	–

INDIVIDUAL CAREER RECORDS – *continued*

ZIMBABWE (*13 players*)

		BATTING AND FIELDING								*BOWLING*					
	M	*I*	*NO*	*HS*	*Runs*	*Avge*	*100*	*50*	*Ct/St*	*Balls*	*Runs*	*Wkts*	*Avge*	*Best*	*4W*
Brown, R.D.	4	4	0	38	93	23.25	–	–	2						
Butchart, I.P.	6	6	2	34*	82	20.50	–	–	2	300	213	3	71.00	2–52	–
Curran, K.M.	6	6	0	73	212	35.33	–	2	–	350	274	5	54.80	3–65	–
Fletcher, D.A.G.	6	6	2	71*	191	47.75	–	2	–	301	221	7	31.57	4–42	1
Heron, J.G.	6	6	0	18	50	8.33	–	–	1						
Hogg, V.R.	2	1	1	7*	7	–	–	–	–	90	49	0	–	–	–
Houghton, D.L.	6	6	0	84	176	29.33	–	2	7						
Paterson, G.A.	6	6	0	27	99	16.50	–	–	–						
Peckover, G.E.	3	3	1	16*	33	16.50	–	–	–						
Pycroft, A.J.	6	6	0	21	71	11.83	–	–	3						
Rawson, P.W.E.	6	4	1	19	24	8.00	–	–	2	373	239	8	29.87	3–47	–
Shah, A.H.	3	3	0	16	26	8.66	–	–	1	45	40	1	40.00	1–17	–
Traicos, A.J.	6	4	1	19	25	8.33	–	–	2	408	202	4	50.50	2–28	–
Extras, subs & run outs.					*168*				*1*		*73*	*1*			
TOTALS	66	61	8	84	1257	23.71	–	6	21	1867	1311	29	45.20	4–42	1

INDEX OF PLAYERS

Every player who appeared in one-day internationals before August 1985 is listed alphabetically within his country's section of the index. The numbers in brackets show the total number of one-day international appearances by the player for that country. The numbers that follow are the reference numbers of the matches in which he played: only the prefix of each match number is listed (e.g. Match No. 77/15 is shown as 77).

ENGLAND (84 players)

AUSTRALIA (85 players)

INDIA (54 players)

NEW ZEALAND (50 players)

PAKISTAN (56 players)

SRI LANKA (40 players)

WEST INDIES (45 players)

CANADA (13 players)

EAST AFRICA (14 players)

ZIMBABWE (13 players)